Dynamics of Effective Teaching

Dynamics of Effective Teaching

THIRD EDITION

Richard Kindsvatter
Kent State University

William Wilen
Kent State University

Margaret Ishler
University of Northern Iowa

Dynamics of Effective Teaching, Third Edition

Copyright © 1996 by Longman Publishers USA.
All rights reserved.
No part of this publication may be reproduced,
stored in a retrieval system, or transmitted
in any form or by any means, electronic, mechanical,
photocopying, recording, or otherwise,
without the prior permission of the publisher.
Longman, 10 Bank Street, White Plains, N.Y. 10606

Associated companies:
Longman Group Ltd., London
Longman Cheshire Pty., Melbourne
Longman Paul Pty., Auckland
Copp Clark Longman Ltd., Toronto

Associate editor: Travis Lester
Production editor: Dee Josephson
Editorial Assistant: Matt Baker
Cover design: Ed Smith Designs
Production supervisor: Winston Sukhnanand
Compositor: Digitype

Library of Congress Cataloging-in-Publication Data

Kindsvatter, Richard.
    Dynamics of effective teaching / Richard Kindsvatter, William
Wilen, Margaret Ishler. —3rd ed.
        p.   cm.
    Includes bibliographical references and index.
    ISBN 0-8013-1565-4
    1. High school teaching—United States.   2. Classroom management—
United States.   3. Motivation in education—United States.
I. Wilen, William W.   II. Ishler, Margaret F.   III. Title.
LB1737.U6K56   1996
373.11'02—dc20   95-20346
                                                                          CIP

1 2 3 4 5 6 7 8 9 10-MA-9998979695

Contents

Chapter 3

DEMOCRATIC CLASSROOM DISCIPLINE 71

Chapter 4

CURRICULUM CONSIDERATIONS 103

Chapter 5   **PLANNING FOR TEACHING   142**

Chapter 6   **BASIC INSTRUCTIONAL TECHNIQUES   178**

Chapter 7

Chapter 8

**TEACHING STRATEGIES
FOR PROMOTING ACHIEVEMENT   289**

Chapter 9

**EVALUATION OF CLASSROOM
PERFORMANCE   329**

Chapter **10**   TOWARD EFFECTIVE TEACHING   357

Preface

As with the previous two editions, we have designed the third edition of *Dynamics of Effective Teaching* for teacher-preparation students in high school or middle school general-methods courses, student or interim teachers who need a solid reference book and a comprehensive set of analysis instruments, and beginning teachers who intend to achieve a level of optimum effectiveness. In a broader sense, though, we believe that any teacher who engages in instruction or supervision will find something of value in *Dynamics of Effective Teaching*. It will appeal to readers who share our views on the following:

> Effective teaching is basically sound decision making.
>
> Teaching is an art informed by science.
>
> A sound knowledge base is the bedrock of every bonafide profession.
>
> Translating this knowledge base into thoughtful classroom practice is the challenge and task of every professional teacher.
>
> Empowering teachers is the key to heightening their esteem and improving the image of the profession.

We have tried to embody these positions in *Dynamics of Effective Teaching* by introducing decision making in chapter 1 as a process fundamental to educators and by revisiting the application of that process in every succeeding chapter. Our view of decision making considers it from a constructivist view of teaching and learning based on reflection and "meaning making." In addition, these positions are built into the structure and organization of the text. Because a strong knowledge base is so important to our vision of decision making, every chapter contains at least one section called "Research and Theoretical Base" that grounds the discussion in the most current thinking and situates readers in their own research. We have updated and given a stronger focus to material throughout these sections. Because they are relatively discrete segments of each chapter, instructors may easily choose how and to what degree they integrate the theory and research into their classrooms. Related sections called "Application to Practice" focus the research findings and theoretical approaches and help readers begin to consider their practical implications. A realistic scenario contained in each chapter serves to add faces, names, and a narrative structure to the issues we present. These scenarios are predicated on our assumption that we often learn most effectively when we feel some sense of connection and personal relevance to the content, and our feedback from instructors using earlier editions has wholeheartedly supported this contention.

In addition, introductory and concluding questions frame each chapter, serving to encourage reflection and personal exploration. Periodic summary points focus reader attention and reiterate important topics. Finally, analysis forms are included at the end of many chapters. We and other instructors have found these worksheets and questionnaires useful for facilitating comprehension by developing personal understanding, promoting a common language for the community of educators, and providing tools for the action research and the teacher-as-researcher approach we hope to stimulate. Altogether, we hope that these various parts of the text will continue to serve to organize instructional methods into a sound and eminently teachable structure that promotes independence, reflection, and discussion.

Of course, our revision has not simply extended to rethinking and revising the pedagogy and skeletal structure of *Dynamics of Effective Teaching*. We have sought out new topics in keeping with our mission and the book's spirit that have become important since the publication of the second edition. For instance, we have expanded coverage of simulation-gaming strategy because it so powerfully lends itself to constructivist purposes, added a chapter on curriculum to highlight the inextricable relationship between curriculum and instruction, greatly deepened the coverage of cooperative learning and performance assessment in light of their wide attention and the testimony to their effectiveness, and broadened the discussion of Outcome-Based Education (OBE).

The text breaks into four large areas. The first, made up of chapters 1 and 2, considers the meaning of teaching and being a teacher. The second—chapters 3 and 4—examines discipline and curriculum, two topics that undergird all other parts of professional instruction. Chapters 5 through 9 present teaching as an integrated process and build on the first four chapters. Chapter 10 both closes the book (temporarily) and shows the openings in the world beyond.

As mentioned above, chapter 1 presents our view of decision making and its importance in the minds of professional educators. We also put forth our view of education as a professional discipline here.

Since all classroom teaching occurs within a social setting, chapter 2 addresses the teacher's role in providing a productive climate and attending to students' motivation. In fact, motivation, in our view, is the most basic task of the teacher, and much of this book is directly or indirectly concerned with the topic.

Classroom discipline has been inserted as chapter 3 in the third edition. Because discipline emerges naturally from our discussion of classroom climate and motivation, and because it is a pervasive aspect of teaching, we have placed it ahead of the chapters on instruction. We have selected pertinent aspects of discipline rather than attempt a broad coverage of this complex topic. We have, however, expanded somewhat the presentation of the myths of discipline, for we consider awareness of the myths to be an important prior step to developing a sound belief system about discipline.

Chapter 4 addresses curriculum. Very simply, in order to teach, one must teach about something. *What* one chooses to teach and *how* one teaches it determine teaching effectiveness. Constructivist approaches that focus on encouraging students to discover personal meaning beyond the accumulation of factual knowledge make the selection of content especially critical.

We see teaching as a three-step process: planning, instruction, and evaluation. Chapter 5's discussion of planning continues the logical transition from chapter 4's discussion of curriculum. We conceive of planning as a human process of decision making rather than only the routine development of written plans. Planning should be the beginning of an adventure in learning for students, so it deserves to be done with a sense of excitement and commitment.

Chapters 6, 7, and 8 deal specifically with instruction—a central focus of this book—as the second component of teaching. We begin this component in chapters 6 and 7 by talking about behaviors and techniques that are the basis for instruction, showing how they evolve into methods and strategies through manipulation by the purposeful teacher. In chapter 8, we stress the elements of effective teaching that have the greatest impact on student achievement and those approaches such as direct teaching and cooperative learning that have the potential to help students find relevance in their learning.

Evaluation, the third component of teaching, is addressed in chapter 9. Like discipline, it is presented concisely. The areas of assessment and evaluation are changing rapidly and much controversy exists here. We have tried to synthesize important traditional and new topics in evaluation to establish a reasonable foundation for further and more specialized exploration in the professional literature.

In the final chapter we describe the use of this book beyond the general-methods classroom. As students become involved with instruction through student teaching, internships, and finally in their first in-service year, the book will continue to be an applicable and useful resource. For instance, the analytical instruments at the end of most of the chapters, especially if they are used in the context of the action research we encourage, will aid in the analysis of the various teaching components in clinical or field settings and will promote improved performance.

As is always the case with projects of this kind, many people have contributed to the final result. We are especially indebted to the colleagues who reviewed the manuscript in its various stages and provided their insight and expertise:

Robert Erbes, Michigan State University

Jerry R. Franklin, Morehead State University

Joel Hausler, Middle Tennessee State University

Elizabeth Manera, Arizona State University

Paul Retish, University of Iowa

William G. Samuelson, Emporia State University

Isabelle L. Shannon, Virginia Wesleyan College
Betty R. Tutt, William Woods College
Bill Weldon, Arizona State University

We know that in teaching, each of us must develop our own most effective style. It is a task that is made more difficult because there is no definition of that style or assurance of the task's completion. The most important purpose of this book is to assist and support you in your quest.

It is informed decision making that is the most credible plank in the argument for teaching as a profession.

Why a chapter on decision making? Farr and Brown (1971) provided a persuasive rationale as they observed that "most instructional decisions are made by forfeit; that is, by not recognizing that a decision can be made or by not being aware of possible alternatives. The usual forfeit 'decision' involves continuation of a practice whether or not it is the most appropriate procedure for the situation" (p. 341). This chapter attempts to guide teachers away from such forfeiting or decision making by default, toward purposeful decision making.

Furthermore, as Hunter (1984) pointed out, professional decision making and effective teaching are interrelated concepts.

Education professionals need to move from the extremes of either intuitive or "recipe-based" behavior to deliberate professional decision mak-

1

ing based on research plus experiential wisdom. There still remains plenty of room for intuition. Clearly, we desire educators who are inspired, empathetic, and sensitive to the needs of students and dedicated to the value of education. Those traits are more likely to emerge and be maintained, however, if educators see that students learn successfully as a result of effective teaching. (pp. 189–190)

Finally, decision making is a thread that links all the topics in this book. Decision making is pervasive, so any improvement that is made in a teacher's decision-making skills will be reflected in every aspect of that teacher's practice. In this respect, any change in decision making has the possibility for a broad-based impact.

FOCUS QUESTIONS

1. Why is pedagogy—the professionally established knowledge base of teaching—considered to be suspect by some teachers?
2. What conditions, professionally considered, would need to exist so that pedagogy would be held in high esteem by all teachers, and be the referent of choice for their decision making?
3. What, in general, would a teacher have to know to be a genuinely informed decision maker?
4. In what ways have theory and research—essential aspects of the knowledge base of teaching—contributed to the practices of informed teachers? And what is their potential to contribute even more?
5. What typical sorts of decisions will you need to make about the major aspects of teaching: planning, instruction, discipline, and evaluation?
6. What will be the referents and the process you use to make teaching decisions?

OVERVIEW

Decision making is personal behavior. It does not lend itself to tightly designed prescriptions. Nevertheless, there are certain common aspects of the process that you as a teacher or prospective teacher should consider. This chapter's most important point is that a well-informed belief system is the most credible basis for rational teacher decisions. The first concern is that you are purposefully aware of the assumptions and beliefs that comprise your belief system. Then, as you develop particular attitudes and habits of practice (i.e., patterns of decision making) based on those assumptions and beliefs that define your personal teaching style, you should examine each one carefully to ensure its conformity to accepted educational principles. As you later plan your instruction, interact in the classroom, and evaluate instructional outcomes, the parameters of thinking you have established will be a safeguard against specious and anti-intellectual reasoning.

ASSUMPTIONS AND BELIEFS

Assumptions and beliefs are the basis for much of our everyday behavior. Assumptions tend to be informal, whereas beliefs are more structured. However, one blends into the other so that, in many cases, it is impossible to distinguish between them.

Teachers make assumptions and depend on beliefs in their everyday teaching lives. For example, a teacher who lectures to a class about a particular topic assumes that the class will assimilate a sufficient understanding of that topic from the remarks. Or the teacher who assigns a detention to a misbehaving adolescent believes that punishment is a deterrent to future misbehavior. Some may not share the assumptions or beliefs of these teachers and would, therefore, use a different approach in these situations.

Decision making, with its attendant assumptions and beliefs, serves as a thread throughout this book. As authors, we realized that we needed to make explicit the beliefs that reflect the particular preferences, perceptions, interpretations, and priorities to which we subscribe. You, as the reader, deserve to be informed about them to understand the decisions we made about the content, tone, and style we used in writing this book.

Belief 1. Quality of teaching is directly contingent on the quality of the decision making that precedes the teaching. Decision making is a process, as will be described in this chapter, but more pervasively it is a concept that integrates the various elements of teaching. Decision making is integral to establishing classroom climate, planning for teaching, interacting with students, and evaluating performance and achievement. It is our intent to convince you, the reader, that decision making deserves your most professional attention.

Belief 2. Teaching is complex behavior. To interpret it in too simple terms leads to misunderstanding. This, in fact, is what is done by many noneducators, and results in distorted notions about the role of the teacher and the needs of schools. More tragically, some teachers are also guilty of this kind of simplistic, if well-intentioned, thinking as reflected in classroom approaches that disregard professionally endorsed pedagogy and rely on unexamined traditional practice and personal intuition. Their concept of teaching is more likely to be a bag of tricks than a synthesis of sound principles.

Throughout this book, we are careful not to take for granted our own impressions of teaching or our collective experience. We have attempted to identify the most pertinent theory and most useful research as the basis for the selection of content. The emphasis on effective teaching research and constructivist learning theory—both elaborated in this book—are examples. As a more specific example, we present a unique approach to lesson planning after finding that research on planning informs us that the most commonly recommended approach has serious limitations.

Belief 3. Teaching is learned behavior. One often hears about the "born teacher," and that nobody had to teach Socrates or Christ how to teach. A charismatic personality, personal sensitivity, or the gift of verbal dexterity contributes to some people's effectiveness in informing and influencing others. Certainly these characteristics are desirable traits in a teacher. However, pedagogy, as the study of education, is based on systematically derived principles that have been established and recorded by thousands of scholars and practitioners. To assume that a teacher can be optimally effective without a reasonably sound grounding in this science is naive. One can draw the analogy of a kindly family doctor, a general practitioner, being called upon to perform quadruple-bypass heart surgery, the task of a highly trained specialist. It is unthinkable. How then can one rationally assume that it does not take extensive preparation to teach with optimal effectiveness?

Brophy and Good (1986), after reviewing the research on teacher behavior, concluded:

> Elitist critics often undervalue teaching or even suggest that anyone can teach ("Those who can, do; those who can't, teach"). The data . . . refute this myth. . . . Although it may be true that most adults could survive in the classroom, it is not true that most could teach effectively. . . . [Teachers] who do . . . these things successfully produce significantly more achievement than those who do not, but doing them successfully demands a blend of knowledge, energy, motivation, and communication and decision-making skills that many teachers, let alone ordinary adults, do not possess. (p. 370)

Pedagogy, which is available to educators in the professional literature of education, deserves a prominent place in your academic thinking and decision making. It brings respectability and dignity to the teaching profession. In fact, without pedagogy, teaching could not claim to be a profession. Throughout this book, we will emphasize that pedagogy takes precedence over personal experience as a referent for teacher decision making.

Belief 4. Instruction should be based on the most effective strategies, methods, techniques, and behaviors as determined by current research and learning theory. Actually, this belief is an extension of statements made in beliefs 2 and 3. A science of teaching, or pedagogy, is derived from research and learning theory and—please take special note of this—is validated by practice. As a professional practitioner, you must have faith in the science of your profession, for without faith you approach it essentially as a craft. A totally personal approach hardly serves in guiding the development of the most complex entity known in the universe—the human mind. In this book we have attempted to translate the most up-to-date, credible ideas from educational literature into practices you can integrate into your own teaching style.

Belief 5. Students must be motivated. This is hardly a controversial statement. In fact, it is so obvious and pervasive that it is regularly taken for granted.

As this book was written, the concept of motivation could not be ignored, any more than any current or prospective teacher can afford to ignore it. Students must be motivated in the areas of emotional and academic needs, interests, and abilities for learning to occur. This is the cornerstone of instruction. Your initial and most essential responsibility as a teacher is to arouse these students' desire to learn. To assume that students should want to learn, or will make the effort—especially if they already lack a personal sense of purpose—is naive. The truest measure of teaching effectiveness is the extent to which a teacher creates conditions that promote student motivation.

Belief 6. The social setting in which learning occurs is a major factor affecting instruction. Admittedly, the possibility of tutorial teaching and independent learning exist, but when one thinks of schooling, one envisions teachers instructing a group of students in a classroom, laboratory, or on the athletic field. The nature of such interaction is termed *group process*. A body of knowledge has been developed on the subject of group process, and principles related to its application have been established. Clearly, the classroom cannot be fully understood solely in terms of intellectual considerations. The quality of life in the classroom is also contingent on social factors. Therefore, the classroom environment as it is affected by group process is the backdrop of productive learning.

In this book, we do not focus specifically on theories dealing with the special area of group process. We have, however, attempted to employ some ideas that involve productive and cooperative interrelationships within the classroom. Discussions on classroom climate and classroom discipline draw heavily on these ideas, and throughout the chapters on instruction they are considered to be implicit.

Belief 7. Teaching is, in the final analysis, a personal invention. Although pedagogy is the foundation of optimally effective teaching, it tends to be more suggestive than prescriptive. Individual teachers, meanwhile, are as different from one another as everyone else in the population is. For example, a teacher who has a highly developed sense of humor may banter with students and use quips, the overall effect of which can be quite positive. A more serious-minded teacher may conduct a more structured class, yet also be effective in helping students achieve intended learning outcomes. Teachers will be most effective if they maintain their own personal identity and integrity while being guided by the tenets of pedagogy. Please note, however, that not all persons, no matter how true to themselves they remain, have personalities that are well suited to the demands of teaching. This is especially true of persons who have limited social sensitivity, or an inordinate need for security, recognition, or authority.

The observation has been made that effective teachers tend to be more diverse among themselves, whereas mediocre teachers tend to be more alike. We believe that teaching is a personal invention for each practitioner, and this book is intended to contribute to the personal inventing process. Throughout this book, the emphasis will be on helping teachers develop their own unique teaching styles within a framework of established principles.

Belief 8. Students learn both individually and as a group. Just as the physicist finds it useful to postulate that light exists in one case as a wave and in another as quantum units of energy, educators find it useful to consider learning sometimes to be a group process and other times to be an individually defined task. The effective-teaching research done in the 1970s and 1980s tended to focus on learning in terms of process and structure within the group. It has been very useful in helping teachers clarify their roles as group leaders. On the other hand, much recent attention has been given to constructivist teaching and learning. This approach commonly engages students as individuals or small groups in personal reflecting and "meaning making." Its intent is to involve students in a dimension of learning that they will perceive to be rich and rewarding. Both of these are powerful means of conceiving effective learning conditions in classrooms. We consider them to be complementary: both necessary, but neither sufficient in its own right to provide optimally effective teaching.

PEDAGOGY: THE DISCIPLINE OF TEACHING

Pedagogy, like mathematics, music, or philosophy, is a discipline, that is, a recognized area of academic study and practice. The term *pedagogy* itself has Greek and Latin origins, and is a reminder of all that was excellent in classical education. In current use, it likewise connotes all that is best in modern education. Whereas educators more commonly use the broader term *education*, *pedagogy* has the advantage of defining more precisely a rational approach to teaching, the opposite of anti-intellectualism. Pegagogy is understood to refer to the discipline of education and not necessarily to all practices that in some way might be associated with teaching. Pedagogy, therefore, defined as an extensive body of knowledge that incorporates those principles and practices that have been validated by research and scholarly scrutiny, is a term that will be used often in this book to convey the ideal of enlightened teaching.

Pedagogy as a formal discipline is not always enthusiastically embraced by teachers. Attitudes range from unconcern through condescension to distrust. When teachers are suspicious of pedagogy, or associate it primarily with scholarly papers and textbooks, they consider the literature to have little relationship to what really happens in schools. Teachers sometimes remark that a particular idea seems "okay in theory, but won't work in the classroom." Such a position reflects a misunderstanding of theory and of pedagogy.

The authors do not maintain that pedagogy implies absolute certainty, but rather that it is currently the most accurate theory known about education. To reject it, or to ignore it and be guided primarily by individual personal experience, is to assume a patently anti-intellectual posture. In doing so, one is in essence saying, "Don't confuse me with the facts."

If teaching is to reach its fullest potential, teacher decision making—the link between theory and practice—must be guided by pedagogy. Hunter (1979) observed, "Now adequate preparation parallels that of medicine, for it requires the professional to learn, internalize and implement the contributions of science to increased productive human functioning" (p. 62).

THE BASIC DIMENSIONS OF PEDAGOGY

Two generalizations emerge from the previous commentary. First, teaching involves a high order of human functioning. The most effective teachers are well informed regarding modern pedagogical principles, and are able to translate those principles of teaching and learning into effective practice. Furthermore, teaching behaviors have many purposes: academic, social, personal, and behavioral. Teachers need a repertoire of skills and methods that will enable them to accommodate a host of instructional demands.

Second, teaching may usefully be conceived as a science that is implemented by artists. Automobile racing serves as an apt analogy. The sophisticated technology involved in modern automotive engineering achieves its potential only in the hands of a talented and skilled driver. Likewise, state-of-the-art pedagogy remains only a promise until it is made functional by competent teachers whose own personalities and perceptions provide the dynamic dimension of pedagogy.

This book uses as its point of departure the beliefs and generalizations presented in this section. The authors have attempted to collect and organize theories, principles, research findings, and practices that usefully elaborate these selected beliefs and generalizations. Again, there is no possible prescription for effective teaching in a direct, one-to-one fashion. However, the authors believe that teachers—and teacher-education students—will benefit from giving careful consideration to the ideas and examples in this book, and translating them within the context of their respective teaching styles and settings.

SCENARIO

Ms. Knettel was listening as her 9th-grade students read aloud from *The Rime of the Ancient Mariner*, one verse per student in succession. The reading was expressionless and halting. Students paid little attention as other classmates read. Squirming and fidgeting created a minor disruption.

In planning this lesson a few days earlier, Ms. Knettel speculated that this poem, in particular, was one to which students could relate. It involves a fierce storm at sea, the curse of a so-called Spirit, shipmates who become zombies, and other miraculous events. The poem has vivid imagery and a readily perceived moral. Although some feel it is not the best of Romantic poetry, it seemed well-suited to acquaint students with the Romantic style.

As she conducted the lesson, Ms. Knettel realized she had overestimated the potential of the poem to capture the students' imagination. She occasionally interspersed questions like, "Why did Coleridge choose an albatross as the bird that was shot?" and "Why was the ancient Mariner telling this tale to the wedding guest, who was a complete stranger?" But the class sat dumbfounded. To continue, she realized, was pointless. Yet what could she do?

An actual crisis had not yet occurred. The students were not out of hand, even though they were restless. She could momentarily continue with the present activity and buy a little time to think about it.

One alternative, she thought, was for students to read silently, and write answers to questions she put on the board. Meanwhile she could circulate throughout the room helping students individually, because many hesitated to ask questions aloud. Another alternative might be to appoint the best readers as small-group leaders, and each group could read through the assignment together. This would provide active involvement of a greater number of students. A third alternative was for students to act out scenes from the poem: shooting the albatross, the vehemence of the crew, zombies sailing the ship, and confronting the wedding guest. For the poor readers, this would be a particularly useful way of presenting the substance of the poem, and everyone would enjoy the poem more.

Ms. Knettel considered the likely consequence of each alternative, but none of them seemed quite right. Then a fourth alternative occurred to her that was even more appealing. Why not have a class meeting to give the students the opportunity to express their perceptions and opinions, and to help her think through the situation? Her long-range intention for the class was that the students become increasingly empowered and responsible, and she was consciously aware that her decision at this point was influenced by that goal.

"Class," she said, "we seem to have gotten bogged down. Do you think it would help if we talked about it? Let's spend the 25 minutes we have remaining in a class meeting. Move your chairs into a circle, like we did the last time, but lift them so we're not too noisy."

Ms. Knettel sat in as a member of the circle, but asked Marge if she would chair the meeting. A lively discussion ensued. Some students felt that *The Rime of the Ancient Mariner* was not "the greatest thing since pizza parties" (their expression), and they didn't see the point in studying it. Other students said they enjoyed the poem, even though they had difficulty expressing a rationale for their position. Finally, Geri asked, "Do you really think this stuff does us any good, Ms. Knettel? How can we ever use it?"

Ms. Knettel had taken the opportunity to reflect and to formulate the outline of her response while the students discussed their views for nearly 20 minutes. Now Geri provided the opportunity to comment.

"As a matter of fact," Ms. Knettel said, "there are few things you learn in school that you use directly. Everything you learn becomes part of what you are, and contributes to broad understandings and appreciations. Remember, *The Rime of the Ancient Mariner* was written about 170 years ago. Many thousands of poems have been written since, yet few of them are known or read today. This poem is still popular, mainly because it tells us with beauty and grace something important about the human condition. For example, we now sometimes use the expression 'a person has an albatross around his neck,' and it has a useful meaning because of the legacy Coleridge left us in his poem. Along with other great literature, this poem has made our thinking and expression much richer."

The students were quiet for several moments. Then Geri and several others agreed that they hadn't thought of it that way before. Todd commented that he still didn't like poetry, in general, but that he could see how somebody might. The bell rang at that point and the students left the room still talking about the possible merits of good poetry.

Ms. Knettel now sensed more interest from the students. The likelihood existed that, for the moment, they were willing to give the poem the benefit of the doubt. She realized that her job was to try to get them to the point of making a reasonable commitment. By tomorrow, she thought, I've got to use a little imagination, and come up with a plan that utilizes this apparent momentum. With that, further decision making was in progress.

RESEARCH AND THEORETICAL BASE

General Perspectives

Ms. Knettel made a timely decision that redirected the activity in her class. She did, in fact, employ a systematic approach to decision making that may not be apparent to a person unfamiliar with the dynamics of the process. These dynamics have their basis, in part, in the knowledge base related to decision making.

Perhaps the single most significant statement in the literature related to decision making was made by Shavelson (1973); he pronounced decision making to be the basic teaching skill. It is a statement that stands unchallenged because it is self-evident. Support for the statement is founded in logic and experience, not in research. In this same vein, Hunter (1984) defined teaching as "the constant stream of professional decisions that affects the probability of learning: decisions that are made and implemented before, during, and after interaction with the student" (pp. 169–170).

While Shavelson and Hunter attested to the critical importance of teacher decision making, Manley-Casimer and Wasserman (1989) were pessimistic about the attention given it. They commented, "Decisionmaking—a profoundly complex process that lies at the heart of virtually all classroom practices—is a wasteland with respect to the professional preparation of teachers. . . . For most teachers, there is no forum that either acknowledges or validates professional decision-making processes—let alone a forum that might help them to sharpen their professional decision-making skills" (p. 293).

This unquestioning, often unconscious acceptance of decision making as a tacit and pervasive aspect of teaching is one reason for the limited amount of research focused on it. Another reason is the intimate nature of decision making. Decision making is wholly internalized, and can be studied only by inference from observed behavior or personal reporting. In addition, decision making is a generic and many-faceted concept. Research has addressed such related matters as teacher beliefs (Sontag, 1968), categories that are used as the basis for teacher decisions (Clark & Peterson, 1976; Herbert, 1974; Rubenstein & Fisher, 1974), and the reliability of teacher decisions (Shavelson, Cadwell, & Izu, 1977). There is, however, no theory or concept that integrates all the parts into a cohesive whole.

Of the several models of decision making presented in the literature, few have been associated with research. An exception is Perkins' (1986) IDEA model. The letters refer to the four steps in problem solving: *Identify* the problem; *Define* the problem; *Explore* strategies to solve the problem; and *Assess* the effectiveness of the solution. Research based on this model was conducted by Cardelle-Elawar (1993). She found that "the most difficult process that teachers encountered was analyzing their own practices objectively; detaching the real problem from other factors affecting the problem was hard" (p. 55). However, she did report that all 11 teachers in the study were successful in applying usefully the IDEA model—that is, through using a systematic approach to problem solving they made decisions that improved their effectiveness in targeted areas.

Shavelson (1983) expressed his concern in his review of the research that, although teachers made about 10 interactive (i.e., during instruction) decisions per hour, they tended to consider few alternatives. They were more concerned with justifying their choices than in examining them critically. In other words, the potential for decision-making skills to contribute to effective teaching is being only marginally realized. While Shavelson reported 10 interaction decisions an hour—one every six minutes—Clark (1988) claimed from his review of the literature that teachers made an interactive decision every two minutes. These researchers may differ somewhat in their perception of interaction decisions, but we can assume from their informed estimates that teachers average an interactive decision every two to six minutes. Therefore, teaching is affected for better or worse by an interaction decision 50 to 100 times each day. Clark said further, "The research on teaching has made an empirical case that the practice of teaching is complex, uncertain, and dilemma riddled" (p. 10). This is a compelling reason to encourage rational and effective decision making as part of professional development in both preservice and in-service programs; informed decision making by teachers is the most credible plank in the argument that teaching be considered a profession.

The decision making of novice teachers has been examined, and the results are not unexpected. Nagel and Driscoll (1992) found in a study of student teachers that the novices had little commitment to practices they had learned in university coursework. Their more important concern was acceptance within the school culture. "Teaching decisions were influenced by field experiences, peers, personal experience in the schools, and the relationship with the cooperating teacher. There was a significant lack of mention of university coursework" (p. 8). Westerman (1991) found that, "In contrast to the model for expert teachers, decision making for novices seems more linear than dynamic . . ." (p. 300). Mohlman Sparks-Langer and Colton (1991), in reviewing the literature on reflective teaching, concluded that experience was the reason experts had rich schemata as compared with the novices, who had less developed schemata. All of these findings remind us that novice teachers present a special case in our efforts to understand teacher decision making.

Decision making undoubtedly is a basic teaching skill, but educators are left essentially to their own devices regarding its application. Evidence of the direct impact of theory and research on teacher decision making is minimal. However, each contribution to the literature on decision making expands our knowledge of it. A critical mass of knowledge may one day exist, signifying a major breakthrough in the skill and application of decision making.

Instructional Perspectives

During the 1970s and early 1980s, process-outcome studies contributed in an important way to the knowledge base of teaching. Generally speaking, this empirical research measured correlations between teacher behavior and student achievement to identify effective teacher practices. Rosenshine (1983) listed some of these effective practices: "structur[e] the learning; proceed in small steps . . . ; provide many examples; ask a large number of questions . . . ; provide feedback and corrections . . . ; have a student success rate of 80% or higher . . . ; . . . provide for continued practice" (p. 336). These kinds of practices were organized into a structured set of functions that provided guidelines for effective teaching:

1. Review, checking the previous day's work
2. Present new content/skills
3. Provide for initial student practice
4. Provide for feedback and correctives
5. Provide for student independent practice
6. Provide weekly and monthly reviews (337)

Much of the research done on effective teaching used population samples from urban elementary school settings. The outcomes were measured by standardized tests. Even though the findings were variably generalizable to other school populations and were important in the development of pedagogy, the limitations of the research became increasingly apparent to educators. The outcomes that were sought and measured involved two factors: essentially convergent thinking that yielded right answers, and acquisition of basic learning skills. Chapter 2 includes an expanded commentary on several aspects of effective teaching, and its applicability to secondary classrooms. The authors acknowledge in this edition, as we did in previous editions of this book, that structured and direct teaching—sometimes called "active teaching"—such as lecture and recitation is an essential set of skills for the fully functioning teacher.

As scholars during the latter half of the 1980s and into the 1990s have proclaimed, another important dimension of learning—students' personal meaning making—is not sufficiently addressed with direct-teaching approaches. National curriculum reports from subject-area learned societies began to appear in the late 1980s, the first from the National Council of Teachers of Mathematics. These reports, while they address their respective disciplines, have many common features (Zemelman, Daniels, & Hyde, 1993, p. 5):

- Less whole class, teacher directed instruction, e.g., lecturing
- Less student passivity: sitting, listening, receiving, and absorbing information
- Less attempt by teachers to thinly "cover" large amounts of material in every subject area
- Less rote memorization of facts and details
- Less tracking or leveling students into "ability groups"
- More experiential, inductive, hands-on learning
- More emphasis on higher order learning
- More responsibility transferred to students for their work
- More enacting and modeling of the principles of democracy in school
- More cooperative, collaborative activity; developing the classroom as an interdependent community

The teaching approach that incorporates these features has come to be called *"constructivist"* teaching. The term is a fairly recent one, but this student-centered approach has its roots in the work of philosopher John Dewey and cognitive/developmental psychologist Jean Piaget, two of the seminal educational theorists of this century. In this mode students become active searchers into knowledge rather than passive receivers of it. They are encouraged to discover their own meanings and develop new understandings through inquiry, reflecting, problem solving, and applying. Brooks and Brooks (1993) listed several characteristics of learning settings that encouraged constructivist learning (p. 21):

They free students from the dreariness of fact-driven curriculums and allow them to focus on large ideas.

They place in students' hands the exhilarating power to follow trails of interest, to make connections, reformulate ideas, and to reach unique conclusions.

They share with students the important message that the world is a complex place in which multiple perspectives exist and truth is often a matter of interpretation.

They acknowledge that learning, and the process of assessing learning, are, at best, elusive and messy endeavors that are not easily managed.

We include this commentary on effective teaching and constructivist teaching in this chapter because they are two major sources within the pedagogical knowledge base that inform teachers' decision making. Throughout this book repeated reference will be made to practices that emerge from these two perspectives on teaching—and learning. We assert in the following section that rational bases for decision making, when they apply, are professionally preferable to intuitive bases. Effective teaching research and constructivist teaching theory are two of these rational bases that will serve reflective teachers well.

APPLICATION TO PRACTICE

The Process of Decision Making

As cited, a persuasive argument has been made for designating decision making as the basic teaching skill. Indeed, effective decisions inevitably precede effective teaching. This is a compelling rationale for both examining decision making and striving to become proficient in its essential skills. But decision making is a subtle concept, and involves skills that are not directly acquired. Instead, the teacher must acquire certain predisposing awarenesses and attitudes, after which an improved decision-making capability is possible and probable.

Impact of Belief System

Teachers accumulate teaching-related ideas over time. Generalized information, attitudes, and assumptions are internalized, and constitute the teacher's belief system. In the classroom scenario, Ms. Knettel wanted her students to be interested in lesson content, and was disturbed that her lesson was proceeding mechanically. She needed to make a decision. But the decision she ultimately made, like most thoughtful decisions, was not based on one identifiable principle or idea, but was the product of a belief system consisting of many integrated ideas. If the ideas from which a belief system is developed are judiciously selected, the decisions that emanate from it will be generally sound. Unfortunately, the judicious selection of ideas is not an easily monitored process, and it requires knowledge and experience.

Part of the skill of decision making, therefore, involves an astute selection of ideas that will predispose subsequent decisions. One can assume that there existed within Ms. Knettel's belief system regard for the democratic process and respect for her students' perceptions and opinions.

Some teacher beliefs are fairly simple: homework should be assigned routinely, for example, or, conversely, routine homework is an unproductive use of students' time. Other beliefs are more elaborate and far-reaching. Some teachers subscribe to the proposition that learning occurs most effectively when the teacher is authoritarian or, again conversely, when the teacher is minimally directive. Such beliefs—some soundly conceived, some only superficially; some clearly defined, some vaguely—characterize individual teaching styles.

Some further examples of teachers' beliefs will help clarify the pervasive, although sometimes subtle, influence of those beliefs on teacher decisions. Some teachers consider punishment to be a deterrent to future misbehavior; others contend that punishment is a negative influence on the classroom climate that increases the potential for misbehavior. Some teachers also believe that meticulous planning contributes to effective instruction; others believe that structured plans inhibit spontaneity. Moreover, some teachers think of grades as ends in themselves; others consider grades to be means for providing feedback and correction. Which beliefs in each of these pairs—and the many more that might be listed—are right? Which can we say with confidence will result in more effective learning? Which may actually undermine students' learning? The task of every teacher is to develop a belief system that is pedagogically sound and personally comfortable. Teachers are more or less successful because of a variety of factors, some of which they cannot personally control. Fortunately, the belief system, one of the most powerful of these factors, can be directly controlled.

Figure 1.1 illustrates an interpretation of decision making that is especially pertinent to the concern raised earlier. The basic process as depicted in the model is familiar in the literature (Cooper, 1982; Hurst, Kinney, & Weiss, 1983). However, the personal belief system is an added feature that has been incorporated by the authors. It has its point of entry in the selection of an approach. Clearly, the belief system as the selection mechanism in decision making becomes a key variable in the process.

The belief system is itself informed from two bases, the intuitive and the rational. Each is comprised of several components. The intuitive components include the following:

> *Experience-based impressions*—teacher's personal judgment regarding what is appropriate or useful practice. Examples: "After 10 years of teaching I know I must get students' total attention before I begin class." "When I send a student to the office, I don't have any more trouble in that class the rest of the day."
>
> *Traditional practices*—common strategies and techniques that are widely accepted in schools and have a rationale rooted in conventional wisdom. Examples: Friday is test day. Students write out the answers to the questions at the end of the chapter. Reading is taught in the morning.
>
> *Personal needs*—personality-related and mental health–related factors that precondition the teacher's perception and behavior. Examples: Students' desks are arranged in rows so that the teacher can control the noise level and direct lessons from the front of the room. All students in industrial arts lab work on the same project at the same time.

Figure 1.1 Process of Teacher Decision Making

Rational components include the following:

Pedagogical principles—those well-established and extensively documented tenets that often have a basis in related areas of study such as
psychology, sociology, communications, leadership, organization, and
group process. Examples: Positive reinforcement promotes the highest
level of student achievement. Students learn best when they perceive
meaning and relevance in a topic.

Constructivist approaches—emphasis on the student as meaning
maker. Example: Students are actively engaged more in inquiry and the
discovery of personal meaning than in being receivers of preorganized
knowledge.

"Teacher effectiveness" practices—effective teachers were found to employ in common certain techniques in their teaching. Example: Students'
learning of unfamiliar material is enhanced by direct-teaching methods.

Research findings—discoveries through systematic methods of research into content of education, instructional approaches, and learning

effectiveness. Examples: Low-ability students learn best from concrete approaches. Task time correlates positively with student achievement.

Scholarly contributions—those essays, models, theories, and judgments of learned academicians that are an essential source of intellectual vigor and developmental thrust. Examples: Gardner's (1985) *Frames of Mind: The Theory of Multiple Intelligences* and the National Commission on Excellence in Education's (1983) *A Nation at Risk*.

Examined practice—the strategies and techniques that have been determined through experience to be effective and consistent with professionally endorsed principles of pedagogy. Examples: A variety of activities that show concern for students' span of attention result in effective teaching. Treating students with respect and sensitivity contributes to the quality of classroom life.

Importance of Using Examined Beliefs and Practices. Even in our modern schools it is not unusual to find teachers whose practice is shaped primarily from their past experiences. Some teachers (also counselors and administrators) are unquestionably effective simply because of their ample intuitive grasp of what their role demands, and their talent for responding to students. These naturally gifted teachers are often referred to as "artist teachers." Less gifted teachers are obviously less effective.

To the extent that teachers operate primarily on the basis of experience, they perform analogously to the tribal medicine man. Through his use of both mystique and proficiency with primitive medicines, he may actually perform a valuable service for his tribespeople. His practice, however, lacks a rationally developed base. Little change occurs in his practice from generation to generation because there is, essentially, no understanding of causes, and instead simply a recognition and treatment of symptoms. This is a casual analogy, and, in all fairness, should not be overstated. Changes have obviously occurred in education over any recent period of time one chooses to examine.

The fact remains that the gap between what is and what might be (real-ideal discrepancy) is a serious professional concern, evident by the 1980s' reports on the condition of schooling: *A Nation at Risk* (National Commission on Excellence in Education, 1983) as reported on by Goldberg and Harvey (1983) and "A Study of Schooling" (Goodlad, 1983). The former study stated that inferior education is one reason for lack of competitiveness with other nations, and that even though mediocrity is the norm rather than the exception, we can—and must—do better. In a discussion of the latter study, Goodlad stated, "The most striking discovery to emerge from the data is what might be called sameness of form in the substance and design of the curriculum whether the subject is English Language Arts, Mathematics, Science or Social Studies" (p. 467).

There are many reasons for the real-ideal discrepancy in the schools, and teachers' use of unexamined beliefs and practices contributes to that discrepancy. Unexamined practice encases our professional feet in blocks of anti-intellectual cement, and makes moving forward both as individual teachers and as a profession very sluggish. If the recommendations in all of the studies of schooling were implemented, but some critical mass of teachers continued to use primarily experienced-based approaches, a real-ideal discrepancy would continue to exist.

Informed Decision Making

A science of education emerges from rational sources. Intuitive sources will inevitably remain as a factor in decision making, but practices based on rational sources should take precedence in any case in which they are available and applicable.

Intuitive sources are, in particular, inclined to reflect bias and self-service. Consider, for example, the case of students in class who make minimal efforts to perform assigned learning tasks. The teacher who makes a superficial evaluation of students may consider them to be lazy. That judgment places the fault—and therefore the responsibility—entirely on the students. The teacher may nag and occasionally reprimand students, or simply ignore them except to assign low marks.

On the other hand, a teacher using a rational perspective is more likely to infer that they lack sufficient motivation, a factor for which the teacher shares responsibility, and may look for causes and solutions to the motivation problem. In Ms. Knettel's classroom scenario, she began searching for causes, rather than assuming that students would take an interest in Romantic poetry. Teachers who acknowledge their responsibility in a situation are more likely to take initiatives to improve the conditions for learning.

If educators were to relate their informed beliefs to their practice, changes would occur in their practice. The following are some possible areas of potential change:

> *Discipline practices*—The recent outpouring of professional literature on the management of student behavior signals a heightened awareness of past inadequacies and provides direction in the development of more enlightened approaches; approaches include the use of reasonable consequences, reality therapy, and behavior modification.

> *Individualization*—New understanding through cognitive-style studies and left brain–right brain experimentation raise expectations regarding the compatibility of teacher strategies with learner assimilation. A particular student's inclination toward intuitive (right hemisphere) or logical (left hemisphere) thinking has implications that are available to teachers to employ in classrooms in a systematic way.

> *Higher-level thinking*—Modern techniques of questioning can significantly raise the quality of students' thinking and increase the potential for a lasting impact. Bloom's taxonomy (1956) stimulated efforts of scholars and practitioners to emphasize the use of information as a means to an end, not an end itself.

Instruction—Discriminating and imaginative use of a variety of strategies, such as those suggested in *Models of Teaching* (Joyce & Weil, 1992) and in *Cooperative Learning: Theory, Research, and Practice* (Slavin, 1990) extend the purpose and range of instruction. Meaningful use of constructivist teaching and of concepts such as time-on-task, direct teaching, instructional cues, and others popularized by research on effective teaching contribute to effective instruction.

Evaluation—Concepts such as nongraded classrooms, mastery-level learning, alternative assessment, contract grading, diagnosis and prescription, connoisseurship, and criterion-norm-person-referenced considerations can help integrate evaluation with instruction.

The previous examples include both some older, familiar ideas and some recent ones. A teacher whose belief system and, therefore, whose practice is informed by such constructs is one for whom theory is—as Dewey (1929) insisted—the most practical of all things. Dewey meant simply that, as a practical matter in effective teaching, a sound conceptual framework (i.e., an informed belief system) is necessary. Without it, teaching is likely to be superficial and lacking in clear purpose.

Clark and Peterson (1986) captured the spirit of informed decision making as it contributes to reflective teaching:

> The maturing professional teacher is one who has taken some steps toward making explicit his or her implicit theories and beliefs about learners, curriculum, subject matter, and the teacher's role. This teacher has developed a style of planning for instruction that includes several interrelated types of planning and that has become more streamlined and automatic with experience. Much of this teacher's interactive thinking consists of routines familiar to the students, thus decreasing the collective information-processing load. During teaching, the teacher attends to and intently processes academic and nonacademic sociocognitive events and cues. These experienced teachers have developed the confidence to depart from a planned course of action when they judge that to be appropriate. They reflect on and analyze the apparent effects of their own teaching and apply the results of these reflections to their future plans and actions. In short, they have become researchers on their own teaching effectiveness. (pp. 292–293)

The remainder of the chapter essentially is an elaboration of this statement.

The Decision-Making Continuum

Virtually all teacher behavior involves choice, including the choice not to make a choice! By the idea of choice we mean that the possibility of alternatives exists, the simplest of which is whether or not to act. Some actions are characterized by the absence of any conscious choice; they represent unconscious behaviors on the part of the teacher. Other actions—and sometimes a complex sequence of actions—are preceded by deliberate reflection, such as the decision of Ms. Knettel to stage a classroom meeting. The range between these extremes represents a continuum of possibilities. Examples of behavior at each of the extremes and at the approximate midpoint will help to clarify different kinds of decision making.

Conditioned responses and unconscious knee-jerk or habitual behaviors are at the absence-of-choice end of the continuum. The repeated use of certain words or phrases (especially "okay" and "you know"), rolling chalk in a hand, and raising the voice to talk over student noise are examples of this behavior. These examples and several other kinds of behavior from this end of the continuum are such a constant part of a teacher's pattern that they help define a teaching style, and in some cases are recognized as a teacher's idiosyncracies.

At the middle range of the continuum, behavior contains a conscious dimension, with some degree of spontaneity as well. Perhaps it is best described as conscious, nonreflective behavior. Examples of this sort of behavior often fall into the category of routine behavior. This behavior includes seating students in alphabetical rows, using the textbook as virtually the sole resource in a course, and starting lessons regularly by reading the answers to the homework.

At the deliberation end of the continuum, decision making is characterized by reflection. If one assumes that some degree of decision making has occurred all along the continuum—any teaching-related action is, by definition, preceded by a decision—the term *purposeful reflection* best describes the mental operation at this far end. Examples of this behavior are unit planning, offering enrichment or remediation to particular students, and using a balance of lower- and higher-order questions in classroom discussions.

Teachers make hundreds of habitual responses and spontaneous choices in the course of a teaching day. For the sake of their sanity, they must. Practicing teachers may remember the mental fatigue they felt at the end of the day before they established a repertoire of effective responses and techniques.

On the other hand, teachers must not take their habitual choices for granted, and thereby engage in glib decision making. To do so inclines them toward the "mindlessness" syndrome observed by Silberman (1970) in so many classrooms in the late sixties, or the "monotonous sameness" reported by Goodlad (1983) in describing classrooms of the late seventies. These findings of mindlessness and monotony are, in part, due to superficial attention to decisions. Teachers should remain aware of the consequences of their decisions as reflected in their emerging teaching styles. A part of any teaching style, in fact, should be to give a full measure of reflection to decision making whenever it is due, as in planning a lesson.

Some situations arise that are unfamiliar and present momentary uncertainty—even for an experienced teacher such as Ms. Knettel. Like Ms. Knettel, a teacher must consider the alternatives, weigh the likely outcomes, and select a course of action. This sequence of mental activities extends beyond spontaneous choice and requires decision making based on principles of education, research findings, and examined practice—the core of pedagogy.

A teacher may encounter the same situation in the future and, having previously made a personally acceptable response, may readily do it again. Therefore, the same teacher behavior (response) that once required reflective decision making may become, at a later date, a simpler matter of spontaneous choice.

In the process of teacher development, both of these types of teacher response—thoughtful and spontaneous—deserve consideration. If the teacher should develop a set of automatic behaviors that are counterproductive, then teacher effectiveness is diminished. For example, a teacher may habitually lecture as a means of covering content, and may exceed student attention span. Or a teacher may frequently threaten students whose behavior is considered inappropriate. These approaches may contribute to the teacher's momentary comfort as a means of responding to the immediate demands of teaching, but the long-term effects on students are contrary to the conditions of productive learning. Continual repetition of such practices can only result in mindless and monotonous teaching.

Choice patterns or sets of responses result from prior decision making, so reflective decision making as the basis for these patterns is an essential step toward successful teaching. It is important to look at the sources from which these first-encounter decisions are made.

The Locus of Decisions

Decisions occur in three different aspects of teaching: planning and preparing for instruction, the interaction phase, and evaluating learning outcomes. Each of these aspects involves different kinds of considerations.

Planning Decisions. Decisions made prior to instruction can be made without haste or a sense of immediacy, and can be made after lengthy reflection. In the process, the teacher has time to pose some searching questions and make use of those educational principles, research findings, and theories that relate to the intent of the instruction. Some of these broad questions are:

Is this the most worthwhile topic or activity for these students at this time?

Do the students have the knowledge and skills necessary to handle the content?

What are students' attitudes about this topic, and what implications evolve from those attitudes?

What broad approaches are likely to induce the greatest motivation within the students?

How does this topic or activity relate to the objectives of this course?

Other more specific questions should also be posed, such as:

> What are some key questions that will direct students' thinking toward the lesson objectives?
>
> What arrangements and support must be provided?
>
> How can individual student differences be accommodated?
>
> What sort of entry will most effectively initiate learning?

Interactive Decisions. Teachers make an average of one interactive decision every two to six minutes (Clark & Peterson, 1986; Shavelson, 1983; Clark, 1988). Furthermore, decisions made during the interactive phase of instruction often must occur rapidly, for time is severely limited. Yet, one's success as a teacher clearly is contingent on the quality of these decisions. The seasoned teacher who has encountered a wide variety of conditions and who has learned appropriate responses by some means—even trial and error—is surely at an advantage. Ms. Knettel made the decision to use a classroom meeting based on prior experience with the activity.

A less experienced, but alert, teacher may speculate about possible situations that will require decisions and think them through beforehand. As situations arise, they will not be quite so strange or puzzling, and can be taken in stride. For example, a teacher may be planning a small-group activity for the following day's lesson. The class has not participated in small-group activities as yet, so the teacher does not know how students will respond. Therefore, the teacher could make an alternate plan, such as an appropriate seat-work assignment, as a contingency.

But no amount of preparation can help the teacher predict every situation that will occur. What then does the teacher do? Several nonspecific strategies are applicable in these cases:

> Simply pause and take a moment to reflect, even at the risk of momentary awkwardness.
>
> Admit honestly to the class that the situation requires some time to think through.
>
> Make a decision, if the consequences are not irreversible, with the intent of reviewing it later.

Any teacher who has a well-informed belief system, and who is in touch with that belief system, has an important advantage in this interactive phase of instruction. When sound educational principles that can be quickly called to use populate the belief system, effective decisions are the probable outcome. Fewer off-the-top-of-the-head judgments will occur. The teacher whose belief system is more intuitively based rather than rationally based, or who simply does not make a sufficient effort to act rationally, will make a large proportion of suspect decisions while teaching that can cause problems for both the teacher and the students.

Evaluation Decisions. Finally, decisions are made following instruction. The teacher must determine the extent to which students have performed according to some standard. The more explicit both the initial objectives for learning and the criteria for evaluation are, the more clear and valid are the decisions regarding students' performance. The teacher who has thoughtfully developed objectives and criteria beforehand will find the postinstruction evaluation decisions simpler to make. On the other hand, a teacher whose evaluation decisions are largely after the fact fails initially to provide students with a clear idea of expectations and is likely to engage in arbitrary, expedient means of assessing achievement. The consequences are predictable: validity of the evaluation is marginal, and the very purpose of evaluation is compromised.

A second set of decisions should be made following instruction, although these are often ignored or done superficially. The teaching process, however, is not complete until the preceding instruction is critically reviewed—at the least casually and sometimes systematically—to provide an analysis. The obvious question is: How effective was this episode or unit of instruction?

For the conscientious teacher, there are several sources that provide immediate answers to this question: student demeanor and initiative, demonstrated student achievement, and the teacher's own sense of how well the students complied with predetermined expectations. The more specific the teacher is regarding predetermined expectations, the more likely that evaluative decisions will be useful.

As the teacher moves toward greater specificity and objectivity, a more systematic means of analysis and data collection is required. Formal approaches, including audio and video recording, are useful for this purpose. They provide a reliable basis for decision making in the interest of improved teaching and for developing a belief system.

SUMMARY POINT

Being aware of decision making as a process and understanding the dynamics of the process does not exhaust the potential of this concept to contribute to effective teaching. Decision making is the professional orientation and a pattern of thinking that undergirds one's instructional style and ensures that teaching will be conducted as a thoughtful practice. To the extent that this occurs, a teacher cannot be comfortable employing unwitting, intuitive responses to the demands of teaching. Rather, rational sources become the only acceptable basis for decisions, and for subsequent related choices. Rational, reflective decision making is the basic teaching skill that, fully developed, is essential to optimally effective teaching.

REVIEW: CONSIDERATIONS IN DECISION MAKING

Optimal teacher decision making involves:

1. commitment to the proposition that decision making is the basic teaching skill;
2. the teacher's conscious desire to be a skilled decision maker;
3. acceptance of the science of education as the basis for enlightened instruction;
4. a belief system informed by the tenets of modern pedagogy; and
5. purposeful use of a systematic approach to decision making in planning, conducting, and evaluating instruction.

QUESTIONS FOR REFLECTION

1. Eight general beliefs are included in this chapter, but these represent only the beginning of a much longer possible list. What are some other teaching-related beliefs that you currently hold?
2. The assertion is made in chapter 1 that decision making is the basic teaching skill. What arguments might be made to support or refute that statement? What, in fact, are the subskills that comprise rational decision making?
3. Teachers must make decisions abut all the aspects of teaching, including physical arrangement of the classroom, climate, lesson planning, instructional style and strategies, testing and evaluation, classroom management rules and routines, and student behavior. What are some typical decisions you as a teacher might make in these contexts, and, importantly, what are your beliefs and motives that underlie them?
4. Personal needs are included in the list of intuitive (unexamined) bases for teacher decisions. What is your own needs profile that is likely to predispose, for better or for worse, decisions you will make as a teacher?

REFERENCES

Bloom, B. (Ed.). (1956). *A taxonomy of educational objectives, Handbook I: Cognitive domain.* New York: McKay.

Brooks, J., & Brooks, M. (1993). *The case for constructivist classrooms.* Alexandria, VA: Association for Supervision and Curriculum Development.

Brophy, J., & Good, T. (1986). Research on early childhood and elementary school teaching programs. In M. Wittrock (Ed.), *Handbook of research on teaching* (3rd ed.). New York: Macmillan.

Cardelle-Elawar, M. (1993). The teacher as researcher in the classroom. *Action in Teacher Education, 15,* 49–57.

Clark, C. (1988). Asking the right questions about teacher preparation: Contributions of research on teacher thinking. *Educational Researcher, 17*(2), 5–12.

Clark, C., & Peterson, P. (1976). *Teacher stimulated recall of interactive decisions.* Paper presented at the annual meeting of the American Educational Research Association, San Francisco.

Clark, C., & Peterson, P. (1986). Teachers' thought processes. In M. Wittrock (Ed.), *Handbook of research on teaching* (3rd ed.). New York: Macmillan.

Cooper, J. (1982). The teacher as decision maker. In J. Cooper (Ed.), *Classroom teaching skills* (2nd ed.). Lexington, MA: Heath.

Dewey, J. (1929). *The sources of a science of education.* New York: Liveright.

Farr, R., & Brown, V. (1971). Evaluation and decision making. *Reading Teacher, 24*(4), 341–346, 354.

Gardner, H. (1985). *Frames of mind: The theory of multiple intelligences.* New York: Basic Books.

Goldberg, M., & Harvey, J. (1983). A nation at risk: The report of the National Commission on Excellence in Education. *Phi Delta Kappan, 65*(1), 14–18.

Goodlad, J. (1983). A study of schooling: Some findings and hypotheses. *Phi Delta Kappan, 64*(7), 465–470.

Herbert, G. W. (1974). Teachers' ratings of classroom behavior: Factorial structure. *British Journal of Educational Psychology, 44,* 233–240.

Hunter, M. (1979). Teaching is decision making. *Educational Leadership, 37*(1), 62–64, 67.

Hunter, M. (1984). Knowing, teaching, and supervising. In P. Hosford (Ed.), *Using what we know about teaching.* Alexandria, VA: Association for Supervision and Curriculum Development.

Hurst, J., Kinney, M., & Weiss, S. J. (1983). The decision making process. *Theory and Research in Social Education, 11*(19), 178–182.

Joyce, B., & Weil, M. (1992). *Models of teaching* (4th ed.). Englewood Cliffs, NJ: Prentice-Hall.

Manley-Casimer, M., & Wasserman, S. (1989). The teacher as decision-maker. *Childhood Education, 65*(5), 288–293.

Mohlman Sparks-Langer, G., & Colton, A. (1991). Synthesis of research on teachers' reflective thinking. *Educational Leadership, 48*(6), 37–44.

Nagel, N., & Driscoll, A. (1992). *Dilemmas caused by discrepancies between what they learn and what they see: Thinking and decision-making of preservice teachers.* Paper presented at the annual meeting of the American Educational Research Association, San Francisco.

National Commission on Excellence in Education (1983). *A nation at risk.* Washington, DC: U.S. Department of Education.

Perkins, D. (1986). *Knowledge and design.* Hillsdale, NY: Lawrence Erlbaum.

Rosenshine, B. (1983). Teaching functions in instructional programs. *Elementary School Journal, 83*(4), 335–351.

Rubenstein, G., & Fisher, L. (1974). A measure of teachers' observations of student behavior. *Journal of Consulting and Clinical Psychology, 42,* 310.

Shavelson, R. J. (1973). What is the basic teaching skill? *Journal of Teacher Education, 24,* 144–151.

Shavelson, R. J. (1983). Review of research on teachers' pedagogical judgments, plans, and decisions. *Elementary School Journal, 83*(4), 392–413.

Shavelson, R. J., Cadwell, J., & Izu, T. (1977). Teachers' sensitivity to the reliability of information in making pedagogical decisions. *American Educational Research Journal, 14*(2), 83–97.

Silberman, C.E. (1970). *Crisis in the classroom.* New York: Random House.

Slavin, R. (1990). *Cooperative learning: Theory, research, and practice.* Englewood Cliffs, NJ: Prentice-Hall.

Sontag, M. (1968). Attitudes toward education and perception of teacher behaviors. *American Educational Research Journal, 5,* 385–402.

Westerman, D. (1991). Expert and novice teacher decision making. *Journal of Teacher Education, (4),* 292–305.

Zemelman, S., Daniels, H., & Hyde, A. (1993). *Best practice: New standards for teaching and learning in America's schools.* Portsmouth, NH: Heinemann.

Building a Climate for Learning

OUTLINE

A teacher's decisions about behavior and academic standards contribute to classroom climate and influence students' attitudes toward learning.

FOCUS QUESTIONS

1. What is meant by school climate?
2. What do you believe to be the most important factor in maintaining a positive learning climate?
3. What are some practices that indicate to students that high standards are being maintained in a classroom?

4. How can the teacher influence the success of the student?
5. What teaching behavior is most consistently related to student achievement?
6. How does one praise effectively?
7. How can students use metacognition to become better learners?

OVERVIEW

You are about to meet Tom Baldino, a master teacher who knows that teaching is more than lesson plans and tests. He will demonstrate his approach to building an effective classroom climate that encourages student learning.

Building a supportive learning environment continues to be an important goal for all teachers to increase student success. Teachers exercise minimal control over many environmental factors. However, beginning teachers can develop an understanding of how the learning environment they are creating contributes to the success of the students. Beginning teachers can learn to develop practices that are supportive of the learner. These practices must be compatible with teachers' knowledge of their students and of themselves as teachers, knowledge of the curriculum, and understanding of the influence of the context in which they are working. Considering all these factors, effective teachers can set up classroom conditions that encourage the learner.

Many studies have examined effective teaching through the process-product (input-output) research of the seventies and eighties. Schools and teachers that were especially successful in promoting student achievement have been studied, and investigations have been made to identify the factors leading to that success.

Although we recognize today that the teaching behavior of successful teachers is only one dimension of the complex spectrum that influences student learning, we still need to consider certain elements of effective teaching that have been repeatedly identified in classroom research over the years as having considerable impact on learning.

This chapter will focus on some of the characteristics of classrooms and teacher behaviors that build a positive climate for learning—an academic climate, promotion of high standards, expectation for success, and provision of feedback and praise that encourages the development of metacognitive skills.

The key to instructional effectiveness is, as ever, a wise and informed teacher–decision maker who considers the school context (setting), student needs, and curricular goals. The complexity of the instructional process is such that no teacher can plug in certain practices and achieve guaranteed success. Rather, this chapter emphasizes the importance of understanding the interaction between teacher and students and the influence that the teacher's decisions about instruction have on student success within the sphere of influence of the classroom and the school.

A climate for learning is the sum of all the students' perceptions and predispositions to their association with schools. Climate refers to the affective aspects of the classroom—such as feelings generated by and about the teachers, the students, the subject matter, and the school—that contribute positively or negatively to the learning environment. Teachers exercise some control over environmental factors. Beginning teachers need to pay attention to factors that affect classroom climate and to notice these factors' impact on students.

SCENARIO

Tom Baldino was meeting his math class for the fourth time in the first week of school. It was a diverse group, with a mix of white students (mainly males), a number of African-Americans, several Latinos, and two American Indians. He knew that a cooperative learning approach would be important to help this group become cohesive. He had his work cut out for him in addressing their math needs, as well. The diagnostic tests he administered during the first class sessions revealed that his students were not up to grade level in their math skills. Basic skills seemed to be in place, but analytical-reasoning skills registered low, as did problem-solving skills. Most of the class had obtained a 6th-grade achievement level, putting them two years behind in math proficiency.

Mr. Baldino smiled at the students as they entered the room. He stood in front of the desks, seating chart in hand, trying to match names with faces. The halls emptied and became quiet as students found their seats.

Chatter subsided because he was standing in front of the class looking at the students. He had explained on the first day that students could talk until he stood in front of the class, ready to start the lesson. Though still unfamiliar with him and with some of the other students, the class was following his rules. He had shared only three rules with them, and he intended to enforce them.

"I've been putting you through your paces the last few days so I could get an idea of your math skills and your knowledge," he said. The class let out a subdued groan and waited expectantly. "Now it's time to get started and use that ability you show to do well in math. How many of you want to do better in math this year?" About half of the class slowly raised their hands. "Well, you've come to the right place. All of you. Baldino-the-Wizard is going to start working his wonders on you—even on those of you who didn't raise your hands. Right here in this room, before your very eyes, and with considerable help from you, you are all going to become good math students. It won't happen overnight, but with some help from both you and the magic hat, it will happen."

Students giggled as Mr. Baldino reached under his desk and pulled out a magician's wand and a tall, black silk hat. Occasionally he had fun hamming it up for the classes, and being an amateur magician helped. All eyes were on him as he stood in front of them, waving his hand over the hat as if he were going to pull out a rabbit. He couldn't help doing a few simple, sleight-of-hand tricks with chalk and pencils, like pulling a pencil out of the ear of a student sitting in the front row. Everyone laughed, and seemed to relax as math class took a turn toward the unexpected.

"Now that I've got your attention, let's see what mysteries the hat holds that are going to turn you into good math students. First, let me check again to make sure I know which students are going to use this magic this year." He peered carefully at the class, trying to contact every eye. "Let's see again those hands of people who want to become good math students this year." This time more hands went up. Only about five remained down—those of five boys in the back. He made a mental note of the boys' reluctance to get involved, and chose one of them to come forward to be an assistant. The student reluctantly agreed and ambled to the front.

"Okay, now that I have some assistance, let's check the magic hat for ways to make our math powers stronger." He had the assistant hold the hat and tap it with the wand as he pulled out a rubber chicken. The class laughed politely.

Baldino admitted to himself the act had gone over much better for the 7th grade, but he was determined to get them started on a higher note. After next instructing the aide to tap the hat twice, Mr. Baldino pulled out a slip of paper that, he explained, contained a magic, coded message. He went to the board and scribbled down some mathematical symbols, and then wrote on the board, "Math Magic. You become a math whiz by doing the following." He did more hamming by chanting mysteriously and waving his arms, and then plunged into the hat for another magic message. This one read: "Homework papers turned in every day Monday through Thursday. On Mondays and Tuesdays students will be responsible to determine their own homework assignments. Homework ideas will be available in the Math Wizard Mystery Book on the teacher's desk. Those who complete the week's assignments receive a magic award of no homework on Fridays." The proclamation was received with some groans and some cheers.

With a flourish, Mr. Baldino pulled out another slip. "All tests will be graded pass or take over. No numerical grade will be given. Students will continue to work on difficult material until able to pass a test."

The list went on to include the following, which were written on the board:

"All students will bring magic tools to class: books, pencils and papers, calculators, and thinking caps."

"Students will develop a goal plan for themselves to chart their progress over the next three months."

"Students will be expected to work in small groups of two or three during weekly practice times."

"Students will be responsible for bringing in once a week for the next month real-life problems that require math problem solving."

When he was finished, the students looked subdued, but they were all watching him. He described the magic fun corner of the room that would be filled with math games and math puzzles to be used for relaxation time after work was completed, or if a special award was given. (He hoped to add a computer to the room the next year. It would be excellent for practice exercises and individual instruction.)

He ended with a pep talk on class attitude, saying that for the magic to work, everyone had to keep believing that they could handle the material. The tests showed they had the ability; now they had to prove it to themselves and to everyone else by following the magic plan.

Mr. Baldino thought through his additional plans. He expected to give a feedback quiz once a week and an exam as students finished units of work. The units would be focused on the topics in the NCTM curriculum (National Council of Teachers of Mathematics). Units would be built around problem solving and inquiry projects that would be interdisciplinary in nature. He would hold periodic review lessons and include items from past units in his tests. He would continually convey to the class and to each individual student his belief in everyone's ability to become a math wizard. He planned to have all students develop math portfolios of their work so that their success profiles could be easily seen. This visible feedback about progress was to be an important part of the magic to make students feel successful. He explained aloud that his magic—and the students' magic—would work together to achieve success.

After emptying the hat, he asked the class if they knew of any other magic formulas to promote success. One boy from the unreceptive group suggested that the teacher teach them how to pull money from people's ears. The class nodded approval. Mr. Baldino located a quarter in his pocket, then seemingly pulled it from the ear of the girl in the front seat while he talked about the introduction to the lesson.

"In order to solve a problem or create magic we must use good thinking. How would you think about solving the problem of how high the ceiling would have to be in a room that contains a stack of 1 million quarters?" The class started to buzz as students got out paper, quarters, and began discussing the problem with each other.

TOPIC 1: ESTABLISHING AN ACADEMIC CLIMATE

RESEARCH AND THEORETICAL BASE

When examining the research on climates that encourage student learning, several factors surface from the effective-schools research (Lezotte, 1984.) One of the factors that has implications for decision making about curriculum and instruction encourages the teacher to focus class activities on the completion of meaningful academic objectives. The teacher presents the learning objectives to the class and helps students reach those objectives to the best of their ability. The issue is not completion of material but of holding students accountable, to demonstrate understanding of the key concepts so they can use the knowledge in meaningful ways. Students are not motivated to learn when they are required to memorize material that they can't apply.

In a research summary of teacher effects on student achievement in urban schools, Brophy (1982) listed emphasis on cognitive objectives within a warm, supportive climate as a key teacher behavior. In another study, Rosenshine (1979) cited a major focus on challenging academic goals as a characteristic of teachers in effective classrooms. He indicated that students learn best in classrooms in which there is both academic emphasis and teacher-directed instruction. The direct-teaching model (teacher interacting with total class) that he observed being employed in effective schools included two practices related to emphasis on academics: (1) teachers placed a clear focus on academic goals, and (2) teachers made an effort to promote extensive content coverage and high levels of student involvement. Today's teachers are advised through findings of recent research and in the standards work of national groups such as the NCTM to reduce content coverage and focus on key concepts in more depth. Less and in-depth is the adage. Deep understanding is the goal (Brooks & Brooks, 1993).

Another factor that contributes to the establishing of an academic climate is the amount of time that the student is involved with the content. The teacher must consider three aspects of the involvement behavior: (1) how much time is provided by the teacher (allocated time), (2) to what degree students are engaged during the time provided (engagement rate or time-on-task), and (3) how successfully students are engaged (academic learning time, that high-quality time in which students devote themselves to and succeed in meaningful tasks) (Fisher et al., 1978).

The importance of on-task time is supported consistently in the literature. In their review of research on teacher behavior and student achievement, Good and Brophy (1994) cited studies showing that academic learning was influenced by the amount of time students spent engaged in appropriate academic tasks. Studies comparing the amount of time low-achieving students and high-achieving students spend actively working with content have revealed that students with more involvement time also have a higher achievement level (Good & Beckerman, 1978; Perkins, 1965).

The National Education Commission on Time and Learning (1994) conducted a 24-month investigation and concluded that the academic-learning unit had been stolen to make room for a host of nonacademic activities. The commission recommended that the academic day needed to provide at least 5.5 hours of core academic instructional time. The expectation was that within those hours teachers should engage students in activities that increase their quality academic learning time.

APPLICATION TO PRACTICE

The following practices are recommended to the teacher for generating an academic climate in the classroom.

1. Be task oriented.
2. Keep students on task.
3. Encourage students to do homework.
4. Encourage students to build their understanding of academic work.
5. Give daily feedback.
6. Convey to students confidence in their ability to succeed.
7. Provide learning activities that offer academic challenges.
8. Support students' efforts.

Be Task Oriented

A task-oriented teacher is aware of both the use of time spent on a lesson and the purpose of that lesson. A major effort is made to keep students productively involved throughout the lesson. The teacher starts class promptly by indicating to the class what needs to be accomplished during a specific time period and the purpose for the day's learning activities. This establishing-set technique is advocated by both Hunter (1994) and Rosenshine (1979). Rosenshine included it as part of the first function—structuring the lesson—in his direct-teaching strategy (see chapter 6). By way of this introduction, the students know what is expected of them and that the teacher will make sure the tasks are accomplished. The instruction portion of the lesson will center on the planned objective(s) and the learning activities (including practice time) that will be used to accomplish the objective. The teacher monitors the students' progress in accomplishing the lesson's objective through feedback, circulating around the room to check on their progress, and collecting, checking, and recording their completed assignments.

Teachers need to become aware of their use of time during the instructional day. Much instructional time is wasted in the classroom by such practices as allocating 20 to 30 minutes in class for students to work on homework, excessive viewing of films, class announcements, attendance routines, and starting class (Lowe & Gervais, 1988). McGreal (1994) reported recent studies showing that the time between the bell ringing in high schools and instruction beginning averaged about 9 minutes out of the 50-minute period.

These time studies make it clear that teachers need to know how time is being used in their classrooms. Through conscious clock watching for several days or by using a student observer, a fellow teacher, or the principal, teachers will be able to gather information that informs them about their use of time. How much time is spent on the opening of class? When do students stop working? Is the time spent on a task in proportion to the importance of the task? How much time do the students spend on teacher materials in contrast to working with the teacher? How much individual attention does a student receive each week from the teacher? How much time during each class period does the teacher spend interacting with the class? How much time does the class actually spend actively involved with the lesson?

Trying to find the answers to these questions through the analysis of the instructional pattern of one's own teaching helps develop a sense of time awareness for the teacher. Teacher and classroom observers can determine the amount of students' engagement time by using uncomplicated observational instruments such as the learning time–analysis chart or the participation ratio grid (see instruments at end of chapters). Percentages can be determined for students' time-on-task during the observation period. Student-engagement time—another term used to describe student on-task time—takes into consideration both time and "engaged time," which is the amount of time the students actually spend working on content during that period. Other methods that can be used to gather time-related information could include the use of Flanders interaction analysis for quantitative time analysis of classroom interaction, time-on-task instruments, teacher notation of time at beginning and ending of instruction segments, student notation of time, or the teacher noting in the plan book the amount of time for each phase of instruction or time spent with certain students for several class periods. Observing academic learning time (high-quality involvement) is difficult unless the observer moves around the room and examines the students' output.

Keep Students On-Task

Moreover, to establish an academic climate and keep students on-task, the teacher must be aware of the class's engagement time and of each student's academic learning time. Academic learning time is that high-quality time when the student is involved with the content and is succeeding. The teacher may have to use a variety of methods to help certain students increase their on-task time, such as calling on students by name, getting students busy with an activity, encouraging group work, focusing on students by moving around the room and checking their papers, interacting with students about the content rather than other distracting topics, and spending little time on organizational and management tasks such as setting up equipment or handing out materials. Use of discipline measures should be limited and employed only to maintain an orderly environment for learning. For example, we sense that Mr. Baldino was task oriented even while maintaining a sense of humor, and that students would have been kept productively occupied throughout the year in his class.

Give Limited and Purposeful Homework

The third practice is assigning homework. Homework received national attention when reports on schools in the early 1980s revealed that little homework was being assigned in U.S. schools, and even less was being completed. The importance of homework was documented in a U.S. Department of Education study (1985) entitled, *What Works*, which cited research showing the beneficial effects of homework on learning. In response, some school districts around the country passed mandatory homework laws that pressured the teacher to assign homework four or five times a week. For example, in 1986 the Chicago Board of Education adopted a policy across all grade levels that homework was to be assigned every night, from 15 minutes of work for kindergarten to $2\frac{1}{2}$ hours of work for high school students (Snider, 1986).

Such actions necessitate caution. Assigning homework will not in itself guarantee academic achievement. Homework activities must be carefully selected by the teacher to accomplish a specific purpose, and should be limited in quantity and tied to course objectives and student outcomes. Homework is best suited for the following purposes: to provide students with more practice, if needed, after a group practice session in class; to provide students more time to develop a paper or project over a period of several days; and to provide students time to become familiar with concepts or themes presented in reading material prior to discussion in class. Routine homework that has no purpose other than to keep students involved with 20 math problems or 5 pages of history every night will not increase achievement or encourage a climate for learning. This kind of busy work just initiates negative attitudes toward homework.

When purposeful homework is assigned, the teacher makes decisions regarding the application of the assignment to the daily lesson and the weight of its evaluation. The teacher needs to go over the work in class to provide immediate feedback to students. Homework should be collected and checked to determine whether it is completed correctly. A teacher's cursory glance over a paper is enough to see if the homework is finished and understood or to check on any problems that a student may have had with the assignment. A check mark in the grade book can indicate that the assignment has been accomplished. Those students who have not turned in homework should be notified they are being held responsible for it. A student's handling of homework assignments should be an appropriately weighted part of the grade-period mark.

A caution to consider on homework is that disadvantaged students—those who are homeless or have no place to study at home, or no computer with which to work—may be treated inequitably through homework assignments. Don't give homework if students won't be able to complete it.

Encourage Students to Master Materials

Students should also be encouraged to master the material by allowing them to advance at their own rate whenever possible. The teacher may have to reteach students until they can acquire the essential skills and knowledge to pass an exam satisfactorily. Some content may have to be eliminated for those who fall behind the rest of the class to allow time for mastery of essential knowledge. Part of the class hour or day may be spent working in small-group sessions of students on remediation or problem-solving activities. In this context it is vital that students know they are being held responsible for mastering the key information. They must sense that they have control over their school progress by meeting their learning responsibilities. Tom Baldino's "magic" rules conveyed to students the emphasis on standards and his intention to monitor work in terms of individual students.

Give Daily Feedback

Another practice in establishing an academic climate is giving daily feedback that includes writing comments on corrected papers and holding conferences with students to discuss their progress and encourage their success. Optimally, the teacher should try to have some interaction with every student each day. The nature of this interaction should provide feedback related to progress, indications of teacher interest and concern for the student, and remediation suggestions. Displaying and sharing quality student work with the class is useful feedback because it reflects a high performance standard, student success, and a student product for peer comparison.

Monitor Progress for Student Success

In addition to promoting academic excellence, each student's potential should be nurtured and monitored. The teacher nurtures students, with the intent to encourage the students to keep trying, by making them aware of their individual progress and potential. A model of frequent quizzes and fewer large exams gives more information to the students and their teacher about the students' learning. Planning conference times with students during the school year or at the end of class several days a month are important ways to support student feelings of success in the class. Results from pre- and posttesting can be shared, along with term grades and samples of student work collected in student portfolios. Conveying confidence in students' ability was perhaps the most impressive aspect of Mr. Baldino's class. His so-called magic was his way of convincing students of their eventual success—the self-fulfilling prophecy.

Provide Academic Challenges

It is also essential to provide students with learning activities that offer academic challenges. A teacher plans activities that involve students with application, analysis, and synthesis experiences as well as with practice with lower-level knowledge and comprehension tasks. Learning activities should be examined to see if they encourage students to use higher-level thinking skills and problem-solving techniques. Extensive unit projects can be developed to provide students with opportunities to expand their thinking. Such activities might include planning and printing a grade-level or room newspaper after studying a journalism unit, or developing a community survey form to focus the town's attention on the recreational needs of youths and senior citizens. Any activity that creates excitement for learning encourages an academic climate. Encouraging student questions and input into projects enables students to challenge themselves, as well.

Support Students' Efforts

All these practices for establishing an academic climate need to be embedded within a warm, supportive learning climate. Such a climate is characterized by teachers with an unconditional positive regard and genuine interest in each child and who make purposeful use of indirect verbal teaching behaviors suggested by Flanders (1970): accepting students' feelings, praising students, using student ideas, asking questions to actively involve students, and encouraging student questions and ideas. If the climate in the classroom created by the teacher's demeanor is cold, distant, controlling, and uncaring, students' motivation to learn will be adversely affected. So whereas creating an academic climate is necessary for academic achievement, it can never be at the expense of affective factors. The most effective teachers are those who are able to make these two essential dynamics of climate—cognitive needs and affective needs—mutually reinforcing while encouraging and supporting students to take charge of their own learning, pursue their questions, become problem solvers, and explore issues.

TOPIC 2: PROMOTING HIGH STANDARDS

RESEARCH AND THEORETICAL BASE

The purpose of this section is to emphasize the importance of individual accountability and high standards but not to sacrifice social responsibility and positive interdependence for academic excellence. The message of Mr. Baldino was not one of competition but rather individual progress and group interaction for learning. Mr. Baldino addressed high standards in his classroom when he announced to the students that all tests had to be passed or taken over until passed. His message was that there would be no failures in the classroom. The goal was understanding and individual progress, not high test scores. If students failed, they would be retaught via programmed materials or through controlled group practice and, later, independent practice (Hunter, 1994). He also stressed the importance of students' goal plans, coming prepared to class with books and paper, and seeking life applications of mathematics. He believed that informing the class of the standards they had to meet was essential.

Mr. Baldino knew that in many groups, including Native American cultures, the achievement of the individual was of less value than the social good of the group. He would emphasize group work frequently, and the progress of the whole class as well as of individuals, so as not to place Native American students in conflict with the mores of their culture (Swisher, 1990).

The issue of establishing higher standards became a nationwide charge in 1983 following the publication of the findings of numerous national reports on the status of public education. The National Commission on Excellence in Education report, *A Nation at Risk* (1983), called for the upgrading of standards by increasing basic academic requirements for graduation. The commission recommended that more rigorous and measurable standards and higher expectations for academic performance and student conduct be adopted by schools and colleges. Rutter, Maugham, Mortimore, and Ouster (1979) supported the call for higher standards in a report defining effective schools as those where "high expectations were the order of the day" (p. 42).

Block (1970) examined the impact that standards had on students' performance and attitudes and found that higher standards resulted in higher cognitive achievement. His study also noted that when required performance standards (that level at which student performance was considered acceptable) were too high, student attitudes were affected negatively. These results indicated the need to establish performance standards that would challenge yet not discourage students.

Levin with Long (1981) pointed out that most researchers agree a 100% mastery standard is neither realistic nor necessary in the classroom. A 70% to 80% performance level is acceptable if that score indicates a student has achieved the essential understanding and is prepared to move ahead in the course. The teacher should recycle through the content students who do not meet the acceptable understanding level. Others who have met the acceptable level should move forward.

To summarize the numerous research studies, one can say that setting reasonable standards for performance in the classroom includes maintaining an acceptable level of performance on everything from conduct to homework and tests. The goal of these standards is to create a climate in the classroom that conveys the following message: The business in the classroom is to learn; students can be and are expected to be successful.

APPLICATION TO PRACTICE

The following practices can convey to students that high standards are maintained in a classroom:

1. Setting an academic performance level that all students must meet.
2. Establishing an organizational system for remediation.
3. Maintaining a standard of performance that acknowledges an acceptable level of understanding.
4. Rewarding excellent work and effort.
5. Maintaining a professional image in the classroom.
6. Encouraging students to discover the excitement of learning through their own inquiry.
7. Requiring a level of work that challenges but does not frustrate.
8. Emphasizing higher-level thinking as well as memory-level and comprehension-level cognitive functioning.
9. Encouraging group work, peer tutoring, and group development of performance criteria.

Setting a Mandatory Performance Level
The teacher should set a performance level for each key objective to indicate at what point each objective has been satisfactorily met. For example, a teacher must decide that an objective has been mastered if students are able to pass a test on the information at the 70% level and explain key concepts, or are able to get 8 out of 10 problems correct and explain the process they used, or write a para-

graph with only two errors in sentence construction, spelling, and punctuation. Below-level students would continue to do remediation work and then be retested on an objective until they met the achievement standard.

Deciding the level at which to set performance standards is difficult for teachers, especially for beginning teachers who cannot rely on past experiences. Research does not reveal appropriate performance levels for optimum learning. Each teacher must determine the level appropriate to challenge—but not frustrate—the class or individuals. Also, the teacher may decide to set individual performance levels. These performance levels may be raised or lowered during the year to improve the learning climate.

Establishing an Organizational System for Remediation

If a teacher defines a performance level for major objectives as recommended in this chapter, an organizational system for remediation will also need to be established. This means that the teacher builds a reserve of additional explanatory materials, practice activities, and tests on key objectives. If some students are unsuccessful in reaching the accepted level of performance, they continue to study and practice until they reach the level or until the teacher decides to move them on to the next phase. (This feature was emphasized in Tom Baldino's approach in the scenario.) A successful remediation program cannot be implemented until the teacher has a supply of materials from reference textbooks, sample texts, and, in those cases where skills and content have not changed, old textbooks from which to draw material and additional practice for the learner.

Using peer tutors and remediation groups is an important part of the remediation system, as well. If this remedial system is in place, the teacher has more time to reinstruct students who have not reached the satisfactory performance level.

The remediation or recycling stage will be most effective if it involves the teacher's controlled practice with a small group or an individual. The teacher conducts the controlled practice to reexplain, model, and illustrate the material. Then the students proceed to small-group practice or independent practice. When this step has been completed successfully, retesting occurs. During those times when the teacher is working with an individual or small group needing remediation, the rest of the class can be involved in group work or independent practice to review the objective or to achieve a new objective. (These practices just described comprise part of the strategies of mastery learning explained in chapter 6.)

Maintaining a Standard of Performance

Teachers who maintain an academic climate use certain pertinent practices in their instructional and management approaches. Homework is collected and checked so students know that homework is a required performance standard and that they will receive feedback on it. Not every homework paper must receive a grade. Other practices used by teachers to convey academic standards include assuring that work missed because of absences is made up; that most class time is spent on academic tasks; and that objectives for learning tasks are shared with students and, at times, developed by students. Rewards are handled carefully. Marginal or wrong answers are not rewarded or criticized; rather, the student learns to analyze incorrect answers to see where the problem occurred and why it occurred. The emphasis is on understanding more than correctness. Excellent work and effort are rewarded.

Rewarding Excellent Work and Effort

A suggested practice for promoting high standards emphasizes rewards. The reward strategies the teacher chooses to use are important in maintaining the success climate in the classroom. Recognition for doing outstanding work can be given in a variety of forms, such as displaying the work in the classroom or on the bulletin board, displaying student work in the school lobby in display cases or on hall walls, sharing the product with the class by reading it or passing it around for examination, and giving special mention of the work to the class by allowing the creator to explain it. Tom Baldino used no homework on Fridays and the magic fun corner as rewards for his class. Students can experience new rewards through encouragement from teachers to submit written work for publication in student anthologies. For example, one of the authors obtained literary recognition for several athletes, all football team members, by encouraging the class to send their poems composed for a poetry unit to the *National Student Anthology of Poetry*. Four of the athletes' poems were published. This recognition caused quite a stir in the school. This example points out that the teacher can enter student work into local, state, and national arenas, where it may receive recognition. Also, the school newspaper may accept written work of general interest to the school.

Maintaining a Professional Image in the Classroom

Another influence on the academic atmosphere in the classroom is the tacit message communicated by the teacher's professional behavior. That behavior indicates acceptable standards for conduct as surely as written rules and procedures given to children. Brophy and Good (1986) reported that teachers who promoted the highest achievement in the classroom were businesslike and task oriented. Such professional teacher behavior evokes respect for the teacher's position.

Teacher behavior that reflects a professional attitude may include such practices as lessons prepared in advance, correct use of grammar, correct spelling, legible writing on both the board and papers, prompt return of student work, and good teacher attendance. A teacher's professional commitment to using class time to concentrate on academic tasks and conducting class in a supportive but businesslike manner impresses students. A professional teacher will also encourage students to provide feedback on how the class is functioning for them. In addition, teachers convey their interest in students' progress by supplying frequent feedback through quizzes, tests, comments on assignments, and daily comprehension checks.

Encouraging Students to Discover the Excitement of Learning

Another practice that effective teachers employ to create enthusiasm for scholarly activity at any grade level is helping students enjoy the excitement of learning. A curious mind can lead to investigation that involves all of a student's higher thinking processes. Creating excitement through discovery and exploration of individuals' questions can stimulate an environment that encourages students to share their ideas and interests. For example, after reading Bill Moyers's *Healing and the Mind* (1994), a teacher discussed some of the information with her biology class. This led to a lively discussion on the use of mind/body medicine and a visit from a guest speaker, a local doctor who used biofeedback in his practice. Encouraging students to share in a similar fashion can be contagious. Students may bring in books on snakes and display some pet snakes to the class. Or, children may show a telescope to the class and explain their study of the evening sky done with parents. A student's stamp collection can lead to a history lesson about famous people the class does not know. Spin-offs into and beyond the established course of study for a particular subject through the sharing of interests can be exciting.

Challenging Without Frustrating

The promotion of high standards also requires finding a level of work that challenges but does not continually frustrate students. Challenging students necessitates that the teacher know the capabilities of each student so that expectations are realistic. This does not mean that less should be required of a slower-achieving child, but rather that the requirements should be different.

Consider the following example. Peter had been struggling with a paper examining the Puritan influence on Hawthorne's writing in *The Scarlet Letter*. The topic appeared too abstract for his thinking, even though the teacher had told him how to proceed. Peter was given a new assignment to investigate what Puritanism was and how it would feel to live as a Puritan in that time period. He was better able to handle the latter, more specific task than the original analytical topic he was assigned.

Emphasizing Higher-Level Thinking

Encouraging thinking at the higher levels of application, analysis, synthesis, and evaluation as identified in Bloom's *A Taxonomy of Educational Objectives* (1956) is a practice essential to promoting achievement and high academic standards. In their planning and questioning, teachers need to remember that recalling information is a necessary, but not sufficient, condition for student success. In addition to the establishment of basic knowledge, opportunities for using information through solving problems, generating hypotheses, analyzing alternatives, and creating imaginative solutions should be available. Bloom's taxonomy can be helpful to teachers when developing objectives and learning activities on higher levels of the cognitive domain.

An academic climate with appropriately high standards can be maintained in any classroom. The climate is promoted by a teacher who conducts class in a businesslike manner—namely, someone who establishes goals and objectives, encourages student goal setting as well, and helps students accomplish those objectives by using class time productively.

Encouraging Group Development of Performance Criteria and Group Work

With the emphasis on group work and cooperative learning today, students need to see that high standards can be upheld within the small groups as well as with whole class work. The quality of the activity that students are doing establishes the performance level to be expected of the group. Authentic cooperative-learning activities that encourage students to demonstrate learning outcomes important to them, with evaluation criteria identified by the group, motivate students and encourage self-directed learning (Putnam, 1993). For example, Putnam reported that students who were learning the scientific method decided to conduct experiments they devised to investigate a question about a subject important to them. One student investigated various kinds of cat food and the container in which she put the food to see how they affected her cats' eating. The class then evaluated each inquiry project to see if it followed carefully the designated steps of the scientific method. Group criteria for products often are higher than teacher-established criteria. The teacher will need to work with the students to help them become proficient in setting group standards and standards for individual performance within the group.

TOPIC 3: EXPECTATION FOR SUCCESS

RESEARCH AND THEORETICAL BASE

In the opening scenario, Mr. Baldino was well aware that by the time many students reach 8th grade, they have poor self-images in mathematics. He knew that to improve their achievement, he needed to promote a successful image for them all. His expectations for students were positive. He had assessed their potential through diagnostic tests and knew they were capable because they had basic mathematical skills even though they had been mediocre achievers in the past. He had formulated plans about the methods he would use to improve their math images.

As was attested by the classic but controversial *Pygmalion in the Classroom* study by Rosenthal and Jacobson (1968), teachers' attitudes toward students do influence student performance. Students in the study who were identified as having a high potential for success achieved at a higher level than would otherwise be predicted. Purkey (1978) related a student's story concerning his inability to sing: "When I was in the 3rd grade, a choral teacher said that I was a good listener (implying a poor singer). Everyone laughed except me. I've never uttered a musical note in public from that day to this" (p. 33). Purkey's book, *Inviting School Success*, also emphasized the importance of sending students verbal and nonverbal supportive messages that encourage them to learn and to succeed.

Research literature is full of studies that substantiate the effect of teacher expectations on student achievement. Good (1981) reviewed 10 years of research on teacher expectations and concluded that teachers behave differently toward different students and affect student achievement accordingly. Over time, student achievement and behavior will conform more and more closely to the teacher's expectations. One finding from a Brophy and Good study (1970) revealed that students for whom teachers held high expectations gave more correct answers in reading groups and achieved higher average scores on a year-end standard test than did students for whom the teacher held low expectations. Again, this study conducted in an elementary classroom has clear implications for secondary classrooms as well.

Good and Brophy (1994) pointed out that teacher expectations affect teacher perceptions and interpretations. Teachers may observe behaviors that they expect to see from certain students and screen out other behaviors that could cause teachers to question their perceptions. Teachers also may interpret what they see in light of their expectations to justify their view of certain students rather than being open to information that could cause them to change their interpretation.

The self-fulfilling-prophecy studies (Rosenthal, Baratz, & Hall, 1974; Rosenthal & Jacobson, 1968) illustrate the need for teachers to be aware of the effect their perceptions and interpretations may have on student behavior. Students may behave in a particular way because the teacher perceives them behaving in that manner. Thus, students who are considered slow by their teacher might consider themselves poor students regardless of their ability, which may indeed be comparable to that of other classmates.

Judgments about students' abilities often are made based on students' cultural differences or socioeconomic background. Hale-Benson (1986) reported that when minority children experienced academic difficulty, the children were more likely to be labeled mentally disabled than white children having difficulties. White children often are considered to be encountering problems with the instructor rather than having mental deficiencies. Minority children are two to three times more likely to be considered educably mentally retarded than white children ("Status of Black Children," 1989).

The effective-schools research conducted by Edmonds (1979), Brookover and Lezotte (1977), and others discovered that raising expectations for success among both teachers and students improved the achievement level of that school. An apparent cause of poor achievement in urban schools is directly related to the low academic expectations teachers tend to hold for pupils in those schools.

The research cited has examined the effect teacher attitudes have on students. The classic Coleman et al. study (1966) upset the educational world because it reported that school-related factors contributed much less than home environmental factors to variability in student achievement. However, student attitudes, whatever their source, have the strongest relationship to achievement. Children who have a sense of control over their environment have a better opportunity to achieve. This means that if children feel their efforts will produce results in schools and the teacher and school are supportive of their efforts, they are more likely to succeed. Coleman encouraged teachers to understand that we must help children develop positive attitudes about themselves as learners.

APPLICATION TO PRACTICE

Effective teachers like Mr. Baldino develop a climate for success in the classroom by doing some or all of the following practices:

1. Develop positive attitudes concerning students' abilities.
2. Develop positive attitudes in students toward their success in the subjects.
3. Help students to understand that success can be reached through their efforts.
4. Demonstrate that the teacher and the school are supportive of student success.
5. Adapt learning activities and materials to fit students' abilities for success.
6. Provide all students with opportunities to be successful.
7. Give effective feedback.
8. Become aware of messages being communicated to students, both verbally and nonverbally.
9. Show interest in all students.
10. Check for each student's understanding.
11. Encourage students to compete with themselves.

An experience illustrating the effect of teacher attitudes on a class was recounted to one of the authors by a friend who was a secondary English teacher. She explained that her third-period class had been giving her headaches because they were not doing their work, talked throughout the class period, and conveyed to her that they did not like English or her. At her wits' end in trying to cope with the situation, she decided to try a positive approach. She began to smile a lot at the class, made positive remarks to individuals, dropped her negative approach to classroom management, praised them for their efforts, and explained that she had been frustrated with them because she knew this class had a high potential but was not reaching it. As a result, the class slowly began to turn around, and within a month she was amazed to find that it was one of her favorite classes. Students were achieving considerably better than in the past. She acknowledged that the experience taught her a valuable lesson in building positive expectations. Clearly what was operating here was that her attitude about the class had led her to treat the class differently. She had been less able to perceive positive behaviors that she had not expected from them—even to the point of distorting what she did see. When she forced herself to perceive them differently, she began to notice the real abilities of the class for the first time and was more able to address the difficulties she had been having with them.

Examining Ability Versus Effort

Recent articles (Murphy, 1993) and books (Goodlad & Keating, 1994) have called our attention to a prevailing American attitude that innate ability—rather than effort, as believed in nations with high academic achievement such as Japan— determines school success. Our tracking system sorts students and encourages them and their teachers to consider students as able or "terminally" unable. Schools' failure to provide or encourage different types of intelligence and learning styles often result in prejudicial practices. In junior and senior high schools the separation of students by curriculum into vocational and academic tracks often results in the vocational group coming from poor and racial minority groups (Goodlad & Keating, 1994). Thus students may decide not to work hard because they and their teachers view their ability to learn as limited rather than capable with ability to make up for the deficits in their experiences and background. The result too often is that students are allowed to waste their time just getting by, to remain unchallenged, and to enter the job market unprepared for meaningful work other than in low-paying service jobs.

Develop Positive Attitudes Concerning Students' Abilities

Teachers need to have positive attitudes concerning students' abilities. Teachers need to believe in their students regardless of their ability levels, backgrounds, or previous records because students look to them for cues about how teachers assess their abilities. A teacher can trap students in poor achievement if little is expected of them because of their ethnic group, academic labeling, or family background. Therefore, teachers must try to keep an open mind and encourage positive behavior in each child.

Help Students Develop Positive Attitudes

Helping students to feel good about themselves, as well as to believe in their ability to be successful in a school subject, is important. The state of low math achievement in the country, as reflected in results of national testing, may be directly linked to the nation's poor self-concept concerning the ability to do well in the subject. Consider how frequently one hears intelligent, successful people admitting in conversations or on late-night talk shows that they were terrible in math. Teachers must help students develop a positive attitude by convincing them of their potential for success through supportive comments, reinforcement, and individual help as needed. Such supportive communications with students may sound like the following:

Your questions during class today were important ones. You asked about key points that were causing others trouble, too. You had more than 70% of your homework correct yesterday. Keep up the good work. Remember, I'll be available to answer your questions if you get confused again.

Relationship of Success to Feelings of Self-Empowerment

Building expectations for student success means encouraging students to understand that success can be reached through their own efforts. Helping students realize that they control their fortunes in school by the amount of time and effort they are willing to put into their work is an important task. This control principle can be impressed on students by having them keep track of the time they spend on a unit or project, as well as by encouraging them to evaluate their work using criteria developed by the teacher or the class. Making students aware of their progress through the use of charts and graphs helps them observe that they have control over their achievement; they realize that the grades they receive are not given by the teacher, but rather result from their own efforts.

The literature gives reports about programs such as the one at Centennial High School in Fort Collins, Colorado (Lamperes, 1994), an alternative school for at-risk students that has turned around a low attendance rate and high dropout rate. The school now boasts that 42% of the students have reached the honor roll (with a grade point average of 3.2 or higher) through the teaching of necessary prosocial skills. Teachers create a culture of interaction that stresses cooperation, positive relationship, and noncoercion, and empower students to determine their own success. The program focuses on positive attending skills, problem solving of critical issues, and promoting the notion that every student can learn. All students are provided with personal knowledge of their learning strengths as well as the teaching styles of their instructors. They are taught how to assess what they need to do to learn and achieve, as well as how to solve their own problems through conflict resolution skills. The success of the school as evidenced by their attendance records and the low number of police visits is attributable to, among several factors, the self-empowerment of the students.

Support for Student Success

As was revealed by the Coleman et al. study (1966), a student needs to feel that the school as well as the teacher supports students and encourages their success. Such conditions as public telephones for student use, an attractive cafeteria setting where students have access to hot and cold drinks during study hours, and attractively decorated classrooms are all examples of messages sent to students about the concern of the school for their welfare. Display cases filled with academic and extracurricular awards and athletic trophies are important. Displays of student pictures and work convey positive messages. Guidance counselors with doors open to students, a student and teacher tutoring system within the school, and teachers with hours available to help students are important for establishing a support network. Peer support networks for at-risk students are an effective human resource, as well. Many schools are establishing close relationships with social service agencies in the community to help support students and their families who have problems that affect the students' success.

In the opening scenario Mr. Baldino let all his students know that during his seventh-hour planning period every day he was available to tutor anyone needing help. He would also arrange tutoring sessions before or after school on request. This type of teacher behavior conveys to students that teachers are concerned about them and are trying to help them.

Adapting Learning Activities
Teacher caring can be reflected by developing activities and materials that fit student needs. For example, a student who may not be able to write an exam, for whatever reasons, may take the test orally. A student who has poor reading ability in junior high may use a different textbook or do different assignments with fewer pages involved. These are straightforward, even obvious, examples. Imaginative, concerned teachers will find many ways to individualize tasks. The point is that teachers must be flexible and willing to adapt to individual needs if all students are going to be successful in the classroom.

Opportunities for Success
To promote success, the teacher needs to structure success experiences so that all students can feel positive about themselves as learners. Students need opportunities to succeed frequently on learning tasks. Teachers need to make sure that students achieve success consistently by encouraging them to meet challenging objectives gradually and to prepare students with tutoring, guidance, and feedback (Good & Brophy, 1994). Teachers need to individualize learning tasks whenever necessary so that students are engaged with tasks and materials suitable for their success rate. Also, each student's success rate should be monitored and used as a basis for decision making about that student.

Effective Feedback
Other suggestions teachers may consider for establishing a success climate in the classroom include giving feedback that informs students how to become more proficient in those areas that have not been successfully learned. The importance of feedback that tells students how and where they need to improve and gives opportunities for additional practice and relearning needs to be understood by all teachers. (See feedback section, topic 4.)

Teacher Messages
Teachers need to become aware of the messages they send to students through their verbal and nonverbal behavior. These messages may reinforce the more academically able and ignore or criticize the weaker students (Good, 1981). Exam-

ples of such debilitating behaviors come from a review of the literature (Good & Brophy, 1994) and include the following:

1. Good students are seated across front and down the middle of the room.
2. Teacher eye contact is mainly with higher-achieving students.
3. Teacher calls on higher-achieving students much more frequently than lower-achieving students.
4. Teacher punishes off-task behavior in lower-achieving students and more frequently ignores it in higher-achieving students.
5. Teacher communication with lower-achieving students is mainly negative and critical.
6. Teacher gives little wait time to lower-achieving students to answer questions.
7. Teacher praises higher-achieving students more.
8. Teacher displays work of only the higher-achieving students.
9. Teacher gives higher-achieving students more cues with which to respond to questions.
10. Teacher requires less effort and work from lower-achieving students.

Show Interest in All Students

By changing the seating pattern to meet students' needs, teachers can convey an interest in students. Those who have difficulty paying attention or seeing the board may sit in the front; talkative students may be mixed with quiet students to encourage better attention. Regardless of the seating pattern, teacher eye contact with students—even those in the back of the room and in the far rows by the windows or doors—needs to include all students so that the teacher can send and receive nonverbal feedback.

Verbal and nonverbal behavior that expresses teacher interest, such as speaking to each student at least once in a period and trying to have some individual communication daily, is important for positive classroom climate. Students with more academic weaknesses or quiet students may sit in class without recognition for a week or more at a time. Part of the communication should be positive feedback given at the appropriate time.

Check for Understanding

Checking for understanding reminds the teacher to monitor a student's progress by constant checks on comprehension of the material. Group comprehension checks can be taken as suggested by Hunter (1994), by having the students raise fingers to indicate their answers to multiple choice or true-false oral questions. One finger is a true response, two is false, and so on. With this method, the teacher can quickly determine whether the class understands a part of the lesson.

Encourage Self-Competition

Encouraging students to compete with themselves requires that the teacher give students frequent feedback about their progress by checking homework, giving quizzes and tests, and writing comments on papers. Through extensive feedback, students can be encouraged to consider their personal progress in regard to objectives rather than to their ranking within the class.

An effective teacher does not have to be a magician, although Tom Baldino used this ploy. However, an effective teacher does need to be able to make purposeful decisions that help establish a climate for success in the classroom. The decisions Mr. Baldino made in approaching his class through one of his hobbies were based on his knowledge that students work harder if the climate in the room is interesting to and supportive of students, and if students know what is expected of them. He understood that in achievement, reinforcement can bring results. He planned to use the puzzles and math games for reinforcement as well as for teaching interested students magic. He would see that students received frequent feedback so that they would know the results of their efforts and the skills they needed to learn. Many math experiences from life situations would be available for group and individual practice. Through practice and self-checking, students would learn at their individual rates.

Students who fell behind would either become a separate group that Mr. Baldino would teach for 10 or 15 minutes each day, or they would be introduced to new material while still being held responsible for learning the material of the previous unit. Promoting student feelings of responsibility to learn the course material was an important goal set by Mr. Baldino. Holding students accountable for practice exercises or for taking tests that would be self-checked encouraged their feelings of responsibility.

Mr. Baldino decided to use much of his class time for working with individuals and small groups on remediation problems as necessary, as well as on enrichment experiences. The beginning of most classes would consist of large-group instruction in which review and introduction of lesson content would occur. Explanation and demonstration would follow, after which groups would work on mathematical problems to demonstrate their understanding. Individual practice would then follow. An important part of the yearly curriculum would be working on problem-solving and analysis skills. He would give frequent quizzes and unit and review tests so that he could monitor class progress. Much feedback and reinforcement would be used to encourage positive feelings toward the subject and to emphasize the standards students should meet. Students would be expected to keep track of their progress in their math portfolios.

Mr. Baldino looked forward to the effect his plan would have on the class. His success rate had been high before. He knew he could encourage success for everyone again, but he knew that for this class, he would have to learn a few new magic tricks himself.

TOPIC 4: PROVIDING FEEDBACK AND PRAISE

Teacher feedback also influences student performance and achievement. Teacher feedback has been mentioned briefly in two previous sections dealing with establishing an academic climate and expectation for success. However, it is also necessary to examine feedback and praise in their own right so that the importance of each in contributing to a positive learning environment can be better understood.

Though the scenario at the beginning of this chapter provides many pertinent examples of the use of the major factors of effective teaching, feedback and praise are not specifically dealt with by Tom Baldino's presentation on "math magic." In the following scenario, feedback and praise are integral and necessary.

SCENARIO

Laura Trilby glanced at the clock—10:55 a.m. She had left 20 minutes for this practice phase of the lesson because she wanted time to work with Bill, Cindy, and Miguel to see if she could help them resolve their problems with the unit. Meanwhile, the rest of the class would review in their groups to reinforce their understanding of the unit.

Mrs. Trilby wondered if she could start moving around the room to determine whether students were working or encountering problems before she pulled the three aside to work with them.

Yes, she decided she needed to travel. Joe and Tom in the back had stopped pushing each other when she looked back at them and were settling down to work. She walked slowly around the room and surveyed each group as she stopped beside their desks. The class seemed to be engaged in the practice activity. Her directions must have been clear because she had been asked to repeat them only once. Tom's group was working on the second question already. They had answered the first one with an appropriate response. "You're working well today, group. I'll be back to see how you do on the seventh question. That's a tricky one." Tom looked up and smiled.

As she moved round the room she reinforced selected students. (Had she spoken to Scott yet today?) "Good response to that question, Scott. You and the group got the point."

A glance at Susan made Susan shove her address book back under the desk and return to her writing. Must remember to check on her group in a few minutes after I see what's happening to Bill, Cindy, and Miguel, Mrs. Trilby thought to herself.

Bill thumbed through the book and appeared to be looking for answers. Jody, who was in his group, appeared to be giving him some assistance. Bill's paper was blank. "Did you finish the chapter, Bill?" Bill reads very slowly, Mrs. Trilby remembered. He probably never finished reading the material. He would have difficulty with the questions in the review. "Keep on reading, Bill. When you finish the chapter you can look over the questions the group is working on and see if you want to add anything to their responses." Mrs. Trilby moved on to Cindy.

The class remained busy except for a few exchanges among the "superstar four" group. Could they be done already?

"Joan, Charlie, Dan, and Steve, when you are finished, please exchange papers with group 2 and check each other's answers. Check them for the following points." She walked to the board and wrote on it: "(1) Do you agree with the answer? (2) Is good form used—complete sentences and paragraphs? (3) Spelling and punctuation correct? (4) Grade you would give paper." She continued, "Please give papers back to their owners after they are corrected and talk to them about any problems you saw. Then you have free time."

Mrs. Trilby checked the rest of the class. Group 4 had been the first to finish. Everyone else appeared to be working. She called Bill, Cindy, and Miguel to leave their groups and come to a table where she could work with them.

Bill's group had been helping him with his writing problems, and Cindy's group read much of the material to Cindy. That practice wasn't helping Cindy with her reading.

A brief thought about her bridge party that night passed through Mrs. Trilby's head. Should she serve dessert; would they like chocolate pie? She let the decision go and moved over to Cindy, who had copied the questions onto her paper. Cindy was always staying busy—bless her heart—but composing answers was difficult for her. "What does that first question ask you to do, Cindy?" Cindy went back to the first question while Mrs. Trilby helped her pick out the key words. "Now tell me what you want to write down."

Cindy responded while Mrs. Trilby turned her head to look at Tom in the back of the room. He saw her glance. He made an exaggerated move to appear as though he were writing very diligently. Joe, beside him, smirked. Cindy finished her explanation. Mrs. Trilby patted her shoulder while saying, "Has your group gotten to the seventh one yet, Tom? I'll be back to check on it in a minute." It takes a lot of attention to keep Joe and Tom ontask, she noted.

She turned back to Cindy. "You answered the questions well, Cindy, because you responded to what the question asked. Now see if you can put that on paper. Use your book to help with the spelling." She moved down the table to give individual feedback to Bill and Miguel and to check their papers.

Five minutes to go. The class was stirring. Most seemed to be done. What to do now? "How many groups have finished the assignment and feel their responses are correct?" About eight people raised their hands. "Okay. Joan, Charlie, Matthew, and Christie [one from each group], please bring your papers here for a check. Then if you have them correct you can share with your group why these are good answers. When the bell rings, everyone please put your papers on the desk. Remember the quiz tomorrow on this chapter."

The practice period seemed to have gone smoothly. Only her usual three appeared to have difficulty. She would have to encourage more peer tutoring for them from their groups. Tomorrow she'd make out a different test for them and put in some challenging practical situations for them to handle.

She moved toward the front of the room. "Look at number 4 again, group 1. Charlie just told you that you missed the point of the question. Check that second line of the question." Silence. "Read that part over again. See if the information is there."

She noted that almost every book was closed now. Her desk had a pile of papers on it. Only 30 seconds until the bell. "Good job today, class. You worked well. Papers look good. Remember the quiz tomorrow."

The bell rang. The room filled with voices, shuffling feet, and desk sounds. Mrs. Trilby smiled at students as they passed her. "All finished, Jeff? Good work today, Tom. Is Northwood going to win on Saturday?" Three students responded to that question as they left. What was she going to do about the difficulties Cindy, Bill, and Miguel were having in analyzing reading material? She'd have to work with their groups to give them suggestions on how to provide feedback to remedial readers. She would talk to the reading specialist about that, too.

Strawberry tart or chocolate pie? Decisions!

Student feedback can provide the teacher with essential information that enables the teacher to adjust instruction. Teacher feedback is being examined in this section. As Laura Trilby worked with her students during the practice phase of the lesson, she not only made decisions to keep students on-task as much as was possible by her teacher behaviors, but she also made decisions to give feedback and recommend corrective procedures to as many students as possible. She decided to spend more time this period with those who needed special help, such as Cindy, Bill (who had reading-comprehension problems), and Miguel. She gave Bill permission to proceed at his own rate. She instructed four students who had completed the assignment to give feedback to others who were finished. She decided she would recheck all the papers later so that she could give everyone corrective feedback on this important phase of the content. She could hand back their papers before the quiz the next day so that they would have some time before the test to learn from the comments on their papers. As she moved around the room she could quickly spot problems that groups were having and help them locate the source of the misinterpretation so that they could rethink their response.

Mrs. Trilby was making decisions about her teaching behaviors based on her understanding that feedback, and especially immediate feedback, was essential to the learning process. She also understood that identification of right and wrong items was not enough. Students must be able to see necessary corrective procedures. In many cases,

Mrs. Trilby could give instructional cues through questioning so that students could locate errors themselves. With some students she would have to identify the problem for them and help them make corrections. Throughout the practice time she would be involved in the feedback process.

RESEARCH AND THEORETICAL BASE

Bloom (1976) cited feedback as the teaching behavior most consistently related to student achievement. Feedback commonly means receiving knowledge of results. However, knowing whether the response is right or wrong is not sufficient for learning. Levin with Long (1981) pointed out that many research studies demonstrated that knowledge of right and wrong answers alone had little or no effect on improving learning. In his theory of school learning, Bloom (1976) emphasized that the student needs to know the corrective procedures to be taken. When teachers are able to provide information about what is left to be learned and corrective measures for students' responses, instruction is more effective. Bloom stated that student learning is dependent on knowledge of results when that knowledge can be used for correction.

As Levin with Long (1981) detailed in *Effective Instruction*, effective feedback contains three components: (1) a definition of correctness or standard of performance to be met, (2) evidence indicating whether the standard was or was not achieved, and (3) corrective procedures as to what must be relearned, and how.

A major form of feedback teachers use is grades, but it is important to realize that grades do not provide the student with all the feedback necessary for learning. Grades do indicate a standard of performance and the student's progress relative to that standard, but they do not indicate the kinds of problems students are encountering or the steps being taken to remediate those problems. Therefore, it is advisable at grading periods for the teacher to provide each student with corrective feedback, as well as to help students increase learning.

Anderson (1989) pointed out that teachers today want students to be able to monitor and regulate their own work. This is a cognitive process called *metacognition*. Students are taught to analyze where they are having difficulties and what they need to do to move beyond the difficulties. Teachers who encourage students' monitoring themselves plan learning activities that promote student responsibility and less dependency on teacher approval.

APPLICATION TO PRACTICE

As research and experience have confirmed, feedback is an essential practice for effective teaching. Anyone who has ever tried to learn a sport, such as golf or tennis, can identify with the frustration one can experience as a learner if the teacher does not give feedback in the practice stage. Learners need to know what they are doing correctly or incorrectly. Otherwise they may be doomed to repeat the same errors unless they can learn how to make corrections. Feedback that announces that one has missed the golf ball or hit the tennis ball into the net is useless in helping a person achieve goals. One needs to know what corrective procedures to take. Similarly, students who receive a test paper marked 55% know that they have not done well, but what to do next remains a mystery. Meanwhile, some of the most useful functions of a test—to correct misunderstandings and guide future learning—are not realized. Thus for several reasons, more informative feedback is necessary.

The following considerations are pertinent regarding the use of feedback and praise:

1. Attend to standards of performance, students' progress, and corrective procedures.
2. Give immediate feedback.
3. Use peer evaluation and self-evaluation as feasible.
4. Use reinforcement, praise, and criticism purposefully.
5. Use students' ideas as reinforcers.
6. Use verbal and nonverbal reinforcers.
7. Avoid the use of ineffective praise.
8. Use the principles of effective praise.
9. Use criticism sparingly.
10. Develop students' metacognitive abilities so that they can provide their own feedback.

Three Parts of Effective Feedback

Effective feedback contains three pieces of information essential to the learner: (1) the standard of performance, (2) the student's progress toward meeting that standard, and (3) corrective procedures to be taken. Examples of effective verbal feedback are the following:

> John, your paper was graded a 65 because you missed so many of the problems with a decimal in the divisor. Let's go over the procedure for working with decimals in the divisor and then you can try this practice exercise to see if you understand it better.

> Your quiz grade is 32%. Your problem seems to be that you didn't read the chapter carefully. Review your outline of the main ideas of the chapter, then reread the chapter. Let's try for a retest on Thursday.

It is important that students know the standards of performance prior to the evaluated activities. The teacher should write on the board the evaluation criteria for a project or give examples of acceptable paragraphs or procedures to follow in writing up a lab report, as well as an indication of the level of achievement required for a passing mark.

A teacher using effective practice relates the student's score or performance to the acceptable level of performance to be met. Some examples are: "John, 80% is expected; you received 65%." "The essay must have four complete paragraphs; you have only three, Betty." "Passing is 70%, Tony; you have 75%." Teachers generally provide this knowledge of results to their students. However, the next step is the critical one—indicating the problem areas and the practice step to be taken. For example: "Four errors in your paragraphs involved run-together sentences, Carla. I will give you some practice papers on writing and punctuating complete sentences that may help you with the problem. Get together with your study partner and go over the papers together." Now the feedback process is complete and provides the student with information that can promote learning.

Wiggins (1993) summarized the characteristics of effective feedback as follows:

1. Provides guidance and confirming or disconfirming evidence.
2. Compares current performance and trend against successful result.
3. Is timely and immediately usable.
4. Measures in terms of progress; assesses the accomplishment; specifies degree of conformance with the goal or standard.
5. Offers specific, understandable diagnoses and prescription.
6. Allows students to see tangible effects from their efforts.
7. Measures the essential trails or key criteria expected.
8. Examines the result in terms of the goal sought.

Give Immediate Feedback

The effective teacher provides regular and immediate feedback. For example, teachers can give oral feedback during recitation and practice. "Everyone close your eyes. Now raise your hand if this response is correct." In her presentations on effective teaching techniques, Madeline Hunter (1994) demonstrated an oral diagnostic technique that gave both the teacher and the students immediate feedback during a lesson. She would ask the audience to raise one finger if they thought the answer to a teacher question was A and two fingers if the answer was B. When more than half the audience would raise the wrong finger to answer a question, she would remark that she would have to give more practice on that phase of class instruction because they had overlooked a key point. She knew they were confused. The audience knew that they had incorrectly interpreted the point she was making and the situation they were examining on the screen. The immediate feedback let them know the technique they needed to reexamine.

Using a simple oral diagnostic tool such as Hunter's "raising fingers" response method is an example of effective and immediate feedback for both the students and the teacher. The teacher discovers whether the students are comprehending while also involving every student in the activity. Other examples include correcting all important assignments, suggesting corrective procedures, and returning papers promptly. Giving frequent quizzes and tests is an important feedback measure and should be used for remediation. Requiring students to make corrections on graded assignments and to return them to the teacher for correction verification can assure the teacher that the students have examined their problem spots and have made the appropriate modifications.

Use Peer Evaluation and Self-Evaluation of Papers

All this feedback can mean mounds of paper for the teacher to examine. Having students engage in peer evaluation and self-evaluation of their papers can be an effective technique as long as the students understand the evaluation criteria. Putting students into small groups of two or three and encouraging them to evaluate each other's work can be valuable for all concerned if students have learned how to handle that responsibility. Teachers can teach their students the procedures for peer evaluation and self-evaluation. Students from the 4th grade upward should be able to handle this type of group-learning experience well as long as the teacher has indicated precisely what is required of the group. The teacher or the students can identify the evaluation criteria. The teacher can provide examples to illustrate the standard for each criterion. Students can then examine each other's work and give each other feedback on how well the papers meet the criteria.

Having a chance to examine each other's work and receive help from peers can be beneficial and effective teaching tools. Teachers can use small groups for peer instruction as well as for feedback. Students can teach each other the main ideas or check each other on vocabulary words, compare responses with the teacher's answer sheet, and help each other with corrections and remediation practice.

Teachers play a facilitator role during this experience by moving among the groups and keeping them on-task, assessing how productively the groups are working, answering questions, and giving judgments when the groups are confused and request teacher input.

Allowing students to check their own papers is a good device to promote independence in the students and to free the teacher to work with individuals. The teacher must learn quickly by observation which students abuse the privilege of marking their own papers and which ones can handle the task responsibly. Self-checking supplies students with immediate feedback from which they can decide whether to proceed or to continue on the current topic or skill.

Student checking does not relieve the teacher entirely from the responsibility of examining student papers, however. The teacher needs to check student papers to learn where errors are occurring. On the basis of that information the teacher then makes decisions concerning reteaching, regrouping, or moving the class along to the next unit.

Use Reinforcement, Praise, and Criticism Purposefully

Other forms of feedback used by teachers are praise and reinforcement (the rewarding of desired student performance) and criticism (the reprimanding or correcting of student performance). The use of praise and criticism should be considered carefully by the teacher as factors having an effect on the climate of the classroom and the self-concept of the individual student. The amount of praise used by the average teacher is between 1% and 2% of total classroom interaction time. Criticism is used twice as much as praise (Amidon & Flanders, 1967). Reinforced feedback is important for the development of student self-confidence and motivation. Criticism is linked negatively to these learning factors. Studies describe criticism as impairing learning because it decreases motivation and damages self-esteem (Levin with Long, 1981). Brookover, Beady, Flood, Schweitzer, and Wisenbaker (1979) found that teachers in effective classrooms used more positive reinforcement to encourage student achievement and used it on a consistent basis. In summarizing the research on effective schools, the *Encyclopedia of Educational Research* (Mitzel, 1982) pointed out that in the more effective classrooms, pupils received more praise and fewer criticisms.

In summarizing research on academic praise, Brophy and Good (1986) found weak but positive correlations tying praise to achievement, particularly for younger and lower-ability students. A caution needs to be raised here because researchers have discovered that teachers can use reinforcement and praise to control students' behavior. Students can be made to feel insecure and dependent on the teacher's feedback if the praise becomes necessary for every student action to assure students they are progressing satisfactorily. Therefore, teachers should understand their use of reinforcement and its intended result. Also, if teachers reinforce by praising every student response, participation is rewarded but encouragement for quality of response is neglected.

Two major points that come from the literature concerning reinforcement and criticism emphasize that students should understand the reason for any given reinforcement and know when and how to modify behavior where appropriate (Levin with Long, 1981). Stallings's (1983) research showed that effective teaching behaviors are those that acknowledge or praise correct responses and probe to help the students examine incorrect responses. The research also pointed out that praise was not necessarily beneficial and more was not necessarily better. It may even be intrusive. Much teacher praise is used as a controlling device rather than expressing admiration for students' accomplishments. Judicious and informed use of praise is recommended (Brophy & Good, 1986).

When giving feedback to students, teachers are likely to include words of praise and reinforcement or criticism. Both are important psychological tools and must be used carefully by the effective teacher. Praise can encourage the development of a positive self-concept, which should increase a student's motivation to learn, to participate, and to become more self-directed. Reinforcement can take on many forms. It can range from praise using one word such as "good" or "great," to using student ideas, to nonverbal types such as a smile or pats on the back. Similarly, criticism can range from verbal chastisement because of failure to perform well, to nonverbal looks of disgust and annoyance. Suggestions on how to use both reinforcers and criticism more effectively to encourage student progress are offered in the following paragraphs.

Reinforcement and praise that benefit the student the most are referenced specifically to the condition or product of merit. One example is, "Good work in our discussion today, Jim. Your comments related very well to last night's reading assignment and to the international trade question I asked today. You provided a good model for the other students to follow in the way you handled the question." Another is, "Sally has an excellent picture here because she kept the outline of the tree but within the tree drew a number of different scenes telling a story. She was very creative."

Use Student Ideas as Reinforcers

Effective praise also includes use of students' ideas. This type of reinforcement acknowledges that a student's contribution is important, thus encouraging more student involvement. Use of a student's comments signals acceptance by the teacher and can give the student a stronger feeling of self-worth. Example: "Good idea, Carlos. Carlos calls our attention to the fact that Mrs. Bennett may not have wanted to accept the money at first. Is there any evidence of her reluctance that you can find in the story, class?" (The teacher restates Carlos's response, then asks a question built on the student's idea.)

In his work on analyzing classroom behavior, Flanders (1970) listed seven categories of teacher behavior, one of which was acknowledging the use of student ideas. He found that this reinforcing behavior conveys to students that their ideas are important enough to be given further consideration. The positive impact of this is greater than that of a one-word reinforcer such as "good."

Rosenshine and Furst (1971) indicated five ways teachers can use student ideas when verbal interaction is taking place in class.

1. *Acknowledging* a student's contribution by repeating the response aloud to the class with the student's name. Example: "Sue said the number is brought to the right-hand side."
2. *Modifying* a student's contribution by putting it into different words to make it more understandable without changing the student's ideas. Example: "I believe you implied, Barry, that the gross national product is not an accurate measure of the economy's health. Is that right?"
3. *Applying* the student's response to some situation, or using it as an explanation for some event. Example: "Remember when Carmen told us that Jack's decision to leave before Todd came home with the news could get Jack into some trouble? Well, here is the trouble."
4. *Comparing* the student's response to something in the text or the lesson, or to a similar event. Example: "Julie said the word was used as an adverb. Let's look in our books on page 37 to see how an adverb can be used and see if we agree with Julie."
5. *Summarizing* students' contributions and using them to make a point. Example: "After examining the comments that Jack, Della, and Maurice just made, I think they may be saying essentially the same thing—that nuclear disarmament plans are meaningless unless they include all nations with nuclear capabilities. This is an important point to consider. Let's examine what it means."

Use Verbal and Nonverbal Reinforcers

Teachers need to guard against the overuse of certain words for praise, which thereby lose their impact. Teachers need to plan a list of reinforcement words they can use, and also plan nonverbal reinforcers such as displaying student work, smiling, nodding, and patting on the back. Both aspects of praise, verbal and nonverbal, need to be used purposefully by teachers.

REINFORCEMENT WORDS

Nonverbal Reinforcers

"Well done. You have [smile and eye contact] an excellent idea."

"Let's see how that fits [pat on back] into what we have said."

Paper displayed in room.

"Good work."

Choosing student for important job.

"Bravo."

"Fine."

Using student's work as model.

"Outstanding."

Finger signal—"O" for okay.

"Right on target."

Putting student response on the board.

"Let's examine the idea Tim just gave us."

Nodding head and listening with direct eye contact.

"Rosa's answer was correct. Can you add more information to it?"

Symbols of approval—stickers, stars, etc.

"Good point—that is the key idea."

A note of warning is in order concerning nonverbal feedback. Many studies of nonverbal behavior have substantiated that nonverbal communication "speaks" louder than verbal. A student will acknowledge messages from a teacher's facial expressions over any spoken messages. Therefore, it is important for teachers to be aware of the use of nonverbal feedback for praise or criticism because a teacher's body language is sending out evaluative nonverbal messages much of the time. Examples of nonverbal behavior that send negative messages to students can include those such as an unwillingness to touch a student of a different race, not making eye contact with certain students, sending only scowling messages to selected students, seldom calling on certain students, not bending over a desk or moving to a student's desk to offer help, and looking at the clock or watch while a student is commenting.

Avoid the Use of Ineffective Praise

Praise also needs to be used discriminately. All students need some praise; some students need more praise and encouragement than others. Higher-achieving students need less praise than slower-achieving students.

Less well understood is the fact that praise can sometimes be detrimental. Teachers need to scrutinize their use of praise as a controlling device to be sure they are not limiting students by praising only those behaviors that reflect their own thinking and ideas. Reinforcement also needs to be given to those students who, at times, display creativity and challenge conventional thinking. Furthermore, praise that is given too quickly or routinely can block the development of student ideas and critical thinking. In short, praise needs to be individualized and adjusted for the situation. The teacher must try to learn the acceptance and encouragement needs of each student and to respond to each one accordingly.

Use the Principles of Effective Praise

A useful set of guidelines for effective praise was developed by Brophy (1981, p. 10). It is especially helpful because it contrasts effective and ineffective praise.

Effective Praise
1. is delivered contingently
2. specifies the particulars of the accomplishment
3. shows spontaneity, variety, and other signs of credibility; suggests clear attention to the student's accomplishment
4. rewards attainment of specified performance criteria (which can include effort criteria, however)
5. provides information to students about their competence or the value of their accomplishments
6. orients students toward better appreciation of their own task-related behavior and thinking about problem solving

Ineffective Praise
1. is delivered randomly or unsystematically
2. is restricted to global positive reactions
3. shows a bland uniformity that suggests a conditioned response made with minimal attention
4. rewards mere participation without consideration of performance processes or outcomes
5. provides no information at all or gives students information about their status
6. orients students toward comparing themselves with others and thinking about competing
7. uses the accomplishments of peers as the context for describing students' present accomplishments

Effective Praise (continued)

7. uses students' own prior accomplishments as the context for describing present accomplishments
8. is given recognition of noteworthy effort or success at difficult (for this student) tasks
9. attributes success to effort and ability, implying that similar successes can be expected in the future
10. fosters endogenous attributions (students believe that they enjoy the task and/or want to develop task-relevant skills)
11. focuses students' attention on their own task-relevant behavior
12. fosters appreciation of, and desirable attributions about, task-relevant behavior after the process is completed

Ineffective Praise (continued)

8. is given recognition without regard to the effort expended or the meaning of the accomplishment
9. attributes success to ability alone or to external factors such as luck or (easy) task difficulty
10. fosters exogenous attributions (students believe that they expend effort on the task for external reasons—to please the teacher, win a competition or reward, etc.)
11. focuses students' attention on the teacher as an external authority who is manipulating them
12. intrudes into the ongoing process, distracting attention from task-relevant behavior

Written comments on papers are an important form of feedback and can offer praise or criticism. Using comments to establish communication with individuals can be a valuable technique for the teacher. They communicate to the student that the teacher is concerned enough to write a message. After surveying a number of studies on the effects of written comments, Levin with Long (1981) emphasized the importance of making comments specific so that students know which response to continue and which areas need to be improved or relearned. Example: "This is not one of your better tests, Rosy. You must have been tired. Notice that you missed four questions and you did not appear to know the main points of the chapter. See me and let's schedule a retest."

Use Criticism Sparingly

Criticism as feedback does need to be considered. There are times when criticism may be appropriate to change the behavior of a student. However, if the criticism is continually repeated, it loses its impact and creates negative feelings. Some points to remember concerning the use of criticism are:

1. Reference it to the action or product that is not acceptable.
2. State the reason it is not acceptable.

3. Indicate what the student can do about it.
4. Get back to a pleasant tone with that student as soon as possible.
5. Never criticize the student, only the action. Example: "Combing your hair during class is unacceptable, Shirley. It disrupts the people around you and I suspect you aren't getting much done, either. Please keep your comb in your purse while you are here. Now, I see you have a good topic sentence written. Do you need any help to proceed with the paragraph?" Example of ineffective criticism: "You are always stirring up trouble in that corner, Peter. I am sick and tired of your disturbance. Get to work!" Such statements may release tension for the teacher but do not help the student because they do not contain any of the recommendations for constructive criticism.

Use Feedback to Develop Students' Metacognition Abilities

Helping students become aware of their own thinking processes and working with them to acquire specific learning skills is an important goal for teachers. Then the feedback the teacher gives is not focused on the "right" answer but rather on helping students to analyze what they are thinking, to make comparisons and distinctions to models the teacher or they may have in mind, to see errors that are occurring in their thinking, and to make self-corrections (Ornstein, 1990). This type of feedback is called metacognition.

Metacognition is a cognitive process whereby students are taught specific learning strategies so that they can sense when they are not learning, or are having trouble learning, and be able to review where problems seem to be occurring. For students to be able to function metacognitively, teachers need to train students to be aware of the objective or goal during a learning activity, to monitor the strategies they are using to reach those goals, to analyze the effects of the strategies they are using, and to decide if they are satisfied with their responses based on the goals they are trying to accomplish (Pressly, Johnson, Symons, McGoldrick, & Kurita, 1989).

The development of metacognition takes time. Students need to develop certain thinking skills and understand clearly what is expected of them. They need to be able to sense when they are getting close to the answer or reaching the goal, or when they are moving farther away. Students need to be able to analyze what part of a problem needs more work and what additional information is needed to solve the problem (Weinstein and Mayer, 1989).

Much information exists on thinking skills. It is important for the teacher to know how to incorporate learning strategies into one's teaching. For example, Charles Letteri (1985) has formed the following list of thinking skills that students need to process and use information:

1. *Analysis*—the ability to break down complex information into component parts for the purpose of identification and categorization.
2. *Focusing-scanning*—the ability to select relevant or important information without being confused by irrelevant or secondary information.

3. *Comparative analysis*—the ability to select a correct item from among several alternatives and to compare information and make proper choices.
4. *Narrowing*—the ability to identify and place new information into categories through its attributes: physical characteristics, principles, or functions.
5. *Complex cognitive*—the ability to integrate complex information into existing cognitive structures and long-term memory.
6. *Sharpening*—the ability to maintain distinctions between cognitive structures (including old and new information) and to avoid confusion or overlap.
7. *Tolerance*—the ability to monitor and modify thinking, to deal with ambiguous or unclear information without getting frustrated.

Feedback that specifically encourages students to use these and other skills to examine areas they do not understand or errors they have made helps them become independent learners. The most effective academic climate teachers can promote in their classrooms is one that challenges students to take charge of their own learning.

SUMMARY POINT

One of the important roles teachers play is that of shaping the classroom learning environment. Teachers create the classroom environment by verbal and nonverbal behavior displayed toward the students and by their professional execution of teaching responsibilities. The decisions teachers make regarding the treatment of students and the standards of the classroom, including behavior and academic standards, contribute to the classroom climate. Within this climate each student's self-image is influenced positively or negatively toward learning.

This chapter on climate included many practices teachers may use to promote a positive learning environment. These practices were detailed to enable beginning teachers to recognize the choices available to them when making decisions about their teaching behaviors. Classroom practices need to be considered in light of the effect they have on creating a favorable learning climate. They need to be kept in mind when planning instruction. Chapter 3 discusses other considerations to keep in mind when planning lessons.

REVIEW: IMPORTANT PRACTICES FOR ESTABLISHING A PRODUCTIVE LEARNING CLIMATE

1. Establish an atmosphere in which academic goals are emphasized.
2. Promote high standards, then monitor and reward achievement.

3. Maintain an orderly environment.
4. Build expectations for success by convincing students of their ability to succeed and providing them with success experiences.
5. Use feedback, reinforcement, and praise to promote student achievement.
6. Encourage student self-monitoring and independent learning initiatives.

Postscript: School Climate

This chapter has addressed the classroom climate that promotes student learning. However, the classroom climate is influenced by the school environment to a considerable degree. School environments for learning differ considerably across the country. Different communities with diverse socioeconomic groups in various geographic regions of the country have schools that look and operate differently from other schools. Even within a school district, schools may differ in terms of their facilities and learning climate.

In *Savage Inequalities* Jonathan Kozol (1991) vividly depicted the squalid conditions that exist in some of our urban schools: plumbing that docs not work, broken windows, and drug pushers hanging around the school grounds. Yet in other city schools, despite the age of the buildings, the facilities are well maintained and well equipped. The physical condition of schools sends a message to the students as to whether they—the students—are important to their community and to society. The conditions create a positive or negative image concerning the value of learning. Unfortunately, many factors, such as segregated housing, low incomes, and school attendance policies, often segregate students so that children who are African-American, Hispanic, or recent immigrants from Asia may attend schools with substandard conditions. Teachers within these classrooms have to overcome the climate set by poor conditions and work harder to create a positive learning environment. Federal money was earmarked in 1994 for school improvement and staff development, particularly for those states with a larger percentage of at-risk children in deteriorating school facilities. Cuts in the federal budget in 1995 and 1996 reduced that aid considerably.

Each school has its own culture that shapes the climate of the building and sends messages to students about what is important in that environment. Ryan and Cooper in *Those Who Can Teach* (1995) point out that schools most often are concerned with efficiency and economy and are less able to accommodate arrangements for privacy or small groups to work together. Through architecture, rules, and schedules, to mention only a few aspects of the institution, the school sends messages as to what is valued that influences the learning climate.

Douglas Heath (1986) has formulated the following questions about the school environment that may help you examine the learning climate of schools you are observing or may be considering for employment purposes:

1. Is this school so big I'd feel lost in it?
2. How proud are the faculty and students about the school?
3. What are the conditions of the bathrooms?
4. Are students I see in the halls aloof, sullen, cheerful, effervescent?
5. Does the principal call students by name? Do any stop us to ask him or her a question?
6. Do faculty greet me warmly in the teachers' room, or do they ignore me?
7. How flexibly, imaginatively, or colorfully have teachers created their work space?
8. How do I feel when I walk into a classroom I am to observe?
9. What do the arrangement of desks, presence of plants, orderliness of the room, and comments on the chalkboard tell me about this teacher's assumptions concerning how students are to behave and learn in the classroom?
10. What does the room tell me about the teacher?

QUESTIONS FOR REFLECTION

1. How important is the teacher's role in making a difference in student achievement?
2. What approaches would you use starting the first day of school to build a positive learning climate?
3. On a typical school day how would you plan the use of time in a 50- minute class period?
4. What attitudes do you need to develop toward children, the curriculum, the school, parents, the community, and yourself as teacher to foster a positive learning climate?
5. Can you recall classrooms that you were a student in or that you visited where the climate was strongly positive for learning? What did the teacher and students do to promote that positive climate?
6. Have you experienced or observed teacher or student behaviors that created a negative classroom climate? What were these behaviors and conditions that created a poor learning environment?
7. In your teaching experiences, what have you observed about your interaction with aggressive male students, quiet and docile female students, minority students, students for whom English is a second language, and students who don't follow directions? (Continue identifying different types of students one would expect to find in the classroom. Consider carefully how you as teacher react or might react to each type of student.) Would your reactions and interactions support or threaten the positive learning climate?

ANALYSIS FORMS

ACTIVITY 1: LEARNING-TIME ANALYSIS

(Adapted from Stallings-Teaching Learning Institute)

Directions: Observe the entire class every five minutes. Code all off-task behavior in seat blocks. Then make a slash mark and show what the student was supposed to be doing. Count the number of times you sweep (observe) class. A summary of the percent of students off-task can be found by using this formula:

$$\frac{\text{the sum of the number of students off-task for each observation}}{\text{the number of students} \times \text{the number of sweeps}}$$

Teacher _____   Date _____

Grade _____   Time _____

Number of Sweeps: _____

| Mrs. Doe | front of classroom |

John	Sally	Bill U/T U/S	Tony U/O M/T D/S
Joe U/I	Rose	Joyce	Mary
Sue	Jose D/T	Carol U/G U/S U/I	Ted
Pete D/S	Steve U/O	Mike U/Q	Stella

Students Off-Task key

S = Socializing
U = Uninvolved or Waiting
D = Disruptive
M = Moving Around Room
P = Personal Needs

Activity Codes

I = Instruction
O = Organizing, Directions
S = Seatwork
O = Oral Reading
G = Group Work

Q = Question, Answer
T = Transition—Changing to Another Activity

ACTIVITY 2: PARTICIPATION RATIO GRID

Directions: Take 10 samples of behavior from the same 10 students at fairly close intervals. Compute the participation ratio from these samples. In the course of a week cover all students. In the example, notice that Suzy was participating 6 out of 10 times. Dividing 6 by 10, her P ratio is 60%.

School_____   Date_____

Observer_____   Time_____

Trials	Names / Suzy Jones										Group Total %
1	P										
2	P										
3	N										
4	T										
5	P										
6	P										
7	P										
8	T										
9	N										
10	P										
Individual % Total	60%										Average

P = Participating (actively involved in learning)
N = Not participating (talking, dawdling)
T = Transient (getting new materials, answer keys, etc.)
P ratio is P/10

ANALYSIS FORM   CLASSROOM CLIMATE

ANALYSIS SCALE

TEACHER _____   OCCURRENCE

OBSERVER _____   1. Not evident
                                2. Slightly evident
CLASS _____   3. Moderately evident
                                4. Quite evident
DATE _____   N Not applicable

TOPIC	OCCURRENCE	COMMENTS

1. ACADEMIC CLIMATE: TEACHER . . .
  a. Fills class time with learning activities
  b. Keeps students on-task
  c. Challenges students
  d. Is businesslike but supportive
  e. Monitors student progress		

2. HIGH STANDARDS: TEACHER . . .
  a. Maintains optimum performance standard
  b. Rewards effort and achievement
  c. Effects a professional demeanor
  d. Promotes higher-level thinking		

3. EXPECTATIONS FOR SUCCESS: TEACHER . . .
  a. Has a positive attitude; encourages a positive attitude in students
  b. Adapts learning activites for increased possibility of student success
  c. Shows interest in all students
  d. Encourages students to compete with themselves		

4. FEEDBACK AND PRAISE: TEACHER . . .
  a. Provides feedback on standard of performance, student's progress, corrective procedures
  b. Provides timely feedback
  c. Uses effective praise
  d. Uses criticism sparingly and judiciously
  e. Encourages student self-monitoring		

REFERENCES

Amidon, E., & Flanders, N. (1967). *The role of the teacher in the classroom*. Minneapolis, MN: Association for Productive Teaching.

Anderson, L. (1989). Learners and learning. In M. Reynolds (Ed.), *Knowledge base for the beginning teacher*. New York: Pergamon Press.

Block, J. (1970). *The effects of various levels of performance on selected cognitive, affective, and time variables*. Unpublished doctoral dissertation, University of Chicago.

Bloom, B. (Ed.). (1956). *A taxonomy of educational objectives: Handbook 1. Cognitive domain*. New York: McKay.

Bloom, B. (1976). *Human characteristics and student learning*. New York: McGraw-Hill.

Brookover, W., Beady, C., Flood, P., Schweitzer, J., & Wisenbaker, J. (1979). *School social systems and student achievement: Schools can make a difference*. New York: Praeger.

Brookover, W., & Lezotte, L. (1977). *Changes in school characteristics coincident with changes in student achievement*. East Lansing: Michigan State University, College of Urban Development.

Brooks, J., & Brooks, M. (1993). *The case for constructivist classrooms*. Alexandria, VA: Association for Supervision and Curriculum Development.

Brophy, J. (1981). Teacher praise: A functional analysis [Review of educational research]. *American Educational Research Association, 51*(1), 5–32.

Brophy, J. (1982). Successful teaching strategies for the inner-city child. *Phi Delta Kappan, 63*(8), 527–530.

Brophy, J., & Good, T. (1970). Teacher communication of differential expectation for children's classroom performance: Some behavioral data. *Journal of Educational Psychology, 61*(5), 365–374.

Brophy, J., & Good, T. (1986). Teacher behavior and student achievement. In M. Wittrock (Ed.), *Handbook of research on teaching* (3rd ed.). New York: Macmillan.

Coleman, J., Campbell, E., Hobson, C., McPartland, J., Mood, A., Weinfield, F., York, R. (1966). *Equality of educational opportunity*. Washington, DC: U.S. Government Printing Office.

Edmonds, E. (1979). Effective schools for the urban poor. *Educational Leadership, 37*(1), 15–24.

Fisher, C. W., Felby, W., Marliane, R., Cahen, L., Dishaw, M., Moore, J., & Berliner, D. (1978). *Teaching behaviors, academic learning time and student achievement: Final report of phase 111–13. Beginning teacher evaluation study*. San Francisco: Far West Laboratory for Educational Research and Development.

Flanders, N. (1970). *Analyzing teaching behavior*. Reading, MA: Addison-Wesley.

Good, T. (1981). Teacher expectations and student perceptions: A decade of research. *Educational Leadership, 38*(5), 415–422.

Good, T., & Beckerman, T. (1978). Time on task: A naturalistic study in sixth-grade classroom. *The Elementary School Journal, 78*(3), 193–201.

Good, T., & Brophy, J. (1994). *Looking in classrooms* (6th ed.). New York: HarperCollins.

Goodlad, J., & Keating, P. (Eds.). (1994). *Access to knowledge: The continuing agenda for our nation's schools*. New York: College Entrance Examination Board.

Hale-Benson, J. (1986). *Black children: Their roots, culture, and learning styles.* Baltimore: Johns Hopkins University Press.

Heath, D. (1986). Developing teachers, not just techniques. In K. Zumwalt (Ed.), *Improving teaching.* Alexandria, VA: ASCD.

Hunter, M. (1994). *Enhancing teaching.* New York: Macmillan.

Kozol, J. (1991). *Savage inequalities.* New York: Crown.

Lamperes, B. (1994). Empowering at-risk students to succeed. *Educational Leadership, 52*(3), 67–70.

Letteri, C. (1985). Teaching students how to learn. *Theory into Practice* (spring), 112–122.

Levin, T., & Long, R. (1981). *Effective instruction.* Alexandria, VA: Association for Supervision and Curriculum Development.

Lezotte, L. (Ed.). (1984). Conducting an effective school program. *The Effective School Report, 2*(10), 1.

Lowe, R., & Gervais, R. (1988). Increasing instructional time in today's classroom. *National Association of Secondary Principals* (February), 19–22.

McGreal, T. (1994, December 2). *The research on good teaching: A practical update on what works and what's new.* Speech given at the Kaleidoscope of Learning Conference, Cedar Rapids, IA.

Mitzel, H. (Ed.). (1982). *Encyclopedia of educational research* (5th ed.). New York: Free Press (division of Macmillan), American Educational Research Association.

Moyers, B. (1994). *Healing and the mind.* New York: Doubleday.

Murphy, J. (1993). What's in? What's out? American education in the nineties. *Phi Delta Kappan 74*(8), 641–646.

National Commission on Excellence in Education (1983). *A nation at risk.* Washington, DC: U.S. Department of Education.

National Education Commission on Time and Learning Fact Sheet (1994). Washington, DC: Department of Education.

Ornstein, A. (1990). *Strategies for effective teaching.* New York: Harper & Row.

Perkins, H. (1965). Classroom behavior and underachievement. *American Educational Research Journal, 2*(1), 1–12.

Pressley, M., Johnson, C., Symons, S., McGoldrick, J., & Kurita, J. (1989). Strategies that improve children's memory and comprehension of text. *Elementary School Journal, 90,* 3–32.

Purkey, W. (1978). *Inviting school success.* Belmont, CA: Wadsworth.

Putnam, J. (Ed.). (1993). *Cooperative learning and strategies for inclusion.* Baltimore: Paul H. Brooks.

Rosenshine, B. (1979). Content, time, and direct instruction. In P. Peterson & H. Walberg (Eds.), *Research on teaching: Concepts, findings, and implications.* Berkeley, CA: McCutchan.

Rosenshine, B., & Furst, N. (1971). Research on teacher performance criteria. In B. O. Smith (Ed.), *Research in teacher education: A symposium.* Englewood Cliffs, NJ: Prentice-Hall.

Rosenthal, R., Baratz, S., & Hall, C. (1974). Teacher behavior, teacher expectation, and gains in pupils' rated creativity. *Journal of Genetic Psychology, 124* (March), 115–122.

Rosenthal, R., & Jacobson, L. (1968). *Pygmalion in the classroom: Teacher expectation and pupils' intellectual development*. New York: Holt, Rinehart & Winston.

Rutter, M., Maugham, B., Mortimore, P., & Ouster, J. (1979). *Fifteen thousand hours*. Cambridge, MA: Harvard University Press.

Ryan, K., & Cooper, J. (1995). *Those who can teach* (7th ed.). Boston: Houghton Mifflin.

Snider, W. (1986, June 11). Chicago board adopts strict homework policy. *Educational Week, 38*(3), 1.

Stallings, J. (1983, June). *Findings from the research on teaching: What we have learned*. Charleston, WV: West Virginia Department of Education.

Status of black children. (1989). *Black Child Advocate, 15*(4).

Swisher, K. (1990). Cooperative learning and the education of American Indian/Alaskan native students: A review of the literature and suggestions for implementation. *Journal of American Indian Education, 29*(2), 36–43.

U.S. Department of Education (1985). *What works*. Washington, DC: U.S. Government Printing Office.

Weinstein, C., & Mayer, R. (1989). The teaching of learning strategies. In J. Sheinker & A. Sheinker (Eds.), *Metacognitive approach to study strategies*. Rockville, MD: Aspen.

Wiggins, G. (1993). *Assessing student performance*. San Francisco: Jossey-Bass.

CHAPTER 3 Democratic Classroom Discipline

Prospective teachers should recognize the value of being well-informed, but that their personal interaction style and level of social development are critical factors as well.

Discipline typically has an ominous connotation for the teacher. The term conjures up an image of misbehaving students frustrating the teacher's sincere instructional efforts. One may be left with the impression that teaching would be more appealing if it were not for discipline. However, this perception takes into account only a narrow—but highly visible—band within the wide spectrum of discipline.

In a more dispassionate and broad-based perspective, discipline is neither good nor bad. It is a necessary and pervasive dimension of every classroom. Within that setting, discipline refers to the inclination of students to comply with the teacher's expectations. Discipline, then, is comprised of factors both external and internal to the student. Understanding discipline and dealing with it requires that both aspects be addressed.

When collective student behavior is "good," that is, when students behave in an orderly and responsible manner, discipline is a tacit matter. Classroom activities proceed in a manner that is satisfying to the teacher and, we usually assume, to the students as well. Little overt attention is given to the subtle factors that result in orderly and cooperative behavior. But when "bad" behavior occurs, whether due to ineffective teacher actions or to conditions internal to students that lie beyond the teacher's immediate control, that behavior calls attention to itself. Dealing with it becomes a matter of urgency on the teacher's part. At the very least it is annoying; it may even be threatening to the teacher and cause an uncomfortable emotional state. Impulsive or irrational discipline-related decisions are likely to occur when a teacher experiences this condition.

When teachers think of discipline, this uncomfortable "bad" condition usually comes to mind. Yet the "good" condition, during which students behave within the limits of teacher expectations, is also a part of discipline. Establishing in the classroom those conditions to which students respond positively is as much a part of discipline as the monitoring, controlling, and intervening behaviors more commonly associated with it. Discipline, in this teacher-oriented sense, refers both to the structure—especially the explicit limits placed on student behavior—intended to produce an optimum learning setting and to the manner in which the teacher's authority will be used.

FOCUS QUESTIONS

1. What are some important ways that research informs discipline-related teaching practice?
2. Teaching, including discipline-related practices, is usually considered to be both an art and a science. While the focus of this chapter is primarily on the science dimension, art certainly has its place. What sort of discipline-related decisions rely heavily on the intuition of the teacher-as-artist?
3. A certain mystique is perceived by some educators to be associated with classroom discipline. Does it, in fact, exist? Should it? What should an informed teacher's position be on this phenomenon?
4. Many persons, including many teachers, think of discipline as a distasteful, even odious, aspect of teaching. How can discipline be construed to be a potentially positive and productive aspect of teaching?

OVERVIEW

An informed belief system is the basis for sound teaching decisions, including discipline-related decisions. Common sense or conventional wisdom for addressing the concerns of discipline is not adequate in the modern secondary classroom. The first step in developing a personal plan for classroom discipline is becoming informed regarding professionally endorsed principles of discipline. The second step is developing a comprehensive set of practices that attends to all four phases of discipline: prevention, management, intervention, and remediation. Finally, acquiring an understanding of the teacher's social power in the classroom is useful in implementing the intended practices. The ideas previously presented on classroom climate (chapter 2) focus on producing the conditions of productive learning. Essentially, they form the foundation of sound discipline. The thrust of this chapter is to help new teachers acquire a framework for decision making about discipline. It stops short of providing prescriptions because these are situational and would require more elaboration than space allows. Many sources in the literature describe practices in detail, and the reader is encouraged to seek those that are compatible with individual needs and preferences.

SCENARIO

Jane DeFederico—"Mrs. D" to her students—was trying some new ideas in managing her general-science class this third year of her teaching. Her first two years had not been all that bad, but she felt that the class could have accomplished much more if she had not had to spend so much time and energy maintaining a reasonable semblance of order. She had attended a course on discipline during the summer and had written a term paper describing a personal discipline strategy based on her new understanding. She would find out whether theory was helpful in addressing her concerns.

She had done some things the first few days of class that she had not done in the past. She established a seating arrangement that provided ready access to all the students but that gave special consideration to students who might need the greatest attention. Expectations, just a few in number and positively stated, had been written on the board, discussed at length, and left there as a continuing reminder. Students were given the opportunity to express what they expected from her. Class routines and signals had been established and practiced. And, importantly, she had installed a system of "behavior citations"—written communication that created an ongoing record—to address chronic and flagrant misbehavior. With these done, she felt more comfortable and in control.

Now the class was in the third week, and Mrs. D was beginning a unit on chemistry. As the bell rang, she stood at the front of the classroom affecting a businesslike demeanor. To her satisfaction, the class came quickly to order. As an advance organizer for the day's lesson she was using the concept of bonding. The class was asked to think of instances that involved an attraction between two things.

Claire called out almost immediately upon hearing the activity described, "My mom and dad."

Mrs. D moved a few steps to the board and tapped purposefully on rule number 3 referring to raising one's hand to be called on by the teacher. Claire raised her hand somewhat sheepishly. "All right, Claire, that certainly is one kind of bond. What are some more, class?" Several hands went up. Mrs. D pointed to Anita.

"People and dogs," answered Anita.

"Well, yes, bonds often exist between people and animals; emotional bonds, I suppose we would call them. Why do these kinds of bonds exist?" Several hands that had been up went down as this higher-level question was posed. As hands began to go up tentatively once again, Mrs. D called on Susan.

"They are attracted to each other." Mrs. D gave an encouraging nod and Susan continued. "Each one gives the other something it wants."

As Susan was answering the question, Mrs. D noticed Andrew and Leslie on the opposite side of the room begin a whispered conversation. She looked in their direction as she continued the discussion. "Yes, that is a key idea, Susan. And it applies to things other than people and animals, class. Leslie, can you think of an example of inanimate things?"

Leslie's attention was quickly drawn back to the class discussion and she remarked, "Magnets stick to our refrigerator door at home. That seems like a bond."

In response to Leslie's example, Ronnie exclaimed in a low but audible voice, "That's dumb." Mrs. D acknowledged Leslie's answer and called on Jeremy for his idea. Meanwhile she arrived at Ronnie's seat and looked sternly at him for a few moments until his eyes dropped. He had gotten the message. The discussion in the class proceeded for several minutes as many examples were given. Finally, Aaron observed that it seemed as though bonding was everywhere.

"Exactly," Mrs. D responded enthusiastically, "and that is just the point. Now we're going to be studying chemistry for the next two weeks. What sort of bonds do you think we are going to be especially thinking about?"

"Mrs. D, my pencil is broken. Can I sharpen it?" interjected Renee as she raised her hand but did not wait to be called on. Mrs. D placed her left hand on her hip and gave Renee a brief, sharp look. Renee put her hand over her mouth and drew in her breath in the realization that her impulsive comment was inappropriate. But throughout the class Mrs. D recognized that there was some fidgeting and straying of attention. She had hoped to continue the discussion for a few more minutes, but realized now that a change of pace and activity was in order to regain students' attention and avoid further possible disruptions such as Renee's, or worse. She proceeded to answer her own question about the bonds they would be thinking about, then pulled down a periodic table chart as a reference for the class. A more direct teaching mode would help, she reasoned; they need some information about the elements so they can begin to understand how chemical bonding creates all the kinds of matter we know. She began a minilecture about the electrical charges associated with protons and electrons that establish the basis for bonding.

This brief glimpse into Jane DeFederico's classroom illustrates her informed systematic approach to discipline. Jane was aided by her term paper that we may assume contained her carefully thought-out design for discipline and the identification of underlying principles and had been shared with and critiqued by other knowledgeable educators. She quickly implemented her plan at the beginning of the year by conducting several activities intended to clarify expectations and reduce the students' need to "test the teacher." When inevitable misbehavior did occur, she was ready to respond. Meanwhile, she would do what she could within the instructional mode to prevent most of the incidental misbehavior.

Jane indicated that she was realistic in her expectations for student behavior and was willing to accommodate as necessary. As a sensitive teacher she became aware during this episode that the class was nearing the end of its tolerance for the discussion mode, even though her plan had been for further use of discussion. A likely response to students' waning attention might have been an expression of dissatisfaction with their off-task behavior. Jane's more enlightened response was to change the pace and shift to a more promising mode. Her informed belief system served her well in this instance of midlesson decision making.

When minor lapses in student compliance occurred, Jane took immediate but judicious action. In each case the lesson proceeded smoothly while Jane dealt unobtrusively with the target student or students. Students received the message that learning was important in this classroom, but that their dignity was important, too. They had probably begun to sense by this third week of class that Mrs. D "had her act together." No serious problem occurred in this episode, and this classroom seemed to have been an unlikely place to expect it. It could happen, of course, but Jane DiFederico seemed prepared to deal competently with it if and when she must.

RESEARCH AND THEORETICAL BASE

Discipline, as a general aspect of every classroom, is difficult to study. Discipline does not exist as a discrete entity but rather as a collection of many factors. Much of the research that is helpful in understanding discipline is more specifically focused on such factors as reinforcement, span of attention, or teacher transitions. Furthermore, this sort of research has as much implication for instruction as it does for discipline.

Clarification of the relationship between instruction and discipline is helpful in understanding the research in areas that affect both. Many of the teacher strategies and behavior that are intended as effective instruction operate simultaneously, but tacitly, to diminish misbehavior. Some teacher behaviors are specifically instructional; others are specifically disciplinary. Between these two extremes is an overlapping area referred to as *classroom management*. Prevention and management strategies such as clearly stating expectations and establishing efficient classroom routines fall within this area. In chapter 2, these strategies are addressed as they relate to classroom climate.

The most extensive available review of the literature on classroom management was conducted by Doyle (1986). While many contributions to the literature on classroom management have been made since then, his work is still the most comprehensive single source, and it continues to be highly relevant. His major conclusions were the following:

1. The teacher's management task is primarily one of establishing and maintaining work systems for classroom groups rather than spotting and punishing misbehavior, remediating behavioral disorders, or maximizing the engagement of individual students.
2. Rules, procedures, routines, and reprimands all have a role to play in sustaining classroom order, but they can only supplement what teachers do to specify and orchestrate programs of action.
3. In situations in which students lack either the inclination or the ability to follow the primary vector of the teacher or the teacher lacks skill in steering the program of action, order is often a protracted struggle.
4. It is difficult and potentially misleading to study management processes without attention to curriculum, or curriculum designs without attention to classroom processes.
5. The use of familiar activities such as recitation and seat work and the standard practice of routinizing most classroom procedures and activities appear to be reasonable strategies for offsetting the inherent delicacy of classroom order.
6. The key to teachers' success in management appears to be their (1) understanding of the likely configuration of events, and (2) skill in monitoring and guiding activities in light of this information.

Kounin (1970), in a series of landmark studies on effective classroom management, developed several key concepts in the area of group dynamics. His studies were conducted using videotapes in elementary classrooms, but the implications clearly extend into the secondary level. Although scholarly work on discipline was published prior to 1970, Kounin's studies at that time marked the beginning of a more intensive scientific approach to discipline.

To describe what he observed in classrooms, Kounin applied terms to discipline in ways that had not been done before, most notably "ripple effect" (p. 2), "withitness" (p. 80), and "overlapping" (p. 85). *Ripple effect* refers to the influence that a control measure applied to one student has on the others in the group. *Withitness* describes teachers' awareness of what is happening throughout the classroom, staying one jump ahead of the students and thereby averting potential misbehavior. *Overlapping* is associated with withitness in that it describes teachers' ability to attend to more than one activity at a time. Kounin also found that both more effective and less effective classroom managers tended to use similar intervention techniques. Prevention, one may conclude, more so than intervention, is the key to effective discipline.

Since 1970, more than a dozen discipline-related strategies of varying degrees of structure have been developed (Wolfgang & Glickman, 1980; Charles, 1985; Duke & Meckel, 1984). These so-called models are not based directly on research as such, but they employ generally accepted social and psychological principles. Wolfgang and Glickman arranged them along a continuum from those that are predominantly student centered and use psychotherapeutic and communications principles to those that are decidedly teacher centered and are based on behavioral psychology.

Perhaps the best known of the formal discipline strategies is Canter's (1976) *Assertive Discipline*. The bases for the model are the teacher-centered premises that the teacher must be in charge in the classroom and no student has the right to interfere with the classroom instruction. Assertive discipline provides for predetermined rewards for compliant behavior and penalties for misbehavior. This model is popular with teachers because it presents a definitive set of procedures that the teacher controls. A certain amount of controversy attends the assertive discipline model, as described in a series of 1989 articles (Canter; Render, Padilla, & Krank; McCormack; McDaniel; Curwin & Mendler). Emmer and Aussiker (1989) concluded after reviewing the studies on assertive discipline that "in spite of teacher and administrator perceptions that are often positive, there is no evidence that Assertive Discipline training results in improved student behavior" (p. 119). Brophy and McCaslen (1992) are more favorable in their assessment in that they conclude that assertive discipline

> can be helpful for teachers who are notably lacking in both confidence and viable strategies for dealing with problem students, and it is an improvement on earlier developed control methods that placed even more emphasis on reward and punishment and less emphasis on helping students to understand the rationales underlying rules in addition to the rules themselves. However, the program emphasizes establishing externally enforced control over problem behavior rather than diagnosis of causes and treatment through long-term change strategies. (p. 61)

Greenlee and Ogletree (1993), in a study of 50 Chicago teachers, reported that "stress related to classroom management is the most influential factor in failure among novice teachers" (p. 14). In 1984, Veenman reported similar findings, and the literature in general reports awareness of this condition. It is a serious problem, one aspect of the larger behavior problem that schools and teachers continue to cope with, but without heartening results. This is, in fact, not just an educator's problem, but a problem of the larger society, and the larger society needs to be part of the solution.

In a study of 51 7th- and 8th-grade teachers, Evertson and Emmer (1982) identified the following practices of effective managers that differentiated them from ineffective managers:

1. Instructing students in rules and procedures. . . . Better managers were more explicit about what was desirable behavior.
2. Monitoring student compliance with rules. . . . (E)ffective teachers noted and reacted to departures from acceptable classroom behavior.
3. Developing student accountability for work. More effective managers . . . had stronger and more detailed accountability systems.
4. Communicating information. Effective managers were more successful in presenting information clearly, in giving directions, and in stating objectives.
5. Organizing instruction. Effective managers wasted less time in their activities and had more on-task time. (p. 9)

As studies such as this show, teachers can acquire skills that contribute to effective classroom management. We must recognize these skills as necessary, but not sufficient, to ensure orderly behavior.

From their review of the research on classroom management, Evertson and Harris (1992) found that certain elements were associated with effective managers. The elements included the following:

- Use time as effectively as possible.
- Implement group strategies with high levels of involvement and low levels of misbehavior.
- Choose lesson formats and academic tasks conducive to high student engagement.
- Communicate clearly rules of participation.
- Prevent problems by implementing a system at the beginning of the school year. (p. 76)

These findings affirm the importance of teachers attending to certain key factors; finding ways to accomplish this is the challenge to the teacher. In this instance both the application and the limitation of research in guiding teacher decision making is demonstrated.

Attribution of the causes of misbehavior was the topic of a study by Brophy and Rohrkemper (1981). They found that teachers tended to assign cause to factors outside themselves, often targeting the students directly. Whereas many factors affect students' behavior, teachers' reluctance to recognize their own culpability diminishes the likelihood that they will make useful adjustments in their classroom practices.

A research synthesis of literature on student discipline and motivation by Cotton and Savard (1984) included as a major conclusion that tangible rewards tended to have a temporary positive effect but often a long-range negative effect. On the other hand, classroom conditions that provided students with academic and social success experiences tended to reduce discipline-related problems. Furthermore, the authors asserted that punishment in and of itself was ineffective. Only when punishment was clearly related to misbehavior and was recognized as such by the student did it have the intended effect.

Much of the attention to discipline in the past has focused on control aspects. However, Gettinger (1988) emphasized that prevention in the form of proactive classroom management had greater potential than remediation for effecting optimum classroom conditions. Proactive management is preventive rather than reactive, integrates instruction and management teacher behaviors, and addresses group dynamics more so than individual behavior. Gettinger stated as a conclusion to her review of the research that "unless teachers use proactive management methods to create positive learning environments that encourage productive behavior, behavior change interventions will have limited long-term effectiveness" (p. 240).

Richmond and McCroskey (1983) examined the teacher-power construct in the classroom. Five types of power are available to teachers: referent (personality), expert, legitimate, coercive, and reward (these terms are defined in the "Teacher Power in the Classroom" section of this chapter). These categories were originally defined by French and Raven (1968) in their research on supervisor style. Of these power types, referent power has the greatest impact on cognitive and affective learning, but expert power also has a favorable effect. Legitimate power and coercive power tend to retard both aspects of learning. Reward power is unrelated to either. Richmond and McCroskey concluded that teachers should attempt to employ referent and expert power, but use reward power in preference to either legitimate or coercive power when possible.

Educators are aware of the disparity between research and practice. Bielefeldt (1988) cited several reasons for this: "lack of time and money for teacher training; the cumbersomeness of certain behavioral techniques; the increased diversity of the school population; socioeconomic conditions; the attractiveness of short term solutions (such as punishment) that have deleterious long term effects; and the fact that some teachers don't get along well enough with students to make a discipline program work" (p. 2). At least three of the aforementioned reasons lie outside direct control by teachers; consequently the gap between research and practice may be diminished, but it is unlikely to be closed.

Much of the research on classroom discipline is not directly translatable into prescriptions for teacher practice. This gives rise to the misconception that research on discipline is not a useful source of information for the teacher. In fact, research as it is initially reported serves to reinforce at the general level certain principles of discipline and clarifies effective patterns of teacher behavior. Knowledge of these principles or patterns is then available to be incorporated into a teacher's belief system. The extent to which this knowledge actually is acquired by a teacher, the priority assigned it, and the extent to which it is reflected in practice remains an individual matter. In this sense, informed teacher decision making must be considered the most basic aspect of effective discipline. Research is a necessary but indirect part of it.

The literature on discipline is far too extensive to present a representative sampling here. However, the authors have selected certain works they hope will convey some sense of its content. On the whole, the literature on discipline includes a great deal of expository commentary relating to theory, principles, and practices. Research is less abundant, and it is mostly descriptive in nature. Almost no experimental research involving manipulation of variables is available. Even with its shortcomings, the literature is the foundation for the knowledge base of discipline. It is an invaluable resource for a teacher's informed belief system.

APPLICATION TO PRACTICE

Classrooms characterized by a positive climate and academically motivated students are those in which misbehavior of consequence occurs infrequently. Realizing this, however, is of little help to those preservice or in-service teachers who feel the need to understand the dynamics of discipline and who want to acquire confidence in their ability to establish order and decorum, and want to deal effectively with misbehavior when it occurs. An important purpose of this chapter is to contribute to the understanding of discipline and to make realistic suggestions regarding discipline-related approaches.

One may wonder why concern with discipline should still be prevalent after so many years of being recognized as a school problem? Writings from ancient Egyptian, Greek, and Roman societies inform us of the recalcitrant nature of students from those eras. For example, an elderly Socrates wrote in the fourth century:

> From the day your baby is born you must teach him to do things. Children today love luxury too much. They have detestable manners, flout authority, have no respect for their elders. They no longer rise when their parents and teachers enter the room. What kind of awful creatures will they be when they grow up?

The question regarding the concern with discipline has no easy response, or it would have been answered long ago. The nature of discipline is such that a final solution is not even possible. Only the sound principles of discipline will remain constant; the application of those principles will vary as the factors and conditions in classrooms vary. The commentary in this chapter is essentially a rationale for this statement.

Discipline is not a neat, discrete concept. It is comprised of a wide assortment of more specific concepts. Addressing the topic of discipline is a multifaceted, complex task. The perennial efforts of educators to oversimplify discipline have led to the emergence of many widely accepted but suspect beliefs about discipline. Raywid (1976) astutely observed that "the most tyrannical of all our beliefs are those which are persistently unexamined—precisely because they appear so patently reasonable as to be mandated by common sense and impervious to question" (p. 37).

The professional literature presents a wide array of definitions of discipline, which may in itself be testimony to the misunderstanding often attending it. As was previously stated, discipline for the purposes of this book refers to the inclination of the students to comply with the teacher's expectations for behavior. Discipline, therefore, is a dynamic set of conditions that exists within students, individually and collectively, the effect of which is revealed in the classroom in terms of order and decorum. Direct implications for the structure established in the classroom and the use of teacher authority stem from these conditions. Discipline is not something a teacher does in the sense that a teacher "disciplines" students. To use discipline as a verb is to confuse it with a teacher's controlling or punishing acts. Discipline recognized as a dynamic set of conditions affecting the pertinent causes, not just the visible symptoms, is clearly the basis for an informed approach.

Addressing the conditions related to discipline greatly complicates the task of the teacher in achieving a desirable level of classroom decorum. It is one thing to tell the class to be quiet, or to confiscate a squirt gun, or to intercept a surreptitiously passed note; it is quite another to create conditions within which these behaviors are neither attractive nor feasible alternatives in the students' view. The relationship of climate and motivation to discipline becomes clearer when one considers that student behavior is in large measure influenced by the quality of the climate and the level of their motivation.

The educational practices associated with effective classroom management are sophisticated. This fact has not been fully appreciated by educators. As a result, personal experience and intuition—sometimes generally referred to as "common sense"—are the basis of many teachers' discipline-related practices. For example, the widespread use of punishment, when defined as retribution involving physical pain or mental discomfiture, is not defensible in a democratically oriented environment (though one must be careful in generalizing out of context). Yet new teachers entering the classroom are socialized compellingly into the use of retributive punishment. (Consider the frequent use of detention.)

A further implication of the sophisticated nature of discipline is addressed by Gage (1978) in his comments on the effect of multiple variables on teacher decision making:

> Scientific method (straightforward application of principles or "laws") can contribute relationships between variables taken two at a time and even, in the form of interactions, three or perhaps four or more at a time. Beyond say four, the usefulness of what science can give the teacher begins to weaken, because teachers cannot apply, at least not without help and not on the run, the more complex interactions. At this point, the teacher as artist must step in or make clinical or artistic judgments about the best ways to teach. In short, the scientific base for the art of teaching will consist of two-variable relationships and lower order interactions. The higher order interactions between four and more variables must be handled by the teacher as artist. (p. 20)

Discipline commonly involves decision making of the "four and more" variable type as already described. In a classroom of 20 to 30 students, each a separate personality with unique perceptions and needs and all involved with the many academic, social, and psychological factors indigenous to that setting, the complexity of achieving and maintaining order is apparent. Gage pointed to the futility of depending on preconceived prescriptions such as those often included in lists of "teacher shoulds." He contended that effective functioning at this level requires an artist dimension, or a level of performance that transcends routine or mechanistic applications. Redl (1966) recognized this same phenomenon when he stated that "for the job of establishing good discipline and maintaining it . . . the personality of the teacher is the most essential factor" (p. 254). This is not to say that teachers do not have much to learn from the professional literature about discipline, but in fact just the opposite. An informed belief system is essential for being aware of—let alone achieving—the desirable outcomes of effective discipline. Prospective teachers should recognize the value of being well informed, but should realize that their own personal interactive style and level of social development are critical factors as well. "Withitness," in other words, is a matter both of possessing social competence and of being well informed.

Dealing with discipline is further complicated by its emotional aspects, especially in the case of teacher interventions with noncompliant students. When students misbehave in classrooms in obvious violation of the teacher's expectation, it may be sensed by the teacher as an affront. Self-esteem is in large measure a function of the teacher's own perceived competence; students' misbehavior signals the teacher's impotence at that given moment. By undermining a teacher's perception of personal competence, students trigger what psychologically are instinctive acts of self-preservation by the teacher (i.e., preservation of the self-concept). Meanwhile, those pedagogical principles relevant to such situations are likely to be ignored in the urgency to restore psychological comfort. Teachers are swept up in a tide of events of which they have only tenuous control and limited understanding—fertile conditions for nurturing a mystique. A succession of these events in the classroom can be devastating to teachers.

The Myths of Discipline

The mystique of discipline resulting from the conditions described has deterred teachers from seeking rational—or pedagogical, if you will—approaches. Some of the expedient approaches that have been devised deserve to be considered as the myths of discipline. The myths are widely accepted and form the basis for many teachers' discipline-related decisions. But these myths simply do not stand up to scrutiny; they are not pedagogically valid. Taken collectively they violate several generally accepted, virtually self-evident classroom principles: Students' worth and dignity must be respected in accordance with democratic ideals; teachers should structure classrooms with the needs and natural inclinations of students clearly in mind; teachers should use authority judiciously in the classrooms; and teachers have a major responsibility for students' motivation. Recognizing the myths for what they are and rejecting them as the basis for one's discipline decisions is necessary for the development of a defensible approach to discipline. Twenty common myths are listed here (adapted from Kindsvatter and Levine, 1980), each followed by a statement that is the pedagogically endorsed counterpart of the myth. These may be helpful in screening new ideas encountered about discipline or in purging ideas that are not sound.

Myth 1: Student misbehavior is self-evidently the student's fault.

Endorsed Principle: Misbehavior may have multiple causes, one of which may include teacher characteristics and/or practices.

Myth 2: Discipline is realistically conceived as a power struggle between the teacher and the students.

Endorsed Principle: Reason rather than coercion is the basis of sound discipline; discipline involves doing something *for* students more than doing something *to* students.

Myth 3: Good control depends on finding the right gimmick.

Endorsed Principle: Good control is achieved through sound judgment grounded in an informed belief system.

Myth 4: Every teacher can become optimally effective in managing classroom discipline.

Endorsed Principle: Teachers will inevitably vary in their potential to become effective classroom managers, especially as their personalities and belief systems vary.

Myth 5: The best teachers are those in whose classrooms students dare not misbehave.

Endorsed Principle: Intimidation is at cross-purposes with humaneness; it only signals the teacher's lack of interpersonal skills or social maturity.

Myth 6: A good classroom is a quiet classroom.

Endorsed Principle: The nature of the learning activity should determine the nature of students' participation, and sometimes participation noise—while it must be held to a reasonable level—is desirable.

Myth 7: The teacher should not smile before Christmas.

Endorsed Principle: A teaching style devoid of a sense of humor and grounded in an adversarial posture is bankrupt.

Myth 8: Teachers' responses to misbehavior should always be directly related to the misbehavior.

Endorsed Principle: Conceiving responses that immediately, directly, and appropriately respond to each specific misbehavior in its context is an impossible task for the teacher. However, the reasonable consequences of student misbehavior may be similar for different sorts of misbehavior; generalized responses stressing behavior remediation are often appropriate.

Myth 9: Punishment is educational.

Endorsed Principle: A reasonable consequence is focused on the student's best interest; punishment serves mainly the punisher. The only certain outcome of punishment is that the person being punished suffers. Respect and worthwhile learning, not fear, should be instilled through discipline; the mindless use of punishment is a travesty in American education.

Myth 10: A teacher has to use harsh punishment because "difficult" students do not respond to less stern measures.

Endorsed Principle: For students who experience harsh punishment at home, it is all the more important that they be treated with compassion and understanding in accordance with the best human-relations principles.

Myth 11: The behavior of teachers can be understood only in terms of their instructional role.

Endorsed Principle: From a personal, human-needs point of view, teaching is an important means in the teacher's life of satisfying certain basic psychological needs such as power, security, and self-esteem.

Myth 12: The behavior of students can be understood only in terms of their role as students.

Endorsed Principle: Students' social and psychological baggage come with them through the classroom door. Further, their felt needs are not so much for academic learning as for socialization and status.

Myth 13: Students do not know how to behave with decorum.

Endorsed Principle: Students do not need to be taught how to behave appropriately nearly so much as they need to be convinced that it is in their best interest to conform to the teacher's and school's expectations.

Myth 14: Students deliberately "test" the teacher to find out what they can get away with.

Endorsed Principle: There is no insidious conspiracy on students' part to test the teacher. But students are not psychologically comfortable until they know the limits—de facto, not just de jure—of their freedom in the classroom.

Myth 15: Teachers should not examine students' records to avoid becoming prejudiced by negative information.

Endorsed Principle: Teachers should know as much as possible about their students to make decisions about them that are in the students' best interest.

Myth 16: Being consistent should take precedence over all other considerations.

Endorsed Principle: Teachers' informed and judicious judgment should take precedence over thoughtless consistency.

Myth 17: Keeping the students occupied will prevent misbehavior.

Endorsed Principle: Keeping students on-task with thoughtful assignments is vitally important for both classroom order and productive learning, but mindless busywork is never justified. Further, busywork induces boredom, which in turn predisposes misbehavior.

Myth 18: Students will comply if they are given sufficient incentive.

Endorsed Principle: Appropriate rewards have their rightful place; however, incentives in the form of bribes are not only unconscionable, but they become a means through which the students manipulate the teacher.

Myth 19: Students will be good for the teacher if they consider the teacher to be "one of the gang."

Endorsed Principle: The teacher's rightful role involves authority and leadership, and the teacher's credibility and effectiveness is undermined by most behaviors that have teacher popularity as their major intent.

Myth 20: All misbehavior should be dealt with swiftly and with finality.

Endorsed Principle: Misbehavior that disrupts learning must obviously be terminated when it is detected. However, some misbehavior alerts the sensitive teacher to the student's need for help, so the teacher should not too quickly default to expedient, self-serving measures that may exacerbate the problem.

Teachers have the responsibility to provide every student with the realistic opportunity for emotional comfort and personal success. It is unrealistic, possibly unethical, to force students to fit the school without regard for any other concerns; to do so is not only self-serving, but the discipline problems that result from this approach underscore its inadequacy.

In the scenario at the beginning of the chapter, Jane DiFederico was depicted as using appropriate approaches to address the disciplinary aspects of her classroom. If she had subscribed to myth number 1 (misbehavior is self-evidently the student's fault), she may simply have proceeded with her lesson as originally planned even as students grew restive. Then, when misbehavior occurred on the part of students whose attention spans had been exceeded, she may have acted in terms of myth number 3 (good control depends on finding the right gimmick) and myth number 9 (punishment is educational). In so doing, she could have assigned a detention to offending students with the rationalization that they deserved it and would know better next time. One does not need to proceed very far with this type of scenario to realize what sort of climate is being created in such a classroom, and that a self-serving teacher is exploiting teacher authority.

Students should be expected to cope with reasonable conditions and responsibilities, and be dealt with firmly when they do not conform with the necessary expectations of a democratic institution. But even more importantly, children need the guidance of enlightened teachers who are free of the shackles of the myths of discipline and who employ practices that reflect the best of both the art and science of teaching.

Principles of Discipline

Discipline is sometimes thought of essentially as reacting to misbehavior and restoring classroom order. When this is the case, the ends may be considered to justify the means, which gives rise to misguided and punitive control techniques. However, an educationally sound approach to discipline has its basis in humane, democratically oriented principles. They function both as a guide and a check in teachers' discipline-related decisions. As examples, therefore, teachers' democratic discipline approaches should have the following characteristics:

1. be conceived on the basis of pedagogical and human-relations principles and in all cases preserve the dignity and personal integrity of students;
2. have a developmental thrust that democratically produces important personal and social-learning outcomes;
3. reflect the belief that promoting self-control in students is at least as important as procuring their compliance;
4. have the intent of doing something for students more than doing something to them;
5. avoid aggravating the problem of an already troubled student.

SUMMARY POINT

Teachers' discipline-related decisions are influenced by philosophical considerations, pedagogical principles, and teacher personality. Purposeful reference to each of these sources is necessary for teachers in the development of their informed approach to discipline.

REVIEW: IMPORTANT CONSIDERATIONS REGARDING DISCIPLINE

1. Discipline is usefully considered to be the inclination of students to comply with the teacher's expectations.
2. Refer to the myths of discipline as an aid in scrutinizing current ideas and selecting new practices.
3. Keep the faith; expedients may seem to serve the moment but they undermine the quality of discipline.

The Phases of Discipline

While becoming aware of the myths and developing an informed belief system, teachers must also acquire a clear understanding of the concept of discipline. As implied by the definition of discipline in terms of student predispositions, it is a neutral concept, a means of categorizing certain factors related to interaction in the classroom. Realistically, however, discipline often has a negative connotation for practitioners because it conjures images of misbehavior, the primary source of teachers' apprehension. Developing an informed, practical approach to discipline requires that one transcend the intuitive, often negative and simplistic, view that frequently exists and acquire a comprehensive awareness of the several interrelated components. A straightforward approach to acquiring a comprehensive view of discipline is to consider in order the nature and implications of its four phases: prevention, management, intervention, and remediation.

Prevention. This phase is first, both logically and intuitively, in the process. The chapters on classroom climate, planning, and instruction address this phase of discipline in important ways. The climate developed over time through the cumulative interactions of teacher and students establishes the social norms that both define and limit appropriate student behavior. The motivation, especially intrinsic motivation, associated with the learning activities energizes both the substance and direction of students' behavior. When this motivation is strong, students' immediate basic drives are satisfied, or at least sublimated, and misbehavior is not an attractive alternative. Thus it is obvious that teachers need to be well prepared, to try to make the topic somehow relevant (otherwise why teach it?), to provide for variety and individual differences, and to be enthusiastic, fairminded, and good-humored. Complying with these conditions is the most crucial aspect of discipline; paradoxically, these conditions do not readily come to teachers' minds when concerns about discipline arise. Rather, teachers are more likely to think of discipline in terms of authority and control.

Motivation. Motivation is so important to prevention, and therefore to positive discipline, that it is given special attention in this section. Ardrey's (1970) theory of motivation provides a useful perspective on the role of the teacher in establishing positive conditions for learning. He postulated that human beings have three basic psychological needs: identity, stimulation, and security. We have extended this list to include the need for power. When these needs are not sufficiently met, deficiency conditions occur, respectively: anonymity, boredom, anxiety, and impotence. If one were to design a situation in which the deficiency conditions were the intention, it is likely that something that looks like a typical classroom would result! Consider the possibilities for relative anonymity in a classroom of 20 to 30 students; for boredom when physically and socially active adolescents are rendered mostly passive and quiet for extended periods of time while they study material about which they have limited innate interest; for anxiety in a setting in which their academic achievement is incessantly tested and their social status is tentative; and for impotence as they are manipulated without personal recourse by the whim of the teacher.

This obviously is a pessimistic view of the classroom, and yet Silberman (1970) and Goodlad (1983) reported through their research that these conditions—characterized as "mindlessness" and "monotonous sameness"—were all too common in U.S. classrooms. That is the bad news; the good news is that teachers can do much to provide for the basic needs of students in the classroom setting in the four critical areas of identity, stimulation, security, and power. In the organization of secondary schools, teachers are inclined to view themselves as purveyors of their subjects. Teachers need to sense what lies beyond that narrow interpretation of their role. Preferably, they should conceive of themselves as agents for enriching their students' lives in many dimensions.

IDENTITY

Teachers can give straightforward help to students in the area of identity by knowing their names and using them outside as well as inside the classroom. A greeting by name from the teacher is very satisfying to a student. Beyond that, knowing students more personally provides opportunities to refer to them in the course of learning activities: Bill is an avid birdwatcher; Jennie is a fine pianist; Danny, who is disfigured from a childhood burn accident, skydives on weekends; Allison has lived in seven different states. Teachers may make special efforts to talk with students, especially shy or unpopular ones. Eating lunch with students occasionally may be appropriate.

By using praise judiciously, a teacher can make a student's day. Supportive notes on students' papers are also helpful. As these suggestions indicate, providing students with evidence of their worth as human beings basically involves the application of effective human relations principles.

STIMULATION

Stimulation is the factor that is most readily associated with motivation. Teaching approaches in achieving it make up much of the commentary on effective teaching. In a sense, one can consider the instructional ideas presented in other chapters in this book as the basis for promoting compliant student behavior. More specifically, teacher enthusiasm and liveliness contribute to stimulation. Providing students with a credible rationale for learning activities and convincing students of the relevance of a topic is helpful. In the course of instruction, teachers should plan for "peak experiences" that will be remembered when the French and Indian War, quadratic equations, gerunds, and sporophytes are forgotten. These might include preparing an ethnic meal, a three-day backpacking expedition, being a quasi-official city or county officeholder for a day, or developing a mural for the cafeteria wall.

Finally, teachers gain credibility by modeling their academic discipline for students: math teachers who are computer specialists; English teachers who publish poetry; or technology teachers who design a simulated automobile electrical system. Being a showman in the classroom helps, but over time being a scholar of substance may be more valuable in stimulating students to achieve academically.

SECURITY

Students' needs for security essentially require that the teacher help them feel confident that they will be able to cope sufficiently with the tasks and challenges of schooling. Providing every student with the reasonable opportunity for success is most important in this regard. This involves recognizing individual differences among students and accommodating them in appropriate—even creative—ways. Such strategies as variable grouping, differentiated expectations and assignments, individual projects and independent learning, peer tutoring and cooperative learning arrangements, and grade contracts with stress on personal goals and personal improvement may be employed. A formative approach to testing that de-emphasizes the competitive aspects of grades and stresses feedback and corrective measures is recommended. Tests then become learning aids instead of simply the basis for grades. Teaching study skills to the students and monitoring their use are straightforward means of contributing to students' confidence in coping with class assignments. The strategies for promoting a sense of security have an effect on students' self-concept and identity, as well. These categories are not mutually exclusive.

POWER

Power, like security, is a need with implications throughout the needs categories, but it has a particular focus that is useful for teachers. By power we mean that people have the need to exert reasonable control over their own life and have influence among associates. Two strategies previously cited regarding the security need, independent learning and grade contracts, are pertinent to satisfying the power need, as well. Students' perceptions and opinions should be sought when feasible and acted on when possible. The classroom should be established as a participatory democracy, but with the necessary limitations imposed by the school organization. Classroom meetings are a common and useful mode for addressing classroom concerns. Within this setting the students are encouraged to own the learning objectives established within the class. Having access to power through these means diminishes students' needs to seek power in less desirable, possibly disruptive, ways, or worse, to experience anxiety from feelings of frustration and develop increasingly negative attitudes over time.

The commentary regarding the four basic needs makes little reference to discipline as such. However, in the classroom, as in a football game, the best defense is a good offense. The teacher who maintains an effective discipline offensive based on the motivation that results from effective instructional practices will engage infrequently in defensive reactions to student noncompliance.

In the scenario we find Jane—Mrs. D—attending to prevention by developing a comprehensive approach to discipline and clearly establishing regularities to facilitate the classroom operation. However, the effect of prevention measures tends to be pervasive rather than specific, and establishes the norm of compliant behavior within the classroom. We can infer from the quality of the interaction that prevention, as defined in terms of classroom climate and student compliance, was acceptably evident, yet it did not totally prevent instances of minor deviation.

Although preventive approaches to discipline occur continuously, they are most essential at the beginning of the year. Based on extensive research, Emmer, Evertson, and Anderson (1980) suggested four principles as being especially pertinent in guiding planning for the first week: (1) resolve student uncertainties— the basic rules and expectations for the routine operation of the class should be explained; (2) help students be successful by planning uncomplicated lessons— the students' immediate success in the academic aspect of the class contributes to a positive attitude about the class; (3) keep an entire-class focus—conduct learning activities during the first week that engage the class as a whole group while students become accustomed to the class operation; and (4) be available, visible, and in charge—during the first week as you establish yourself as the group leader, keep students alert to your presence, your influence, and your willingness to help.

The concern for clear expectations deserves elaboration because of its special importance. Classroom order depends on clear, explicit rules. The students may be involved as much as possible in developing these rules to promote ownership of them. Most recommendations in the literature are for a few general rules stated in a positive way rather than a lengthy list. Such rules might include: Respect the property of others; help maintain a quiet and orderly classroom; and be responsible for keeping your own work space tidy. Once developed, the rules should be permanently displayed in full view. Most importantly, perhaps, students should be taught what the implications of the rules are for their behavior in an initial discussion, and in later discussions as behavior warrants. When all this has been done, the teacher must be consistent in enforcing compliance and dealing with noncompliance.

Management routines are closely associated with rules. These involve establishing early and clearly procedures for such things as accomplishing routine tasks, speaking to the teacher or other students, going to the rest room or library, sharpening pencils, and using learning centers, then carefully monitoring the implementation of the procedures. Students' awareness of guidelines for operating an efficient classroom contributes to their sense of well-being.

Management. The demarcation between prevention of misbehavior and maintenance of acceptable behavior is hazy at best. However, management behaviors of the teacher are generally those things a teacher does in addition to instructional behaviors and are intended to keep students on-task. As a first order of concern, this requires having a businesslike, purposeful (although certainly not humorless) approach to learning activities. Furthermore, it involves moving around the room during the course of the lesson, maintaining eye contact with students, noting any occurrences of incipient misbehavior, citing instances of exemplary behavior, actively involving as many students as possible in the learning activity, and stating expectations as appropriate. These behaviors reflect the teacher's "withitness." Monitoring students' behaviors and conducting classroom meetings, referred to as prevention practices, would in some instances be more appropriately considered as management activities.

The managing behaviors a teacher engages in are in essence a combination of instructing and controlling behaviors. Figure 3.1 depicts management as a roughly defined area in the middle of a continuum between instruction and discipline. This indicates that a classroom can be managed using strong, authoritarian discipline, much as we would expect in the military. Control problems are minimal and are handled quickly and efficiently. This figure also suggests that a classroom can be managed using instructional practices. We can envision an industrial arts laboratory where all the students are busy working on their individual projects at their stations while the teacher confers with a small group of students needing assistance. In the real world of the classroom, though, students are managed through a combination of a teacher's instructional and discipline-related behaviors. According to the research, effective teachers rely more on instructional behaviors to manage the classroom. This can be accomplished by creating the conditions for a good learning environment and thereby increasing the probability that discipline problems will be prevented. Effective teachers are effective managers; effective managers prevent potential problems.

The learning environment requires purposeful attention. The effective manager physically organizes the classroom to implement learning activities efficiently. For example, desks are arranged appropriately for discussion, lectures,

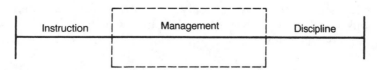

Figure 3.1 Classroom Management as a Function of Instruction and Discipline

and small-group work. The learning environment can also be structured psychologically by setting expectations for student learning and behavior. As an illustration, the teacher might say, "Today we are going to do some role playing to try to understand how teenagers make decisions about their social lives. In order to be able to accomplish this, I will need your cooperation. Role playing is a very effective method to learn and feel what others are experiencing—but only if everyone is listening and paying attention." Rules can be set and routines can be established to help guide students as they go about their learning tasks.

The effective managing teacher has planned to vary instruction to achieve learning objectives in different ways and for the purpose of stimulating students' interest and involvement. When students are faced with the same instructional method or strategy each day in one class, they become bored. Boredom provides opportunities for students' minds to wander and become preoccupied with other students and nonacademic activities. Teachers need to maintain command of a repertoire of methods and strategies to provide a stimulating instructional environment. The great variety of techniques, methods, and strategies presented in chapters 6 through 8 should contribute significantly to a teacher's repertoire of instructional approaches. Teaching must also be focused to maintain students' attention and involvement. Preplanned specific objectives are essential to provide instructional direction and focus.

There is a concern with the management phase because teachers tend to take students' behavior for granted by shifting the major responsibility for behavior to the students. Students should be responsible up to a reasonable point and should be given as much responsibility (and corresponding freedom) as they can manage. However, the students deserve the teachers' systematic attention to management tasks to diminish the temptation of and opportunity for misbehavior. Therefore, teachers should develop complementary instructional and managerial strategies designed to promote a smooth-running, orderly, productive classroom (Evertson & Emmer, 1982; Evertson & Harris, 1992). For example, teachers should move about the classroom and have intermittent eye contact with every student while they conduct an interactive lecture, a recitation, or a guided or reflective discussion. The teacher should move to a distant part of the room as a student responds or comments so the student will speak loudly and the teacher will be able to view most of the class. If the teacher is incompetent in this regard, should students nevertheless be expected to remain continuously forgiving and compliant? Only if they are zombies! The most important day of class in terms of its potential impact is the first day of school. Students acquire their first impressions at this meeting, the tenor of the class is established, and momentum is initiated. This day should be more carefully and purposefully planned than any other. Although no formula exists for conducting this meeting, a likely sequence of events might be the following:

1. Conduct introductions, beginning with the teacher's, in which some appropriate bit of personal information is shared.

2. Present a course overview and rationale, highlighting interesting and relevant activities.

3. Present academic expectations and the grading policy, accompanied by a rationale.

4. Present behavioral policies, expectations, and conventions, including a brief list of general rules, and directions regarding how to enter and leave class, obtain a pass, be recognized to speak, use the pencil sharpener, pass papers in, obtain materials—whatever a comprehensive classroom-management plan requires. This may extend over a number of days.

5. Provide an opportunity for the students to express their expectations for the teacher, with the possibility of mutual verbal contracting.

6. Assure students they will be successful learners in your class.

7. Begin studies during the first meeting. The students will get the message that you consider class time to be precious and irretrievable, that it must be protected and used purposefully.

8. Attend to filling in seating charts, handing out textbooks, and making an initial study assignment. More than one period may be needed to complete the entire agenda, but it will be well worth whatever time it takes.

In Mrs. D's room, the management phase of discipline was readily evident. She commenced class in a businesslike way as she assumed a posture that clearly communicated her expectation. Students' participation was encouraged and supported so that they would stay with the lesson. Through alert monitoring, two instances of incipient misbehavior were detected and quickly defused. Meanwhile she enforced the rule about the raising of hands. She changed the mode when restlessness occurred but did not chide the students about it. She displayed the all-important quality of "withitness" to an admirable degree.

Intervention. This is the phase generally associated with discipline by teachers. New teachers frequently ask: What can I do when these kids won't be quiet, or are insolent, or are always fooling around? Some colleagues respond with their favorite approaches, although sometimes these have a basis in conventional wisdom. Better-informed colleagues tend to hedge their answers, realizing there are no guaranteed effective approaches. They leave the new teacher not only frustrated, but questioning the credibility of pedagogy in the area of discipline. The problem does not necessarily lie in the colleagues' practices, which seem to work for them, nor in the pedagogy. The problem is in the question itself, for it essentially addresses symptoms rather than causes. A more appropriate question, at least to begin what could be an extended process, is: What are the conditions, internal and external, that are causing this situation? When the question is thus posed, productive problem solving can begin.

More than a score of books and many dozens of articles have been written focusing on this particular phase of discipline. We could hardly do justice to the topic if it were our intention to pass along all the sound advice and suggestions included in the literature. A few important considerations are presented here, but wider reading on the topic is necessary to supplement this commentary for the reader who has a special interest in this area.

When the indirect and tacit techniques of the prevention and management phases are insufficient to preserve order, intervention is necessary. Preservice teachers often have difficulty in learning about appropriate interventions from effective teachers because effective teachers only occasionally need to use them. The teachers who need to use them frequently, on the other hand, are not the preferable role models. Therein lies a paradox: Interventions, or overt teacher intrusions, are least well-learned from the most effective practitioners. Furthermore, some research indicates that less effective classroom managers cannot be reliably distinguished from more effective ones by the nature of their intervention practices (Emmer, Evertson, & Anderson, 1980; Kounin, 1970). So whereas judiciously selected intervention techniques should be part of every teacher's repertoire, they are always expedients and not the definitive aspects of a teacher's style.

By definition, interventions, or teachers' efforts to stop disruptive behavior, are expedients, so they should be used frugally and with discretion. An important consideration should be initially to use the mildest form of intervention that is likely to be effective, and resort to more stringent forms only as necessary. It is useful to consider the more seriously misbehaving student to be a troubled child exhibiting the symptoms of a personal problem rather than a bad kid who needs to be straightened out. The teacher then approaches the situation as a "therapist" rather than a "disciplinarian," and uses as a matter of personal style the science and art of pedagogy instead of the raw power with which the teacher role is endowed. Teachers in these circumstances might share the oath of the physician: *primum non nocere*, or, "the first thing (is) to do no harm." We affirm, however, that firmness is an essential quality for effective discipline.

Teachers need to have skill in applying a graduated set of interventions. But remember, clear rules and expectations must already be in place so that the errant student may be referred to them. The preferable approach to dealing with a nonattentive or mildly disruptive student is to use a question or some other instructional cue to enlist the student's active involvement in the lesson. This may be considered as much a management activity as an intervention. If this is not possible, and the teacher notices incipient misbehavior, nonverbal interventions such as eye contact and a "teacher look" should be used. If a look doesn't suffice, then moving to the target area in the room provides a stronger signal. The proximity of the teacher to restive students is usually sufficient to quell a minor disturbance. When these means have not been sufficient the teacher may catch the student's eye and gesture with the head or hand, indicating that a particular behavior is inappropriate. Or, if the teacher is in the immediate vicinity of the misbehavior, touching the student lightly but meaningfully, or opening the book on the student's desk, sends an unmistakable signal.

When these unobtrusive, nonverbal approaches fail or are not feasible, a verbal reminder is necessary. Initially, just saying the student's name, perhaps accompanied by shaking the head, should be employed. If the misbehavior is moderately disruptive or persistent, using the student's name followed by a redirecting statement may be effective. If these approaches are unsuccessful, the teacher should approach the disrupter and quietly but firmly direct the student to another seat, a time-out site, or whatever else is appropriate under the circumstances. This is the point where the teacher may feel anger at having been affronted by the student. Resist it! Remain calm and in control. Above all, avoid a confrontation of any sort. It is a no-win situation for the teacher.

Teachers' responses to student misbehavior must qualify as reasonable consequences related to the behavior. Arbitrary punishments, such as remaining standing, writing a phrase repeatedly, serving a detention, or receiving an angry reprimand, rarely if ever meet the test. They tend to be retributive, and have no redeeming social or educational value. Despite teachers' common belief, research shows that such punishments are largely ineffective as deterrents of future misbehavior. On the other hand, reasonable consequences sometimes appear superficially to be similar to a punishment (i.e., mild reproval may be appropriate or a student may be directed to take another seat). The difference lies in whether the student recognizes the consequence as being directly and logically related to the misbehavior, and whether it is a potential learning experience for the student. Furthermore, punishment tends to satisfy the needs of the teacher, but a reasonable consequence attends to the needs—at least the predicated needs—of the student.

Many kinds of misbehavior obviously have no readily conceivable direct and reasonable consequence. For example, a student may have a habit of calling out, using profanity, or intimidating other students. A more generalized and systematic teacher response is useful for such behavior. A program using behavior citations might be established. Such notices serve as a record of the incident and incorporate a graduated set of consequences. The first might involve a brief conference in which the teacher tries to help students develop insight into their behavior and make a commitment to more appropriate conduct. The second citation would repeat the procedure and intent of the first, but involve a more extensive conference and possibly a written contract as well. A third citation would build on the first two, and perhaps involve a third party—parent, administrator, counselor—as appropriate. A fourth citation would signal a serious behavior problem and involve referral to a specialist. If this approach is adopted schoolwide, especially at the secondary level, it should involve in-school suspension, but with counseling available to the student as an integral aspect of that suspension. Any teacher—or school—that adopts a program based on these general guidelines has to work out the specifics accordingly. The advantages are that it does qualify as a reasonable set of consequences of misbehavior, emphasizes the developmental thrust of democratic discipline, and is consistent with the humane, democratic principles espoused by modern-thinking educators.

Mrs. D had generally compliant students in her classroom, better this year than in her first two years because of her new, well-planned approach to discipline. Nevertheless she did use several nonverbal interventions. When Claire called out an answer, Mrs. D tapped rule number 3 on the board specifying that students should seek permission by raising a hand. A question addressed to Leslie on the topic was, in fact, an intervention into Leslie's whispered conversation. Ronnie received a "visit" from Mrs. D as she strategically positioned herself at his desk and caught his eye. And Renee, who asked impulsively to sharpen her pencil, elicited the teacher's assertive posture and sharp look. All of these unobtrusive interventions occurred without missing an academic beat. Mrs. D had become proficient in using nonverbal measures. Inevitably, verbal reminders will be required on occasion, and sometimes even stronger measures. Hopefully, she will employ these with the same measured restraint and judgment.

Remediation. The purpose of behavior remediation is to diminish—and ideally eliminate—a student's disposition to noncompliance. As was noted earlier, it may begin as an extension of the teacher's intervention and incorporate follow-up as the consequences of the citations are applied. This is the phase of discipline within which important student-learning outcomes may occur. Teachers are not trained therapists, and they must recognize their limitations in dealing with pathologically induced behavior. Nevertheless, as well-informed, compassionate adults, teachers have the potential to affect students' attitudes and behaviors in beneficial ways. Teachers can help students realize that behaviors have reasonable consequences. They may also help students gain insights into the underlying reasons for their behavior, and thus be better able to control their own lives. Furthermore, for the remedial aspect of the behavior-related contracts, teachers can help students consider alternative behaviors and monitor their compliance to the contract. How much time can a teacher spend in this sort of activity? It is a matter each teacher must work out individually. But it is a means of effective change in the lives of some students who greatly need to change.

Teacher Power in the Classroom

The commentary in the previous section described classroom conditions and teacher behaviors associated with a comprehensive approach to discipline. The final section of this chapter presents another perspective on teachers' discipline-related behaviors. In any social situation in which a leader exerts influence on the other members of the group, power is involved. As noted in the research section, five kinds of power are possible: referent (personality), expert, legitimate, coercive, and reward (French & Raven, 1968). Each of these dimensions of power has implications for the teacher (Richmond & McCroskey, 1983). Students' behavior can be related to their perception of the teacher's use of these different types of power. The teacher who is aware of the uses and possible pitfalls in the application of each type of power has, therefore, a cogent decision-making rationale for selecting appropriate discipline-related practices.

The concept of power does not itself constitute an approach to discipline.

Rather, power is a dynamic within the process. Understanding its role and effect helps the teacher acquire a more in-depth understanding of discipline. With this understanding, the teacher can more knowledgeably recognize optimum and inferior modes of discipline-related interaction and establish teacher-behavior goals accordingly. Any approach to discipline will be enhanced when the teacher refines discipline decisions by using insights into the power dynamic.

Referent Power. This is probably more readily understood if it is thought of as the influence one has through personality. Referent power is especially related to the interpersonal and communication dimensions of the classroom. A teacher who is endowed with or acquires a generous measure of referent power may be expected to have a high degree of social poise, exhibit a healthy sense of humor, maintain a respect for the feelings and rights of students, and be reasonably stable and consistent in demeanor. The teacher remains aware of the impact of each verbal interchange and demonstrates to the students sincere concern for their best interests. The outcome of these characteristics is a comfortable classroom climate and students who identify with and even sincerely want to be good for the teacher.

In the scenario, Mrs. D can be assumed to have relied to some extent on referent power as she took a position at the front of the room to begin the class session. The students' respect was implied as they quickly came to order. As we get a sense of the kind of teacher she is in the remainder of the scenario, there is no hint that other kinds of power are necessary. Referent power, however, is often subtle in its effect.

Expert Power. The competence of the teacher in conducting the tasks of managing the classroom and guiding learning is the basis for this power. The teacher, therefore, must be an informed scholar who is an advocate of the subject and is able to select aspects of it that are appropriate for the students to bring it alive, flesh it out, and help students recognize its relevance and possibilities.

Other aspects of expertise are manifest in the teacher's classroom-management practices. Systematic approaches are evident in much of what routinely occurs, such as making seating arrangements, establishing expectations, keeping records, marking and evaluating students' work, and passing out papers. The teacher's instruction is characterized by variety and student involvement. Students sense a certain ownership in the learning objectives and activities. In addition to the typical teacher-dominated presentations, one might also expect to find role playing and simulations, projects, learning centers, hands-on opportunities, and independent study. Higher-level thinking will occur as students reflect on important ideas. The concept of individualization will be applied as special-purpose groups form and disband, and enrichment and remediation are available to students as needed. Motivation will be an overriding concern of the teacher, who realizes that instruction without motivation is bankrupt. In describing expert power, we are, in effect, describing effective instruction. The implication is not that a teacher must be unusually talented to be reasonably successful. We do believe, however, that a mediocre teacher cannot depend on control measures to compensate for an inability or unwillingness to provide effective instruction.

Even in expert teachers' classrooms, misbehavior occasionally occurs. Expert teachers maintain a calm demeanor, quickly evaluate the situation and decide what approach will interfere least with the ongoing learning activity, then respond firmly yet respectfully to the student. When students realize the teacher is purposeful, assured, and unflappable (getting to be this way should be every teacher's developmental goal), they are less inclined to misbehave.

Mrs. D displayed her expertise in the instructional dimension as she began the chemistry unit with an advance organizer, then proceeded to develop the topic using the students' ideas. Later in the class she changed instructional modes as some students' span of attention ran out. These are expert instructional behaviors that have a positive impact on students' behavior, as well. As a competent classroom manager, she attended to seating arrangements, classroom expectations, class routines, and a systematic plan to cope with serious misbehavior. Her students undoubtedly—albeit tacitly—recognized Mrs. D's competence and considered her acceptable in the teacher role. This positive attitude, in turn, inclined them to generally compliant behavior.

Referent power and expert power together create a charisma that endows the teacher with virtually all the power needed to manage successfully in the classroom. Achieving some degree of charisma might well be a goal of every teacher and, in this fashion, operate as a general guide for the teacher's professional growth.

Legitimate Power. As far as misbehavior is concerned, charisma operates primarily as a preventive influence. Realistically, however, the teacher must expect that misbehavior will occur and intervention will be necessary. In such cases, other types of power are available. One of these is legitimate power. This power is inherent in the teacher role, just as it is for a police officer, lifeguard, or military officer, and it is the basis for their authority.

Students ordinarily submit to legitimate power and respond to it readily. For this reason legitimate power is attractive to people with a special need to wield power. It could become, in effect, an end in itself and result in abuse of power. The existence of this condition may be inferred from an inordinate number of rules, unreasonable expectations for decorum, rigid classroom structure, gimmicky means of control, or teacher nagging about student behavior.

Legitimate power used appropriately involves establishing reasonable, minimal expectations for order and procedure, monitoring student behavior, and keeping students on-task through nonverbal cues and mild verbal reminders or restraint. In cases of serious misbehavior or persistent disruptive behavior, the wise use of legitimate power involves follow-up in determining causes and using well-thought-out behavior-remediation techniques with the student.

Mrs. D used legitimate power when the indirect influence of referent and expert powers was not a sufficient deterrent. She did diligently monitor the classroom and used unobtrusive reminders as appropriate. On the other hand, she was careful not to use legitimate power injudiciously. She seemed to recognize the point at which its use was counterproductive.

Coercive Power. The point where legitimate power ends and coercive power begins is not clearly discernible. In practice it can be the point at which the teacher's voice rises from normal volume to louder than normal or when the teacher asks the class in an exasperated tone for the third time to be more quiet. If teachers make direct reference to their authority or threaten or use punishment, coercive power is clearly being used.

Coercive power is necessary on rare occasions in the classroom. When students are fighting, are openly defiant, or are endangering themselves or others, the teacher must take appropriate coercive action because the time for reason and mild authoritarian action has passed. The intervention should employ the minimum force necessary to restore normal conditions—for example, separating the fighting students, requesting that a defiant student go to a designated place, or insisting that firecrackers be relinquished.

Coercive power, as an extension of legitimate power, is highly subject to abuse in the hands of teachers with personalities that incline them to its use. Punishment is the means such teachers use to attempt to gain control over students' behavior. But coercive power, in general, and punishment, in particular, is far less effective than conventional wisdom would suggest. Teachers who are routinely dependent on punishment to achieve a semblance of order are essentially failing in their instructional or managerial performance. On the other hand, when students do misbehave they should expect to confront the reasonable consequences of their behavior. The astute teacher recognizes the difference, which is sometimes subtle, between punishment and reasonable consequences, and between measures that are merely self-serving and those that are educationally sound.

Reward Power. The use of rewards is the final application of power. Rewards are actually an integral part of expert or referent power as a teacher approves students' commendable performance. Reward in the form of deserved praise or other appropriate recognition of achievement has a positive overall effect and, in fact, is probably necessary for optimum teaching effectiveness.

Although rewards properly employed are recommended, incentives—rewards not intrinsically related to performance—should be used with discretion. They may serve to initiate student efforts toward achieving some performance goal, but at some point internal sources of motivation should supersede. Otherwise, the performance remains only a means toward an end and learning is incidental rather than purposeful. The use of grades as incentives is probably the most common form of this type of suspect practice.

Rewards can take the form of a bribe or bargain, particularly in regard to discipline. For example, a teacher might offer to let students go to lunch early if they are quiet during the lesson. In this case, they are being quiet for the wrong reason, and a reward is used as a substitute for effective teaching. The insecure teacher who runs a popularity contest with students is especially prone to misuse rewards. In general, when rewards are used to manipulate students, or for any other ulterior motives, it is a misuse of this type of power. Furthermore, incentives diminish in effectiveness over time, and ultimately impede learning.

Mrs. D limited her use of reward power in the scenario to praising the ideas presented by two students. In each case the praise was low-key and emerged as a natural part of the interaction in the class. These instances are examples of the appropriate use of extrinsic reward. Such thoughtful use of reward power contributes over time to students' inclination to be active participants and contributors.

SUMMARY POINT

The complex nature of discipline may be readily inferred from this chapter. Some teachers have a naturally occurring, mature interaction style that serves them well in the disciplinary aspects of teaching. Although these teachers may acquire useful insights and skills from experience, much remains to be learned about discipline by any teacher. Anti-intellectualism, more pervasive within discipline than any other aspect of teaching, has inhibited the attainment of a norm condition characterized by fully professional practices. The ideas presented in this chapter can be helpful in transcending the empirical level that is characteristic of current practice and in convincing educators that discipline is not a dirty word.

REVIEW: IMPORTANT CONSIDERATIONS REGARDING DISCIPLINE

1. Effective discipline and effective instruction are inseparable.
2. Plan a comprehensive, pedagogically sound approach to discipline addressing, in particular, the four phases: prevention, management, intervention, and remediation.
3. Use the five types of teacher power as a means to select appropriate behavior modes within the broad strategies employed.
4. Nothing is so strong as gentleness; nothing so gentle as real strength (Indian proverb).

QUESTIONS FOR REFLECTION

1. What instances of misbehavior do you recall from your own classroom experience that were well handled or poorly handled by the teacher?

Evaluate the respective behaviors based on the principles and approaches presented in this chapter.

2. The personality of the teacher is identified as a major factor in a teacher's ability to be an effective classroom leader, especially regarding discipline-related matters. Evaluate your own personality as you project yourself into the managing role of the teacher.

3. The literature presenting the theory and research on discipline was described as being informative at the policies/program/principles level, but rarely prescriptive at the incident-by-incident level. How will you use the literature in your development as a classroom manager? What are the limitations of the literature for that purpose?

4. List the five propositions in the order of their importance that will form the foundation of your philosophy of discipline.

5. As you anticipate developing a plan for having positive and effective discipline in your prospective classroom, what will be its major features in the areas of prevention, management, intervention, and remediation?

REFERENCES

Ardrey, R. (1970). *The social contract*. New York: Atheneum.

Bielefeldt, T. (1988). The challenge of classroom discipline [monograph]. *Oregon School Study Council, 32*(4), 2.

Brophy, J., & McCaslen, M. (1992). Teachers' reports of how they perceive and cope with problem students. *Elementary School Journal, 93*(1), 3–68.

Brophy, J., & Rohrkemper, M. (1981). The influence of problem-ownership on teacher perceptions. *Journal of Educational Psychology, 73*, 295–311.

Canter, L. (1976). *Assertive discipline: A take charge approach for today's educator*. Seal Beach, CA: Canter and Associates.

Canter, L. (1989). Assertive discipline: More than names on the board and marbles in a jar. *Phi Delta Kappan, 71*, 57–61.

Charles, C. (1985). *Building classroom discipline*. New York: Longman.

Cotton, K., & Savard, W. (1984). Student discipline and motivation: Research synthesis (Prepared for Northeast Regional Educational Laboratory, April 1982). In R. Reitz and A. Fink (Eds.), *Discipline*. Bloomington, IN: Phi Delta Kappa.

Curwin, R., & Mendler, A. (1989). We repeat, let the buyer beware: A response to Canter. *Educational Leadership, 46*(6), 72–75.

Doyle, W. (1986). Classroom organization and management. In M. Wittrock (Ed.), *Handbook of research on teaching* (3rd ed.). New York: Macmillan.

Duke, D., & Meckel, A. (1984). *Teacher's guide to classroom discipline*. New York: Random House.

Emmer, E., & Aussiker, A. (1989). School and classroom discipline programs: How well do they work? In O. Moles (Ed.), *Strategies to reduce student misbehavior*. Washington, D.C.: U.S. Department of Education, Office of Educational Research and Improvement.

Emmer, E., Evertson, C., & Anderson, L. (1980). Effective classroom management at the beginning of the school year. *Elementary School Journal, 80*, 219–231.

Evertson, C., & Emmer, E. (1982). Preventive classroom management. In D. Duke (Ed.), *Helping teachers manage classrooms*. Alexandria, VA: Association for Supervision and Curriculum Development.

Evertson, C., & Harris, A. (1992). What we know about managing classrooms. *Educational Leadership, 49*(7), 74–78.

French, J., & Raven, B. (1968). The bases of social power. In D. Cartwright & A. F. Zander (Eds.), *Group dynamics: Research and theory* (2nd ed.). Evanston, IL: Row Peterson.

Gage, N. L. (1978). *The scientific basis of the art of teaching*. New York: Teachers College Press.

Gettinger, M. (1988). Methods of proactive classroom management. *School Psychology Review, 17*(2), 227–242.

Goodlad, J. I. (1983). *A place called school*. New York: McGraw-Hill.

Greenlee, A., & Ogletree, E. (1993). Teachers' attitudes toward student discipline problems and classroom management strategies [Monograph]. Chicago Public Schools (ERIC: ED 364 330).

Kindsvatter, R., & Levine, M. A. (1980). The myths of discipline. *Phi Delta Kappan, 61*(10), 690–693.

Kounin, J. (1970). *Discipline and group management*. New York: Holt, Rinehart & Winston.

McCormack, S. (1989). Response to Render, Padilla, & Krank: But practitioners say it works! *Educational Leadership, 46*(6), 77–79.

McDaniel, T. (1989). The discipline debate: A road through the thicket. *Educational Leadership, 46*(6), 81–82.

Raywid, M. A. (1976). The democratic classroom: Mistake or misnomer? *Theory into Practice, 15*(1), 37–46.

Redl, F. (1966). *When we deal with children*. New York: Free Press.

Render, G., Padilla, N., & Krank, M. (1989). What research really shows about assertive discipline. *Educational Leadership, 46*(6), 72–75.

Richmond, V., & McCroskey, J. (1983). *Power in the classroom: Two studies*. Paper presented at the annual meeting of the Association for Teacher Education, Orlando, FL.

Silberman, C. (1970). *Crisis in the classroom*. New York: Random House.

Veenman, S. (1984). Perceived problems of beginning teachers. *Review of Educational Research, 54*(2), 143–178.

Wolfgang, C., & Glickman, C. (1980). *Solving discipline problems*. Boston: Allyn & Bacon.

4 Curriculum Considerations

OUTLINE

Well-informed teachers know about the curriculum changes taking place today and examine those changes as to how they can help students' learning.

FOCUS QUESTIONS

1. What is the relationship of curriculum to instruction?
2. What national standards have been developed and how will they impact school curriculum?
3. What does a constructivist approach to teaching mean?
4. What five areas are important to consider in the education of multicultural students?
5. What is the role of pedagogical content knowledge in effective teaching?
6. How can a teacher help students understand the structure of the knowledge they are experiencing? Why is this important?

OVERVIEW

Planning for teaching necessarily involves curriculum; that is, one must plan to teach *something* for some *purpose*. Both the "something" and the "purpose" are the curriculum; the "something" part is the most obvious. A popular view of curriculum is that it is a plan for learning, a written document with objectives that determines what learning is important (Wiles & Bondi, 1989). The plan is a linear view that defines curriculum as a sequence or progression of content-learning goals and activities that move toward an end. The purpose often remains tacit in teachers' minds, with curriculum guides and textbooks uncritically accepted as the content to be taught. Curriculum in this view is specific, externally imposed, and prescriptive.

Another, broader view of curriculum, based on John Dewey's thoughts in *Experience and Education,* is that it is the *experiences* of the learner that comprise the curriculum. This definition describes curriculum as "all the experiences children have under the guidance of teachers" (Caswell & Campbell, 1935). This definition is one that elementary teachers and middle school teachers may find more comfortable because it emphasizes the importance of the total school environment and the role of the teacher in planning active participation for the students.

In considering the purpose of curriculum, Eisner (1990) takes the broadest view of curriculum and defines the purpose idealistically as "to free the mind from certainty, to liberate children and adolescents so that they can consider options not entertained by their parents . . . to help children become what we are not" (p. 62). In this view the purpose of prime importance and the role of the teachers is to uncover, as much as it is to cover, the curriculum. The teacher is not just a conduit and a guide to students' discovery. The teacher helps students explore experience and search for personal meanings within and beyond the curriculum.

Eisner's view of curriculum encourages the constructivist approach to instruction: "to have students take responsibility for their own learning, to be autonomous thinkers, to develop integrated understanding of concepts, and to pose—and seek to answer—important questions" (Brooks & Brooks, 1993, p. 13). This textbook supports that view of curriculum and teaching yet recognizes that national curriculum standards, state curriculum frameworks, and local scrutiny of curriculum may make teachers feel locked in to a curriculum that is assessment driven for high achievement. Indeed, chapter 8 (on teaching strategies) identifies strategies that increase achievement. However, the authors acknowledge the discrepancy and respond that our approach to instruction, in keeping with the reform movement in education, is a transitional move from behaviorist certainty to emphasis on personal meaning through curriculum built on large concepts, interdisciplinary exploration, scope and sequence that acknowledge children's developmental level, and interactive teaching. The text informs teachers of theories, research, and principles of instruction, with the understanding that interpretation into teaching approaches and student-learning activities is the essence of teaching. In the final analysis, the success of any teacher is determined by the teacher's ability to involve students in learning activities that they perceive to be meaningful.

Most of us are far more familiar with a teacher's performance than with the performance of a symphony conductor. Yet the symphony conductor's performance is more readily visible, more cleanly articulated. As such it provides a useful analogy for understanding the relationship of the teacher and the curriculum.

Can a conductor of a symphony who has been given a detailed score function creatively? I don't think it takes too much reflection to recognize that conductors not only can but do. A score is a set of directions subject to the conductor's interpretation. The length of time that notes are held, the dynamics the conductor directs the symphony to create, the tempo used in particular symphonic sections, the balance between sections of the orchestra, the color and timbre created, and the general mood within the movements of the symphony are all subject to the conductor's control. Composers provide scores; conductors amplify the material received and in the process put their own imprint on the work. Making the judgments necessary to create a musically important rendition of a score requires a musical imagination, the ability to hear in one's auditory memory what the music might become, and an ear to know if and when it has been attained. The conductor is the first listener (Eisner, 1990, p. 64).

In some regards, the curriculum is similar to the musical score. However, the curriculum that defines a unit of study is much less precise and confining than a musical score. Teachers have far more latitude in interpreting the intent of the curriculum and having their individual impact on it. When teachers understand curriculum as a *referent*—not the whole plan—for this instrumental decision making, they are less intent to be bound to a textbook or a feeling of being manipulated. Their approach can be proactive rather than reactive, developmental rather than technical. The teacher's ear, like the conductor's, becomes attuned to listening for the meanings being generated by the learner. These understandings are the basis on which more complex meanings and interrelationships are built— and on which one's personal curriculum grows.

For the beginning teacher we describe formal curriculum as based on the values and needs of society, adhering to state standards and district guides, with a scope and sequence attuned to learner development. Within that framework the teacher and the students can develop curriculum together as the students construct their own meanings.

A number of curricular movements that started in the 1980s are developing in the country today. Teachers need to have some knowledge of these movements so that if their district is making a decision to adopt a particular approach, they have some familiarity with the movement and the possible impact it may have on curriculum and instruction. Several of these important movements are examined in this chapter including national goals, the national-standards movement, constructivism, interdisciplinary curriculum, whole language, and multicultural and international education. The second part of the chapter discusses aspects of curriculum that need to be considered in instruction today, such as pedagogical content knowledge, the structure of knowledge, and concept mapping.

SCENARIO

Rebecca Hager and Al Marzano were looking over the material on national curriculum standards in the professional library corner of the teachers' lounge. Al was examining the *NCSS Social Studies Curriculum Guidelines* because he taught 8th-grade social studies. Rebecca, a science teacher, was interested in *Project 2061 Benchmarks for Science Literacy*. They were waiting for the arrival of Angeletta Rodrigo, the 8th- and 10th-grade English teacher, to make plans for an interdisciplinary unit they wanted to try to develop on cultures.

The idea to try an interdisciplinary approach to a unit grew out of an excellent in-service workshop they had attended right after the Christmas break. With the Martin Luther King Jr. celebration occurring in January, they had been expressing their disgruntled feelings that the middle-level curriculum gave only superficial treatment to multicultural foci, and that mainly through the social studies. That was when they decided that given the information from the workshop, and their present concerns about the lack of multicultural treatment within their curriculum guide, they would try to develop a new unit with a multicultural theme to follow their state curriculum framework and their district curriculum guide. The state framework was built on national curriculum standards, and their district guide had been updated in 1995 as part of the district's school improvement plan. They both worked on the revision so they were knowledgeable about the various curriculum standards. Angeletta, the English teacher, had shared with them that she was planning a poetry unit on voices from various cultures that might fit in well with their plans.

Another factor that encouraged them was that basically the same group of students were in Rebecca's second period and Al's third period, so they could try to do some team teaching. Unfortunately, Angeletta did not have the 8th graders until fifth period, but she would integrate the information or projects into her class whenever possible.

Building on Angeletta's unit on poetry voices, Rebecca and Al were thinking of taking the theme—"Voices from the Culture"—and examining the culture of various countries through the people of those cultures. As represented in the stories, music, historical reports, case studies, and leaders' speeches, students could examine cultural patterns in use of land, settlement patterns, customs and ideas, and ecosystem changes. A chapter on "Human Social Benchmarks for Science Libraries" would supply some ideas concerning cultural effects on behavior and the impact landforms, weather, and climate have on human life and the shaping of cultures. Genetic inheritance, social inheritance, and life experience could be examined. Rebecca told Al she would like to have students examine census reports and do some data gathering and analysis, as well. She needed to speak with Carl Bowdin in mathematics.

Both Al and Rebecca agreed that technology would be important in the unit. Students would need to talk with other students in other places and through the Internet perhaps speak with a state university sociologist and a poet in residence. The World Wide Web could take them into communities around the country and the world to visit museums, even to see images of famous paintings and sites, as could programs on videodiscs.

Ideas were beginning to flow rapidly. Rebecca cautioned them to keep the unit flexible so students would interact and ideas could be plugged in. For now they needed to start identifying the key concepts they wanted to cover.

Rebecca and Al looked at each other, pondering whether they could get the unit ready by April. They'd have to see if Angeletta would delay her unit until . . . .

Rebecca looked at her watch. Fourth period was about over.

Al, Rebecca, Angeletta, and Carl Bowdin would need to spend much planning time together. She looked up to see Angeletta coming through the door. Perhaps they should start with a smaller two-week unit . . . .

PART I: UPDATE ON CURRICULAR MOVEMENTS

Although this book concentrates on instruction, one cannot teach in isolation from content or curriculum. Every teacher, as does every curriculum developer, must wrestle with the basic questions of what knowledge is important for all to know, what the purpose is of the curriculum, how we can ensure that the curriculum is equitable, and how appropriate the curriculum is for our students' needs. Every teacher must answer these questions, or someone else will provide answers for them. These questions feature largely in teacher decision making: What should students learn? What is the purpose of our school? How do my beliefs about education influence my instruction? Educators continually search for the curriculum that responds to society's expectations to ensure that all students meet district and state standards, and grow into productive, well-balanced individuals. The following curriculum movements are providing their own answers to these questions. Beginning teachers need to examine the movements' influences on their district's educational plan and staff-development initiatives—and most importantly, on their own instructional decisions.

NATIONAL GOALS

In 1994, the U.S. Congress adopted eight goals to provide direction and focus in improving the educational performance of students. These goals grew from the Governors' Educational Summit in 1989 in which the state leaders—including then-governor Clinton from Arkansas—and President Bush announced that the nation must establish cooperative educational goals if it is to face the technological, scientific, and economic challenges of the 21st century (National Education Goals Panel, 1994).

Because of public concern about low levels of student academic performance and the poor showing of students' performances in international assessments, the eight goals were identified to provide educators, community members, and legislators with a yardstick with which to measure the progress of our educational systems in promoting high student achievement. Funding to support the goals was to be allocated to the states through the reauthorization of the Elementary and Secondary Education Act with Title III funding. Each state was to submit an improvement plan that could include identified content standards or student outcomes as well as "opportunity to learn" standards. Individual districts were to draw up school-improvement proposals that could include plans for staff development and preservice teacher improvement (Early, 1994).

Federal funds were allocated to the states that submitted plans. The states in turn allocated money to districts, which applied for funding to improve their elementary and secondary schools. Participation was voluntary; no state was required to participate in this funding initiative.

As this book goes to press, the federal government has begun to provide start-up funds for state and local school improvement. Support in the coming years may be cut considerably given the conservative nature of the majority of federal legislators.

Politics aside, it appears clear that the following education goals that President Clinton, on March 31, 1994, signed into law (Goals 2000: Educate America Act [P.L. 103-227]) will influence school curriculum and assessment into the 21st century. The national education goals, to be achieved by the year 2000, are as follows (National Education Goals Panel, 1994):

1. All children in the United States will start school ready to learn.
2. The high school graduation rate will increase to at least 90 percent.
3. All students will leave grades 4, 8, and 12 having demonstrated competency in challenging subject matter including English, mathematics, science, foreign languages, civics and government, economics, arts, history, and geography. Every school in the United States will ensure that all students learn to use their minds well, so they may be prepared for responsible citizenship, further learning, and productive employment in the nation's modern economy.
4. The nation's teaching force will have access to programs for the continued improvement of their professional skills and the opportunity to acquire the knowledge and skills needed to instruct and prepare all American students for the next century.
5. U.S. students will be first in the world in mathematics and science achievement.
6. Every adult American will be literate and will possess the knowledge and skills necessary to compete in a global economy and to exercise the rights and responsibilities of citizenship.
7. Every school in the United States will be free of drugs, violence, and the unauthorized presence of firearms and alcohol and will offer a disciplined environment conducive to learning.
8. Every school will promote partnerships to increase parental involvement and participation in promoting the social, emotional, and academic growth of children.

NATIONAL STANDARDS

With the advent of national education goals through Goals 2000, the need arose to have voluntary national standards in the content areas. With the exception of mathematics, no national standards in the late eighties had been identified to guide curriculum planning in determining what students should know and be able to do by the time they graduated from high school. In 1992, the National Council on Educational Standards and Testing, a group authorized by Congress to help move national reform forward to accomplish the Goals 2000 mandate, recommended that voluntary national standards and a national system of assessment be implemented.

This voluntary national movement to identify content standards, provided mainly by content-specific professional organizations, has been having considerable impact on the country's curriculum. Throughout the remainder of this century and into the next millennium, national standards that identify key content and outcomes in subject fields will be the major influence in school curriculum, textbook composition, and assessment measures.

The National Council of Teachers of Mathematics (NCTM) led the way by releasing their content standards in 1989. In 1991, the NCTM published *Professional Standards for Teaching Mathematics*, their vision of the direction mathematics instruction should take. Their publications have served as models for other subject-area associations and councils developing standards. By 1994, the U.S. Department of Education was funding projects in a number of the disciplines. In 1995 there were 14 different standards-setting initiatives in progress in various subject areas, though not all funded by the government. In addition, in 1994, 45 states were reported planning, developing, or implementing new curriculum standards (Cross, 1994). This activity means that in all likelihood, the district that employs you now or in the future may be implementing new curriculum to meet national-content standards or new state curriculum frameworks.

What is meant by national standards? Do they identify the essential knowledge that all students need to know? Do they define the level of achievement all students are to meet to demonstrate mastery? To address these questions the National Council on Education Standards and Testing recommended that national standards include *content* standards specifying what students need to know and be able to do, *performance* standards identifying the level of competence the student and the school system need to reach for achieving high standards, and *school-delivery* standards to judge whether schools are providing students the opportunity to reach those standards (O'Neil, 1993).

What do these national standards look like? The standards, most of which were to have been completed by 1995, have been developed by various national professional groups such as the National Council of Teachers of Mathematics, National Council of Geographic Education, National Council for the Social Studies, National Council of Teachers of English, and International Reading Association. The National Science Education Standard project was supported by the National Research Council, and the Project 2061 was developed by the American Association for the Advancement of Science.

Differences are apparent among the various efforts. Mathematics delineated 40 curriculum standards for grades K–12. History standards included many more. Social studies standards (National Council for the Social Studies, 1994) were developed around 10 themes and 10 skill areas. Also, on the issue of student performance, there is considerable difference among the projects. Standards in history and science have identified one set of performance criteria for all, while other standards identified two or more levels of performance criteria (O'Neil, 1993).

How should standards be assessed? Congress has made it plain that it has no desire to be involved in national testing. It has resisted the establishment of a mandatory national curriculum and national examination (O'Neil, 1993), leaving assessment up to the states to set their own processes. One national venture in assessment—The New Standards Project, a joint venture of the Learning Research and Development Center at the University of Pittsburgh and the National Center on Education and the Economy—was launched in 1991 with 17 states and 6 school districts enrolled. The project, an outgrowth of the 1991 report *America's Choice: High Skills or Low Wages*, has concentrated on changing the way students are assessed by using tests that include performance tasks, projects, and portfolios. This system permits states and districts to determine whether their students meet national standards of performance (O'Neil, 1992).

K–12 curriculum during the last years of the century is being influenced considerably by national standards. However, these standards pose more challenges for teachers as they deliberate in so many subject areas the essential knowledge to be learned. There simply isn't enough time to teach all the knowledge identified in the standards. The result could be a fragmented, chaotic curriculum for a state or district (Cross, 1994). Some states, such as Maine, have identified common multidisciplinary cores. But many have not. Those who dream of educational equity in which all students learn a common body of knowledge and, hence, have the same opportunity for jobs and college placement despair that a national curriculum has not been enacted.

Application to Practice

One element remains clear in all of these debates concerning national standards—you, the teacher, need to be conversant with the various national standards and also have the ability to approach the standards in interdisciplinary or multidisciplinary teaching. You will need to be better educated in the areas of concept learning, problem solving, and the development of thinking skills. You must be able to use alternative forms of assessment, such as performance tasks and portfolios. Understanding how to deliver learner-centered education is a necessity. The school district must be held accountable to help you help all students to accomplish the established goals of the school.

CONSTRUCTIVISM

When we study reforms in education through the curriculum standards established by national professional organizations such as the National Council for Teachers of Mathematics and the National Science Teachers Association, we encounter a student-centered, active-learning approach to instruction that some educators refer to as constructivism. Constructivism is influencing the teaching of reading and writing (Tierney, 1990) and other subject areas (Newman, Griffin, & Cole, 1989). Constructivist teaching and learning, introduced in chapter 1 in this text, recognize that knowledge is created in the mind of each learner and that effective teaching approaches delve into the learner's mind through active learning; learner-generated inquiry; concrete, authentic experiences; collaborative investigations and discussions and reflection; and structuring learning around primary concepts. Much of the change initiatives taking place in school reform advocate practices that are considered constructivist teaching practices.

Constructivism is not a method or a strategy as defined in these chapters, but rather a theory about knowledge and learning that is changing how teachers perceive their instructional roles and their students' roles. Teachers are to help students relate new content to the knowledge they already know, as well as to have them "process and apply the new knowledge" (Good & Brophy, 1994, p. 414). Before students can solve problems and generate fresh approaches, they must examine the new content in relation to what they already know and build new knowledge structures (Resnick & Klopfer, 1989). "Subject matter topics are not something to be covered by the teachers and passed to students, but areas of experience and ideas to which students relate their own associations and concepts for these topics" (McNeil, 1995, p. 4).

Research and Theoretical Base

The research and theory base of constructivist approach is not about teaching but rather about knowledge and learning (Brooks & Brooks, 1993). It has its roots in the work of Jean Piaget, a Swiss scholar concerned with cognitive development and the formation of knowledge. He examined how people came to know their world.

As explained by Brooks and Brooks (1993), Piaget (1952) saw the "human mind as a dynamic set of cognitive structures that help us make sense of what we perceive. These structures grow in intellectual complexity as we mature and as we interact with the world . . . through maturation and experience, the groundwork for new structure is laid" (p. 26). A number of cognitive theorists have built on Piaget's work to explain how learners actively construct their world (Bruner, 1964; Siegel & Cocking, 1977; Von Glasersfeld, 1981; Copple, Sigel, & Saunders, 1984). These emergent theories about how we learn recognize that knowledge is not a substance that can be transferred from the teacher's head to the students'. Rather, knowledge must be constructed individually by every student (Lockhead, 1985). From this view of learning comes the term *constructivism*.

Two other important educators from the past, Henry Pestalozzi and Frederick Froebel, promoted the learner-centered activity learning by doing, the approach that characterizes constructivist teaching. Pestalozzi stressed initial concrete experiences by exposing the learner to the environment that would make a personal impression. Froebel (founder of the kindergarten movement) believed in relating the inner world of the child to the powerful principles of the universe. He instituted an activity curriculum for young children that provided opportunities for self-expression (McNeil, 1995).

Application to Practice

Constructivist teachers are concerned about teaching for understanding, meaning that they expect their students to be able to explain, find evidence and examples, generalize, apply, and represent the concept or principle in a new way (Perkins & Blythe, 1994). They give assignments that push students to use what they have learned, such as planning a playground for a new neighborhood apartment complex. Such an assignment challenges students to use their knowledge in geometry, health and human development, general mathematics, design, and science.

The Association for Supervision and Development reported in the February 1994 issue of *Educational Leadership* about the Teaching for Understanding Project, a five-year study conducted by the Harvard Graduate School of Education and teachers in the Boston area (Perkins & Blythe, 1994). Researchers developed a four-part framework to encourage teaching for understanding in a constructivist way (pp. 6–7):

1. *Use generative topics*—Teachers and students generate topics that are essential to a discipline, meaningful to the students, and connectable to topics inside and outside the discipline. These might include patterns in art, mathematics, and poetry, or conflicts of people against themselves in literature.

2. *Develop understanding goals*—Teachers and students need to identify a few key goals for a topic, such as that the students will understand the responsibility of the individual in a democracy, that students will be able to understand several points of view, or that students will appreciate the power of the individual in a democracy. The purpose of the goals is to focus instruction. Within these goals teachers may ask students to formulate more specific learning objectives for themselves or their group.

3. *Plan understanding performances*—Teachers design experiences that support their knowledge of understanding goals. The experiences may culminate in a final challenging performance of understanding, such as a project demonstration or an original skit presented to the class. The experiences should be active and interactive and should involve inquiry prompted by students' questions and research activities using primary sources of data. For example, Robin Woods (1994) explained how he taught a unit on electricity using student predictions and conductivity laboratory experiences to test their predictions and review their initial theories. Teachers also must be sensitive to student responses that can create new performances in different directions than planned.

4. *Conduct ongoing assessment*—In constructivist classrooms with emphasis on understanding, students need regular feedback and opportunity for reflection on their progress in learning. Teachers will either encourage students to develop the criteria that can measure their learning progress or develop the criteria themselves.

The experiences of one English teacher in the Teaching for Understanding Project were described by Rebecca Simmons (1994). The teacher was working in the unit "Trials and Literature: Who Determines Justice and How?" Students read such books as *To Kill a Mockingbird, Mutiny on the Bounty, Inherit the Wind*, and *Twelve Angry Men*. As students read they kept charts to identify justice themes. They used the charts in their papers and in debates held near the unit's end. They also kept journals with their responses to higher-order questions, as well as to their own questions and reflections. The teachers ask such questions as the following: "Which of your questions can be answered definitely? Which might have several answers? Were some answers better than others?" (Simmons, 1994, p. 22). A final paper on justice using two or three of the books students had chosen was the culminating performance. (For more in-depth treatment of constructivism, see Brooks & Brooks, 1993, and McNeil, 1995.)

Another example of this student-centered active-learning approach is Doreen Nelson's "modern city building" (1985) curriculum that requires the students to learn content and skills from different subject areas as they develop a scale-model city. Students start off studying their own community, drawing scale maps of the major features—streets, main buildings, parks, and so on. From these maps, students draw up plans for a new city and form a city council that will hear the plans for city development and handle questions such as: Where should the industrial park go in relation to environmental factors? Will there be a transport system and where will it be located? What park areas will be planned? Questions such as these require students to learn much about city government, ecology, landscaping, and city aesthetics. Math skills are important when students build their city to scale. This approach uses an integrated curriculum and cooperative learning with students divided into groups to build the various sections of the city.

Teaching for understanding in a constructivist classroom means using instructional strategies that move a learner from giving "information" to knowing the deep understandings through their own questioning, exploration, testing out of ideas, making connections among content areas, and working cooperatively with peers and adults to prepare to be lifelong learners (Brooks & Brooks, 1993).

Characteristics of constructivist classrooms are as follows (Brooks & Brooks, 1993, p. 17):

1. Curriculum is presented with emphasis on big concepts.
2. Pursuit of student questions is highly valued.
3. Curricular activities rely heavily on primary sources of data and manipulative materials.
4. Students are viewed as thinkers with emerging theories about the world.
5. Teachers behave in an interactive manner, mediating the environment for students.
6. Teachers seek students' points of view to base future lessons on student conceptions.

7. Assessment is interwoven with teaching and occurs through student exhibits and portfolios.
8. Students work primarily in groups.

INTERDISCIPLINARY CURRICULUM

One of the characteristics of school restructuring is the implementing of interdisciplinary curricula, either through teams in high school, such as in the scenario, or through the planning by one elementary teacher of interdisciplinary units. By having subjects combined around themes, wherein the subjects are connected rather than studied in isolation, students can begin to see meaningful relationships. These themes enable students to delve into concepts and generalizations that have been identified in subject standards, to deal with big questions and larger perspectives, and to develop their ability to learn through exploration. The learning rather than the subject matter becomes the center of attention (Martinello & Cook, 1994). The learners' questions, activities, and projects become more important than internalizing facts from one discipline area at a time.

Students may study a unit on a topic such as the prairie, if they live in the Midwest, and become very involved in examining the history of the land in their area, efforts to restore or safeguard prairie land, and the grasses and wildflowers of the prairie. They may read books, visit museums, talk to grandparents about life on the prairie. With a theme topic, students can decide what subtopics they want to know about, and the academic disciplines can be the sources and tools for learning rather than the content to be mastered. Their textbooks become reference sources. The curriculum may be built around themes, problems, or local issues that are important to that particular site and group of students; hence it has high interest for the students.

Research and Theoretical Base
The theoretical base for interdisciplinary curriculum comes from the works of John Dewey and other educators whose writings were part of a reform movement in educational, social, and political affairs during the early part of the 20th century called the progressive movement. The early progressive thinkers placed heavy emphasis on *how* to think rather than on *what* to think. The curriculum was interdisciplinary in nature, with subject matter as part of the learning process rather than the source of ultimate knowledge. The teacher's role was to guide students in their problem solving and scientific inquiry (Ornstein & Hunkins, 1993).

The other research base is in constructivist theory, which maintains that students construct their own understanding of the world. Experience is the key, and learners understand according to analysis of their own experiences.

The major research study that examines the results of interdisciplinary curriculum is the famous "eight year study" (1932–1940) that researched the effect of a nontraditional education in progressive schools with largely interdisciplinary curriculum to that of education in traditional subject-centered programs. The findings of the study were that students in the progressive schools were as well prepared for college as those prepared in traditional schools (Ornstein & Hunkins, 1993).

Application to Practice

The interdisciplinary approach is popular today, particularly in the middle school curriculum. Some schools, as part of their reform, have implemented interdisciplinary team teaching such as called for in New York State's "Compact for Learning" (Darling-Hammond, 1993).

Jacobs (1989) identified four steps for developing integrated interdisciplinary units. They involved (1) selecting an organizing center, such as a theme, topic, problem, or concept; (2) brainstorming associations from the perspective of different fields, with the graphic representation of the brainstorming depicted with a *webbing*—a wheel with spikes and subspikes—on which topics or information related to the center hub are written; (3) the establishing of guiding questions to provide a framework; and (4) designing activities to explore the questions.

Martinello and Cook (1994, p. 60) gave a longer list of steps to designing theme studies that may prove useful as teachers attempt this innovation to curriculum and teaching. Their guidelines for designing interdisciplinary theme studies are as follows:

1. Select a theme.
2. Develop a web, or build other designs to generate a wealth of ideas.
3. Identify questions through the lens of different disciplines.
4. Identify concepts; formulate generalizations within the theme.
5. Meet local curriculum requirements and the framework of the district and the state.
6. Map out or draw the general sequence.
7. Formulate with the students the questions to explore.
8. Develop ideas for a learning activity—clusters of ideas around concepts.
9. Identify content and process objectives.
10. Design learning activities.
11. Choose culminating projects.
12. Use resources to explore questions.
13. Decide on record keeping, reporting, and assessment measures.

WHOLE LANGUAGE

Another curricular innovation that has had considerable impact on the teaching of reading and language arts, particularly in the elementary schools, is whole language. Whole language is a rapidly expanding approach to literacy development (Ellis & Fouts, 1993). Although whole language is practiced more in the primary grades, it has extended into the upper elementary and middle school grades in some districts. It is also an approach that holds merit for adult literacy development. The whole-language approach to reading maintains that students are active learners and learn language in a natural way (Lemlech, 1994). It is compatible with constructivist philosophy, which maintains that learners construct their own knowledge and therefore should have exposure to broad ideas and meaningful, authentic learning experiences.

Research and Theoretical Base

Ellis & Fouts (1993) reported that the research base for whole language was very broad and included research from many different fields including linguistics, psycholinguistics, sociology, anthropology, philosophy, child development, curriculum, composition, literary theory, and semantics. They mention that the *Administrator's Guide to Whole Language* (Heald-Taylor, 1989) contains a chapter with more than 50 studies of related topics in the areas of reading, writing, oral language, and developmental studies that make up the research base. However, Ellis and Fouts (1993) point out that the applied research does not show that whole language has any more positive or negative impact than basal programs on children's literacy.

Application to Practice

The whole-language curriculum emphasizes forming discussion groups, accepting developmental spelling, focusing on reading and writing in all subject areas, and using many trade books in place of basal readers. Whole-language classrooms encourage children to choose the books they read, write their own books, and do meaningful activities in every subject area to achieve an integration of reading, writing, and speaking. The activities are to be fun and thought provoking, an outgrowth of student interests. Skills are taught as they are needed.

Whole language has been criticized by those who subscribe to a skills approach to reading and writing. For example, critics advocate the consistent teaching of phonics, correct spelling, and grammar along with prescribed texts and materials. In whole language, phonics instruction is de-emphasized but not discarded. Phonics are introduced according to an individual student's needs.

Ellis and Fouts (1993) explained that whole language became important in school curricula because of a reaction to the skills-focused language arts curriculum that emphasized phonics rather than extensive use of language, and because of recent information from cognitive science with new theories of learning that are compatible with the approach.

MULTICULTURAL EDUCATION

How would you respond on a scale of 1 (strongly disagree) to 7 (strongly agree) to the following statements (Cushner, 1986):

1. I enjoy studying about people from other cultures.
2. I enjoy being with people from other cultures.
3. I think about living within another culture in the future.

Considering that the United States and other world societies are changing rapidly and dramatically, future teachers responding negatively to these questions are clearly going to be out of step with current multicultural and international trends. When planning curriculum and instructional units, as well as daily lessons, it is important to integrate intercultural and international concepts and values to prepare students to live in a society of interdependent cultures.

Consider these statistics compiled for a research study (Haberman & Post, 1990):

> By 2010, there will be 62,644,000 school age children in the United States, over 38% of whom will be minority. More than half (32,392,000) will live in nine states: California, Texas, Florida, New York, New Jersey, Pennsylvania, Illinois, Michigan, and Ohio. Of these, almost half (15,000,000) will be minority. In many districts and in the entire states of California, Texas, Arizona, New Mexico, and Florida, minority students will be the majority. Minorities already constitute a majority of students in 23 of 25 largest districts. (p. 32)

The state of New York serves as a good illustration of the coming intercultural era. More than 1 million students representing 85 different language backgrounds have limited English proficiency. In New York City alone, one child in four is an offspring of non-English-speaking immigrant parents. While numbers are growing, the problem remains that attitudes toward students representing diverse populations have not changed. As a result, New York's Department of Education has revised its social studies curriculum to emphasize multicultural and international education (Sobol, 1990).

Research and Theoretical Base

The essence of understanding multiculturalism and internationalism is understanding the concept of *culture*. One contemporary definition of culture is "the learned, shared, and transmitted social activities of a group, the human-made part of the environment that satisfies all basic needs for survival and adaptation to the environment" (Bennett, 1986, p. 7). In their review of the literature, Cushner, McClelland, and Safford (1993) examined many definitions and identified three major themes: "culture as a socially constructed and dynamic phenomenon, culture as shared by a group which decided through a process of interaction what ideas, attitudes, meanings and hierarchy of values belong to that group, and culture as a set of ideas which is passed on to the young as a means of nourishing the next generation" (p. 56).

Although all cultures from different parts of the world share common characteristics including language, communication patterns, forms of aesthetic expression, and social, political, economic, and religious systems, there are many cultures within each culture. Pasch, Sparks-Langer, Gardner, Starko, and Moody (1991) distinguished between *macrocultures* and *microcultures*. Whereas the dominant culture, or macroculture, of the United States is Anglo–Western European, many microcultures, or groups of people having unique cultural patterns, exist within the country. Ethnic groups, made up of people from the same race, religion, or nationality with the same culture, are microcultures. Examples include African-Americans, Jewish-Americans, and Latinos. People incorrectly often use the terms *culture* and *ethnicity* interchangeably.

The United States is a culturally pluralistic, or multicultural, society where different racial and ethnic groups are encouraged to maintain their individual cultures within the broader culture. It was not always this way. During the great immigration period of the late 19th and early 20th centuries, an assimilationist philosophy prevailed. Schools were expected to assimilate immigrant children into the mainstream American culture as quickly as possible. The term *melting pot* was used to describe the process of different ethnic groups giving up their cultural characteristics to become new Americans.

More appropriate as an analogy for cultural pluralism is a salad bowl. Cultural pluralism accepts, encourages, and celebrates cultural diversity. While people maintain their unique identities, they also adopt traits of the broader American culture. There is a balance between cultural similarities and differences, and heritage is seen as a source of the nation's strength. Regarding the role of education in this process, Banks (1993) suggested that the major goal needed to be to change the entire educational environment so that it promoted a respect for a wide range of cultural groups and assured equal educational opportunity for all. Cushner et al. (1993) elaborated on the school's role:

> The children of diversity who are coming into our schools are unlike any previous generation of students seen in American public education. Today, more than ever before, we have the obligation and responsibility to address the needs of children and youth from a variety of backgrounds. At the same time, we must begin to prepare the youth in our charge with the perspectives, attitudes, knowledge, and skills which will enable them to interact effectively, satisfy their own needs, as well as work with others to solve the common problems which face a global, interdependent society. . . .
>
> The bottom line is that, like it or not, teachers will encounter people who increasingly are not like themselves. Our schools, our nation, and our world are becoming increasingly diverse, not only in terms of cultural difference, but difference in terms of ethnicity, class, race, religion, gender, exceptionality, and lifestyle and mobility as well. We must learn to work effectively in a world of transition, of change, and difference. (p. 23)

The multicultural education research shows that five areas matter a great deal in the education of multicultural students (Ladson-Billings, 1994). Area 1 is teachers' beliefs about students. Winfield (1986) pointed out that teachers often perceive African-American students as incapable of meeting high academic standards. Such negative attitudes lower teacher expectations and, in turn, lower the achievement of minority students and their educational opportunities (Lipman, 1993).

Area 2, which is crucial in multicultural education, is the content and materials used. Superficial celebration of ethnic holidays and heroes trivializes multicultural education. Instead, multicultural emphasis needs to be an ongoing part of the regular curriculum (Ladson-Billings, 1994). Also, "a realistic image of ethnic and racial groups should be included in teaching materials in a consistent, natural, and integrated fashion" (Banks, 1993, p. 253).

Area 3 addresses instructional approaches that ensure equitable pedagogy. Teachers need to examine their instruction to use the best instructional methods that will not handicap or discriminate against any group. Equitable pedagogy may mean using peer tutors for all students or cooperative learning groups. Learning to speak to children in their own language could be a powerful learning tool, as well.

Area 4 is educational settings. This area refers to the fact that even though schools are desegregated today, most students of color attend segregated schools. Even if they are in desegregated settings, tracking practices often put them in low-ability groups (Oakes, 1985).

Area 5 is teacher education, crucial in multicultural education and cultural variations in teachers' preservice preparation (Zeichner, 1992). Research shows that many teachers receive little information about multicultural education. Therefore, they may express their biases in discriminatory ways through the handling of or perceptions they have about their students without realizing their practices may be causing differences in student performance and achievement.

Application to Practice

Martorella (1991) suggested that effective educational programs emphasizing intercultural understanding and growth might incorporate the following experiences:

1. Learning how and where to obtain objective, accurate information about other cultural groups.
2. Identifying and examining positive accounts of other cultural groups or individuals.
3. Learning tolerance for diversity through experimentation in the school and classroom with alternative customs and practices.
4. Encountering, where possible, firsthand positive experiences with different cultural groups.
5. Developing empathic behavior . . . through role playing and simulations.

6. Practicing using "perspective glasses," that is, looking at an event, historical period, or issue through the perspective of another cultural group. (p. 312)

INTERNATIONAL EDUCATION

Along with the multicultural approach in the curriculum comes international education or global education to expand the world view of students. Although all subject areas of the school curriculum will need to be involved in international, or global, education for a more realistic perspective of the world to evolve, by the nature of its content the social studies area has demonstrated the most commitment to achieving this goal. Therefore it seems fitting to start with a definition of global education by the National Council for the Social Studies (1981):

> Global education refers to efforts to cultivate in young people a perspective of the world which emphasizes the interconnections among cultures, species, and the planet. The purpose of global education is to develop in youth the knowledge, skills, and attitudes needed to live effectively in a world possessing limited natural resources and characterized by ethnic diversity, cultural pluralism, and increasing interdependence. (p. 1)

Another narrower, but more publicized, definition of global education that focuses on global economic interdependence can be found in the report of the National Governors' Association (Fleming, 1991). The report advocated an education much more in tune with global changes because "world trade and financial, economic, and political developments have transformed disparate economic systems into a highly interdependent global market place. Today, the nations that inhabit the planet are often more closely linked than neighboring states or villages were at the turn of the century" (p. 11).

Research and Theoretical Base

Why has the United States become more dependent on other nations, particularly during the past decade? The reasons strongly suggest that developing our students' international awareness and involvement is imperative at this time in our history. Anderson (1991) provided a three-point argument to support his rationale for global education. First, several major historical developments have converged to cause changes in the world's social structure. One development was the growth of global interdependence that has accelerated and become worldwide during the modern era, particularly since 1900. This interdependence is noticed in the "expansion of technological, political, cultural, economical and ecological networks connecting different peoples, cultures, civilizations, and religions" (p. 14). A second historical development was the erosion of Western dominance. Contributing factors include the decolonization of the world since 1900, assertion of long-dormant, old cultures and religions, and the decline of the

Atlantic Basin in economic importance. A final historical change is the decline of U.S. influence in the world. At the end of World War II the United States was the world's hegemonic state. From then until the early 1970s, it dominated world production, commerce, and finance. Since the early 1970s the United States has declined in these areas as other nations have caught up.

In addition, these changes have greatly accelerated the globalization of the U.S. economy, politics, demography, and culture (Anderson, 1991). In terms of the economy, international trade has substantially increased, multinational corporations dominate production, and foreign investment has grown significantly and has impacted all sectors of our economy. U.S. political life is paralleling economic life by becoming more internationalized. This is evident in the growing number of state and municipal governments that are becoming increasingly involved in international economic policy and the growing number of foreign firms becoming indirectly involved in U.S. politics. The American people are also becoming more globalized because, through immigration, we are becoming a multicultural society. In many respects, "we are becoming a world nation within a world system" (p. 29).

The literature on global education suggests that much needs to be done to help students adopt a more realistic, and less ethnocentric, perspective of the international situation. Luckily the educational programs in the schools have the potential to facilitate the necessary changes. Dhand (1986–1987) reported on generalizations drawn from two reviews of the literature and research on global education. One was that students' perspectives on the world are largely shaped by the end of grade 9. Another generalization was that American children believed the United States was the "best" country in the world. Another was that teachers appeared to be more global minded than their students but showed the same propensity to express an ethnocentric view of the world. There appears to be a strong relationship between global attitudes and global knowledge. The more students know about global affairs, problems, and issues, the more positive are the attitudes (Dhand, 1986–1987, p. 73).

Application to Practice

What should be the content of global education? The National Council for the Social Studies (1994) identified the importance of "global connections and interdependence" as strand nine of the ten-strand network. The council's curriculum standards recommended that students in early grades

> examine global connections and basic issues and concerns, suggesting and initiating action plans. In the middle years, learners can analyze interactions among states and nations and their cultural complexities as the response to global events and changes. At the high school level, students can think systematically about personal, national, and global decisions, interactions, and consequences, including addressing critical issues such as peace, human rights, trade, and global ecology. (p. 29)

The council's study included the following performance expectations for global study:

1. explore ways that language, art, music, belief systems, and other cultural elements may facilitate global understanding or lead to misunderstanding;
2. give examples of conflict, cooperation, and interdependence among individuals, groups, and nations;
3. examine the effects of changing technologies on the global community;
4. explore causes, consequences, and possible solutions to persistent, contemporary, and emerging global issues, such as pollution and endangered species;
5. examine the relationships and tensions between personal wants and needs and various global concerns such as use of imported oil, land use, and environmental protection;
6. investigate concerns, issues, standards, and conflicts related to universal human rights, such as the treatment of children, religious groups, and effects of war. (National Council for the Social Studies, 1994, p. 70)

Teaching multiculturalism and global education involve identifying the pertinent concepts and generalizations to be incorporated within units and lessons, devising and selecting appropriate instructional methods and strategies to teach them, and planning for their use. Effective short- and long-term planning with an emphasis on students' thinking about what they are learning and making personal connections with the content increases the probability that they will be better prepared to assume an informed and active role in our modern multicultural, global society.

SUMMARY POINTS

Effective teachers are familiar with the national curriculum standards developed through the early nineties. These standards can be a guide to identify key concepts to teach.

Constructivist teaching, a learner-centered approach, emphasizes teaching for understanding and acknowledges that students construct knowledge for themselves based on the knowledge they already have.

Interdisciplinary curriculum is important today because it connects knowledge and builds relationships rather than having knowledge learned in isolation.

Whole language is a philosophical approach to literacy development that emphasizes the learning of language in a natural way throughout the curriculum with many reading, writing, speaking, and listening opportunities.

Multicultural and international education must be an essential part of the curriculum because our country has many diverse cultures and ethnic groups.

International education emphasizes the interconnectedness among cultures throughout the globe.

PART II: VIEWING CURRICULUM THROUGH INSTRUCTIONAL EYES

SCENARIO

Angeletta Rodrigo was ready to introduce the concept of poetry to her high school English class. She knew that they all had read and perhaps studied poetry elements before. This unit, however, would focus on extending and refining their knowledge while examining poetry cross-culturally. She had selected a few poets to start with—Langston Hughes, Emily Dickinson, and Luis Rodriguez.

She had instructed the students to bring in poems that told them something about a person and his or her life experience. She wondered how many rap poems would be submitted. She had already decided that as the unit moved along they would spend some time looking at rap as poetry, the origin of rap, rap themes, and rap within a cultural concept. She smiled as she anticipated a lesson she had already outlined in her head—"Shakespeare Meets the Rappers." They could examine Shakespeare's Elizabethan England and its culture, as expressed through its poetry, while examining the African-American experience in cities today as expressed in rap music and lyrics. Maybe students might even want to take that experience to the performance level with a production to be presented to the other English classes—a production with music and costumes and. . . .

Angeletta refocused her thoughts again. The anthology assigned to this level's English class had an introduction-to-poetry section with definition and characteristics of poetry. However, she needed to find out what students already knew about poetry. She would write the term *poetry* on the chalkboard after starting class with one of her favorite poems about youth and love—certainly she would include Housman's "From A Shropshire Lad." She would then ask students to write characteristics of poetry on their papers. She knew they would add more than characteristics. Perhaps they would include a poet's name, or an adjective expressing a like or dislike. She would accommodate all these groupings when the class and she put together their web.

Next she would ask students to share aloud some of the written characteristics, and she would record the elements on the chalkboard. With a few lists to examine, she and the class would group elements into categories. Then she would ask the class to group their individual lists. When lists had been grouped and labeled she would draw a web for the groupings on the chalkboard. At the same time students would draw webs for their groupings.

She would encourage the class to examine the definition and characteristics in the text with their lists. How did the approaches differ? A discussion would follow on how poetry is like a short story, what students' experiences were with poetry, and what three things they would like to learn about poetry in this unit. What poem could she give those who responded with nothing? She would find one that would speak to Thaddeus and Roseanne.

Student webs would be important for her to see in order to learn what her students knew, and to sense their feelings about poetry, and even maybe to learn some of their favorite poets. She would start their critical thinking by asking them to think about why poetry was studied in school. Does it play a role in the culture? From there a cultural exploration through poets' voices could begin.

What poems would come from the students' voices? Angeletta felt her excitement growing about the unit ahead.

PEDAGOGICAL CONTENT KNOWLEDGE

As Angeletta considered the content she wanted to include in her unit, she had to make decisions about meaningful ways to help students understand poetry as a mode of communication through the ages. What teaching activities would help her students develop the understanding and appreciation she had as her goals for the unit? She had to consider carefully the interface of the curriculum and her unstructured decisions.

Curriculum and instruction are separate entities, but there is a necessary relationship between them. They have been studied and described separately perhaps more than any other elements of the teaching process. However, the relationships between them have not received nearly as much attention. Shulman (1987) used the phrase *pedagogical content knowledge*—a jargony-sounding but usefully descriptive phrase that refers to the linkage between content and delivery. It implies a teacher's in-depth grasp of the subject matter, sensitivity to the possibilities and limitations of the students as learners, and skill in the use of a variety of teaching modes. With the concept of pedagogical content knowledge we may envision the fully functioning teacher who senses the potential within the subject matter of students' optimal learning, and who is able to follow through in designing pertinent learning activities.

Research and Theoretical Base

Recent research shows that beginning teachers have incomplete and superficial levels of pedagogical content knowledge (Feiman-Nemser & Parker, 1990; Gudmundsdottir & Shulman, 1987; Shulman, 1987). Grossman (1989) found that first-year teachers who had master's degrees but no teacher-education training were less prepared to handle student needs than beginning teachers who had completed teacher training. The former teachers, unable to decide what instructional practices to use, attributed students' lack of understanding to inattentiveness or lack of motivation.

Hashweh (1987) investigated three experienced physics teachers and three experienced biology teachers as to the impact their subject knowledge had on their teaching. When teaching in their field they knew the problems learners had with the content and were more able to provide a variety of accurate examples, analogies, and demonstrations than when they taught outside their field.

Although this research is new and limited it does show that pedagogical content knowledge is related to knowledge of the content. But it is much more than that. It is knowing how to teach the content in a manner compatible with the subject area (Cochran, DeRuiter, & King, 1993).

Application to Practice

The assumptions of pedagogical content knowledge may at first be discouraging to the prospective or novice teacher. A bachelor's degree preparation for teaching is obviously not sufficient to prepare one to comply fully with the expectations implied by pedagogical content knowledge. However, it suggests a direction for the continuing development of every teacher, that is, the acquisition of increasingly effective ways of contributing to students' intellectual maturation. Fenstermacher (1986) made the point that teacher education is not intended to prescribe ways of teaching as such but more importantly to show prospective teachers how to think about teaching.

Shulman (1987) suggested a process that he called *transformation*, whereby teachers would address the task of transferring the learning possibilities they conceived to the minds of the learners. He stated that transformation occurred through some combinations of the following steps rather than rigid adherence to an explicit ordering (p. 16):

1. Preparation (of the given text materials) including the process of critical interpretation.
2. Representation of the new ideas in the form of new analogies, metaphors, and so forth.
3. Instructional selections from among an array of teaching methods and models.
4. Adaptation of these representations to the general characteristics of the children.
5. Tailoring the adaptations to the specific youngsters in the classroom.

He added that "these forms of transformation, these aspects of the process wherein one moves from personal comprehension to preparing for the comprehension of others, are the essence of the act of pedagogical reasoning, of teaching as thinking, and of planning—whether explicitly or implicitly—the performance of teaching" (p. 16).

Some examples of pedagogical content knowledge will be helpful in further understanding the concept. Consider Sally, a 7th-grade mathematics teacher, who became aware that many students were experiencing difficulty with understanding the concept of percent. After talking with several students who were having difficulty, she realized that to them percent represented a new level of abstraction in mathematics. Percent did not refer to absolute quantities like all the mathematical constructs they had studied up to that time, but rather to an implied ratio that had meaning only as it was applied (usually) as a multiplication factor. Repeating "percent means hundredths" many times during each class meeting proved to be ineffective. What, wondered Sally, existed in their experience that would help them make a connection with percent? It occurred to her that the idea of 100 cents to a dollar would be familiar to them. Sally provided those students who continued to have problems with packets of pennies, and gave them the tactile and visual experience of manipulating the pennies as she guided them in thinking in terms of percent. As a result, all her students achieved the mastery-level working knowledge of percent. Meanwhile, the remainder of the class had gone on to work with decimal percents and finding a number when a percent of it is given, based on problems the students cooperatively made up.

In this relatively simple example, Sally used her understanding of percent and her ability to think from her students' perspective to create an effective learning activity. The idea for the activity emerged from the combination of the topic and a relevant learning principle—using past learning as a connector to new learning—to create a bridge to students' new learning. Further, Sally did not feel constrained to keep the class together, which would have resulted in either the quicker students becoming bored or the slower ones being left behind.

Another example (Parrish, 1991) involves a case in which Clark, a social studies teacher, wanted his students to comprehend the concept of invention, and the role of inventions in contributing to the evolution of a society. He asked the class members to play a mind game and invent something that would make life easier. As an example he suggested a machine that would grade essay tests. The students responded with ideas such as a time machine that would allow one to go back and undo the effects of bad decisions, a golf club that eliminated hooks and slices, a three-dimensional television, and a fold-up parking meter that could be used anyplace free of charge. Clark selected two of them to discuss in terms of their advantages and disadvantages. It came as a surprise to the students that seemingly desirable inventions had a negative side, as well. When this had been established, the students were prepared to understand the effect of the cotton gin on the South at the turn of the 19th century. Along with the effect of bringing high profits to the plantation owners, it raised the value of slaves and stimulated the slave trade. And, because cotton is hard on the land, much land was depleted by overgrowing cotton. In subsequent units, when such inventions as the steam engine and sewing machine were important topics, the students would better understand their effects.

Clark might simply have had the students read about these events in their history books, or he might have talked about them in a lecture. But allowing the students to "develop" their own inventions and determine their effects lent a dimension of personal meaning that would otherwise not have existed. Clark understood his topic well, and realized that a powerful insight lay beyond the fact of the cotton gin, so he employed a method that tapped into the potential of the topic. This, indeed, is an application of pedagogical content knowledge.

A final example of this bridge between content and instructions is of Judy's general science class. In a unit on astronomy Judy wanted students to acquire an elementary understanding of the relationship of Earth with the visible bodies in the universe. One of the bodies that has special significance is Polaris, the North Star. It would have been a simple matter to explain the facts related to Polaris, but as she considered her objective, she felt it might be more effective if she presented it as a discrepant event that needed to be investigated further. And so she told the class that of the 6,000 visible objects in the sky, only one appeared not to move, that it was always in the same position when we looked for it. She told the class they could ask questions, but she would answer only yes or no until they could determine the reason for this discrepant event and identify the particular body.

The process of inquiry is used all too rarely in classrooms. Yet it is a powerful mode of thinking and learning that contributes to students' reasoning powers. When the nature of the content is such that it lends itself to inquiry, the teacher who has a sufficient measure of pedagogical content knowledge will recognize it and conduct the inquiry that will be both motivating and useful to the class.

Pedagogical content knowledge is a powerful concept in the interest of educators as they aspire to move education to the status of a major profession. According to Shulman (1987),

> Pedagogical content knowledge is the category most likely to distinguish the understanding of the content specialist from that of the pedagogue. . . . We expect a math major to understand mathematics or a history specialist to comprehend history. But the key to distinguishing the knowledge base of teaching lies at the intersection of content and pedagogy, in the capacity of a teacher to transform the content knowledge he or she possesses into forms that are pedagogically powerful and yet adaptive to the variations in ability and background presented by the students. (pp. 8–15)

In a further commentary on this idea, Shulman (1990) noted,

> Aristotle was right: the deepest understanding one can have of any field is an understanding of its pedagogy, because pedagogical understanding is predicted on the kind of multiple readings, the kind of contingent understanding that reflect the deep objectives of a liberal education. Deep knowledge is never enough for rich pedagogy. Advanced skill in the process of teaching will not suffice either. To teach the highest level of competence as an educator . . . demands a melding of knowledge and process. (p. 14)

Therefore, as you plan for instruction, to translate your discipline into powerful learning experiences for your students and make the curriculum come alive in young minds, you will need a generous measure of pedagogical content knowledge.

STRUCTURE OF KNOWLEDGE

To be an effective teacher with pedagogical content knowledge, one must have a thorough understanding of one's content area, a knowledge that will keep learners designing or redesigning their cognitive structuring of important content. Gardner (1991) points out that information is transformed into understanding when the mind creates new cognitive structures or reshapes present ones. (Angeletta Rodrigo in the scenario knew the importance of building a knowledge structure for concepts that she taught as she decided to make that structure graphic with a web.)

Traditional education approaches often present broad coverage of subject areas and encourage memorization or repeating of chunks of information. The curriculum is broken down into pieces and students concentrate on learning these pieces without seeing how the pieces fit together and what the structure of the whole is. Facts remain facts and are not tied into concepts. The emphasis is on basic skills, fact-driven content, and proceeding "part" to "whole." In constructivist classrooms the curriculum is presented "whole" to "part," with emphasis on big concepts. Constructivist teachers organize information around concepts with conceptual clusters of problems, questions, and discrepant events (Brooks & Brooks, 1993). This approach is consistent with the new findings about learning from cognitive science (Doyle, 1992). "Structuring curriculum around primary concepts is a critical dimension of constructivist pedagogy" (Brooks & Brooks, 1993, p. 46). When students can break down the concept into parts that they can see and understand, they then can make sense of the concept. Curricular activities designed by both the teacher and the students around broad concepts can help students with understanding.

Whether teachers intend to teach in the constructivist approach or combine traditional and constructivist practices, they must understand the structure of the knowledge that they are teaching to be effective with content pedagogy. In other words, when planning instruction, teachers think about the subject matter they are going to teach. They then are operating in the cognitive domain—the domain of learning that focuses on academic or intellectual content. The structure of that content can be examined as facts, concepts, and generalizations. Forming that content into various intellectual operations from which objectives are formed can be examined using Bloom's taxonomy (see chapter 5). Forming objectives will be described in chapter 5, which deals with planning.

This structure of knowledge can readily be illustrated by a pyramid (Figure 4.1) that visually displays the relationship of facts to concepts and generaliza-

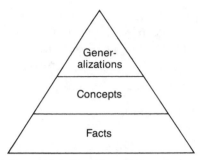

Figure 4.1 Structure of Knowledge

tions in terms of quantity and quality. There are billions of isolated facts but there are fewer concepts because concepts are formed from facts and serve as their organizers. Generalizations are at the top of the pyramid because there are even fewer generalizations than concepts. Generalizations are statements expressing the relationship of concepts. Another reason generalizations are at the top is because they are the most abstract form of knowledge generally studied by elementary and secondary students. Formal theories are actually the highest form of knowledge but are not generally studied until the college level. As abstractions, generalizations are more easily transferred to other situations, which makes them more applicable and useful for learning. Whereas facts are specific and have the least generality, concepts involve some degree of generality, and generalizations are compounded concepts. Most of the instructional content taught in elementary and secondary schools is from the factual and conceptual levels.

Facts

A fact is a "statement about concepts that is true or verified for a particular case on the basis of the best evidence available" (Martorella, 1991, p. 150). Factual knowledge "consists of specific data about events, objects, people, or other things that can be or have been verified by the senses" (Banks & Clegg, 1990, p. 86). In addition, facts are restricted to a particular time and place. There is a major problem with teaching facts as the basis of identifying and organizing content because they have little transfer value from situation to situation. Facts best serve to illustrate concepts and support generalizations. When planning units and lessons, the concern should be to identify those facts that are useful to teach a particular concept or generalization (Armstrong, 1980). This not only suggests that the only worthwhile facts to teach are those that serve as evidence for higher forms of knowledge, but also that those taught in isolation of concepts and generalizations will not contribute to meaningful learning. Facts taught in isolation may be memorized and retained for a short time but, without linkages to concepts and generalizations, tend to be forgotten soon after the test.

Concepts

"Concepts are the ideas or abstractions formed as a result of categorizing data from a number of observations" (Gunter, Estes, & Schwab, 1990, p. 98). They are names given to categories formed as factual information is classified. Concepts enable us to group together different things that have some similarities. In a sense, concepts are created to help people be more efficient in their communication. They help us sort out the many events, people, ideas, objects, and other phenomena with which we come in contact daily, formally and informally. Martorella (1990) remarked that "concepts allow us to organize and store similar pieces of information efficiently. Once formed, they eliminate our need to treat each new piece of knowledge as a separate category. In a sense, concepts are hooks on which we can hang new experiences" (p. 190). This sorting-out process, or categorization, helps us reduce the complexity of our environment. Comprehension is enhanced because concepts facilitate communication and, most importantly, they assist in the transfer of learning. This is the primary reason why concepts, as a higher form of learning, should become the basis of the content to be taught and the focus of teaching (along with generalizations).

We now have reached a general consensus through cognitive science that every human being constructs his or her own meanings about knowledge and how things work in the world on the basis of knowledge already possessed. We organize that knowledge into concepts and subconcepts. Concepts are labeled events or records of events or objects that we can define and understand because they occur with regularity.

Acquiring new concepts is done either by *discovery*, the way young children learn, or by *reception learning*. Reception learning is the way many students learn in schools—by memorization of concepts or processes, but students may not see the regularities in events, objects, or relationships designated by these new concepts (Novak, 1991). This is rote learning without understanding. Understanding enables the student to see the regularity in the event or the activity. Rote learning does not build on prior knowledge and is not influenced by misconceptions that we all hold about how things work. Novak (1991) points out that rote memory knowledge is usually retained for only two or three weeks and is not stored in long-term memory because it is not attached to our past knowledge structures. Therefore students who do poorly on science or math achievement tests may not have developed an adequate concept structure. Even repetition of science information from year to year will not help if understanding of concepts is not present.

Generalizations

Generalizations are broad statements that serve as principles expressing the relationship of two or more concepts. Facts are different because they are based on single events; generalizations emerge from a large body of information. Generalizations are similar to facts in that they "are propositional in nature; that is, they

Table 4.1   Facts, Concepts, and Generalization

GENERALIZATION WITHIN EMBEDDED CONCEPT	EXAMPLES OF RELATED FACTS
All *matter* in the *universe* is affected by *gravity*.	Jupiter's gravitational pull keeps its moons in orbit around it.
Different kinds of *materials* respond differently to *electric forces*.	In metal materials, electric charges flow easily. In glass, electric charges can hardly move at all.
One may divide the category of *motion* into steady motion, speeding up, and slowing down.	Newton developed the laws of motion.
Fundamental *forces* of nature include *gravitational* and *electromagnetic* forces.	The earth moves at a rate of 67,000 m.p.h.

are true only so far as available evidence continues to support their truth" (Armstrong, 1980, p. 31). Like facts, generalizations are verifiable and a doubted generalization becomes a hypothesis to be tested with data. Generalizations hold power for teaching because they are inferences based on large sets of data that can be used to make predictions. Predicting is a higher-level critical-thinking skill. Moreover, because generalizations have predictive qualities, they are easily transferable to other situations. "The synthesis represented by a generalization provides the student with a broad, wide-reaching state that applies to the past and the present and to all cases everywhere" (Martorella, 1991, p. 153).

Table 4.1 shows the relationship of facts, concepts, and generalizations through illustrations adapted from a science curriculum.

CONCEPT MAPPING

Consider now a technique that enables students to chart the structure of new knowledge for themselves. The technique is called *concept mapping*. Concept mapping is an educational tool that one of the authors is using in her courses to help students see the structure of key concepts and fields in which they will be teaching. Concept maps can be used with any subject matter. They are most effective when students construct their own personal concept maps for topics they are studying. The practice takes time as students struggle with key ideas and definitions to fit them into what they already know and then begin to see new relationships, new meanings.

The author's experience is that each time she teaches a course she constructs a concept map that continues to change with the added insights gained from the previous teaching experiences. Students are asked to design their own concept maps of the content as the course progresses. A map for a single class session may include many concepts and subscripts. Having students draw the map at the end of a session in which new information is introduced is a good way to check on their understanding.

Research and Theory Base

Concept mapping is based on Ausubel's (1968) assimilation theory that what is most important in learning is what the learner already knows and how the new learning will interface with or relate to previous knowledge.

Joe Novak and associates at Cornell introduced concept mapping in 1972. Since then it has gained acceptance particularly by science teachers in many parts of the globe (Okebukola, 1992). Some of the research claims for the effectiveness of concept mapping in learning science have been reported by Okebukola (1990), Novak (1990), Wandersee (1990), and Jegede, Alaiyemolo, and Okebukola (1990).

Application to Practice

The pattern to use in making concept maps was originated by Novak (1990) and Wandersee (1990). Okebukola (1992, p. 218) reported the steps the student should take as follows:

- The student notes the keywords/concepts, phrases, or ideas that are used during the lesson or read in the text.
- The student arranges the concept and main ideas in a hierarchy from the most general, inclusive, and abstract to the most specific and concrete.
- The student draws circles or ellipses around the concepts.
- The student connects the concepts (in circles) by means of lines or arrows accompanied by linking words so that each branch of the map can be read from the top down.
- The student provides examples, if possible, at the terminus of each branch.
- The student cross-links hierarchies or branching of the map where appropriate.

Figure 4.2 is an example of a concept map.

For a more simplified approach to concept mapping called *webbing*, try these four generalized steps that are a part of the Novak steps but do not require as much specificity. This approach works well with concepts that are not made up of parts that can be arranged in a hierarchy. Linking words are not used in this approach. The four steps in webbing include the following (Morine-Dershimer 1990):

1. List all the words or phrases connected with your topic or concept.
2. Group the words or phrases together in an order that makes sense to you.
3. Label your groups according to the characteristics your groups have in common.

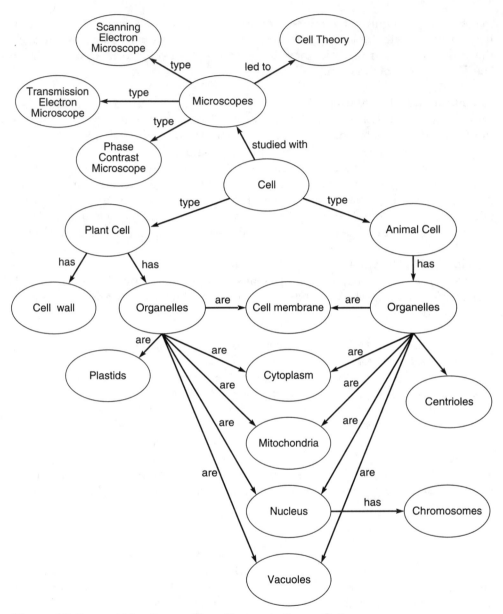

Figure 4.2 Concept Map From a Class Demonstration on Cells
(Reprinted by permission from Lynne Anderson-Inman & Leigh Zeitz, Computer-based concept mapping: Active studying for active learners, *The Computing Teacher*, August/September 1993, 21(1), 8.)

4. Draw a web that shows your groups and subgroups in relation to each other and to the major concept or topic.

(Note that Angeletta Rodrigo in the scenario was using this webbing approach in her introduction on poetry.)

Figure 4.3 is a student's webbing done on teacher planning using these steps.

Our experience has been that when students are required to construct their own personal concept maps or webs for topics they are studying, they find new meanings in the subject and new ways to relate what they already know to the content they are learning. In short, concept maps constructed by students help them to learn meaningfully. Subject matter ceases to be a mass of definitions to be memorized or problems to be solved by the routine plugging in of numbers or symbols into abstract formulas.

Concept maps are no magic bullet. It usually takes several months of regular practice and feedback to teach students how to construct good concept maps; webs are easier to form. The teacher must also take the time to learn how to teach students to do concept maps and to learn to become a constructive critic, allowing students to create maps meaningful to them.

SUMMARY POINTS

Pedagogical content knowledge is the intersection of curriculum and instruction wherein teachers use their grasp of content and the students' understanding or misunderstanding to transform the content into forms that are easily learned. Teachers employ pedagogical content knowledge to present content in suitable classroom representations.

The structure of knowledge in school curriculum is displayed in facts, concepts, and generalizations. A fact is a statement about a concept that present evidence verifies as true. A concept is the key to our understanding. It is the form in which we categorize knowledge. Generalizations are broad statements that express the relationship between two or more concepts.

Concept mapping is an educational tool that helps students see the structure of key concepts and topics. Webbing is a simplified approach to concept mapping conducted by listing key words connected with the concept, grouping words in a sensible order, labeling groups, and drawing a diagram that shows the groups and their relationships to each other.

QUESTIONS FOR REFLECTION

1. Why do you believe the authors included a chapter on curriculum in a book on effective teaching? What other topics might you have included in the chapter?

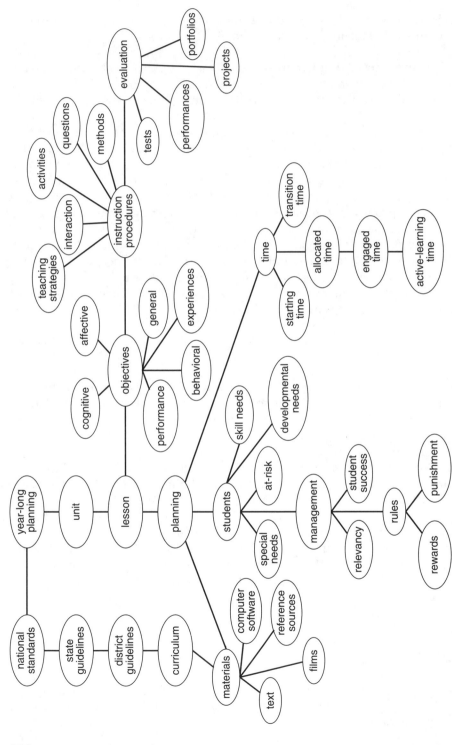

Figure 4.3 Student's Webbing of Teacher Planning

2. Do you believe that national curriculum standards and assessment are important for the country to accomplish Goals 2000?

3. How do you see the constructivist approach to education differing from the traditional approach? What do you see as advantages and possible disadvantages of the constructivist approach?

4. Do you have to develop an interdisciplinary unit in your methods class? If so, what is the planning procedure you are going through? Do you believe that you are able to address the concepts and skills you consider important as effectively as you could focusing on them in isolation? What do you see as the advantages and disadvantages of interdisciplinary curriculum?

5. Have you visited a whole-language classroom? What were the signs in the classroom that indicated emphasis was being placed on reading, writing, speaking, and listening throughout the curriculum? How frequently did the teacher do phonics lessons? What do you see as the advantages and disadvantages of whole language?

6. How are you preparing yourself to address multicultural education in your classroom?

7. What example can you give to demonstrate your understanding of content pedagogy?

8. How would you explain the student webbing on planning in the section on concept mapping? What additional subconcepts might you add or what subconcept relationships might you draw differently?

9. Have you tried drawing a concept map or web for effective teaching? What big ideas would you include in it?

10. How do you see K–12 textbooks structured? Are they emphasizing concepts and the connection of concepts, or do you get the feeling that they are presenting many facts that are disconnected? Would they be helpful to you if you were teaching for depth rather than breadth?

REFERENCES

Anderson, L. F. (1991). A rationale for global education. In K. Tye (Ed.), *Global education: 1991 Yearbook of the Association for Supervision and Curriculum Development*. Alexandria, VA: Association for Supervision and Curriculum Development.

Anderson-Inman, L., & Zeitz, L. (1993). Computer-based concept mapping: Active studying for active learners. *The Computing Teacher, 21*(1), 6–10.

Armstrong, D. (1980). *Social studies in secondary education*. New York: Macmillan.

Ausubel, D. (1968). *Educational psychology: A cognitive view*. New York: Holt, Rinehart & Winston.

Banks, J., & Clegg, A. (1990). *Teaching strategies for the social studies*. New York: Longman.

Banks, J. (1993). Multicultural education for young children: Racial and ethnic attitudes and their modification. In B. Spodek (Ed.), *Handbook of research on the education of young children*. New York: Macmillan.

Bennett, C. I. (1986). *Comprehensive multicultural education: Theory and practice*. Boston: Allyn & Bacon.

Brooks, J., & Brooks, M. (1993). *The case for constructivist classrooms*. Alexandria, VA: Association for Supervision and Curriculum Development.

Bruner, J. (1964). The course of cognitive growth. *American Psychologist, 19.*

Caswell, H., & Campbell, D. (1935). *Curriculum development*. New York: American Book.

Cochran, K., DeRuiter, J., & King, R. (1993). Pedagogical content knowing: An integrative model for teacher preparation. *Journal of Teacher Education, 44*(4), 263–272.

Copple, C., Sigel, I., & Saunders, R. (1984). *Educating the young thinker*. New York: D. Van Nostrand.

Cross, C. (1994). Implications of subject-matter standards. In N. Cobb (Ed.), *The future of education*. New York: College Entrance Examination Board.

Cushner, K. (1986). *Inventory of cross-cultural sensitivity*. Unpublished manuscript, Kent State University, Kent, Ohio.

Cushner, K., McClelland, A., & Safford, P. (1993). *Human diversity and education: An integrative approach*. New York: McGraw-Hill.

Darling-Hammond, L. (1993). Reframing the school reform agenda. *Phi Delta Kappan* (June), 753–761.

Dewey, J. (1938). Experience and education. New York: Macmillan.

Dhand, H. (1986–1987). Recent research on global education. *History and Social Science Teacher, 22,* 71–73.

Doyle, W. (1992). Curriculum and pedagogy. In P. Jackson (Ed.), *Handbook of research on curriculum*. New York: Macmillan.

Earley, P. (1994). *Goals 2000: Educate America act—implication for teacher education*. Washington, DC: AACTE.

Eisner, E. (1990). Creative curriculum development and practice. *Journal of Curriculum and Supervision, 6*(1), 62–73.

Ellis, A., & Fouts, J. (1993). *Research on educational innovations*. Princeton Junction, NJ: Eye on Education.

Feiman-Nemser, S., & Parker, M. (1990). Making subject matter part of the conversation in learning to teach. *Journal of Teacher Education, 41*(3), 32–43.

Fenstermacher, G. (1986). Philosophy of research on teaching: Three aspects. In M. Wittrock (Ed.), *Handbook of research on teaching* (3rd ed.). New York: Macmillan.

Fleming, D. B. (1991). Social studies reform and global education. *The Social Studies, 82,* 11–15.

Gardner, H. (1991). *The unschooled mind: How children think and how schools should teach*. New York: Basic Books.

Good, T., & Brophy, J. (1994). *Looking into classrooms* (6th ed.). New York: HarperCollins.

Grossman, P. (1989). A study in contrast: Sources of pedagogical content knowledge for secondary English. *Journal of Teacher Education, 40*(5), 24–31.

Gudmundsdottir, S., & Shulman, L. (1987). Pedagogical content knowledge in social studies. *Scandinavian Journal of Educational Research, 31,* 59–70.

Gunter, M., Estes, T., & Schwab, J. (1990). *Instruction: A models approach.* Boston: Allyn & Bacon.

Haberman, M., & Post, L. (1990). Cooperating teachers' perceptions of the goals of multicultural education. *Action in Teacher Education, 12*(3), 31–35.

Hashweh, M. (1987). Effects of subject matter knowledge in the teaching of biology and physics. *Teaching and Teacher Education, 3,* 109–120.

Heald-Taylor, G. (1989). *The administrator's guide to whole language.* Portsmouth, NH: Rich C. Owen, Publisher.

Jacobs, H. (1989). *Interdisciplinary curriculum: design and implementation.* Alexandria, VA: Association for Supervision and Curriculum Development.

Jegede, O., Alaiyemolo, F., & Okebukola, P. (1990). The effect of concept mapping on students' anxiety and achievement in biology. *Journal of Research in Science Teaching, 27*(10), 951–960.

Ladson-Billings, G. (1994). What we can learn from multicultural education research. *Educational Leadership* (April), 22–26.

Lemlech, J. (1994). *Curriculum and instructional methods for the elementary and middle school* (3rd ed.). New York: Macmillan.

Lipman, P. (1993). *Teacher ideology toward African-American students in restructured schools.* Unpublished doctoral dissertation, University of Wisconsin, Madison.

Lockhead, J. (1985). *New horizon in educational development: Review of research in education.* Washington, DC: American Educational Research Association.

Martinello, M., & Cook, G. (1994). *Interdisciplinary inquiry in teaching and learning.* New York: Macmillan.

Martorella, P. (1990). Teaching concepts. In J. Cooper (Ed.), *Classroom teaching skills* (4th ed.). Lexington, MA: D. C. Heath & Co.

Martorella, P. (1991). *Teaching social studies in middle and secondary schools.* New York: Macmillan.

McNeil, J. (1995). *Curriculum: The teachers' initiative.* Englewood Cliffs, NJ: Prentice-Hall.

Morine-Dershimer, G. (1990). Instructional planning. In J. Cooper (Ed.), *Classroom teaching skills* (4th ed.). Lexington, MA: D. C. Heath & Co.

National Council for the Social Studies (1981). *Global education: Position statement.* Washington, DC: Author.

National Council for the Social Studies (1994). *Expectation of excellence: Curriculum standards for social studies.* Washington, DC: Author.

National Council of Teachers of Mathematics (1989). *Cumulative and evaluation standards for school mathematics.* Reston, VA: Author.

National Council of Teachers of Mathematics (1991). *Professional standards for teaching mathematics.* Reston, VA: Author.

National Education Goals Panel (1994). *The national education goals report.* Washington, DC: Author.

Nelson, D. (1985). *City building education.* Los Angeles: Center for City Building Education Programs.

Newman, D., Griffin, P., & Cole, M. (1989). *The construction zone: Working for cognitive change in school*. Cambridge: Cambridge University Press.

Novak, J. (1990). Concept maps and vee diagrams: Two metacognitive tools to facilitate meaningful learning. *Instructional Science, 19*, 29–52.

Novak, J. (1991). Clarify with concept maps. *The Science Teacher, 58*(7), 45–49.

Oakes, J. (1985). *Keeping track: How schools structure inequitably*. New Haven, CT: Yale University Press.

Okebukola, P. (1990). Attaining meaningful learning of concepts in genetics and ecology: A test of the efficacy of the concept-mapping heuristic. *Journal of Research in Science, 27*(5), 493–504.

Okebukola, P. (1992). Concept mapping with a cooperative learning flavor. *The American Biology Teacher, 54*(4), 218–221.

O'Neil, J. (1992, October). National system of standards, exams piloted. *Update, 34*(8), 1–5.

O'Neil, J. (1993). Can national standards make a difference? *Educational Leadership, 50*(5), 4–8.

Ornstein, A. & Hunkins, F. (1993). Curriculum-foundations, principles, and theory, 2nd ed. Boston: Allyn and Bacon.

Parrish, C. (1991). Unpublished lesson plan, Kent State University, Kent, Ohio.

Pasch, M., Sparks-Langer, G., Gardner, T. G., Starko, A. J., & Moody, C. D. (1991). *Teaching as decision making*. New York: Longman.

Perkins, D., & Blythe, T. (1994). Putting understanding up front. *Educational Leadership, 51*(5), 4–7.

Piaget, J. (1952). *The origins of intelligence in children*. New York: International University Press.

Resnick, L., & Klopfer, L. (Eds.). (1989). *Toward the thinking curriculum: Current cognitive research: 1989 Yearbook of the Association for Supervision and Curriculum Development*. Alexandria, VA: ASCD.

Shulman, L. (1987). Knowledge and teaching: Foundation of the new reform. *Harvard Educational Review, 57*, 1–22.

Shulman, L. (1990). *Aristotle had it right: On knowledge and pedagogy* (Occasional Paper No. 4). East Lansing, MI: Holmes Group.

Siegel, I., & Cocking, R. (1977). *Cognitive development from childhood to adolescence: A constructivist perspective*. New York: Holt, Rinehart & Winston.

Simmons, R. (1994). The horse before the cart: Assessing for understanding. *Educational Leadership, 51*(5), 22–23.

Sobol, T. (1990). Understanding diversity. *Educational Leadership, 48*(3), 27–30.

Tierney, R. (1990). Redefining reading comprehension. *Educational Leadership, 47*(3), 37–42.

Von Glasersfeld, E. (1981). The concepts of adaptation and viability in a radical constructivist theory of knowledge. In I. Sigel, B. Brodinsky, and R. Golinkoff (Eds.), *New directions in Piagetian theory and practice*. Hillsdale, NY: Lawrence Erlbaum.

Wandersee, J. (1990). Concept mapping and the cartography of cognition. *Journal of Research in Science Teaching, 27*(10), 923–936.

Wiles, J., & Bondi, J. (1989). *Curriculum development: A guide to practice* (3rd ed.). Columbia, OH: Merrill.

Winfield, L. (1986). Teacher beliefs toward at-risk students in inner-urban schools. *The Urban Review, 18*, 253–267.

Woods, R. (1994). A close-up look at how children learn science. *Educational Leadership, 519*(5), 33–35.

Zeichner, K. (1992). *Educating teachers for cultural diversity*. East Lansing, MI: National Center for Research in Teacher Learning.

CHAPTER **5** Planning for Teaching

Plans are the extension of the teacher's personality and instructional style.

All teachers plan. No teacher enters the classroom without having an idea of what to present (except perhaps those unfortunate substitute teachers who arrive at the school and find that no plans are available for their use). However, the nature of plans differs widely from teacher to teacher. Some plans may be quite structured and comprehensive, such as when a physics teacher prepares students to engage in a complex and intricate laboratory experiment. Others might be less structured, such as when a government teacher prepares questions for guiding a discussion to help students develop meaning about a civic issue. Other plans might exist only as vague intentions in the mind of the teacher. Teachers who are particularly glib may consider winging it without benefit of much deliberate planning to be a sufficient practice. Few conscientious educators would agree.

Sound planning contributes to good teaching. Claims to the contrary are likely to involve self-serving rationalizing, if not outright naivete. The issue is not whether one should plan, but how one should plan. No single answer fits all cases. Some teachers, especially inexperienced teachers, are likely to find rather detailed plans to be beneficial. Other teachers may find that less specific plans, but plans that nevertheless contribute to purpose and direction in the lesson or unit, are more useful.

To some extent, plans are the extension of the teacher's personality and instructional style. As Hoover (1972) observed, they are, in that sense, a personal invention on the part of each teacher. The teacher who is basically a structured person will take a different approach to planning than a free spirit will. One could hardly use the plans of the other effectively, even while covering the same topic. The approach taken in this book attempts to accommodate a wide range of personalities, teaching styles, grade levels, subject areas, and teacher experience, while stressing the necessity for conscientious, soundly conceived planning.

Many different approaches to planning are practiced by teachers. Planning, broadly defined and encompassing many differences, includes those teacher activities that organize school- and student-related activities (Clark & Yinger, 1980). A general definition such as this takes into account the diversity of teachers' personalities and styles: formal, detailed planning for highly structured teachers and more informal approaches for those who are less structured. From this perspective, it is relatively easy to adapt a broad definition of planning to the more specific task of instructional planning. Within this context, plans are designs for guiding students' involvement in learning activities.

As a framework, consideration should be given to (1) the objectives of the lesson, (2) the sequence of methods and strategies to be employed by the teacher, and (3) the extent to which the students have achieved the objectives. These three major aspects are a part of every teacher's preparation for instruction, although they may not be accorded equal importance or receive equal attention. The unit and daily plans designed as preparation for instruction are dependent on the intuitive and rational decisions made by teachers about their students, the content and skills to be taught, and the instructional style and situation.

FOCUS QUESTIONS

1. What are some general conclusions about teacher-planning practices that can be drawn from research?
2. What are the differences between goals and objectives, and how are they essential to the planning process?

3. How do the different domains of learning contribute to the complexity of student learning and behaving?
4. How do the selection and sequencing of instructional techniques, methods, and strategies contribute to effective teaching?
5. Why is planning so essential to reflective decision making about instruction?

OVERVIEW

Starting with the premise that effective teaching in large part reflects careful planning, this chapter endeavors to describe the three major components of plans—objectives, instructional approaches, and evaluation—and to explain the different types of long- and short-range planning. Emphasis is given to how teachers can use this information to make reflective decisions about the plans they design to guide instructional efforts.

SCENARIO

Virginia Grove is a 5th-year social studies teacher at a large suburban high school. It is the last period of the school day. Virginia's study hall is small and the students are occupying themselves with completing homework assignments. The two students in the back of the room talking quietly are not a disruption, so she has some time to reflect on how she can wrap up the Civil War unit the class has been studying for the past two weeks. For the past several years she has done this by reviewing the major battles and discussing the surrender of Lee to Grant at Appomattox Courthouse in 1865. Last year she had enough time to show a short film of the war based on original Mathew Brady photographs.

As Virginia reflects on the class's activities up to this point, she is concerned that most of the time has been spent on political and military aspects of the war, such as the causes, elections, comparisons of the North and South, and the battles. She recalls that in a Civil War history course she had in graduate school last year, the instructor, in his lecture on the final campaign, aroused her feelings about the tragedy of war. Her students, she felt, should learn about war in its most basic human terms. Does the school library have a copy of Grant's memoirs and another source documenting common soldiers' experiences and attitudes? Grant's perceptions of the surrender and the soldiers' feelings would help her communicate to students the emotional dimension of war. She makes note of several questions that might serve as the basis of a discussion of feelings about war and to stimulate higher-level thinking about war's futility. Could she use a small group activity to share feelings and ideas? Why not have the students assume the role of a Southern or Northern soldier who thinks about returning home after the surrender is announced? The small groups could compose hypothetical letters expressing their feelings about war as related to the feelings the soldiers might have had. She wonders if the "think-pair-share" cooperative-learning approach would work to structure the sharing a little more?

As the period draws to a close she recalls that the public library has a large history section. Surely she can find some primary sources there if the school library does not have them. Virginia starts toward the library. Better check whether Wednesday would be okay to have her students in the library to do a short research project comparing the American Civil War with recent civil wars in other countries. This will give her two days to have the students explore the concept of "civil war" using several past and present conflicts. Virginia smiles at the thought of this assignment because the in-service day speaker on the new curriculum standards for social studies had stressed the importance of relating the past to the present to help students construct meaning about the relevance of U.S. history. What was the name of the recently published diary written by a young Bosnian teenager in the siege of Sarajevo? Apparently some reviewers had said it was great insight into the horrors of war and were comparing it to the *Diary of Anne Frank*. She thinks about seeing Amanda White, the new English teacher, to find out more about this book and to see how it might be integrated into the Civil War lesson. What about the possibility of doing an integrated social studies–English unit with Amanda?

As she says hello to the principal in the hall, it occurs to her that she should check the newly revised U.S. history course of study to be certain that she has fulfilled all of the objectives listed for the Civil War. She begins to feel very good about the upcoming lessons.

RESEARCH AND THEORETICAL BASE

Virginia Grove used a systematic approach to planning the end of the Civil War unit. She carefully considered instructional methods used in the past and what the students had learned during the unit to design lessons based on students' needs and interests. Decisions related to planning were made reflectively. In addition, several characteristics of Virginia's approach to planning can be supported by current principles and research on planning.

The precept that effective planning is essential for effective teaching is a familiar one to teachers. In the past, so little research was done on planning that this was a statement of faith rather than certainty. Although a substantial body of research exists relating teacher behaviors and techniques to achievement, it has only been within the last 15 years that significant research has been conducted on planning. Most of it has been descriptive and has been conducted at the elementary school level. Generalizations based on this research must be considered tentative, but they do have implications for teachers preparing unit and daily lessons on the secondary level.

Historically, methods texts have consistently recommended a remarkably similar format for planning unit and daily lesson plans. One universally accepted principle has been that objectives must be specified first to provide direction for the teacher and students as learning activities are implemented. Decisions then need to be made about the content and about which instructional approaches should be used to achieve the objectives.

What does research say about teachers' actual planning practices? In a review of research on planning, Clark and Yinger (1979) found that teachers generally have not faithfully applied the principles advocated by teacher educators. In general, the studies conducted by Peterson, Marx, and Clark (1978) and Morine (1976) in a variety of settings with a range of pupils showed that teachers considered content and instructional strategies before objectives as they planned for classes. Most of the time that teachers spent on planning was used in making decisions about the instructional context; far less time was spent on objectives and evaluation.

Such findings bear careful scrutiny in light of research on effective teaching that has identified a focused approach to instruction as a characteristic of effective teachers. Levin with Long (1981) analyzed a substantial number of studies relating students' knowledge of instructional goals to achievement. Although some disagreement occurred, generally it was found that students achieved more if the teacher had informed them of the objectives in specific terms. It was concluded that instructional objectives facilitated learning when students were shown what was to be accomplished and how they were to do it. Objectives in these studies apparently served to provide students with a sense of direction and security.

Teachers also consider classroom-management approaches when planning. Thornton (1991) found, in his review of research, that teachers planned with multiple goals primarily related to subject matter and classroom management/socialization. Sometimes these goals were competing, and the latter area may have become more influential in determining the direction of planning.

Some other interesting conclusions have been made based on research about teachers' planning practices. Clark and Yinger (1980) found that teachers spent approximately 12 hours per week engaged in instructional planning. The planning process begins with a general idea that moves through phases of continual modification and elaboration. Teachers' written plans reflect only a small portion of the total plan. Most remain in the teacher's mind. Clark and Peterson (1986) concluded, "Substantial teacher energy is devoted to structuring, organizing information, and managing limited instructional time" (p. 260).

In a study conducted by Earle (1992), experienced elementary and secondary teachers were surveyed and interviewed about their planning practices. One very interesting finding was that many teachers used mental imagery in the planning process. They visualized what the lesson would be like and how it might unfold in practice, including anticipating problems. Consequently, planning goes on more in the mind than on paper for many teachers.

It has also been found that the development of routines in planning increases teacher efficiency and flexibility. To a great degree, routine helps reduce the complexity and unpredictability of teaching, thereby allowing teachers more time and energy to devote to other activities. Beginning teachers in particular should also realize that long-term benefits can be derived from concentrated planning during the first weeks of the school year. During this time teachers develop a workable system of procedures, time allocations, groupings, schedules, and outlines. For the most part, their established systems remain in effect for the entire school year (Evertson & Emmer, 1982).

Two studies conducted several years ago compared the planning habits of novice and experienced elementary teachers. Westerman (1991) analyzed information from five experienced suburban teachers and their student teachers. She found that experienced teachers had a more comprehensive view of the knowledge taught and of the learners. Novices narrowly focused their planning on achieving objectives rather than accommodating student needs by making connections with what they already knew. This instructional component of comprehensively viewing the classroom and integrating new information with old are basics of constructivist pedagogy.

In a second study comparing the planning practices of experienced and novice teachers, Tyson (1991) found that experienced teachers tended to tailor their lessons around important and difficult components of the subject matter, thus giving them greater emphasis. Novice teachers rarely did this. Also, experienced teachers were more willing to check for student understanding of skills that had been previously taught rather than assuming they all learned as novice teachers tended to do.

Another thrust of educational research has been determining which teacher-controlled learning-environment variables have an impact on students' achievement. Weil and Murphy (1982) reviewed teacher-effectiveness research and found that students tended to achieve more in teacher-directed and controlled learning environments. Within these environments a strong academic focus is evident, students are actively involved in learning with minimal off-task behavior, and the teacher holds students accountable for their work. Brophy and Good's (1986) review of research on teacher behaviors and student achievement supported this closely related finding: The teachers producing students who achieved most had planned and organized daily prior to instruction.

Cooper (1990) defined an effective teacher as "one who is able to bring about intended learning outcomes" (p. 3). Given the current findings from research and the complexity of decisions that must be made anticipating and reacting to the immediate classroom situation, it is extremely difficult to visualize an effective teacher at work in the classroom who has not made careful decisions about evaluation procedures, goals, methods, and strategies.

APPLICATION TO PRACTICE: PLANNING DIRECTION

Decision Making as the Basis for Planning

In one sense, as was implied in chapter 1, life is inevitably a series of decisions. Every conscious behavior one engages in follows a decision to perform that behavior. But most decisions occur as habit, conditioning, or simple response. In teaching, examples of such habit decisions include calling for order when the bell rings, taking attendance, recognizing students who raise their hand to ask a question, and watching the clock to make sure the lesson is completed in time. None of these decisions requires reflection.

At a somewhat higher level, decisions require some reflection, and involve making fairly straightforward choices. Some examples of reflective decisions are choosing whom to call on to answer a particular question, determining the point at which a source of disruption requires overt attention, and deciding whether a particular item should be included on the unit test.

At the highest level, decisions require extensive reflection, often involving synthesis and evaluative thinking. The decisions made at lower levels might generally be characterized as process oriented. At the highest level, the decisions are more likely to be purpose oriented. Some examples of this type are determining what seating arrangement best facilitates instruction, choosing the appropriate referent to evaluate particular episodes of learning, and selecting certain remediation activities for children with particular learning difficulties. This level of decision making was evident in the scenario, in Virginia Grove's approach to planning the culmination of the unit.

Planning requires attention at the highest level of decision making. When planning is ineffective or marginally effective, very likely it is because that planning has received perfunctory attention rather than serious reflection. The "mindlessness" that Silberman (1970, p. 10) recognized in classrooms and that Goodlad (1983) implicitly reaffirmed could be due in large measure to the lack of thoughtfulness that teachers have given planning. Therefore, teachers should give deliberate attention to the following questions as they develop their plans.

What concept, topic, or skill is most important for the students to learn at this time in this class? It is quite possible, given a particular textbook, syllabus, or past practice, to proceed to the next unit of work without any serious consideration of whether it is the most appropriate one. What then is the rationale for each particular unit and the sequences that are planned? Is this the most defensible unit, given all feasible alternatives? Furthermore, do students have the appropriate prior ability and knowledge to achieve the goals of the unit?

How can the teacher ensure students' motivation for studying this topic or unit? Motivation is arguably the most basic factor in students' learning. Ultimately, students choose what they learn, and the extent to which they learn it. Their values and priorities are inevitably involved. To take students for granted, to predicate their interest or intent, is a self-deception of which teachers are occasionally guilty. Thus, how can the teacher initiate momentum in studying and learning, given a particular group of students (each unique), with their background, interests, and predispositions?

What methods and strategies should be employed in teaching this topic or unit? This question is, in large measure, complementary to the motivation question, but does deserve separate consideration. If the most effective long-term learning results when students find personal meaning in the outcomes, then what approaches are likely to result in achieving personal meaning? Those methods that only expose students to ideas are efficient in terms of time, but unlikely to make a strong impact. For example, Virginia Grove could have concluded the Civil War unit with a lecture reviewing the important facts related to the war.

At the other end of the continuum, those methods that involve the students experientially require large expenditures of time, but are more likely to be peak experiences that will affect students in significant ways. This theory is the reason Virginia chose to expose her students to primary accounts of Civil War soldiers' feelings and experiences and to make connections with their feelings about war in general. Given time considerations and the importance of outcomes, what should be the balance among strategies? Furthermore, given students' different learning styles and spans of attention, what variety of methods will optimize outcomes?

How should students' progress in achieving the goals of the unit and lesson objectives be determined? Teachers need to know the extent to which students are learning the content, knowledge, skills, and attitudes being taught. Without this feedback on a regular basis, planning lacks specific direction. How often should the students be evaluated? What means might be used to assess, informally and formally, students' effort and progress?

Planning Act

Planning begins as the teacher initiates thinking about possible learning activities for subsequent classes. The procedure for such planning appears to be straightforward, systematic, and logical. It involves developing objectives, selecting subject matter and associated materials, choosing strategies and methods to be employed, and deciding how to evaluate the achievement of intended outcomes. This approach is typically recommended in textbooks on instruction and by methods-course instructors. Preservice students and student teachers, in particular, are pressured to comply with this rational model.

Ultimately, the plan actually written by the teacher may reflect a format somewhat similar to that already described. But planning is essentially the intellectual process that occurs in the mind of the teacher, more so than the mechanical process of writing it. As previously mentioned, research indicates that teachers rarely plan according to this approach. Objectives, as such, play a very little part in planning (although they are subsequently useful for communicating learning intentions to students). However, they can be a valuable focus for the lesson, particularly for the beginning teacher.

Although textbooks and instructors apparently subscribe to the assumption that planning is self-evidently a logical process, in actual practice planning is more psychological and intuitive. It is more analogous to developing one's own original cocktail sauce than baking a cake from a recipe. Therefore, as one engages in serious planning, it should be done in a natural way, while considering knowledge to be taught, ability and interest of students, time constraints, and materials available.

Consider Virginia Grove's situation described at the opening of this chapter. Virginia had reason to believe that the way she had been teaching the final campaign of the Civil War had been fairly successful. Students had been nominally interested, more so even than with some of the earlier lessons within the unit dealing with the causes, battles, and other aspects of the war.

Nevertheless, Virginia had the nagging sense that somehow this was not enough. The unit had taken on the form of a dispassionate narrative of political and military events rather than a dramatic and dynamic conflict of values. The students had too little realization of the bitterness and agony that had gripped a young, uncertain nation. Unfortunate as the ugly episode was, there were useful insights that the students may have acquired from studying it. As high school students, they were capable of perceiving the Civil War and, as an extension, any war in its tragic human terms. The Civil War may serve better than any other war for this purpose, for it placed Americans in the position of methodically killing other Americans—an unthinkable and outrageous act in conditions other than war.

With this new perspective in mind regarding the potential the Civil War unit could serve, Virginia realized that the instructional methods she had used previously, primarily involving reading, lecture, recitation, guided discussion, and films, were inadequate to stimulate students' expression of feelings. Students needed to become involved with more than the simple processing of knowledge that had characterized most of the unit. A vicarious association with one who suffered the most from the consequences of war—the common Northern or Southern soldier—had to be established. She chose the small-group method to allow students to express and share feelings elicited by composing a soldier's letter.

The chapter began with the statement, "all teachers plan." By now it should be apparent that a major requisite for effective teaching is a consistently conscientious effort toward planning. This effort was quite evident in Virginia's preparation for wrapping up the Civil War unit. The decisions she made regarding content and instructional approach for the lesson were based on her judgments about students' progress and the balance of the kinds of learning and experiences they had to date. The result was a dynamic and innovative plan.

Long- and Short-Range Planning

It is time now to examine more closely the structure of a typical lesson plan. The format is easily recognized by teachers. Following it as one plans will greatly increase the probability of a beneficial learning experience for students.

A useful way of analyzing teacher plans is initially to separate them into three broad categories: long-range plans, unit plans, and daily lessons. Each has a different purpose, a different level of generality, and covers a different time span.

Long-range plans are generally developed for a semester, a year, or perhaps longer. They are called by various names such as course of study, syllabus, or curriculum guide. They usually include global course or program goals, a content or topic outline, major concepts and generalizations, and a proposed weekly time schedule. In Virginia Grove's case, the curriculum guide is for 11th-grade U.S. history.

Unit Plans. Unit plans are the intermediate stage of planning. They reflect several long-range course goals and are the means of organizing a discrete aspect of the course of study. Unit plans serve as a basis for developing a set of related daily teaching plans, and may extend from one to six weeks, or longer. Unit plans can include general goals, a rationale, major generalizations and concepts, diagnostic tests, instructional methods and strategies, evaluation procedures, and learning resources. At the middle or junior high school level, an example unit is "Uses of Fractions"; a high school example is "The Legacy of the Transcendentalists." The title of Virginia Grove's unit was "The Civil War."

Some teachers simply plan day-to-day without first developing a unit plan. Often the textbook is the only source for these plans, which in this case consists of only an outline of content. Without the unit plan to aid in organizing ideas and approaches, teaching is likely to lack cohesiveness, continuity, and relevance. A unit plan is essential to maximize a teacher's, particularly a beginning teacher's, influence as a facilitator of students' learning and experiencing. Table 5.1 shows a sample unit plan, adapted from one developed by Nona Chambers of Anaconda, Montana.

Daily Plans. The daily teaching plan takes as its point of departure the general goals and broadly defined instructional strategies of the unit plan. In effect, it is a schedule of teacher approaches and student learning activities described in some detail. The lesson plan provides the teacher with organization and specific direction daily. The daily teaching plan includes one or more specific objectives, a sequential arrangement of instructional methods and strategies, and a procedure for evaluation.

Widespread differences occur among teachers regarding the exact form and degree of detail in daily planning. Experienced teachers generally do not need to prepare extensive daily lessons because they have taught similar lessons previously. Their daily plans may be brief outlines of objectives, methods, and evaluation and can be recorded in a typical lesson-plan book. The beginning teacher, however, has very little experience on which to draw for effective instructional approaches. For this teacher, thorough planning must compensate for experience, suggesting that the beginning teacher needs more than a brief outline. Plans developed in some detail—and this will vary from teacher to teacher—are necessary to increase the probability of effectiveness. Examples of daily lesson-plan

Table 5.1   Example Unit Plan

Unit Focus: Aging

Grade: 6

Subject: Multidisciplinary, with emphasis on reading

Unit Duration: 2 weeks

I. GOALS

The students will:

become familiar with the variety of personalities of the elderly;

infer the importance of art as a means to bring together the older and younger generations;

understand the role advertisements play in stereotyping the elderly;

determine how current music has depicted the elderly;

analyze the ways in which the elderly interact with other members of the family;

realize the possibilities for a productive life in old age;

understand the contributions of the elderly from a historical perspective;

realize how young and old people can relate socially;

become aware of how people deal with the death of a loved one and one's own dying;

speculate how people in their homes and community can help and learn from the elderly.

II. TOPICS

Different kinds of grandparents

Art as a bridge to understanding being old

Stereotyping of the elderly through advertising

Elderly in today's music

Elderly in family settings

Creativity in old age

Famous oldsters

Relating to the elderly

Death and dying

Helping the elderly

III. INSTRUCTIONAL PROCEDURES

    A. Discussion based on students' differing perceptions, ideas, and feelings related to the issues and personalities in the book *Grandpa*.

    B. Students create their own self-portraits using a variety of art mediums and draw pictures of what they expect to look like when they are about 70 years of age. Individual discussions with students on differences between portraits.

    C. Students locate advertisements that show how society depicts the elderly, share with the group, make judgments about stereotyping, and speculate how the advertisements could be changed to a more positive view of the elderly.

    D. A variety of songs will be played related to the elderly ("When I'm 64"— Beatles; "Old Folks"—from *Jacques Brel Is Alive and Well and Living in Paris*; "It Was a Very Good Year"—Sinatra; etc.). Students will share their opinions through discussion about the meanings of the words and how the elderly are depicted.

    E. Role playing will be used to depict the elderly and analyze how the elderly interact with members of the family. Several reenactments will take place based on students' impressions, opinions, positive and negative stereotypes, and perceptions of reality.

    F. Individual student reports on famous oldsters including inferences about their motivations to be productive and creative beyond 70 years of age. Optional activity is student sharing of reports to class.

    G. Students will view the film *Peege* about an elderly woman experiencing isolation in a nursing home. After students respond individually to questions in written form about the film, small groups will be formed for students to share responses, experiences, and attitudes.

    H. Students read the book *About Dying*. Discussion on the feelings about the characters, their opinion about the book, and their own personal experiences with death such as with a relative, friend, or pet.

    I. Unit culmination: Review of students' learnings and appeal to students to become actively involved in activities and programs related to the elderly in the community. Perhaps the inquiry method can be used if the class perceives an issue that they care to investigate formally or a problem they wish to attempt to solve.

IV. EVALUATION

    Informal observation of students within large- and small-group discussions and during listening (records), viewing (film), and doing (art) activities.

    Formal evaluation of students' written reports on famous oldsters. Students' advertisements brought to school will also be graded.

(continued)

153

Table 5.1   Example Unit Plan (continued)

V. RESOURCES

    A. Books. *Grandpa*, Barbara Borack; *About Dying*, Sara Bonnett Stein; *The Family at Sunday Dinner*, Marcia Cameron; *Age and Youth in Action*, Gray Panthers; *Getting Beyond Stereotypes*, George Maddox

    B. Records. "When I'm 64," Beatles; "Old Folks,"from *Jacques Brel Is Alive and Well and Living in Paris*; "Hello in There," Bette Midler; "Old Friends," Simon and Garfunkel; "No Time at All," from *Pippin*; "And When I Die," Blood, Sweat, and Tears; "It Was a Very Good Year," Frank Sinatra

    C. Film. *Peege*, Phoenix Films

formats are included in Table 5.2, and two illustrative secondary lesson plans are included in Table 5.3.

Goals and Objectives in Planning

As has been stated, goals and objectives tend to come after the fact, even though they are usually incorporated as the first section of a formally written plan. As investigation of teachers' planning habits reveals, if objectives are not usually used as a basis for developing learning activities, they are helpful later in making explicit what otherwise are only implicit intended outcomes from studying a given topic or unit. Writing objectives after determining what subject matter is to be dealt with helps teachers clarify in their own minds the most appropriate outcomes of a unit or lesson. When these objectives are in turn communicated to the students, they provide a focus for their learning. Research on effective teaching verifies that incisively stated and clearly communicated objectives function as useful cues for students.

Learning Outcomes. Outcomes-based education (OBE) is a current, and controversial, approach to defining educational direction for students. Essentially, learner outcomes are broad program goals that students are to attain. Further, they are to demonstrate the achievement of these goals as a result of classroom instruction. Although this sounds like a sensible and logical way to structure curriculum and instruction, the problem is that all kinds of questions emerge: To what extent should outcomes reflect values? What are the levels of student competency to be demonstrated? How can they be assessed? For example, goal number 3 of Ohio's "Model Competency-Based Social Studies Curriculum" is "to enable learners to work with others, make informed judgments and decisions; act in accordance with democratic processes and principles" (Ohio Department of Education, 1994, p. 10). Two learner outcomes associated with this goal are "construct reasoned judgments to support, reject, or generate alternative issue positions; and advocate a choice (using evidenced-based decision making) and act accordingly"

Table 5.2 Examples of Daily Lesson-Plan Formats

These formats are designed particularly for planning the use of the four primary instructional methods presented in chapter 7.

FORM 1 (LECTURE):

    I. Objectives
    II. Instructional Approach
        A. Entry: Preparation for Learning
        B. Presentation
        C. Closure: Review of Learning
    III. Evaluation

FORM 2 (INQUIRY):

    I. Objectives
    II. Instructional Approach
        A. Entry: Preparation and Clarification of a Problem, Issue, or Query
        B. Formation of Hypotheses
        C. Collection of Data
        D. Test Hypotheses
        E. Closure: Drawing Conclusions
    III. Evaluation

FORM 3 (DISCUSSION):

    I. Objectives
    II. Instructional Approach
        A. Entry: Identification of Problem, Issue, or Topic
        B. Clarification
        C. Investigation
        D. Closure: Summary, Integration, Application
    III. Evaluation

FORM 4 (SIMULATION GAMING):

    I. Objectives
    II. Instructional Approach
        A. Entry: Orientation
        B. Participant Preparation
        C. Simulation/Enactment Operations
        D. Closure: Debriefing Discussion
    III. Evaluation

Table 5.3 Example Lesson Plan (Reflective Discussion)

SECONDARY SCIENCE

I. OBJECTIVES

    A. The students will suggest solutions to a hypothetical community-pollution problem.

    B. The students will appraise the proposed solutions and select the most feasible one.

II. INSTRUCTIONAL METHODS AND LEARNING ACTIVITIES

    A. *Entry: Identification of Problem, Issue, or Topic*—Students read a hypothetical account of a local gas station owner who knowingly pollutes the stream flowing behind the station by emptying gas and oil wastes into it daily.

    B. *Clarification*—Ask questions to have students review the facts of the hypothetical account. What wastes were dumped into the stream? How much was being dumped daily? What was the noticeable effect on water life? How did the owner rationalize his actions?

    C. *Investigation*—Ask questions to have students speculate about possible solutions to the problem: If you were a member of the community and knew the owner was violating the law, what could you do about it? What are the alternatives? What might be some consequences of the alternatives? Do the consequences conflict with your values? What might be some legal implications?

    D. *Closure: Summary, Integration, Application*—Have students appraise the suggested alternative solutions and decide on one approach: Which do you consider the best and why?

III. EVALUATION

Students write a brief paragraph summarizing their selection of a problem solution and providing support.

MIDDLE SCHOOL READING

I. OBJECTIVES

    A. The students will explain why moral issues are difficult to resolve.

    B. The students will evaluate Joey's circumstances and decide whether they would keep the $5.00 he found or return it to the stranger who lost it.

II. INSTRUCTIONAL METHODS AND LEARNING ACTIVITIES

    A. *Entry: Identification of Problem, Issue, or Topic*—Students read the short story (or teacher reads the story), "Finders Keepers?"

    B. *Clarification*—Ask questions to have students review the facts of the hypothetical account of a stranger who unknowingly drops a $5.00 bill out of his pocket. Joey notices. Does he have a dilemma? If so, what is it?

    C. *Investigation*—Ask questions to have the students determine alternatives open to Joey: What could Joey do? What might the man say to Joey if he returned the $5.00? What could Joey buy with it?

    D. *Closure: Summary, Integration, Application*—Ask questions to have students decide what they would have done in the same situation: What would you do? Why do you feel that way? Has this ever happened to you?

III. EVALUATION

The thoughtfulness of the students' answers will indicate the extent to which they can deal effectively with the moral issue.

(p. 10). While both are clearly designed to prepare students for active citizenship, they are also value related and difficult to assess. The problem is that certain special-interest groups are objecting to schools teaching anything other than cognitive knowledge and basic skills and assessing in any way other than tests.

OBE has attracted a number of special-interest groups dissatisfied with the current state of education in the United States. They are interested in the wide range of issues associated with designing learner outcomes: "OBE has become a lightning rod for criticisms that opponents have about many different school practices" (O'Neil, 1994, p. 4).

Rather than focus on learner outcomes as the basis for designing units and lessons, we have decided to continue the practice of emphasizing goals for unit plans and different types of objectives for daily lessons.

Program Goals. Those broad and general objectives written to cover units of instruction are often termed *goals*. Very often they incorporate verbs such as *understand, comprehend, know, realize, appreciate*, and *create*. Goals often deal with the intended learning at the level of concepts to be acquired. For example:

      The students will know the parts and operation of five power woodworking machines (industrial arts).

      The students will realize the purpose for conducting lab experiments using a systematic-analytical approach (science).

The students will understand how values are formed (social studies).

The students will perceive how the concept of role is used to create credible and consistent characterization in a story (English).

Although there is no research that supports one preferable style of expressing goals, the convention adopted by most authors in the professional literature is useful. If nothing else, it tends to lend credibility to the objectives as they are reviewed by other knowledgeable educators (e.g., the principal or supervisor who has occasion to examine the teacher's plans).

The convention involves simply (1) using "students" as the subject of the statement, that is, posing the students as the actors rather than those acted on; (2) having each goal statement express just one broad outcome or learning task; and (3) keeping this statement as brief and precise as possible. Although at first glance this may seem simple enough, some practice is necessary to master the skill. A friendly, knowledgeable critic can be helpful in this regard. The following is a list of several social studies goals that might have been presented in Virginia Grove's U.S. history curriculum guide for the Civil War:

The students will experience the feelings soldiers have about war.

The students will know the major issues and events that led the United States into the Civil War and other wars.

The students will become familiar with the major historical schools of thought and their interpretations related to the causes of wars in which the United States participated.

The students will know the strategies, leaders, and outcomes of major battles of wars.

Goals are a generally accepted part of a unit plan. No particular controversy exists over whether or not they should be used or how they should be stated. The situation is not so placid with objectives, which are more explicit statements of outcomes of particular lessons. For years, a major controversy has existed over whether objectives must be stated behaviorally. The argument is made that learning is defined as a change in behavior, and objectives, therefore, should describe the expected change in observable terms. Only when this approach occurs can teacher accountability be straightforwardly assessed. Opponents of behavioral objectives contend that many important learning outcomes cannot feasibly be measured, that many learning outcomes cannot even be anticipated, and, in any event, that learning is highly individual.

The authors have no final resolution for this long-standing controversy, and research provides no definitive answer. Any answers, it seems, are likely to be more related to individual choice than to general consensus. Nevertheless, the authors offer some suggestions for consideration in the matter of writing objectives.

Instructional Objectives. Objectives at higher levels of thinking are more difficult to specify in precise form. Making overly precise statements in these instances is a forced, artificial task for the teacher. Furthermore, learning at these levels becomes more individualized. Working routine mathematics problems produces a similar skill in each of the students involved; deriving meaning from a story has as many outcomes as there are students reading it. Therefore, where the learning experience provides for a range of outcomes or variability based on the perceptions of the learners, instructional objectives are most appropriate. The term means their use is predicated on the assumption that the act of engaging in certain learning experiences is important even though the outcome is not specifically predictable. The degree of achievement of these objectives is difficult to measure, as pointed out by proponents of behavioral objectives. However, the value of an objective is not so much whether it can be measured as whether it guides students toward worthwhile learning and informs students of the teacher's intent for their learning. The instructional objective is specific and relates to singular subjects and grade levels. It includes the following parts:

1. *Audience*—who is to do the task?
2. *Behavior*—what is the task to be completed?

The parts can easily be identified in an example instructional objective:

Students will write their own ending to the story "The Lady and the Tiger."

Some additional examples of these objectives are listed here:

(Audience)   (Behavior)
Students will *summarize the meaning of "The Fox and the Grapes" in two or three sentences.*
Students will *state one example different from any previously given about how they have applied math in an important way for personal purposes.*
Students will *defend a position they take on dealing with illegal aliens in the United States.*

Virginia Grove might have used the following instructional objectives in her planning:

(Audience)   (Behavior)
Students will *compare the role of women in new fields during the Civil War with their role during World War II.*
Students will *write a hypothetical letter home after Lee's surrender to Grant based on accounts of the Civil War recorded by common soldiers.*
Students will *explain why the Civil War strengthened the national government.*

Note that instructional objectives often may be read as activities as much as outcomes. There is less precision, and even the possibility of ambiguity, in such statements. However, some kinds of activities may be considered ends in themselves. To have simply attempted to find a personal meaning or develop a sound position on an issue are worthwhile intellectual activities.

Behavioral Objectives. In instructional instances in which the outcomes are clearly observable and quantifiable, objectives written in terms of pupil performance provide the clearest possible learning cues for students. These are called *behavioral objectives* and are sometimes referred to as *pupil-performance objectives.* When the learning involves, for example, working mathematics problems correctly, identifying direct objects, placing living organisms in appropriate taxonomic categories, or typing some average number of words per minute, specific statements of competency levels are especially useful. Behavioral objectives include the following parts:

1. *Audience*—who is to accomplish the task?
2. *Behavior*—what is the task to be accomplished?
3. *Condition*—what are the circumstances for performing the task?
4. *Degree*—at what level of proficiency is the task to be accomplished?

The parts can easily be identified in an example objective:

(Audience)   (Behavior & Degree)   (Condition)
Students will correctly *complete eight addition problems* on *a quiz that includes 10 problems.*

The following are several other examples of specific behavioral objectives:

> *Students* will correctly *identify at least four direct objects in context given a news item from their* Scholastic Magazine.

> *Given a list of five living organisms, students* will *key them into the appropriate family.*

> *Students* will *type copy in standard form at 40 words per minute with a maximum of two errors per minute of typing.*

Virginia Grove might have used these if she had been using the behavioral format for objectives:

> *Students* will *identify four of the five provisions of the Compromise of 1850.*

> *Students* will *write a 500-word essay comparing the Civil War with one civil war in a foreign country since 1945, incorporating within the narrative at least four similarities.*

Domains and Levels

As teachers devise goals and objectives for their unit and daily teaching plans, another fundamental consideration must be addressed: What level of student learning will be targeted? In other words, will the information, attitudes, or skills to be learned be offered at introductory and basic levels, at more advanced and abstract levels, or, more likely, somewhere in between? Goals and objectives can be classified by areas or domains. Each domain reflects a particular set of beliefs and assumptions about how students learn and behave:

> *Cognitive domain*—objectives that have as their purpose the development of students' intellectual abilities and skills.
>
> *Affective domain*—objectives that have as their purpose the development of students' emotional growth and values development and clarification.
>
> *Psychomotor domain*—objectives that have as their purpose the development of students' motor and coordination abilities and skills.

Each domain consists of a hierarchy of levels that reflect a range of student behaviors from simple to complex. As objectives are devised, knowledge of the domains and levels are useful in providing students with opportunities to engage in a wide variety of behaviors to accommodate their diverse interests, needs, and abilities. Knowledge of the levels also assists teachers in making decisions about individualizing instruction. The three domains and their hierarchies of levels are presented with an emphasis on the cognitive domain because of its wide acceptance and application. Examples of educational goals and objectives are provided.

Cognitive Domain. Bloom (1956) provided teachers with a taxonomy, or hierarchy, of objectives appropriate for classifying behaviors in the cognitive domain. The taxonomy consists of six levels ranging from *knowledge*, with a focus on eliciting facts-oriented reproductive thinking, to *evaluation*, which represents sophisticated, high-level productive thinking. The levels, which all relate to developing students' intellectual abilities and skills, are as follows:

1. *Knowledge*—emphasis on remembering information. Characteristic student behaviors include: define, state, name, recall, identify. Examples:

   The students will know the characteristics of Impressionistic paintings (program goal).
   The students will correctly identify 45 out of the 50 state capitals (behavioral objective).

2. *Comprehension*—emphasis on understanding and organizing previously learned information. Characteristic student behaviors include: relate, describe, rephrase, compare, summarize, interpret, translate, explain. Examples:

   The students will understand the rules of soccer (program goal).
   The students will translate the given paragraph from English into French (instructional objective).

3. *Application*—emphasis on using information in pertinent situations. Characteristic student behaviors include: give an example, apply, solve, demonstrate, compute, prepare, classify, use. Examples:

The students will solve two-digit-by-three-digit addition problems (program goal).
The students will write 200-word essays on the topic of the role of the modern woman, applying the pertinent rules of grammar and logical sentence structure (behavioral objective).

4. *Analysis*—emphasis on thinking critically about information by studying its parts. Characteristic student behaviors include: give a reason, analyze, conclude, infer, generalize, identify causes and motives, support, provide evidence. Examples:

The students will distinguish between the use of melody and harmony in musical pieces (instructional objective).
The students will analyze the Secretary of the Interior's two motives in leasing federal government lands to the oil companies from the documents presented to show their understanding of the influence of the business community (instructional objective).

5. *Synthesis*—emphasis on original thinking about information by putting its parts into a new whole. Characteristic student behaviors include: develop, predict, create, synthesize, compose, devise, build, solve, write, paint, produce, speculate, hypothesize. Examples:

The students will propose a plan to support the development of a new recycling center in the community (instructional objective).
The students will design a solar home that includes the three essential factors to demonstrate their understanding of the application of passive solar energy principles (behavioral objective).

6. *Evaluation*—emphasis on making judgments about information based on identified standards. Characteristic student behaviors include: decide, opine, evaluate, appraise, judge, assess, select, agree/disagree, take a position for/against. Examples:

The students will evaluate the contribution of selected books to the development of American fictional literature (program goal).
The students will express reasons for their choice of a favorite color from the chart to demonstrate the range of preferences (instructional objective).

Affective Domain.   Although the primary emphasis in the schools has traditionally been on the development of students' cognitive learning, attempts have been made to balance intellectual learning with affective learning. Krathwohl, Bloom, and Masia (1964) classified students' attitudes, feelings, interests, and values into five levels of affectivity. The range of behaviors is from simple awareness or perception of something to internalizing a phenomenon so that it becomes a part of one's lifestyle. All the levels relate to developing students' emotional learning. Only the first three levels are presented because of their potential to be practically applied in planning for classroom instruction.

1. *Receiving*—emphasis on becoming aware of some communication or phenomenon from the environment. Characteristic student behaviors include: attend, listen, describe, identify. Examples:

    The students will acquire an awareness of different artistic expressions ranging from realism to surrealism (program goal).
    The students will listen for the different sounds characteristic of the season of spring so they may develop an awareness of sound as a form of communication (instructional objective).

2. *Responding*—emphasis on reacting to a communication or phenomenon. Characteristic student behaviors include: read, write, tell, practice. Examples:

    The students will show interest in mystery stories (program goal).
    The students will participate in a community action project to demonstrate their commitment to active citizenship (instructional objective).

3. *Valuing*—emphasis on attaching worth to something from the environment. Characteristic student behaviors include: appreciate, follow, form, justify, choose, demonstrate, show, value. Examples:

    The students will demonstrate respect for other students' property in school (program goal).
    The students will police their own and others' laboratory behaviors to show they value safety (instructional objective).

The remaining two levels of the affective domain are generally not associated with realistic goals and objectives in the secondary classroom. They involve very high-level affective structure and internalization: organization, or emphasis on organizing values into a system, and characterization, or emphasis on developing an internally consistent system by which one lives.

Psychomotor Domain. Classification of goals and objectives in the psychomotor domain is especially appropriate of the objectives generally associated with motor- and muscular-skill development at the elementary and secondary levels: art, music, physical education, business, industrial arts. Specific units within language arts (writing skills), mathematics (computers), and science (microscopes) also might emphasize the development of student behaviors in this domain.

Several approaches have been developed to classify goals and objectives in the psychomotor domain. One taxonomy has been developed by the American

Alliance of Health, Physical Education, and Recreation (Jewett & Mullan, 1977). The three major levels are (1) generic movement—emphasis on becoming aware of and displaying basic movements; (2) ordinative movement—emphasis on organizing perceptual-motor abilities to accomplish particular physical tasks; and (3) creative movement—emphasis on creating physical movement in personally unique ways. Another taxonomy was developed by Harrow (1972) that focuses on observable behaviors ranging from simple to complex: reflex movement, basic fundamental movement, perceptual abilities, physical abilities, skilled movements, and nondiscursive communication.

Applying a taxonomical, hierarchical approach to classifying goals and objectives when preparing units and daily lessons enhances teacher decision making. The nature of three different but related domains, each with many levels, suggests alternatives from which teachers can choose. Choice also increases the probability of variety in teaching and thereby the accommodation of a wide range of students' abilities, interests, and needs. Meeting individual differences in the classroom results in more effective teaching.

Sequencing of Instruction

The instructional sequence is closely related to the student learning level to be targeted during the planning stage. At this stage the teacher's concern is how the content and methods should be optimally organized to achieve the objectives established for the lesson. Another concern is arranging the objectives themselves to increase the probability that the unit goals will be attained.

Designing a logical sequence of instruction involves an analysis of the content to be taught, whether it is representative of the cognitive, affective, or psychomotor domains. The process for the teacher in teaching a generalization, for example, is to build the simpler facts and concepts into more complex relationships to enhance students' comprehension. The same process would also apply to a skill. As an illustration, social studies students would not be expected to engage in decision making that might lead to social action without first understanding and practicing the skills associated with the decision-making process. Those skills would include defining the decision to be made, identifying alternatives, examining their possible outcomes, evaluating alternative decisions, selecting the best alternative, implementing the decision, and assessing results of the action. In summary, the skill of effective decision making is complex, and for students to learn it, the teacher needs to determine the subskills involved and to sequence them in a logical order.

SUMMARY POINT

Effective teachers approach planning systematically using rational decision making. Research supports the relationship of student achievement and teachers who have planned and were organized. Selecting and devising goals and objectives are important parts of planning. Goals and objectives serve as student learning outcomes necessary to provide instructional direction for the teacher.

REVIEW: IMPORTANT PRACTICES IN PLANNING

Plans

1. Develop long-range plans (courses of study, syllabi, or curriculum guides) to cover a period of a semester or a year.
2. Develop unit plans to cover a period of one to six weeks or more.
3. Develop daily plans for a period of one to several days. Include specific objectives, methods and strategies, and evaluation.

Objectives

4. Incorporate within written program goals an audience (who is to accomplish the goals?) and a broad outcome (what is to be accomplished?).
5. Incorporate within instructional objectives an audience and behavior.
6. Incorporate within behavioral objectives an audience (who is to perform the behavior?), behavior (what is the task to be accomplished?), condition (what are the circumstances for performing the task?), and degree (at what level of proficiency is the task to be accomplished?).

Domains

7. Consider the level of student learning to be targeted when planning goals and objectives.

Sequencing

8. Use a systematic approach to planning for sequencing instruction.

APPLICATION TO PRACTICE: PLANNING FOR INSTRUCTION AND EVALUATION

The primary role of teachers in the schools is instructional, whatever form that may take. What is instruction? In its broadest definition, it is the systematic use of selected techniques, methods, and strategies to create a dynamic interface between the curriculum and the students.

Research has demonstrated that teachers generally think of the content of the lesson and the learning activities before forming objectives when making decisions about lesson planning. In general, they consider the instructional context to be the most important part of planning. This section will examine the instructional and evaluation components in the decision-making process.

Techniques, Methods, and Strategies

A major component of the instructional context is the act of instructing. The curriculum component answers the question, What shall be taught? The instructional component answers the question, How shall it be taught? They are complementary; teaching would not be possible without both of these components. To illustrate this relationship, imagine a large group lecture to high school science students. The guest speaker is using both facial expressions to communicate feeling about a topic of deep concern and gestures to emphasize major points. Overhead transparencies are used extensively to clarify and illustrate ideas. It seems to be an interesting presentation. But no words are heard and the transparencies are blank. This is instruction without content.

Now imagine a 6th-grade teacher sitting with a small group of remedial students in a circle. Each has a book of readings and a specific story has been assigned. When the reading has been completed, the teacher collects the readers and passes out mathematics books. No questions are asked by the teacher to determine the extent to which students understood the plot, nor are comments made to clarify characters' actions. Students' comments and questions are not entertained. This is content without instruction. Instruction and content are, self-evidently, inseparable.

Decisions about the instructional approach involve a consideration of three major, closely related components: techniques, methods, and strategies. As a teacher plans a lesson, these components are generally considered together. Instructional techniques are a part of every method, and methods are combined to form strategies. The question confronting every teacher planning a lesson is: which technique(s), method(s), or strategy(ies) will enable me to achieve my instructional objectives?

Techniques. Instructional techniques are combinations of teacher behaviors and skills essential for the implementation of methods and strategies. The teacher behaviors comprising techniques are relatively specific in that each one can generally be observed and analyzed in the classroom setting. Behaviors are the focus if the teacher intends to engage in a self-analysis or shared analysis of performance so as to gather systematic information to use as a basis for improving instruction. Examples of the more widely applied techniques include:

1. *Information giving*—the teacher verbally provides students with explanations and directions necessary to conduct the activities of the lesson. Skills include clarifying, providing student feedback, and using audiovisual aids.
2. *Motivating*—those verbal and nonverbal teacher behaviors that stimulate students' attention, interaction, and participation. Skills include physical movement, voice, pacing, and body language—that is, gestures, posture, facial expression, and eye contact.

3. *Supporting*—teacher uses verbal and nonverbal reinforcement and encouragement of acceptable student behaviors. Skills include the use of praise, words of courtesy, acceptance, and use of feelings and ideas.
4. *Listening*—teacher uses primarily nonverbal behaviors communicating to students that the teacher is attending to what is being said. Skills include physical distance, eye contact, silence, and facial expressions.
5. *Questioning*—teacher use of verbal statements that have an interrogative function generally requiring students to engage in specific levels of thinking. Skills include formulating convergent and divergent questions, probing, wait time, and phrasing.
6. *Managing*—teacher uses verbal and nonverbal behaviors to control student behavior and ultimately to encourage students to control their own behaviors. Skills include physical position and movement, eye contact, and facial expressions. (These are explained more fully in chapter 3.)

Although these techniques are applied by teachers as instructional methods in the classroom, not all need to be directly considered each time a lesson is planned. The extent to which techniques need to be planned will depend on the objectives of the lesson.

Methods. An instructional method is an organized arrangement of instructional techniques that is intended to achieve a discrete learning outcome. Examples of primary methods used by many teachers at all levels include:

> Formal lecture
>
> Interactive lecture
>
> Demonstration
>
> Recitation
>
> Guided discussion
>
> Reflective discussion
>
> Small-group discussion
>
> Guided inquiry
>
> Open inquiry
>
> Individualized inquiry
>
> Simulation
>
> Role playing

Although instructional methods are presented in more depth in chapter 7, several implications for planning are noted here. Methods are the backbone of instruction because they are the most basic way students have traditionally been taught. Teachers understand the nature of methods and can anticipate their positive and negative impact on students. Teachers have a preference for a method(s) most suited to their classroom situation and personality. Although teachers have specific preferences for particular methods, the variety of students' learning styles, interests, and needs within any one class suggest very strongly that they should plan to use a variety of methods. This will increase the probability of holding students' interest and attention. Teachers should also consider the different methods that can be used to attain the same objective.

Strategies. An instructional strategy is a sequential combination of methods designed to accomplish learning objectives. The methods Virginia employed to achieve the objectives associated with expressing and sharing feelings are activities that could also be considered part of a strategy. This relationship of methods and strategies is illustrated in the introductory scenario. For the past several years, Virginia Grove employed a general strategy consisting of a combination of several methods to review the final phase of the Civil War. From what can be inferred, recitation was used to review the major battles, followed by discussion to involve students in higher-level thinking about the surrender at the Appomattox Courthouse. This strategy incorporated a film that probably served the purposes of information giving and enrichment.

This year Virginia is planning to alter her approach because her objectives have changed, partially as a result of the above-average level of the students. She has tentatively decided to employ another strategy to achieve her goal of helping students to understand war in its most basic terms. First she intends to read selections from several primary Civil War sources. This is to be followed by a discussion to stimulate students' feelings about war. An alternative she is considering is to have the students form small groups in which to conduct their discussions. As a follow-up, she also thought of having each small group write a hypothetical letter that they would then share and discuss.

As she employs the discussion method, we can envision a natural emphasis on the use of the techniques of questioning and listening. If she decides to form the students into small groups, we can envision her relying on the techniques of information giving to provide students with structure and direction for the small group task and managing in an effort to keep students on-task. In summary, the strategy Virginia was planning to use consists of several methods sequentially arranged: teacher reading, large- or small-group discussion, student group writing, student reporting, and follow-up discussion.

Virginia had also begun planning an instructional approach to achieve a follow-up objective—of the students examining the concept of civil war by relating causes and results of the American Civil War with causes and results of civil wars occurring in the 1980s and 1990s. We can imagine a strategy centering on the use of inquiry in which students hypothesize commonalities of civil wars, with small groups carrying out their investigations in the library. She might then use a cooperative-learning approach to have students socially construct knowledge as they teach each other about the different civil wars they investigated. Perhaps a guided discussion, during which students predict countries and ethnic/racial groups of people potentially headed for civil war based on their findings, might wrap up the two days' work. Her instructional strategy for this final phase of the Civil War unit consisted of the use of the inquiry and guided-discussion methods and the cooperative-learning strategy.

Although most strategies are devised by teachers in this manner, a number of strategies have been formally designed and labeled by educators. Joyce and Weil (1992) identified 16 teaching models drawn from the work of educators, sociologists, psychologists, and curriculum specialists. They have assigned the models into different groups characterized by a different genre of learning goals.

This book focuses on another group of more formal strategies that have evolved from the effective-teaching research and emphasize higher student achievement. They are as follows:

1. *Active teaching*—academically focused, teacher-directed classroom instruction using sequenced and structured materials.
2. *Mastery learning*—an individualized diagnostic approach to instruction in which students proceed with studying and testing at their own rate to achieve the prescribed level of success.
3. *Cooperative learning*—the use of peer tutoring, group instruction, and cooperation to encourage student learning.

All this implies that teachers involved in daily and long-term planning need to be aware that a variety of instructional strategies exist that they can use to meet their objectives, classroom situations, and students' abilities, interests, and needs. These strategies can be informal or formal. (Additional commentary on techniques, methods, and strategies and their relationship can be found in chapters 6, 7, and 8.)

Given the wide variety of techniques, methods, and strategies from which to choose when planning a unit or daily lesson, beginning and experienced teachers should be able to understand why decision making is so important. A systematic approach to decision making becomes more valuable as the choices in a situation increase. The following are some of the questions a teacher needs to consider when choosing the instructional approach:

1. Which combination of methods and/or strategies is best to achieve the objectives of the lesson?
2. How much time is available during class for implementation of a particular method and/or strategy?
3. To what extent should the methods and/or strategies be adapted to individual students or small groups of students?
4. How can transitions between the use of methods and strategies be made smoothly and beneficially to enhance students' understanding?

5. To what extent will students be actively and passively involved during the implementation of a particular method and/or strategy?

Lesson Presentation

Planning for instruction—the implementation of specific techniques, methods, and strategies—also involves consideration of several other generic or basic teaching concerns. The preparation of objectives for the purpose of specifying learning outcomes, which provides direction for instruction, has already been discussed previously in this chapter. Similarly, content within the major domains of learning has been discussed. Other considerations, referred to as lesson presentation skills by Shostak (1990), include entry into the lesson and closure. Entry and closure generally occupy the first and last five minutes of a lesson, respectively, and are potentially the most powerful influences on students' learning. Each of these important factors should be accounted for when decisions are made about how the lesson should be presented in class.

The intent of a lesson entry is to focus students' attention on the lesson. This can be accomplished in several ways. The teacher can inform students of the goals and of what is expected of them within the lesson. In this sense the entry serves as an organizer to prepare students for an upcoming activity. Another way a teacher can focus students' attention on the lesson is to stimulate their interest as a means of getting them involved. This can often be accomplished by attracting students' attention with something puzzling, an artifact, or a problematic situation naturally related to the lesson. The entry is usually associated with the beginning of the lesson, but it can also be used to introduce a new topic within a lesson.

We can now imagine Virginia's entry to the final lesson of the Civil War, where she wanted to convey the strong feelings associated with ending the war. Perhaps she might read from Grant's *Memoirs* of his reflections while conversing with Lee over the Confederates' surrender at Appomattox Courthouse. Likewise, a dramatic reading from Zlata Filipovic's diary regarding her feelings as an 11-year-old trapped in a war she could not understand might serve as a powerful entry into the follow-up lesson relating the Civil War to the Bosnian War.

Closure also needs to be considered when planning a daily lesson. It is the wrap-up to the lesson. The teacher's intention in the closing stage of the lesson is to reinforce the key elements of the lesson and to help students transfer what they learned to the next lesson. In many respects, the closure is the complement to the entry. The closure to Virginia Grove's lesson after students shared their hypothetical letters written by Northern and Southern soldiers might be for the students to generalize the major feelings expressed in the letters. Perhaps she could leave them with a question to think about for the next day's lesson: To what extent would the feelings Civil War soldiers had in 1865 be similar to those in 1995 of Serbian and Bosnian soldiers as they think about the end of the conflict and peace in their land? This closure would help bridge the lesson to the upcoming library assignment Virginia was planning. (For a more detailed explanation of the skills, see chapter 6.)

SUMMARY POINT

Planning for instruction involves making decisions about the selection of an appropriate variety of techniques, methods, and strategies to achieve the goals and objectives of units and lessons. Research reveals that teachers actually consider instructional approaches and content before objectives when planning lessons. An appropriate sequence of planning events is: (1) consider the content to be taught and the objective(s) to be achieved simultaneously; (2) establish the method(s) necessary to achieve the objective and teach the content; (3) if appropriate, devise or select the strategy(ies) within which the methods are subsumed; (4) consider the techniques necessary to implement the methods/strategies successfully; and (5) prepare an entry to initiate learning and a closure to reinforce the impact of the lesson.

REVIEW: IMPORTANT PRACTICES IN PLANNING FOR INSTRUCTION

Content

1. Select content to be taught with careful consideration given to balancing the domains of learning: cognitive (facts, concepts, ideas, generalizations), affective (values, attitudes, feelings), and psychomotor (skills).

Techniques

2. Plan to use instructional techniques to help create the cognitive climate of the classroom.

Methods

3. Plan to incorporate a variety of instructional methods to increase students' interest and attention while striving to achieve objectives.

Strategies

4. Build a variety of instructional strategies into unit plans to meet the needs of a generally diverse student population.

Lesson Presentation

5. Decide how to focus students' attention on the lesson (entry) and how to wrap up the lesson (closure) during the planning stage.

Planning for Evaluation

Another major planning component is evaluation. Teachers need to give as careful consideration to this area as to the formation of objectives and selection of instructional approaches. Evaluation is the process of forming judgments about student progress. These judgments collectively serve as a basis for making decisions. The question facing teachers daily is the extent to which students attained the objectives set for the lesson. Over a longer period of time, teachers are concerned with achieving broader unit goals. Evaluative data gathered in response to these questions are determined by the appropriateness and specificity of the objectives, and the quality of instructional methods and strategies employed. In many respects, the outcomes of student evaluation can be a direct reflection on the teacher's effectiveness in the classroom. Consequently, the evaluation component deserves considerable attention.

Evaluation involves making judgments in the form of reflective decisions about instruction. To make decisions to redirect instruction, data need to be gathered. The major part of the evaluation process, and the most time-consuming element, is gathering information about student performance and progress. The decisions a teacher makes based on the data gathered are reflected in both short- and long-term planning.

Planning for evaluation is primarily conducted at the unit-plan and daily-lesson levels. The major concerns teachers have while planning units are determining the time when assessments of student progress should take place, the nature of the evaluation instruments, and how to interpret and represent student progress. At the daily-lesson level, teachers are primarily concerned with how data regarding student progress should be collected.

Unit Evaluation. One of the first concerns teachers have while planning for evaluation at the unit level is incorporating diagnostic and summative evaluation. Diagnostic evaluation is the formation of judgments about a student's learning potential prior to instruction. The data gathered at this preinstructional stage can be useful in helping a teacher plan to meet students' varying abilities.

Summative evaluation is the most common approach used by teachers in assessing students' performance. It is generally conducted when the students have completed an instructional unit. The most common form of summative evaluation is a written test. We can imagine Virginia Grove's two-week unit test on the Civil War consisting of a mixture of objective and subjective (essay) items. (Diagnostic and summative evaluation are further explained in chapter 9.)

Judgments resulting from summative evaluation assess the degree to which students have attained the learning objectives of the unit. Postinstructional decisions have a direct bearing on the objectives and instructional approaches to be used in the next unit. Other important decisions relate to how this same unit will be taught even more effectively in the future.

Another major concern teachers have about the evaluation process when designing a unit plan is interpreting and representing the information gathered about student performance. Interpretation is necessary to make judgments about the assignment of values (generally in the form of grades) that are representative of students' levels of progress over a specified period of time or unit of study. The teacher's basic responsibility is to decide whether to assign marks based on a comparison of individual student performance to group performance, a comparison of progress to a predetermined standard, or a comparison to past individual performance. Although the first approach has deeper historical roots and is better known, the other two approaches have had important applications over the years. (These approaches—norm-referenced, criterion-referenced, and self-referenced, respectively—are described more fully in chapter 9.)

Daily Evaluation. Daily judgments made by the teacher during instruction are part of formative evaluation. These judgments serve as a basis to make decisions about the objectives and instructional approach guiding students' learning. Daily evaluation conducted during the midinstructional phase is important so that modifications can be made in the program to increase the probability that the objectives will be achieved by the students. The major concern teachers have while planning for daily evaluation is how the student progress data should be collected.

Appropriate techniques must be selected or devised to determine whether students have achieved lesson objectives. A wide range of techniques are available for teachers to use formally or informally. When daily lesson plans are made, evaluation can be formal or informal, depending on the means used to gather data. Informal approaches might include observations of student behavior, analysis of students' contributions to group discussions, conferences with individual students, brief reviews of written homework assignments, and impressions of performance. Formal techniques might range from a test to a checklist used to judge students' contributions in a class debate. Other formal approaches might include quizzes, rating scales, and attitude-measuring instruments. However, despite these numerous choices, what is essential when evaluating students' progress is for the technique employed to provide data directly related to the objective being evaluated. Thus, evaluation, like instruction, must be planned.

SUMMARY POINT

The decisions teachers make about planning for the evaluation of students' progress are important and require thoughtful consideration. The evaluation component of planning exists as a means to determine if the goals of the unit or the objectives of the lesson were achieved. As such, the outcomes of student evaluation are a direct reflection on the effectiveness of teachers. Decisions need to be made about the timing of evaluation, the techniques used to gather information on student progress, and how to interpret and represent student progress. Each component needs considerable thought and expression in sufficient detail to be beneficial to students and teachers.

REVIEW: IMPORTANT PRACTICES IN PLANNING FOR EVALUATION

1. Give attention to planning for evaluation along with instructional approaches and planning for goals and objectives.
2. At the unit level, plans need to be made for gathering information about students' learning potential prior to instruction and assessing students' performance at the completion of the unit.
3. At the unit-planning level, decisions also need to be made about interpreting and communicating the information about student performance.
4. At the daily-lesson level, decisions need to be made regarding which formal and informal techniques will be used to gather information regarding students' progress.

QUESTIONS FOR REFLECTION

1. Based on what you have learned about the scenario teacher, Virginia Grove, and her plans for the upcoming lessons ending the Civil War unit, do you think she is a good teacher? Why?
2. Locate a methods text representing your major certification area. How does what it recommends in terms of planning units and daily lessons compare with the research findings reported in this chapter?
3. How does the content of the textbook you use in one of your preparations compare with the content listed in the department's curriculum guide or course of study? What content do you teach and why?
4. Think about teaching a concept or generalization in your subject area at the grade level of your choice. To what extent can you visualize the lesson unfolding in your mind's eye as you teach it in your classroom?
5. How well do you know your subject matter? Do you have to rely on the text or do you incorporate information from a variety of additional sources as you plan lessons?
6. Do you agree that effective teaching is based on effective planning, or are there more influential practices contributing to good teaching? If so, what are they?
7. Assume that you agree with the assertion that motivation is the most basic factor in students' learning. What might you do during planning to ensure that students' motivation will be accommodated?
8. Can you recall a peak experience for you during your years in school? Why do you consider it a peak experience and how might you adapt it for use in your own classroom?

9. To what extent is the planning process logical and to what extent is it intuitive based on your own frame of reference and experience?

10. Secure a copy of a teacher's unit plan. How does it compare with the format suggested in the chapter? What improvements to the unit-planning format can you suggest?

11. What instructional approach might you build into the example unit plan on aging that would encourage 6th graders to construct meaning about what it is like to grow old?

12. Which of the two forms of objectives suggested in the chapter, instructional objectives and behavioral objectives, is most appropriate for your teaching area? Or will you use both? Why?

13. Why does education seem to emphasize achieving goals and objectives representative of the cognitive domain over those of the other domains?

14. How much time should you plan to achieve objectives representing each of the domains (cognitive, affective, and psychomotor domains)?

15. Think of instruction as you experienced it throughout your schooling. What kind of definition of instruction might you synthesize based on your experience? How does it compare with the definition presented in the chapter?

16. Of the instructional techniques presented from which you will draw as you plan to implement lessons, which one do you think is most characteristic of your instructional style or approach? Why? Which one would be a close second?

17. Think of a local, national, or international current event in the papers today. What instructional strategy might you devise to teach it during a 15-minute segment of a lesson? What methods are a part of your strategy and how does each contribute to achieving the objective you have in mind?

18. How important do you consider the entry to a lesson to be? What is one entry to a lesson that you can recall a teacher using from your schooling that grabbed and held your attention? Why was it so effective?

19. Imagine going into class without a plan, without any idea what you are going to do. What problems can you imagine unfolding during the course of the 45 minutes?

20. Suppose you were either student teaching and being observed by the college supervisor or being observed by the principal as a nontenured teacher. What might he or she say in the conference after the observation that is the best evidence that you have planned well for the lesson?

REFERENCES

Bloom, B. (Ed.). (1956). *A taxonomy of educational objectives: Handbook I. Cognitive domain.* New York: McKay.

Brophy, J., & Good, T. L. (1986). Teacher behavior and student achievement. In M. Wittrock (Ed.), *Handbook of research on teaching* (3rd ed.). New York: Macmillan.

Clark, C. M., & Peterson, P. L. (1986). Teachers' thought processes. In M. Wittrock (Ed.), *Handbook of research on teaching*. New York: Macmillan.

Clark, C. M., & Yinger, R. J. (1979). Teachers' thinking. In P. L. Peterson & H. J. Walberg (Eds.), *Research on teaching: Concepts, findings, and implications*. Berkeley, CA: Mc-Cutchan.

Clark, C. M., & Yinger, R. J. (1980). *The hidden world of teaching: Implications of research on teacher planning* (Research Series No. 77). East Lansing, MI: Institute for Research on Teaching.

Cooper, J. M. (1990). The teacher as a decision maker. In J. M. Cooper (Ed.), *Classroom teaching skills* (4th ed.). Lexington, MA: Heath.

Earle, R. S. (1992). *The use of instructional design skills in the mental and written planning processes of teachers*. Paper presented at the convention of the Association for Educational Communications and Technology, Iowa (ERIC Document ED347 987).

Evertson, C. M., & Emmer, E. T. (1982). Effective management at the beginning of the school year in junior high classes. *Journal of Educational Psychology, 74*, 485–498.

Goodlad, J. I. (1983). A study of schooling: Some findings and hypotheses. *Phi Delta Kappan, 64*(7), 465–470.

Harrow, A. J. (1972). *A taxonomy of the psychomotor domain: A guide for developing behavior objectives*. New York: McKay.

Hoover, K. H. (1972). *Learning and teaching in secondary school*. Boston: Allyn & Bacon.

Jewett, A. E., & Mullan, M. R. (1977). *Curriculum design: Purposes and process in physical education teaching-learning*. Washington, DC: American Alliance for Health, Physical Education and Recreation.

Joyce, B., Weil, M., with Showers, B. (1992). *Models of teaching* (4th ed.). Englewood Cliffs, NJ: Prentice-Hall.

Krathwohl, D. R., Bloom, B. S., & Masia, B. B. (1964). *A taxonomy of educational objectives: Handbook II. Affective domain*. New York: McKay.

Levin, T., with Long, R. (1981). *Effective instruction*. Washington, DC: Association for Supervision and Curriculum Development.

Morine, G. (1976). *A study of teacher planning: Beginning teacher evaluation study* (Tech. Rep. No. 76-3-1). San Francisco: Far West Laboratory for Educational Research and Development.

Ohio Department of Education (1994). Model competency-based social studies program [Draft]. Columbus: Ohio Department of Education.

O'Neil, J. (1994). Outcomes-based education comes under attack. *Update, 36*(3), 1, 4–5, 8.

Peterson, P. L., Marx, R. W., & Clark, C. M. (1978). Teacher planning, teacher behavior, and student achievement. *American Educational Research Journal, 15*, 413–432.

Shostak, R. (1990). Lesson presentation skills. In J. M. Cooper (Ed.), *Classroom teaching skills* (4th ed.). Lexington, MA: Heath.

Silberman, C. E. (1970). *Crisis in the classroom*. New York: Random House.

Thornton, S. (1991). Teacher as curricular-instructional gatekeeper in social studies. In J. Shaver (Ed.), *Handbook of research on teaching and learning in the social studies*. New York: Macmillan.

Tyson, P. (1991). Talking about lesson planning: The use of semi-structured interviews in teacher education. *Teacher Education Quarterly, 18*(3), 87–96.

Weil, M., & Murphy, J. (1982). Instructional processes. In H. Mitzel (Ed.), *Encyclopedia of educational research* (5th ed.). New York: American Educational Research Association.

Westerman, D. A. (1991). Expert and novice teacher decision making. *Journal of Teacher Education, 42*(4), 292–305.

CHAPTER **6** Basic Instructional Techniques

OUTLINE

Review
Questions for Reflection
Analysis Forms
References

Enthusiastic teachers who demonstrate their enjoyment of the subject and teaching have a considerable advantage in commanding student attention and stimulating their involvement.

The following three chapters comprise the central focus of the book: instruction. The first several chapters have provided ideas, information, and practice related to those components considered to be the foundation of instruction. Decision making is the most pervasive component of instruction, so much so that effective teaching is inevitably the outcome of effective decision making. Consideration of classroom climate is critical within the instructional process because optimal learning occurs only in a setting of optimal conditions. Optimal conditions also include establishing good classroom discipline for instruction and learning to take place. The foundation also necessarily includes curriculum, since instruction is focused on teaching content in one form or another. Planning is essentially a description of the instructional decisions intended to be implemented in the classroom. Instruction, as a logical consequence, is the direct application and testing of the decisions made about students, environment, content, and method.

Instruction has generally been defined as "a process by which knowledge and skills are developed in learners by teachers" (Hawes & Hawes, 1982). While the proponents of constructivism have been emphasizing the encouragement of students to assume more responsibility for their own learning, clearly the person responsible for initiating, maintaining, and evaluating the instructional process in the school is the teacher. As a process, instruction can be depicted as consisting of teacher behaviors, techniques, methods, and strategies. Basic, physical teacher behaviors comprise the primary instructional techniques of informing, motivating, supporting, questioning, and listening. A sampling of these behaviors includes gestures, voice volume, divergent questions, physical movement, and eye contact. Varying degrees of all these techniques are a part of every instructional method teachers employ in classroom settings. Guided discussion, demonstration, recitation, interactive lectures, guided inquiry, and small groups are among the most commonly used methods today. Methods are selected and sequenced by teachers during planning to form strategies that are the most comprehensive forms of instruction. Strategies can be informal and formal. Informal strategies are the most common and are extemporaneously devised during the planning phase of a lesson. Formal strategies are research based and are more highly structured. An example of a formal strategy is cooperative learning. Entry and closure are the two critical lesson-presentation components to be considered when im-

Figure 6.1 Instructional Model

plementing methods and strategies. The relationship of all these instructional components is depicted in Figure 6.1. Notice the indication of which chapters in this book provide analyses of each element.

FOCUS QUESTIONS

1. How can teachers plan entries and closures to lessons and use motivating skills to stimulate students to achieve learning goals?
2. Why is teachers' classroom questioning considered among the most influential teaching acts?
3. What is the relationship between the different types of questions teachers can ask and patterns of student thinking?
4. How can a teacher's use of supporting skills contribute or detract from the class's social-emotional climate and student learning?

5. What can teachers do to present information in the classroom in an effective way?

OVERVIEW

This chapter focuses on instructional techniques and lesson-presentation components. The research reviewed is drawn, in large part, from the so-called process-product, or process-outcome, research conducted during the past 25 years. This research has focused on determining the effect of specific teacher behaviors and instructional techniques (process variables) on students' learning outcomes (product variables). Most of the research has been concentrated on academic achievement because it is the most obvious and readily measured aspect of learning. The result of researchers' efforts has been the identification of a series of teacher behaviors and techniques that positively correlate with students' achievement. The findings of several major reviews of research and other specific research studies are reported here, supporting the contention that effective teaching consists of, in part, the purposeful and consistent display of presentation skills and specific instructional behaviors and techniques.

While the instructional techniques that serve as the focus of this chapter are those that research has found to influence students' learning of subject matter significantly, they are also key in enhancing students' understanding of what they have learned. Traditional teaching has emphasized content coverage and learning of basic facts and concepts. Textbooks have been the major source of curriculum, and teachers have relied heavily on interactive lecture and recitation as the primary teaching methods. A more contemporary view of teaching is an emphasis on covering less content and exploring topics in greater depth through the use of a variety of teaching techniques, methods, and strategies. The intent is to help students understand what they have learned by processing information at higher cognitive levels and connecting it to their experiences and what they know. Good and McCaslin (1992) referred to this form of instruction as "active teaching." It is generally associated with achieving goals related to the constructivist view of learning and teaching.

> The concept of active teaching implies that instruction becomes less direct as students mature and develop increased ability to direct their own learning, as attention changes from cognitive to affective outcomes, and as the class moves through units and shifts from a focus on lower level knowledge and skill to higher level application, analysis, synthesis and evaluation outcomes. (Good & McCaslin, 1992, p. 1376)

As teachers move from traditional to active teaching, they will need to engage in more extensive decision making, particularly during the planning stage. This is because the constructivist view requires the application of a greater variety of student-oriented instructional approaches and learning activities. The instructional techniques presented in this chapter (entry, closure, motivating, questioning, supporting, listening, and informing) have the potential to contribute toward the teacher's creation of a constructivist classroom environment in which students are challenged to learn through understanding and application.

A series of teaching-analysis instruments is included in this chapter, and in chapters 7 and 8, on effective teaching elements, methods, and strategies. These data-gathering forms are intended to be used by teachers and their support personnel (colleagues, team leaders, departmental chairs, and supervisors) as they begin to inquire formally into the nature of their teaching. The purpose of this inquiry is for teachers to become more informed and reflective about their instructional behaviors and approaches. Ultimately the data gathered can be used effectively to make decisions about improving instruction.

SCENARIO

Richard Taylor wondered how his students would react to the lesson he had planned for the day as they drifted into his 7th-period earth science class. For the past three weeks they had been studying the earth's environment, particularly its renewable and nonrenewable resources and energy. The focus had been on learning how people depend on the environment and how they can influence it. As a major goal, though, he wanted his students to participate in identifying environmental problems in Norwood, their local community. Wouldn't it be wonderful if the students actually wanted to make an effort at solving one of the problems they identified?

As the bell signaled the beginning of class, his thoughts drifted to the state science teachers' conference he attended the month before and to the session on encouraging high school–age students to become actively involved in resolving local community environmental problems. Two boys continued talking in loud voices as the period began, and several others still had not taken their seats. Generalizing from this capricious behavior, he realized that his students were probably still too immature to be interested in dealing with community problems.

"Dave and Todd, I would appreciate your attention so we can get started." Once Mr. Taylor was sure everyone was ready, he told the students, with excitement in his voice, to close their eyes and imagine an environmental crisis taking place in Norwood. After about 20 seconds he asked students to share their imagined catastrophes with their neighbors in pairs and then with the large group. Barbara described her family getting a letter from the Environmental Protection Agency (EPA) informing them that their immediate neighborhood was likely to have been built on a toxic waste dump left from an old paint-manufacturing plant that had gone bankrupt 30 years ago. Jim graphically described an imagined killer smog that enveloped their community for five days, killing several older people and a number of animals and making many people sick. It had been caused by an air inversion that created a pocket of trapped waste gases from the steel mill down the river. Shawn talked about not being able to swim in the nearby lake that summer because of the high level of pollution, and Judy thought a crisis for Norwood might be a monstrous trash-and-garbage accumulation caused by a prolonged strike by sanitation workers. Two other students volunteered to share their crises.

As Mr. Taylor slowly moved around the room maintaining eye contact with the participants of the discussion, he noticed that for several students interest was beginning to wane. He commented about the participants' vivid imaginations, thanked them for their contributions, and mentioned that they were going to be focusing on Norwood's environmental problems. "Yesterday we finished with our discussion of the dangers of nuclear energy and the problems faced by that industry. Now we need to bring our focus down to the community level. Let's leave our imagined crises for the moment and get back to reality by thinking about the present environmental situation in Norwood." He told the students their objective over the next two days was to identify at least three environmental problems Norwood was facing. "I would like you to get out your journals and take two minutes to write down either one environmental problem you think Norwood is experiencing right now or one that Norwood could realistically be facing in the near future." When the students began the assignment, Mr. Taylor circulated among them to assist individual students and keep others on-task.

"What are some of the problems you think we have?" he asked. One cited several abandoned houses in the south section of town that looked like they were ready to collapse. Another student added that they were also dangerous because they weren't boarded up. Mary thought Norwood needed to do more to promote solar-energy conservation. "Using solar energy makes so much sense, but we only have one solar home in town," she said. Harold said that he thought there was too much trash on the streets and that maybe the street cleaners were not doing their job. After some further encouragement, several other students volunteered contributions related to the lack of parks, the foul-tasting tap water, and the need for more trees and flowers downtown. Mr. Taylor wrote the last of the students' ideas on the board.

Mr. Taylor complimented the students on how observant they were of the community. "I didn't think you would have come up with the number of problems you did. Well done!" He then asked, "How do we know if these are really problems that Norwood should do something about?" After a sufficiently long pause he called on Jim, who seemed to be deep in thought. Jim commented that he thought many people in the community would have to consider something a real problem before the city government would do anything about it. "In other words," Mr. Taylor said, "a problem to one person may not be a problem to others. Would you agree?" Jim agreed and Lynn quickly opined that she didn't think a majority of people needed to consider something a problem before the city government did something about it. After all, she couldn't remember Norwood voting on an environmental problem, yet changes seemed to have come about.

Mr. Taylor could hardly contain his enthusiasm for Lynn's insight. "You have just hit on one of the major things I wanted you to learn by the end of the unit! That is, the responsibility city government has in dealing with environmental problems." Moving to the side of the room, he then took some time to describe why the city council passed legislation creating the recycling plant the previous year. The point was that the decision was made without initiation from the people and without a vote because the city council, after gathering information from a consultant, was convinced that it was environmentally beneficial to the community. Both individuals and government are responsible for the condition of the environment.

Realizing that several students were either glancing at the clock or gazing out the windows and that there were 20 minutes left in the period, Mr. Taylor decided to quicken the pace of the lesson. "How many remember the definition of a scientist's hypothesis?" Several hands went up and, after pausing, he called on Julie. She replied that it was a solution to a problem. Jim quickly added that it was a guess or proposed solution that needed checking. "How are your ideas about Norwood's environmental problems and hypotheses related?" After getting no responses, Mr. Taylor asked Chris if he had an idea.

Chris, a capable student but mentally lazy at times, responded with, "I don't know."

Mr. Taylor attempted to lead him to the idea he had in mind. "Could the class's thoughts about Norwood's environmental problems be considered hypotheses?"

"I guess so," was the reticent student's response.

Mr. Taylor confirmed his minimal response and asked the class for an explanation. David responded that the problems the class proposed were only guesses at that point because more information and opinions were needed. "Thanks, David," said Mr. Taylor.

"For homework tonight I would like you to find out if your parents agree with you." Mr. Taylor explained that the students were going to investigate a problem just like scientists, gathering data to support or refute their hypothesized environmental problems. He passed out a survey rating form for students to write down the proposed environmental problems and record parents' responses. "Tomorrow, with your help, we'll know a little more about our community's environmental condition."

During the remaining 10 minutes, Mr. Taylor had the students read a short article from the *Journal of Environmental Education* on a western community's successful attempt to make its environment safe for its citizens. He thought the article would be appealing to the students because of the dramatic confrontation between the mayor and the representatives of several self-serving special-interest groups at one of the town council meetings.

With one minute left before the bell was to ring, Mr. Taylor asked the students to pass their copies of the article to the front of the room. "Christine, which of the problems we identified do you think your parents will consider the most critical?" She thought the lack of parks and recreation areas was a real concern. Mr. Taylor was able to direct the question to two other students before the bell rang. "I think tomorrow's class will be very interesting because of the information you will be bringing in. See you then."

RESEARCH AND THEORETICAL BASE: ENTRY, CLOSURE, MOTIVATING SKILLS

The growing research related to instructional techniques, teacher behaviors, and presentation skills is influential. Attempts to discover factors that constitute effective schools and effective teaching have provided the major impetus for this body of research. School districts and university teacher-education programs have become increasingly aware of these research findings and are incorporating them into in-service and preservice programs to disseminate information on effective teaching skills that enhance students' learning.

Presentation skills are displayed in one form or another in every lesson. Based on his review of the literature, Shostak (1990) found that the entry and closure of the lesson are among the most frequently researched lesson-presentation skills. The entry is the students' first contact with the content and the methods to be used by the teacher. However, teachers infrequently introduce lessons with students' motivation in mind. The majority of teachers' task-presentation statements are neutral, and many are negative (Brophy, Rohrkemper, Rasid, & Goldberger, 1983). In their extensive review of the research, Brophy and Good (1986) concluded that students learn more efficiently and their achievement is maximized when the teacher structures the new information by relating it to what they already know.

This form of entry has been termed *set induction* (Allen & Ryan, 1969). In a series of studies conducted by Schuck (1985), it was found that students achieved and retained more knowledge when their teacher used set-induction techniques. Another consideration in the entry is novelty. Based on his review, DeCecco (1968) suggested teachers should incorporate discrepancies and the element of surprise into lessons to attract and stimulate students' attention and interest. The decisions teachers need to make about the entry to a lesson center on structuring the lesson to relate new information to previous learning and introducing topics and lessons in atypical and interesting ways. Waxman's (1987–1988) review of research on lesson entry strongly supports the positive and influential impact entries have on students' achievement.

All lessons achieve closure by virtue of the fact that finite periods of time govern lesson length. Although logic suggests that a lesson needs a closure to complement the entry, little research has been conducted on the impact of closure on student learning. Based on their review of research, Gage and Berliner (1992) concluded that closure is an important part of an instructional repertoire and teachers need to make decisions regarding how the lesson will be wrapped up and how the bridge to the next lesson will be made.

Of all the major techniques the teacher uses to teach in a classroom setting, the skills associated with motivation are the most important in terms of encouraging and stimulating students to attain lesson objectives. In a recent and exceptionally extensive meta-analysis of more than 300 research sources, Wang, Haertel, and Walberg (1994) found motivation to be one of the most significant influences on student learning. The research literature on motivation has focused on, among a variety of variables, the teacher's role in projecting an enthusiastic image. Good and Brophy (1994) identified two major aspects of enthusiasm: dynamics in presenting the material—which they called intensity—and interest in the subject matter. Both contribute toward maximizing student achievement, especially for older students (Brophy and Good, 1986). Gage and Berliner (1992) reviewed several major studies demonstrating that student learning is affected positively as teachers employ a variety of expressive behaviors the reviewers labeled as the "teacher's style." Decisions about motivation primarily center on two elements: which verbal and nonverbal behaviors to employ in the classroom to convey enthusiasm for the subject matter being taught, and which behaviors are necessary to maintain student interest and attentiveness throughout the lesson.

Motivation can also be gained by varying the instructional approach. Research supports teachers' use of instructional variety and flexibility as a means of maintaining students' attention and increasing achievement (Gage & Berliner, 1992). Based on their review, Good and Brophy (1994) found that in terms of sustaining students' interest, a variety of methods is better than the extended use of one method. Furthermore, research also suggests that the decisions a teacher makes that are related to instructional "activity structures," or methods, also influence students' attitudes and behavior, and this has an impact on instruction (Berliner, 1984). Teachers need to decide how their lessons will vary in terms of the number and kind of instructional methods and strategies to be used and the time necessary to employ them effectively within each class session.

APPLICATION TO PRACTICE

Entry

The first few minutes of a class are the most crucial times in relation to teacher impact. The entry to a lesson is generally recognized as the first instructional phase implemented immediately after the teacher has gained the attention of the students. This usually commences at the beginning of the class period. An entry can also occur several times during a lesson as the teacher makes transitions and introductions to discrete segments of any single lesson. Both of these forms of instructional entry share the common purpose of setting the learning process in motion.

The primary purposes of the entry are to focus students' attention on the learning activity, prepare them for what they are going to learn, and encourage them to get involved. Too often classes begin with statements such as, "Okay, take out your homework," or "I'm going to pass out some material I want you to read now," or, "C'mon class, let's get going. We've got a lot of material to cover before the end of the period." Although these statements may accurately inform and direct the students, they quickly become routine and boring to those who may not have a high level of intrinsic motivation. One way to capture students' attention is for the teacher to make casual or personal comments that indicate respect for students or interest in them. A comment of this type contributes toward a positive social-emotional climate and enhances student-teacher relationships. Examples are: "Weren't Chris and Jenny great in the Thanksgiving play yesterday?" or "I understand that the vocational electronics class needs some broken radios and televisions to repair. How many have one at home they can contribute?"

Another approach to focus students' attention is to use a *springboard* to induce them to get involved with the objectives of the lesson. This can be accomplished by connecting the content to their lives and experiences, which is a major emphasis of constructivist ideals. Examples include: "How many have seen at least one of the *Rocky* films and would like to describe a major fight scene?" (springboard for a sociology lesson on violence), or "Who would like to tell about a book you read over Christmas vacation?" (springboard for lesson on reading skills). Springboards such as these serve to focus students' attention and stimulate them to get involved.

A more sensational, and perhaps more effective, way to get students involved with the learning activity is to do something unexpected. This entry can take many forms, such as starting the class by solving a challenging puzzle related to a math concept to be taught during the lesson. Another approach is to play a discovery game such as having students guess what lesson-related object the teacher possesses (perhaps ration stamps as an introduction to the home front during World War II). Occasionally a shock statement can be used such as, "If you are an average group of students in this school, then two girls in here have had abortions" (as an introduction to a health-class unit on birth control). Anything that stimulates students' curiosity, suspense, or creativity is a possible means to get students directly or indirectly involved with the content to be taught.

One approach to lesson entry that many teachers use fairly consistently is preparing students for the upcoming learning activity. The extent to which students are prepared for the ensuing activity directly affects an entry's effectiveness in orienting them and setting the learning process in motion. Ideally this phase of the entry would include a review and preview to prepare students for new learning. The review consists of the important facts, concepts, and skills learned from the previous lesson. In this way the immediate lesson would be placed into context and cumulative learning would be encouraged. An example is the following statement: "In the last several lessons we have tried to show how some great thinkers, in speaking to the men of their times, were in fact speaking to people of all times. Today we shall begin to try to discern that much of their wisdom is still pertinent for us more than a century later."

During the preview, the teacher describes what the class will be engaged in during the period, the objectives pertinent to the lesson, and a rationale. Although it seems the preview involves extensive teacher commentary, it can be effectively accomplished in a short period of time. For example: "Today if we get through the vocabulary drill and reading section, we can spend the last part of the period playing French bingo. Our primary objective is that you will be able to pronounce correctly the 20 new vocabulary words from the story, 'Jeanne d'Arc.' Although the story is historical, the key words that we will focus on are ones you will find in everyday conversational usage."

It is important to keep in mind that the entry to a lesson is a means to an end, not an end in itself. The effectiveness of the entry is directly dependent on how well the students have been prepared for the upcoming learning activity and how highly they are motivated to pursue the objectives. The decisions a teacher makes during the planning stage are crucial because the impact of the entry will directly affect students' attitude. Their attitude, to a large degree, determines how interested they are in attaining the objectives and how conscientiously they engage in the planned learning activities.

Mr. Taylor, in the illustrative scenario, implemented an interesting and relatively thorough lesson entry. Approximately 10 minutes passed from the time he gained the attention of the students at the beginning of the class session to when he stated the objective. The students certainly did not expect to close their eyes at the beginning of the lesson as Mr. Taylor directed them to do. The effectiveness of this approach was enhanced as the students thought about something quite unusual—a hypothetical environmental crisis in Norwood. Judging from student involvement, the springboard succeeded. After a brief review to link the previous lesson to the new one, Mr. Taylor mentioned what they would be doing during the day in class. The entry culminated with his statement of the objective: over the next two class sessions, to identify at least three environmental problems Norwood was experiencing. The only phase of the entry lacking in Mr. Taylor's lesson, when comparing his approach to the ideal, was a rationale for the objective. Perhaps he could have mentioned that responsible citizens are aware of current issues and problems and many become actively involved in resolving them for the betterment of the community.

The entry is the initial contact students have with the teacher and the planned learning activity. During these first few minutes teachers have the opportunity to focus students' attention on the learning task in an interesting—

and perhaps exciting—way and to prepare them adequately for new learning. In many respects, the entry to a lesson sets the tone for the entire lesson. Because of this, it is important for teachers to take extra care during the planning stage.

Closure

The closure to a lesson is the counterpart to its entry. With a closure, the instructional cycle of a lesson is completed. Whereas the goal of the entry is to focus, prepare, and stimulate the students, the closure serves to reinforce learning outcomes, integrate what has been taught, and make the transition to the next lesson. Unfortunately, classes sometimes stop abruptly without any wrap-up or transition. Teachers who have not planned for closure may stop teaching when the material runs out, then make lame, time-filling comments or inform students that they may have the rest of the class to start their homework. Occasionally the bell rings and cuts activities short. Either way, the students are left to tie everything together into something meaningful. This implicit faith in the students' ability or inclination to synthesize information from a presentation meaningfully is largely unfounded.

Usually the closure occurs at the end of the lesson. Yet often several "miniclosures" are used to terminate segments of a lesson. Just as there can be several entries within any one lesson, there should be complementary closures. The extent to which closure is used will more than likely depend on the ability and interest level of students, the complexity of the content to be covered and the objectives to be achieved, and the time limitations.

One of the major purposes of closure is to reinforce the important learning outcomes that have occurred during the lesson. This can be accomplished by organizing student learning through the use of summary and review. The teacher uses review to reinforce major terms, facts, and concepts. There may be reference to notes on the chalkboard, overhead transparencies, or handouts. Questions are often asked in order to determine the extent of student knowledge and understanding. Higher-level information and ideas from the lesson are summarized by the teacher or students. During this phase of the closure, teachers begin to determine if their objectives have been attained.

Learning is further reinforced as ideas are integrated within students' cognitive structures. Higher-level ideas are synthesized to clarify relationships, to illustrate concepts and generalizations, or to lead students to insights or self-realizations. New learning also needs to be integrated within the unit. The teacher refers to the overall unit goals in an effort to make the link—for example, "Today we have studied the conditions under which conifers develop. This, then, should help you understand one more factor of the overall ecological development of a free-growth region. We have another factor, deciduous growth, to cover for a complete understanding." The most influential form of integration occurs when students attempt to apply learning. In this case, the teacher provides an incentive by referring to some practical and immediate use of the information or skills learned—for example, "Now that you know the long-range effects of marijuana on your mental and physical well-being, you have evidence for formulating your own attitude about its use," or, "Within a week you should be able to tune up your own car."

The closure to a lesson should also facilitate the transition from one lesson to another. The transition helps students understand the larger picture within which the immediate lesson fits. In terms of lectures, Gage and Berliner (1992) referred to this aspect of closure as *interlecture structuring*. The teacher attempts to build a bridge from one lesson to the next by giving a preview of the next lesson, by asking the students to think over a pertinent issue or problem, or by suggesting an assignment using divergent thinking that will prepare the student for involvement in the next class. This aspect of closure implies more than the routine assignment of homework. For example, "By the next class period, make a note of as many causes of inflation as you can think of, and suggest a way that each might be controlled. We can consolidate our ideas, and decide what the government should be doing. Then maybe we'll write our congressperson if you like."

Reference to the accomplishments made by the students during a lesson should also be part of the closure, particularly if the lesson was a good one. Comments such as this contribute significantly in producing a positive social-emotional climate in the classroom. The teacher indicates to the class the extent to which the objectives have been achieved or the amount of material that has been covered, especially as this is determined relative to some predetermined guideline. For example, "You people have done nicely to have already gotten through the fourth step of the experiment, and we should have no problem completing the final two steps during the next lab period."

Mr. Taylor used formal and informal approaches to bring closure to the lesson. He began his closure approximately 10 minutes before the end of the period by informing students of the homework assignment that required them to apply what they learned in the home setting. In addition, the assignment helped serve as a bridge to the next day's lesson because of the continuing nature of the students' inquiry. More directly, he indicated that they will know more about their community as a result of the data they gather. Mr. Taylor had the students write the proposed environmental problems on the survey rating form he distributed. This activity seemed to serve as a very informal review of major learnings. In this case it was the tentative identification of Norwood's environmental problems that related directly to his goal for the lesson. Students' thinking might have been extended with the reading of the article, but there is no evidence that it will be pursued further.

His culminating activity, which involved students in making the transition from class to the home, was particularly effective. Asking them to form judgments about how their parents might react to their tentative list of environmental problems was an excellent way to stimulate higher-level thinking. Mr. Taylor also indicated that he thought the class was interested and he was looking forward to the next day.

SUMMARY POINT

The lesson-presentation skills of entry and closure are important instructional components. With the entry, momentum is established with a purposely designed lesson component. With the closure, students are provided with a "kicker" to reinforce the learning that has occurred. Continuity with previous and upcoming lessons is also made during the entry and closure. Research suggests that students learn and achieve more when teachers plan and use entries to lessons. Teachers are also more effective when closures are used. Reflective decisions about each lesson's entry and closure need to be made by the teacher during the planning stage in order to enhance the learning of their students.

REVIEW: IMPORTANT PRACTICES IN LESSON ENTRY AND CLOSURE

Entry

Purpose is to focus students' attention on the learning activity, prepare them for what they are going to learn, and encourage them to get involved.

1. *Casual or personal comments*—assists in establishing a comfortable climate for learning.
2. *Springboard*—focuses student attention on objectives by relating the content to students' lives.
3. *Attention-getter*—stimulates students' curiosity, suspense, or creativity.
4. *Review*—relates past learnings to current lesson.
5. *Preview*—lesson objectives and rationale are presented.

Closure

Purpose is to reinforce learning outcomes, integrate what has been taught, and make the transition to the next lesson.

1. *Summary*—review of important lesson learnings.
2. *Integration*—lesson is related to previous learnings and unit goals.
3. *Application*—learnings are applied to the real world of the student.
4. *Transition*—preview of next lesson.
5. *Reference to accomplishment*—reinforcement of students' contribution to attaining lesson objectives.

Motivating Skills

The conscious attempt by teachers to stimulate students in the classroom to achieve learning goals is a complex process. Students' attitudes and needs are diverse within any one class, and the teacher's attitude and personality have vary-ing effects. It is self-evident that all students are motivated in some way. For the teacher facing 25 to 35 students in five or six classes each day, the question quickly becomes, "Motivated to do what?" It should be obvious that teachers be-come frustrated when students are motivated into active pursuit of interests un-related to the lesson's objectives. Enthusiastic teachers who demonstrate their en-joyment of the subject and teaching have a considerable advantage in commanding student attention and stimulating their involvement. Likewise, teachers whose behavior is complacent will probably have problems in encourag-ing students to get mentally and physically involved.

From an instructional point of view, the effect of the teacher's motivation-related behavior is reflected in the students' inclination to attain the lesson ob-jectives. Motivating behaviors may take many forms. Instructional style deter-mines the motivational techniques that are characteristic of a particular teacher. The most pervasive form of teacher motivational behavior is the use of a variety of verbal and nonverbal behaviors to create a dynamic presence in the classroom. The teacher who purposely uses a wide range of behaviors to display interest in the subject and the students is displaying a certain presence that contributes to enthusiasm.

The range of motivating behaviors displayed by teachers is influenced con-siderably by their personality and attitude. Another major approach teachers can use to stimulate student interest and involvement is the use of a variety of teach-ing strategies, methods, and techniques. Although sensitivity to the instructional flow influences the extent to which teachers shift gears within and between lessons, other factors such as knowledge of instructional practices and time for preparation play an important part.

A highly motivating teacher consistently displays dynamic personal behav-iors in the classroom. Students and fellow teachers describing that person would probably use descriptors such as *enthusiastic, energetic, exciting*, and *stimulating*. The teacher with a high degree of presence is visually and auditorily dynamic. Four major areas that contribute to presence are: physical movement, nonverbal behaviors, lesson pace, and voice quality.

A motivating teacher moves about the classroom. This teacher avoids pat-terned pacing, but moves purposefully about the front and, when possible, to the sides, rear, and through the rows to give students a "moving target." This teacher also remains at a distance from a reciting student to encourage the student to speak loudly. This often requires retreating from a student who is responding. The teacher refrains from sitting on the desk for more than a few minutes at a time, and avoids sitting at or standing behind the desk or demonstration table ex-cept as necessary. A spatial mapping category system has been devised to help chart patterns of observed teacher classroom travel (Susi, 1985, 1986).

A motivating teacher uses nonverbal behavior to create presence. Research has indicated that nonverbal behaviors have a powerful impact in the classroom. Besides moving about the classroom, this also includes using a variety of facial expressions, maintaining eye contact, using a variety of gestures, using body movements such as nods and head shakes, and placing a hand on a student's shoulder or moving into close proximity to students. The teacher's mode of dress and grooming also send nonverbal messages to students. A neatly dressed and clean teacher will command more respect than one who does not seem to care about appearance. There is an overall impact, a cumulative effect, of the teacher's nonverbal behaviors that will hopefully leave students with the impression that their teacher is an enthusiastic and dynamic person who enjoys both the subject and the work.

Motivating teachers also use their voice effectively. The voice is the most obvious instrument with which the teacher conducts the business of teaching. Ideally, the teacher's voice should be strong (not just loud), and have pleasant tonal qualities. The use of inflection should complement the meaning of words being spoken. The voice should not have shrill or strained qualities, or obvious impediments, which cause the listener to experience discomfort or difficulty. A teacher's vocabulary should be appropriate for the students. The teacher's mode of delivery should be smooth and mature, without the annoying repetition of particular words or phrases, or the use of adolescent speech habits (e.g., "like," "you know," "stuff," and "you guys"). And, it should go without saying, the use of correct pronunciation and grammar is essential.

A motivating teacher controls the pace of the lesson. Controlling the pace helps to maintain student attention and accomplish objectives. Pacing in the classroom results from the teacher's sensitivity to the tenor of student behavior. Although changing mode is a means to control pace, pacing occurs intramodally as well. In a foreign-language drill, for example, students are pushed to the limit they can tolerate; in a discussion in science, patience is exhibited while students reflect on responses. Stepping to the board to write important information is an effective means of adjusting pace, because it "freezes" student thought on a point for a few deliberate moments. The teacher moderates the students' excessive exuberance, but makes deliberate efforts to provide stimulation when the class lags. The teacher's actual behaviors in the interest of pacing may take many forms; it is important that the teacher behaves deliberately to maintain that optimum learning pace.

A teacher also motivates students by varying the instructional mode. Instructional mode refers to the techniques, methods, and strategies used. Just as a teacher commands student attention through personal behaviors, a teacher also sustains attention through instructional behaviors. Attention span is an important consideration, and changing the instructional mode is one means of coping with it. This is most often accomplished by using a particular teaching mode for only a limited period of time, then moving to another mode. There should be at least one major shift during any given class period, and possibly as many as three or four depending on the nature and level of the class.

The most effective shifts are those that vary the learning stimulus of the students. For example, students in a high school government class might listen to a lecture on the concept *compromise* and how the process plays a crucial role in government and the formation of laws today. To demonstrate a historical application of the concept, the teacher might then organize students into small groups to read about, discuss, and report on several of the specific compromises of the Constitutional Convention of 1787. A shift from a lecture to small-group interaction is better than a shift from a lecture to a film on the convention, for example, because students move from passive to active involvement. The occasional rearrangement of chairs in the classroom to fit the nature of the learning activity is also involved in changing mode.

As best as we can tell from a written transcript as the only data source, Mr. Taylor seemed to create a relatively stimulating teaching environment through his use of personal and instructional behaviors. At the beginning of the period he entered the lesson by telling the students "with excitement in his voice" to close their eyes and imagine a crisis taking place in their community. With some imagination we can almost visualize the altered facial expressions and inflection in his voice on the word *crisis* as one way to depict excitement. Later in the lesson he complimented the students on their speculations about community problems. Perhaps we can imagine a lowering of the voice for most of the compliment and a louder and inflected voice as he said "Well done!" We do have a strong indication, though, that Mr. Taylor was concerned about contributing to the students' motivation through varying the pace of the lesson and his physical position in the classroom. He was aware that several students were losing interest at two points during the lesson, and in response to the last observation, he purposely quickened the pace of the lesson to finish what he had planned in the remaining 20 minutes.

A major strength of Mr. Taylor's lesson in terms of the students' motivation that we can determine from the transcript was the significant variety of instructional shifts he employed to sustain students' attention and interest. The lesson was initiated with a brief discussion followed by an equally brief, individually oriented writing exercise that shifted senses. He then continued with discussion involving considerable interaction related to the environmental problems Norwood was facing. At one point he incorporated information giving in the form of an extended explanation and then shifted again to discussion. Senses were shifted once more after he presented the assignment and students had to write on their forms. During the closure he had students read a short article and then wrapped up the lesson with a brief interchange of viewpoints. There were three major instructional patterns: discussion-writing-discussion, explanation-writing-explanation, and a reading-discussion shift. Minor patterns also occurred.

RESEARCH AND THEORETICAL BASE: QUESTIONS AND QUESTIONING SKILLS

The most basic way teachers stimulate interaction, thinking, and learning in the classroom is through the use of questions. The research literature on questions and questioning has grown since the 1970s primarily because of the movement to identify those teacher behaviors and techniques that contribute to students' learning gains. Today, interest in teacher and student questioning continues to grow because researchers are now more interested in the role of questioning within the context of classroom interaction, particularly as the primary means to encourage discussion. Discussion is viewed as an important alternative instructional method to teacher lecture and student recitation because of its potential to promote student understanding of societal issues and problems, in science and social studies classes, for example, and how this might lead to reflective decision making. Constructivist teachers encourage active participation during discussions through the use of open-ended questions designed to challenge thinking (Zemelman, Daniels, and Hyde, 1993).

The following are generalized research findings drawn from several reviews of research (Wilen, 1991 & 1994; Wilen and White, 1991) about teachers' and students' use of questioning in classrooms. The findings support the assertion that questioning is one of the most influential teaching acts because of its potential to stimulate student interaction, thinking, and learning.

1. Questioning can be used to accomplish a wide variety of instructional purposes in the classroom. Purposes include reviewing materials previously read or studied; diagnosing students' abilities, attitudes, and preferences; stimulating critical and creative thinking; arousing interest in a topic; encouraging reflective discussion on an issue or problem; probing students' thoughts and expressions; personalizing subject matter; supporting students' contributions during a recitation or discussion; assessing progress toward attaining lesson and unit objectives; and managing and controlling students' behavior.

2. Questioning positively influences students' achievement. Researchers have found that high frequencies of teachers' oral questions correlate with gains in student achievement. Several questioning techniques also positively correlate with students' achievement gains: asking clearly phrased questions, probing students' responses to questions, redirecting questions to other students, balancing the responses of volunteering and nonvolunteering students, using wait time after asking a question and after a student has responded, and providing feedback primarily in the form of acknowledgement after a student responds.

3. Questioning can be used to get students more actively involved in classroom interaction. Researchers recommend that teachers organize the students' seating in a circle or semicircle to facilitate communication and to create a more student-oriented, conversational atmosphere, one in which the teacher does not dominate the interaction. In a conversational atmosphere the questions are more personal, students' responses are not evaluated, and students have control over speaking turns. Extended wait time increases the quantity and quality of student utterances. Students should be encouraged to ask questions, since they respond in more complex ways to each other than to a teacher's questions. Using nonquestioning alternatives—such as different statement forms—during interaction may

result in a less threatening environment and more student participation. (Nonquestioning alternatives are discussed later in this chapter and in chapter 7 as an important component of the discussion method.)

4. Questioning can be used to encourage students to think. Researchers suggest that recitation is not an appropriate method to encourage students to think because of the emphasis on asking many questions at a low cognitive level within a highly structured interaction pattern controlled by the teacher. Students have little opportunity to use language to think and express ideas. Researchers recommend the use of higher cognitive level questions if developing critical-thinking skills is an important curricular goal. Researchers also recommend extending wait time after questions, since students' responses become more complex and reflective. Use of a variety of teacher and student questioning, and alternative nonquestioning techniques such as the use of statements, are also suggested to encourage higher-level thinking. One problem, though, is that there is only an approximate 50-percent congruency between the cognitive level of teacher questions asked and the cognitive level of students' responses. This correspondence can be increased as teachers use cues to clarify expectations for thinking and to reduce ambiguity. Follow-up probing is especially useful for this purpose.

5. Students can ask more and better questions. Researchers have shown that while teachers ask a high frequency of questions (two to four per minute), students ask few information-seeking questions. Researchers recommend that teachers reduce the number of questions they ask and have students formulate more questions. Teachers should share information about their approach to questioning with students to help the students understand the teachers' expectations regarding the kind of thinking necessary to answer questions. Teachers should consider preparing their students to identify key words within questions that suggest how to process them and the kind of thinking necessary to answer them. Other suggestions center on encouraging students to assume teaching roles. Teachers might train students to generate questions that become the basis of student-led recitations or a part of discussions. Also, teachers might encourage students to engage in reciprocal teaching, or "playing teacher," as they formulate and ask questions after reading text sections.

APPLICATION TO PRACTICE: QUESTION LEVELS

Since the time of Socrates the questions a teacher asks in the classroom and the techniques used to stimulate interaction have been considered essential components of the instructional process. Questions are essential because teachers can conveniently and effectively use them to engage students' thinking about issues, problems, and topics under discussion. Although the congruency of the thought level of teachers' questions to students' responses is not 100 percent, teachers still have considerable impact in their ability to control the thought levels of students in the classroom. As a result, teachers need to pay attention to the questions they ask and the way they ask them.

Once the teacher realizes there are different cognitive levels of questions and that a relationship between questions and student thinking exists, decisions need to be made about the proportion of time students will spend engaged in lower- and higher-level thinking. These decisions will take into account the objectives of the lesson and the method(s) employed to achieve these objectives. Practically every method and strategy that a teacher can employ with individuals or groups of students involves questioning. Two of the most common methods are recitations involving primarily low-level convergent questions to get students to recall important facts and concepts related to an issue or topic, and guided discussions that are designed to encourage students to begin thinking as they apply what they have learned. (These and other methods that rely on questioning are presented in chapter 7.) As teachers plan lesson objectives, and methods and strategies to achieve them, decisions will be made about the balance of thinking levels and the corresponding kinds of questions needed to be asked.

The following classification scheme for identifying and devising cognitive levels of questions is based on Gallagher and Aschner's (1963) well-known adaptation of Guilford's (1956) "structure of intellect" model. The levels have been initially categorized as convergent and divergent to correspond to narrow and broad student thinking, and then subdivided into two additional levels that reflect the hierarchy of thinking levels. Convergent questions serve the important purpose of determining students' basic knowledge and understanding, and are the basis for subsequent higher-level thinking. Therefore, lower-level questions should rarely become ends in themselves; they should serve as a means to achieve higher-level thinking. Divergent questions serve the purpose of requiring students to process what they have learned by thinking critically, creatively, and evaluatively. Students need opportunities to practice higher forms of thought if they are expected to become independent and reflective thinkers. Each of the four cognitive levels is accompanied with a definition, example student behaviors, and illustrative questions (Wilen, 1991). In addition, corresponding levels to Bloom's taxonomy (1956) are identified because of teachers' familiarity with this system. Bloom's taxonomy was used as the basis for devising instructional objectives and goals in chapter 5.

Before proceeding with the introduction of the category system, a word should be said about the importance of identifying example student behaviors, referred to previously in the review-of-research section as "key words" and "clues," and emphasizing the use of these in the planning and asking of questions. Thinking involves the processing of information and questioning helps facilitate this. Costa and Lowery (1989) advocate the use of such clues to communicate to students the types of thinking a teacher wants. Action verbs embedded in the questions can cause students to "use their senses; recall from memory; process the ideas; use or apply the knowledge in some action; and transfer or evaluate those relationships in new or hypothetical situations" (p. 25). A conscious use of key words as part of questions increases the probability that a teacher's intention and expectations will be congruent to students' performances as noticed in their responses.

Level I—Low-Order Convergent: questions requiring students to engage in reproductive thinking. The teacher's intention is to have students recall or recognize information. Emphasis is on memorization and observation, so students' responses can easily be anticipated. Level I corresponds to the "knowledge" level of Bloom's taxonomy.

Example student behaviors (clues): define, recognize, recount, quote, identify, list, recall, answer "yes" or "no."

Example questions: Who invented the sewing machine? How many colors are on the chart? What is the definition given in your book of photosynthesis?

Level II—High-Order Convergent: questions requiring students to engage in the first level of productive thinking. The teacher's intention is to have students go beyond recall and demonstrate understanding of information by mentally organizing material. Students also apply learned information. Although more thinking is involved at this level, student responses still generally can be anticipated. Level II corresponds to Bloom's "comprehension" and "application" levels.

Example student behaviors (clues): describe, compare, contrast, rephrase, summarize, explain, translate, interpret, relate, apply, use, provide an example, solve.

Example questions: What is an example of cooperation in your home? How are these numbers related? How would you solve this problem using the accounting procedure we just discussed? In your own words, according to the story, how did Tom Sawyer convince his friends to whitewash the fence?

Level III—Low-Order Divergent: questions requiring students to think critically about information. The teacher's intention is to have students analyze information to discover reasons or causes, draw conclusions or generalizations, or to find evidence in support of opinions. Higher-level productive thinking is involved; thus students' responses may or may not be anticipated. Level III corresponds to Bloom's "analysis" level.

Example student behaviors (clues): identify motives, reasons, or causes; draw conclusions, inferences, or generalizations; provide evidence; support ideas; analyze information.

Example questions: Now that you have completed the experiment, what is your conclusion about why the substance became denser? Why do you think the girl ran away from home? What evidence can you provide to support your view that the constitutional power of the president has diminished over the years?

Level IV—High-Order Divergent: higher-order questions requiring students to perform original and evaluative thinking. The teacher's intention is to have students make predictions, solve lifelike problems, produce original communications, and judge ideas, information, actions, and aesthetic expressions based on internal or external criteria. This level represents the highest form of productive thinking; consequently, students' responses generally cannot be anticipated. Level IV corresponds to Bloom's "synthesis" and "evaluation" levels.

Example student behaviors (clues): produce original communications, predict, propose solutions, create, speculate, hypothesize, synthesize, construct, devise, write, design, develop, judge, value, choose, opine.

Example questions: How would you rate the effectiveness of the Environmental Protection Agency? What is a good title for this story? How can we raise money to support the recycling center? What is your favorite orchestral instrument and why?

Questioning Circle

The "questioning-circle" system is a very effective approach to use in planning, observing, and analyzing teachers' and students' classroom questions. While the previous question-classification system is appropriate for teachers to use when designing constructivist-learning situations, the questioning-circle system may be even better. In addition to encouraging teachers to plan for questions to stimulate students' critical thinking, the questioning-circle approach encourages teachers to personalize subject-matter content. A main tenet of constructivism is that students learn by making connections between new subject matter and their current knowledge and experiences. The more teachers can relate the content to students' lives the more they will understand it and be able to process and apply it in new situations. Questioning can help accomplish this.

The questioning-circle approach provides a flexible format for questioning by not assuming a sequential and hierarchical thinking pattern. The circles are represented on a plane, with no single type of question "better" or "higher" than another. Christenbury and Kelly (1983) depicted different areas of questioning in the form of overlapping circles, each representing different aspects of reality: (1) the matter—subject of discussion (e.g., topic, concept, issue, problem), (2) personal reality—student's relationship with the subject, and (3) external reality—broader, more worldly view of the subject. Questions are devised based on the circles and their intersections. The most significant question is the central intersection because it requires a synthesis of thinking from all the areas. The questioning circle is shown in Figure 6.2, with sample questions representing the circles and their intersections related to the topic of acid rain*:

1. The matter: What are the causes of acid rain?
2. Personal reality: Have you personally seen acid rain damage and, if so, how would you describe your experience?
3. External reality: How has the acid-rain problem influenced the policies of other countries?

---

*Thanks is extended to the teachers participating in William Wilen's thinking-and-questioning workshop (Lake School District, Ohio) for devising these questions.

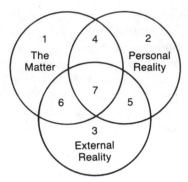

Figure 6.2 Questioning Circle

4. The matter/personal reality: How might you personally be affected by the acid-rain problem?
5. Personal reality/external reality: What could you do to bring the issues and problems associated with acid rain to the attention of other people?
6. The matter/external reality: What are the issues affecting the relationship between Canada and the United States related to the acid-rain problem?
7. The matter/personal reality/external reality: Why should we as citizens of a global society care about acid rain?

APPLICATION TO PRACTICE: QUESTIONING SKILLS

The formation of questions appropriate to desired objectives is extremely important, but no more so than the questioning process. The teacher's effectiveness as a questioner depends not only on devising good questions, but also on the way questions are asked. The skillful application of questioning techniques is essential if the questions are to serve the purposes for which they are intended. Effective application of a series of questioning techniques can make the difference between a class of students who are passive, confused, frustrated, and mentally unchallenged, and a class of students who are active, stimulated, and reflective.

The following is a list of questioning techniques synthesized from a variety of sources on questioning and reported in Wilen (1991). Many of these, based on the effective-teaching research reported previously, are positive correlates with student achievement (Wilen, 1987; Wilen & Clegg, 1986). In addition to the questioning techniques, the nonquestioning alternative of the use of teacher statements has been added. Although there is no research to link the use of statements directly to gains in student achievement, there is a tendency for them to encourage student participation and thinking, particularly during discussion (Dillon, 1988, 1990).

Question Phrasing

Questions need to be phrased clearly to communicate response expectations precisely to students. Vague or ambiguous questions self-evidently lead to student confusion and prolonged frustration if the practice becomes a regular occurrence. A vague question such as "What about the law Congress passed?" forces students to try to guess what the teacher wants rather than thinking of and formulating a direct response to the question. Another source of ambiguity is the run-on question. This occurs as two or more uninterrupted and often incomplete questions are asked in a series. Frustration develops as students try to guess which question to answer. This implies that key questions need to be planned because these are often on a higher cognitive level. Divergent questions need more planning because of their difficulty. This also implies that teachers may need to acquaint students with the different levels of questions to increase the probability that expectations might be communicated more clearly.

Adapting Questions

Questions need to be adapted to the language and ability level of the class and, in many cases, individual students within the class. Most classes are heterogeneously grouped, so questions need to be phrased in natural, simple language to increase the probability that they will be understood by all. Within classes, language will need to be simplified for slower students or certain mainstreamed students and made more thought provoking for gifted students. A question for a lower-ability student might be, "From the article you have just read, how does the demand for a product affect its supply?" To higher-ability students, the question might become, "Going beyond the article a little, how does price affect supply and demand, and at what point is market equilibrium reached?" An important implication for teachers is the need to get to know their students to adjust their questions and thereby increase comprehension.

Question Sequence

Asking questions in a planned and patterned sequence, particularly in preparation for guided and reflective discussions, will enhance student thinking, comprehension, and learning. Random questioning rarely communicates a clear focus or intent. The primary factors influencing the choice of question sequence include the objective of the lesson, ability level of the students, and prior knowledge and understanding students have of the content being discussed. Some sequences will begin with lower-level questions and will progress to stimulating, higher-level thinking. Others will start with higher-level questions and stay there.

Asking lower-level questions will quickly determine the extent to which they understand the content. For example, consider the following episode: After having the students read an article on proposed changes in immigration laws, the teacher asks the question, "Should the United States permit the immigration of unlimited numbers of refugees from war-torn countries?" Students give minimal support for the opinions they express. The teacher then asks these review-oriented questions: "What is the number-one problem the author associates with immigration?" and "What do the current immigration laws say about refugees from nations involved in war?" Accordingly, if teachers intend to ask questions, they should plan the pattern of those questions, particularly those at the higher cognitive levels.

While planning a sequence of higher-level questions in preparation for a guided discussion is useful and advised, planning such a sequence for an open discussion may not be realistic. Open or reflective discussions are more natural and possess the characteristics of an instructional conversation. This form of discussion, by its very nature, is less structured, with students' responses driving the direction of the inquiry and interaction. The teacher's role is to facilitate and to be responsive to students' comments, questions, and ideas as they develop meaning. Although the teacher certainly has planned one or more objectives to achieve as a result of engaging students in a reflective discussion and has planned a few key, thought-provoking questions, the teacher will need to be more flexible in the sequence of questions and statements to move the students toward understanding.

Balancing Cognitive Levels of Questions

Balancing questions designed to stimulate convergent and divergent thinking will enhance the possibility that a greater range of student cognitive abilities will be developed. Research has demonstrated that teachers at all levels tend to ask predominantly lower-level questions, with an emphasis on Level I convergent questions. Convergent questions should serve the purpose of determining students' basic understanding so they can apply their knowledge by engaging in subsequent higher-level thinking. Critical and creative thinking is stimulated with divergent questions. Teachers can use information about the levels of questions presented previously to plan an optimal balance of convergent and divergent questions to achieve unit goals and lesson objectives.

Student Participation

Student involvement in classroom interaction can be increased by balancing responses from volunteering and nonvolunteering students, redirecting initially unanswered questions to other students, and encouraging student-student interaction. Too often, only a few students participate in class discussions and recitations, and therefore dominate the interaction. Every student can make a contribution to class interaction, and teacher alertness is necessary to perceive verbal and nonverbal cues from reticent students, such as a perplexed look or partially raised hand. Discretion should be used regarding the difficulty level and intimacy of the questions when calling on nonvolunteering students. The argument has been made by Kelly (1993), though, that calling on nonvolunteering students is a democratic practice because citizens, just as students, have a democratic responsibility to participate in public talk.

Another useful approach to stimulate a response and thinking is to direct one question to several students. The redirection could be prompted by an unanswered question, an incorrect response, or a desire to get additional responses to the same question. Redirection can involve volunteering and nonvolunteering students. Participation during discussions, particularly, can be stimulated by encouraging students to interact with each other. Sometimes there is a delicate balance between teacher intervention and teacher facilitation. "Jim, how do you react to Mary's point of view that *The Catcher in the Rye* is an example of pornography?" is one way to stimulate student-student interaction. Most interaction is of the teacher-student-teacher type. Student-student interaction involves more students, increasing the probability of a greater diversity of ideas, perspectives, and judgments that are appropriate during a discussion. Thus, the way interaction is encouraged and conducted communicates expectations to the students. More students will get involved in interaction if they are encouraged by the teacher.

Probing Responses

During discussions in which the emphasis is on stimulating more complex student thinking, students sometimes lack skill and confidence in expressing themselves at the higher cognitive levels. Resulting responses to questions can be ambiguous, incomplete, or superficial. In these cases teachers need to follow up with probing questions or comments to encourage students to complete, clarify, expand, or support their answers. Probes to encourage students to complete and clarify responses are often necessary with younger learners as they begin articulating the basics of reflective thinking, or with older learners at the upper grades who have not been sufficiently exposed to higher-level questions. Probes are often useful to encourage students to elevate thinking to higher cognitive levels. Comments beginning with such phrases as "What if," "Suppose," or "How about" are common during discussions in which teachers are challenging students' thinking. Probably the most common probes during discussion are those that request learners to support their points of view, opinions, or judgments with evidence from internal or external sources. Comments such as "Why?", "What evidence do you have?", and "How can you support your view?" are common in reflective discussions. This means that learners' initial responses to questions must be heard before probes can be used. Listening skills are very important. Also, to be effective, probes must be nonthreatening and used in a supportive manner.

Wait Time

Students require more time to formulate thoughtful responses, particularly during discussions, because of the complexity of thinking required by teachers' divergent questions. Although students need more time to think, research shows that teachers wait only approximately one second after asking a question before calling on a student and one second after a student responds before probing the response, rephrasing the question, redirecting to another student, or providing the answer (Rowe, 1974).

Teachers can use wait time at least two different ways to increase the probability that students' responses will be more acceptable. The first, postquestion wait time, is the pause after a teacher asks a question and before a student responds, and the second, postresponse wait time, is the pause after a student responds and before the teacher reacts. Waiting three to five seconds improves the quantity and quality of students' responses, thereby increasing the probability of reflective thinking and effective discussion (Atwood and Wilen, 1991). Rowe (1987) found in her research that the lengths of students' responses increased, responses reflected higher-level thought, failures to respond decreased, student-student interaction increased, and the frequency of student questions increased as a result of expanding wait time. Higher-level questions will be minimally effective in stimulating participation and thinking unless students are allowed time to think. Teachers need to remember to pause after asking a question and after a student responds, particularly during reflective discussions.

Student Questions

Students generally expect to answer questions in most classes, not to have to ask them. They rarely ask questions, except when they do not understand something or need more information. Students should be encouraged to formulate questions because they become more actively involved in the learning process. Just as importantly, as students ask questions at higher cognitive levels, it can be reasonably assumed that corresponding levels of thought are stimulated. For example, suppose students in a Spanish III class have been studying the culture of Latin America. The teacher requests that each student devise two questions to ask a hypothetical visitor from Mexico to acquire a deeper understanding of the lifestyle of Latin Americans. The questions are shared and answered cooperatively by the teacher and students. Teachers should consider if they have underestimated students' ability to generate thoughtful questions and if they need to plan ways for students to get more involved in this manner. Two useful sources for approaches that teachers might use to encourage student-generated questions are *Questioning and Teaching: A Manual of Practice* (Dillon, 1988) and *Teaching Thinking Through Effective Questioning* (Hunkins, 1989).

Teacher Statements

It has been only within the last 15 years that nonquestioning alternatives advocated by Dillon (1988, 1994) have seriously been considered as techniques to enhance classroom interaction, particularly during discussions. In addition to wait time, student-generated questions, and signals that teachers communicate indicating that they are listening to and receiving students' responses, the use of statements by the teacher are suggested. The rationale for using statements is that students respond to them, and perhaps more so than to questions. In fact, Dillon urged that nonquestion alternatives be used in place of questions. Among the types of statements that teachers might use to stimulate student participation and thinking are: (1) declarative statement—stating a thought that occurs to you in relation to what the student has been saying; (2) reflective restatement—repeating, paraphrasing, or characterizing what the student has just said; (3) statement of interest—stating what you are interested in hearing more about related to what the student has just said; and (4) speaker referral—stating the relationship between what the student has just said and what a previous student has said. Instead of replacing questions with nonquestioning alternatives, teachers might find it more practical to use them with questioning techniques during recitations and discussions. A further step is to experiment with different combinations of techniques to see which have the most impact on students' involvement and thinking during classroom interaction.

Scenario Analysis

In the illustrative scenario, Mr. Taylor involved his students in several reflective minidiscussions during the course of the period. The discussions were interspersed with learning activities designed to structure students' critical thinking about their community's environmental problems. The vast majority of questions he asked were at the divergent level, and the questioning techniques he employed were realistic and conducive to a reflective discussion. He initiated a discussion at the beginning of the period after having the students imagine an environmental crisis taking place in their community. The question—it is actually an implied question—is classified at Level IV because original thinking was required as students engaged in speculation. Several students responded with their thoughts. Asking students what problems they think their community is facing requires analytical and evaluative thinking. Students are making generalizations based on observations of their surroundings, and making a judgment as to which observation is most important. This question could be categorized at Level III, although there is no indication that all students supported their responses with evidence.

During the next questioning sequence, Mr. Taylor used several questioning techniques. It was initiated with a Level III question, "How do we know if these are really problems that Norwood should do something about?" This requires students to draw conclusions, a characteristic of analytical thinking. After using wait time, he called on a nonvolunteer who appeared "deep in thought." Mr. Taylor proceeded to probe Jim's response to expand his thinking on the issue by requiring that he make a judgment. Several other students then offered their points of view. Approximately halfway through the period, Mr. Taylor asked students to recall the definition of "hypothesis." Defining is a characteristic of Level I thinking. There was also an indication he purposely used wait time. In attempting to get the students to relate the definition to their guesses about their community's environmental problems, he called on another nonvolunteer with little success. Even with a probe, the student responded minimally. The question was then redirected to another student who gave a more complete response. After assigning homework and having the students read a brief article, Mr. Taylor directed a Level IV divergent question to a student. She was asked to make a judgment about her parents' perception of the most critical environmental problem.

In regard to the other questioning techniques, there was evidence that the questions were phrased well and adapted to this average group of students. Although all the questions stimulated primarily divergent thinking, a sequence of questions is evident based on logical thinking about solving problems. Because of the capabilities of the students, Mr. Taylor needed to spend only a minimal amount of time reviewing facts. Therefore, a balance of questions was not necessary. He did not consider it pertinent to have the students devise questions during this lesson.

RESEARCH AND THEORETICAL BASE: SUPPORTING SKILLS, INFORMATION SKILLS, LISTENING SKILLS

Information giving is another technique that teachers regularly employ in the classroom. Teachers generally give information informally over short spans of time, such as when directions are given for an assignment. More formal information giving is used, for example, in the lecture method. Information giving as a technique focuses on short-term purposes—the emphasis in this section.

The available research on information giving centers on the value of structuring new information for students. One of the 14 major findings from the Beginning Teacher Evaluation Study suggested that structuring lessons for the students and giving directions on task procedures were positively correlated with high student success (Fisher et al., 1980). Brophy and Good (1986) found that students learned more efficiently when teachers structured new information for students. The decisions teachers make about the information they will present should address the provision of an appropriate form of structure to enhance students' understanding.

Research supports the important role teachers' listening behaviors play in interactive learning situations with students in the classroom. Strother (1987) defined listening as "the process by which spoken language is converted to meaning in the mind" (p. 625). In her review of the research, she found that 45 percent of total time devoted to classroom communication was spent on listening, 30 percent was used for speaking, 16 percent was used for reading, and another 9 percent was spent writing. Flanders (1970) found that teacher verbalizations that indicated acceptance of students' feelings and use of their ideas contributed significantly to a positive social-emotional classroom climate. For teachers to genuinely express empathy or paraphrase students' ideas, for example, effective listening behaviors are essential. Garrett, Sadker, and Sadker (1990) further substantiated the need for teachers to display regularly such attending behaviors as eye contact and facial expressions as teachers listen to and communicate with students in group discussions and individual conversations. Furthermore, if teachers expect students to be aware of and regularly display good listening skills, they must also model careful listening behaviors in the classroom (Good & Brophy, 1991).

Teachers' display of support for students' responses and activities is primarily noticed in the form of feedback encouraging them to continue their efforts. Support usually takes the form of reinforcement such as praise, acknowledgment of correct responses, and assistance with incorrect answers. Teachers are also supportive when they accept and use students' feelings and ideas. Chance (1992), based on his review of research, considered the many different forms of extrinsic reinforcers among the most powerful tools teachers could use. He concluded that teachers must supplement intrinsic rewards with extrinsic rewards to influence student behavior effectively. Brophy (1981), though, found that praise was not always effective in stimulating students' learning gains. A high rate of praise defeats its purpose and therefore does not always serve as reinforcement. Simple use of acknowledgment can often be used to communicate acceptance of students' contributions in place of praise. On the other hand, Gage and Berliner (1992) explained that the discriminating use of praise, use of corrective feedback, and a teacher's use of student ideas showed a positive relationship with students' achievement and attitudes. Good and Brophy (1994) found that the most effective form of praise is that which specifies to the student the reason for the praise. Teachers should provide feedback to students regarding their performance to encourage them to achieve goals.

APPLICATION TO PRACTICE: SUPPORTING SKILLS

The extent to which a teacher provides cognitive and emotional support to students in the classroom is based primarily on the kind of climate that has been created. *Climate* is perceived as "the generalized attitudes, feelings, and actions that prevail in a class" (Levin with Long, 1981, p. 206), resulting from a variety of physical, psychological, social, and intellectual stimuli. A classroom's climate is, in many ways, its character or personality, and climate has an impact on learning in significant ways.

The teacher is primarily responsible for establishing the classroom climate. If a positive social-emotional climate has been created, the students feel supported by their teacher. For example, if the teacher regularly displays behaviors suggestive of a positive attitude toward learning and school in comments to students, promotes cooperation among the students, and is accepting of students' feelings and ideas, students will feel a sense of belonging and will develop respect for the teacher and for each other. In addition, they will be stimulated to participate in class activities.

Several supportive teacher behaviors contribute to the creation of a positive climate. They have been identified by Flanders (1970) as acceptance of students' feelings, praise, encouragement, and use of students' ideas. An additional area of support is the use of courtesy. Teachers can demonstrate acceptance of students' feelings by making those feelings explicit, whether they are positive or negative. Teachers can do this with individual students or with the entire class. For example, imagine a group of excited 6th-grade students returning from a special assembly. To get them focused on the task, the teacher might say (with facial expressions depicting enthusiasm), "You must have really enjoyed the presentation. I would like to hear your thoughts before we go back to our work." In this case the teacher has been supportive by displaying acceptance of students' feelings.

Verbal praise is probably the most commonly and frequently used form of reinforcement and support by teachers in classrooms at all levels. Praise can be expressed as comments ranging from brief expressions such as "good" and "right" to extended judgments including the specifics of the accomplishment. An example of the latter situation is, "That was an outstanding report, Jimmy. You not only organized it well and presented it neatly, but also you drew some very interesting conclusions about global warming that we will discuss in class."

Students' contributions and achievements are often taken for granted. Praise has a significant effect on student behavior, so teachers should remain constantly aware of opportunities to praise students in a genuine manner. But keep in mind that the focus must be on the quality of praise. When quantity is the major emphasis, praise does not always have the effect of reinforcement, thereby defeating the teacher's intent. Several rules of thumb have been offered: deliver praise simply and directly in a natural tone of voice; specify the accomplishment; make sure nonverbal behaviors are congruent with the verbal praise; and use a variety of expressions (Good & Brophy, 1994).

Encouragement of student behaviors is similar to the use of praise in that it may have the same supportive effect. However, praise is an expression of a teacher's value judgment. The intent of expressions of encouragement is to stimulate a student to initiate or continue with a learning activity or task related to the objectives. Examples include continuing with a response to a question, further pursuit of an investigation in the library, attempting a new skill, and considering a different approach to solve a problem. Expressions such as "you're on the right track," "keep going," "you almost have it," "okay, how about a little more?" are relatively common. Using wait time (pausing) after students have made responses might encourage some to continue their responses with a new perspective at a higher level of cognition. Expressions of encouragement such as eye contact and a hand on a shoulder communicate support for students' efforts and motivate them further.

Moreover, a teacher can create a supportive climate by using students' ideas. The expression of ideas by students is an inevitable occurrence in the classroom and, when feasible, the teacher should capitalize on these ideas. Repeating a student's answer serves to give emphasis to it. When a student has given a somewhat lengthy answer, the teacher may respond with paraphrasing for both clarification and emphasis—for example, "Am I correct that you meant . . . ?" On the occasion when a student has introduced a pertinent idea in the classroom, the teacher may elaborate further, even at some length, as is appropriate. Finally, the teacher may recall students' ideas introduced earlier in the class, giving credit by name when possible, as they pull together ideas into meaningful generalizations.

A teacher's display of courtesy also contributes to creating a positive social-emotional climate in the classroom. It is a natural way to support students' participation in learning activities and other contributions. The idea is simple: Teachers should be courteous to students because they expect courtesy from them. Research reveals that modeling has the potential to influence students markedly. Thanking students for their point of view during a discussion might be more appropriate than using praise, particularly if the teacher did not want to express a judgment on the opinion. By telling a small group of students their effort on a project is appreciated, a teacher can encourage students to repeat the behavior.

While a teacher's use of supporting skills has always been important, they may be even more essential today with the growing emphasis on constructivism and teaching for understanding. Constructivist teachers attempt to create a classroom social environment that encourages sustained dialogue to promote understanding. Discussion becomes a primary method of teachers as they involve students in interaction with them and with each other. Supporting students' contributions to discussion—by accepting and using their ideas and feelings—and using praise are essential to sustain classroom discourse.

Mr. Taylor displayed a variety of supportive behaviors that were conducive to the creation of a positive social-emotional climate. Early in the lesson there was an indication that he maintained eye contact with students as he listened to and reinforced their contributions. He wrote students' opinions about community environmental problems on the board, a demonstration of support for students' ideas. At one point he expressed considerable enthusiasm for a student's insight, and one can imagine the animated behaviors accompanying the supportive comment, "You have just hit on one of the major things I wanted you to learn by the end of the unit!" The remaining supportive comments were basically expressions of courtesy. He complimented students on how observant they were of the community, and toward the end of the lesson he thanked David for his opinion. The only praise we can find in the scenario occurred at the end of the lesson when Mr. Taylor commented that he thought the lesson had been interesting and he expected it to be much the same the next day.

SUMMARY POINT

The instructional process consists of techniques, methods, and strategies that teachers have at their disposal as they make decisions about how to plan to meet unit goals and daily objectives in their classrooms. The most basic elements in this process are teacher physical behaviors that, for the most part, can be observed, analyzed, and evaluated. Instructional techniques consist of a series of skills that, in a sense, represents groups of teacher behaviors. Major techniques have been identified and varying degrees of all these techniques are used in each method and strategy teachers employ in the classroom.

Three of these techniques are motivating skills, questions and questioning skills, and supporting skills. Research confirms the importance of these techniques as part of a teacher's instructional repertoire. Student motivation is influenced by the teacher's display of verbal and nonverbal behaviors related to enthusiasm and the use of instructional variety. A teacher's application of a variety of question levels and techniques directly influences the degree of student thinking and participation in the classroom. Support, primarily noticed through the teacher's use of praise, has a significant impact on the classroom's social-emotional climate and student learning.

REVIEW: IMPORTANT MOTIVATING SKILLS, QUESTIONS AND QUESTIONING SKILLS, AND SUPPORTING SKILLS

Motivating Skills

Purpose is to stimulate students to attend and get involved in a lesson to achieve its objectives. Components include:

1. Physical movement—teacher varies positions to heighten student attention.
2. Nonverbal behaviors—teacher uses body language to create a dynamic presence.
3. Voice—teacher varies volume and inflection to stimulate student attention.
4. Lesson pace—teacher changes pace in response to student reaction.
5. Instructional mode—teacher employs variety to stimulate learning.

Question Levels

Purpose is to encourage students to engage in a balanced variety of thinking levels. Components include:

I. Low-order convergent—students recall or recognize information.
II. High-order convergent—students demonstrate understanding.
III. Low-order divergent—students think critically about information.
IV. High-order divergent—students perform creative and evaluative thinking.

Questioning Skills

Purpose is to encourage students to participate and think by engaging in group interaction. Components include:

1. Phrasing—teacher asks clear questions.
2. Adapting questions—teacher adjusts questions to language and ability of students.

3. Sequence—teacher asks questions in a planned and patterned order.
4. Balance—teacher asks convergent and divergent questions.
5. Participation—teacher stimulates a wide range of student involvement.
6. Probing—teacher follows up initial questions to encourage students to complete, clarify, expand, or support responses.
7. Wait time—teacher pauses after asking questions and student responses.
8. Student questions—teacher encourages students to ask questions.
9. Teacher statements—teacher uses statements as a nonquestioning alternative to encourage student interaction.

Supporting Skills

Purpose is to create a positive social-emotional classroom climate. Components include:

1. Acceptance of feelings—teacher recognizes and accepts students' feelings.
2. Praise—teacher verbally and nonverbally reinforces students' contributions.
3. Encouragement—teacher verbally encourages student participation.
4. Use of ideas—teacher accepts and uses students' ideas.
5. Courtesy—teacher expresses thanks or appreciation for students' help or contributions.

Information-Giving Skills

Information giving, as a technique teachers regularly display in the classroom, is basically a shortened and informal form of the lecture. Teachers frequently give information spontaneously, for example, in response to student questions and comments, when presenting an assignment, explaining something, giving short directions, and introducing a film or speaker. Information giving can also be more formal and involve more planning, such as when introducing a unit or summarizing learnings, demonstrating a skill or process, giving involved and extended directions, or presenting a formal explanation. Information giving might last from a brief moment to as long as 10 minutes. The lecture, in contrast to information giving, is generally more highly structured, more formal, and may last from approximately 10 to 45 minutes in a middle school or secondary classroom, depending on the situation.

Although most information giving takes place in unanticipated situations and therefore opportunities for planning are almost nonexistent, several considerations will increase the effectiveness of the communication. Spontaneous responses to questions, explanations, directions, and introductions need to be clearly understood by the students. Approaches to increase the probability of clarity include defining difficult terms and concepts as part of the commentary and providing examples and illustrations to aid comprehension. Feedback should also be solicited from the students. This can be accomplished by simply asking students if they have questions regarding the information given, requesting students to summarize key points, or asking students specific questions as part of a review. Much depends on the ability level of the students, the complexity of the content being presented, and time limitations.

Preparation for more formal information giving is similar to preparing for a lecture. The primary differences are the length of time of the information giving, and therefore, ostensibly, the time necessary for planning the presentation. This form of information giving might properly be termed a *minilecture* involving approximately 5 to 10 minutes. In addition to clarifying the lesson content and obtaining feedback characteristic of spontaneous information giving, additional considerations for formal information giving include, first, providing for an introduction, second, organizing the content, and, third, wrapping up with a brief closure.

The introduction to a minilecture should precisely communicate to students what content will be covered, why it is important to know it, and how it fits into the lesson or unit being studied. This need not take any more than one to two minutes within a brief 10-minute information-giving session.

Organization refers to the presentation of the content in a logical way, moving from simple facts, concepts, skills, or ideas to more complex ones. Starting with what the students know is a logical basis for presenting new information. This is the body of the minilecture. The intention of closure is to review what has been presented, determine the extent to which students understood what was covered, and make a tie-in to the next learning activity. Clearly the more time devoted to information giving, the more structured and formal the presentation must become in order to increase the probability that the students will understand what is being taught. Suggestions for conducting effective lectures are presented in chapter 7.

In addition to the aforementioned skills, other more personally related behaviors and skills influence the effectiveness of information giving. These behaviors have been previously presented and discussed as part of the technique of motivation in this chapter. Overall, a teacher presenting information, even for a short period of time, must be concerned with providing an enthusiastic image to focus and sustain students' attention and interest. Of course, the display of motivating skills becomes more essential as information giving turns into a lecture. Physical movement, use of nonverbal behaviors, and voice are among the most important motivating skills. If the teacher has the freedom to move during a short information-giving session, the probability for student attention to be maintained is increased. Nonverbal behaviors contribute to creating a dynamic presence, and are, therefore, an interesting and appealing focus for student attention. Naturally, voice volume and inflection are critical when presenting information.

Mr. Taylor's lesson was primarily discussion and activity oriented. Thus, he engaged in only two instances of information giving. The first time he reacted spontaneously to a student's insightful comment by providing reasons why their community initiated environmental legislation and how it was done. This took less than five minutes. The second time he explained their homework assignment. The assignment explanation, including passing out and clarifying the use of the survey form, took no longer than three to four minutes. Minimal information giving was required, primarily because the majority of Mr. Taylor's students had prior knowledge and experiences with their community's environmental problems, and they were interested in the topic.

Listening Skills

Another essential component of classroom interpersonal communication is the regular display of a teacher's listening behaviors. Primarily nonverbal in nature, they influence all forms of teacher-student interaction and contribute to the social-emotional climate of the classroom. As a result of teachers' impact on communication, it is important that they are aware of their use of listening behaviors and model them for students in class. Teacher modeling will also serve to encourage students indirectly to display appropriate listening skills.

The display of effective listening behaviors is dependent on the implementation of a series of skills. Seven behaviors have been identified by Garrett, Sadker, and Sadker (1990): eye contact, facial expressions, body posture, physical space, silence, brief verbal acknowledgments, and subsummaries. Maintaining eye contact with a student who responds to a teacher's question tacitly communicates the teacher's interest in what is being said. Having a personal knowledge of the respondent is important because some are uncomfortable with direct eye contact. A teacher's facial expressions provide the student with feedback about the teacher's reaction to what is being said. A smile as compared with a frown, for example, communicates a different mood and reaction to students. Overdoing facial expressions could also be distracting and hinder communication. Body posture can determine the formality the teacher intends for the situation, and body gestures communicate meaning. Gestures include the position of the arms, hands, and fingers, as well as touching. Communication can be quite varied, depending on how gestures are used, in what classroom situation, and with whom. The physical distance between the teacher and student(s) is also influential in communicating how close a teacher wants to be to the students; close proximity communicates intimacy, whereas distance communicates separateness. All of these nonverbal behaviors need to be closely monitored when working with groups and individual students because of their implicit positive and negative messages and potential impact on students.

The displays of verbal behaviors, particularly in conjunction with the aforementioned nonverbal behaviors, are effective in communicating to students that a teacher wants to hear what is being said and encourages continuance. The behavior most often associated with teacher listening is silence. Silence, or wait time, has already been discussed as an effective teacher questioning technique. It communicates interest and respect for what is being said and stimulates reflection. Too much silence can be awkward, and can hinder communication. Brief verbal acknowledgments uttered by the listener during discourse can communicate interest and concern to the speaker. For verbal acknowledgments to be effective they must be brief and infrequent. Examples include "hmmm," "I understand," and "okay." A brief verbal summary of what has been said may also be useful. Subsummaries are the least used of the listening skills, but occasionally summarizing for the speaker what has been said clarifies the message and supports the speaker (Garrett, Sadker, & Sadker, 1990).

Although we can readily imagine Mr. Taylor engaging in a variety of listening behaviors during the lesson depicted in the scenario, there was no direct indication that he used any specific listening skill. Indirect clues are the success he had in stimulating responses to his questions—many at the divergent level— and the respect students apparently had for him as indicated by the lack of classroom management problems. Mr. Taylor has established a positive climate for learning. One major characteristic of such a climate is the mutual respect between teacher and students. The congruence of the willingness to listen to one another and the display of listening skills is a contributing factor in the development of respect between teacher and students.

SUMMARY POINT

In addition to motivating skills, questions and questioning skills, and supporting skills, two other major instructional techniques are found in every effective teacher's instructional repertoire: information-giving skills and listening skills. Varying degrees of all these techniques can be found in each method and strategy teachers employ in the classroom. Research supports these techniques as effective teaching practices, and because of this, teachers need to consider these techniques carefully while making decisions about instructional variety during the planning stage. Skills associated with information giving have been positively related to students' learning efficiency and success. Listening skills contribute significantly to classroom communication and to a positive classroom climate. The decisions a teacher makes regarding the use of instructional techniques are critical because of their resulting impact on classroom climate, learning activities, and student outcomes.

REVIEW: IMPORTANT INFORMATION-GIVING SKILLS, LISTENING SKILLS, AND MANAGING SKILLS

Information-Giving Skills

Purpose is to provide students with limited amounts of information spontaneously or, more formally, to assist in attaining lesson objectives. Components include:

1. Clarity—teacher delineates content precisely, relates it to objectives, avoids irrelevant discourse.
2. Feedback—teacher obtains feedback from students during or after information giving.
3. Introduction—teacher prefaces minilecture with an introduction.
4. Organization—teacher presents content in a logical and purposeful manner.
5. Closure—teacher concludes or causes students to wrap up the lesson with reference to primary learnings.

Listening Skills

Purpose is to communicate to students that a teacher is interested in what a student is saying and that what is being said is important. Components include:

1. Eye contact—teacher maintains eye contact with students.
2. Facial expressions—teacher uses a variety of positive facial expressions in response to students' communications.
3. Body posture—teacher uses positive posture and a variety of gestures.
4. Physical distance—teacher adjusts position vis-à-vis students according to the conditions of instruction.
5. Silence—teacher maintains silence while the student is the active communicator.
6. Verbal acknowledgments—teacher uses brief appropriate verbal acknowledgments while listening to students.
7. Subsummaries—teacher interjects brief minisummaries while listening to students during lengthy communications.

QUESTIONS FOR REFLECTION

1. If you were a science student, would you like to be in the class of Richard Taylor, the scenario teacher? Of the techniques he displayed as he taught the lesson, which appeal to you the most and why?
2. What do you recall from your secondary school days was the most influential springboard or attention getter used by one of your teachers as an entry to a lesson? In what way was it influential?
3. Naturally it would be ideal if all teachers were motivating in terms of their personal and instructional behaviors. Which of the two, a teacher's dynamic display of verbal and nonverbal behaviors or a teacher's use of a variety of instructional techniques and methods, do you consider more important in terms of motivating students to participate and learn, and why?

4. Do you agree with some that questioning may be the most influential teaching behavior? Why?

5. In what ways might a teacher manage and control students' behavior using his or her questions in class?

6. What are some specific approaches that you might use to encourage students to generate questions that are related to content you might be teaching?

7. When you are involved in a conversation with friends, try using wait time to determine its impact on the interaction. Purposely pause three to five seconds after asking a question (wait time 1) and try pausing after getting a response (wait time 2). Was there a greater quantity and quality of responses?

8. Do you think that calling on nonvolunteering students is right? Under what circumstances would you call on and not call on nonvolunteering students? Do you agree that this is a democratic practice because all students have a democratic responsibility to participate in public talk? Why?

9. Which type of question do you feel more comfortable asking—closed (low and high convergent) or open-ended (low and high divergent)? Under what circumstances might you feel comfortable asking the other type of question?

10. Do you think that your participation in class is influenced by praise from the teacher? Or do you prefer another form of reinforcement? To what extent do you need praise? How would you characterize students who are motivated by extrinsic motivation? Intrinsic motivation?

11. Which teacher verbal and nonverbal behaviors have the most impact on you in terms of creating a dynamic teaching image? Why? Which ones, when overdone, turn you off and influence you negatively?

12. Have you noticed the different types of verbal and nonverbal behaviors talk-show hosts engage in to create interest and excitement about the topic for a particular show? In what ways might you and other teachers learn from the approaches that talk-show hosts take to whip up enthusiasm?

13. Suppose you are looking at a videotape of yourself teaching a class of your choice. What would you see in terms of your verbal and nonverbal strengths, and what is one area that you need to develop further? How might you develop it further?

TEACHER _____

OBSERVER _____

CLASS _____

DATE _____

ANALYSIS SCALES

OCCURRENCE	EFFECTIVENESS
1. Not evident	1. Not effective
2. Slightly evident	2. Slightly effective
3. Moderately evident	3. Moderately effective
4. Quite evident	4. Quite effective
N Not applicable	N Not applicable

CATEGORIES (Parts A + B Correspond to Occurrence and Effectiveness in the Analysis Scale)	A. OCCURRENCE	B. EFFECTIVENESS
1. CASUAL OR PERSONAL COMMENTS: A. Teacher makes casual or personal comments intended to affect the lesson entry. B. Teacher establishes a friendly, comfortable climate for learning.		
2. SPRINGBOARD: A. Teacher uses a springboard in the entry. B. Teacher establishes relevance of the content to arouse interest in the current lesson.		
3. ATTENTION GETTER: A. Teacher does something unexpected or sensational in the entry. B. Teacher stimulates students' curiosity, suspense, or creativity to focus attention.		
4. REVIEW: A. Teacher reviews learning from previous lesson. B. Teacher presents a well-organized, succinct review of pertinent learning that provides momentum for the new lesson, or teacher asks incisive review questions to begin the new lesson.		
5. PREVIEW: A. Teacher previews upcoming lesson. B. Teacher states the objectives pertinent to the lesson, presents the rationale, and describes enthusiastically the learning activities that are imminent.		

REFLECTIVE CONSIDERATIONS

Describe the entry used.

How much time was devoted to the entry?

What was the student response to the entry?

Why did you decide on this entry? (self-analysis)

To what extent did you achieve your purpose with this entry? (self-analysis)

ANALYSIS SCALES

TEACHER ———————————————

OBSERVER ——————————————

CLASS ———————————————

DATE ———————————————

	OCCURRENCE	EFFECTIVENESS
1.	Not evident	Not effective
2.	Slightly evident	Slightly effective
3.	Moderately evident	Moderately effective
4.	Quite evident	Quite effective
N	Not applicable	Not applicable

CATEGORIES (Parts A + B Correspond to Occurrence and Effectiveness in the Analysis Scale)	A. OCCURRENCE	B. EFFECTIVENESS
1. SUMMARY: A. Teacher summarizes or causes the lesson to be summarized. B. Teacher and/or students synthesize important points from the lesson; this includes more than only repeating the information in the lesson.		
2. INTEGRATION: A. Teacher cites the broad context within which the lesson is a part. B. Teacher meaningfully relates the lesson to the goals of the unit and to students' previous learnings.		
3. APPLICATION: A. Teacher mentions possible uses of the topic/skill learned. B. Teacher makes convincing suggestions regarding the intended immediate or long-range application of the learning outcomes.		
4. TRANSITION: A. Teacher builds a bridge to the next lesson with comments or an assignment. B. Teacher previews coming learnings/activities in a manner that piques student interest; teacher makes a thought-provoking assignment in anticipation of the next class meeting.		
5. REFERENCE TO ACCOMPLISHMENT: A. Teacher comments on accomplishment(s). B. Teacher analyzes the class's progress in terms of the learning objectives; teacher gives specific praise as deserved or encouragement as appropriate.		

REFLECTIVE CONSIDERATIONS

Describe the closure used.

How much time was devoted to the closure?

What was the student response to the closure?

Why did you decide on this closure? (self-analysis)

To what extent did you achieve your purpose with this closure? (self-analysis)

218

ANALYSIS FORM   MOTIVATING SKILLS

ANALYSIS SCALES

TEACHER _____

OBSERVER _____

CLASS _____

DATE _____

OCCURRENCE	EFFECTIVENESS
1. Not evident	1. Not effective
2. Slightly evident	2. Slightly effective
3. Moderately evident	3. Moderately effective
4. Quite evident	4. Quite effective
N Not applicable	N Not applicable

CATEGORIES (Parts A+B Correspond to Occurrence and Effectiveness in the Analysis Scale)	A. OCCURRENCE	B. EFFECTIVENESS
1. PHYSICAL MOVEMENT: A. Teacher uses movement purposely. B. Teacher successively repositions self in a manner that heightens students' attention and serves the monitoring function; does not pace nervously.		
2. NONVERBAL BEHAVIOR: A. Teacher uses a variety of nonverbal behaviors to create a presence. B. Teacher uses facial expression (laughs, smiles, frowns, scowls, looks inquisitive) for effect and emphasis; gestures, nods, points, touches; creates a dynamic presence.		
3. VOICE: A. Teacher uses voice to attract students' attention. B. Teacher has a pleasant voice with a meaningful tone that expresses confidence and competence; easily heard; inflection evident; speech pattern is appropriate for the level of class.		
4. LESSON PACE: A. Teacher varies the lesson pace. B. Teacher moderates or stimulates the flow of activity for optimum learning; adjusts pace in response to evidence of boredom, confusion, or frustration.		
5. INSTRUCTIONAL MODE: A. Teacher varies the instructional approach during the lesson. B. Teacher changes methods and learning activities with appropriate frequency; varies nature of student participation.		
6. ENTHUSIASM: A. Teacher embodies the qualities of liveliness and personal interest. B. Teacher employs a combination of verbal and nonverbal behaviors, lesson pacing, and lesson modes that visibly affect students' attention and participation.		

REFLECTIVE CONSIDERATIONS

What aspect of the lesson created the most motivation within the students?

How do you know?

ANALYSIS FORM   *QUESTION LEVELS*

TEACHER _____   CLASS _____

OBSERVER _____   DATE _____

COGNITIVE LEVELS—

	NUMBER OF QUESTIONS ASKED	PERCENTAGE OF TOTAL	ESTIMATED % OF TIME DEVOTED TO EACH LEVEL
LEVEL I—LOW-ORDER CONVERGENT: Requires students to recall or recognize information. Emphasis on memorization and observation. Responses can easily be anticipated. Students define, recognize, quote, identify, recall, and answer "yes" or "no." Corresponds to Bloom's "knowledge" level.		%	%
LEVEL II—HIGH-ORDER CONVERGENT: Requires students to demonstrate understanding and apply information. Students describe, compare, contrast, rephrase, summarize, explain, translate, interpret, relate, apply, use, provide an example, and solve. Corresponds to Bloom's "comprehension" and "application" levels.		%	%
LEVEL III—LOW-ORDER DIVERGENT: Requires student to think critically about information, ideas, and opinions. Students discover motives, reasons, or causes; draw conclusions, inferences, or generalizations; provide evidence or support for conclusions, inferences, or generalizations. Corresponds to Bloom's "analysis" level.		%	%
LEVEL IV—HIGH-ORDER DIVERGENT: Requires students to perform original, creative, and evaluative thinking. Students produce original communications, make predictions, propose solutions, create, solve lifelike problems, speculate, construct, devise, write, design, hypothesize, synthesize, develop/judge ideas and problem solutions, express opinions, and make choices and decisions. Corresponds to Bloom's "synthesis" and "evaluation" levels.		%	%
Totals		%	%

REFLECTIVE CONSIDERATIONS

What indications did you notice that students were engaging in critical thinking?

To what extent were students' responses congruent to the levels of the teacher's questions?

ANALYSIS FORM   *QUESTIONING SKILLS*

TEACHER _____

OBSERVER _____

CLASS _____

DATE _____

	OCCURRENCE	EFFECTIVENESS
	1. Not evident	1. Not effective
	2. Slightly evident	2. Slightly effective
	3. Moderately evident	3. Moderately effective
	4. Quite evident	4. Quite effective
	N Not applicable	N Not applicable

CATEGORIES (Parts A+B Correspond to Occurrence and Effectiveness in the Analysis Scale)	A. OCCURRENCE	B. EFFECTIVENESS
1. PHRASING: A. Teacher uses questions. B. Teacher phrases questions so that response expectations are clearly communicated to students; no run-on questions.		
2. ADAPTING QUESTIONS: A. Teacher adapts questions to the class. B. Teacher adjusts questions to the language and ability level of the students.		
3. SEQUENCE: A. Teacher asks questions sequentially. B. Teacher asks questions in a patterned order indicating a purposeful questioning strategy.		
4. BALANCE: A. Teacher balances convergent and divergent questions. B. Teacher uses questions at appropriate levels to achieve the objectives of the lesson.		
5. PARTICIPATION: A. Teacher uses questions to simulate a wide range of student participation. B. Teacher encourages student involvement by balancing responses from volunteering and nonvolunteering students; redirects initially answered questions to other students; encourages student-student interaction particularly appropriate during a discussion.		
6. PROBING: A. Teacher probes initial student responses to questions, particularly during discussions. B. Teacher follows up initial student responses with questions that encourage students to complete, clarify, expand, or support their responses.		
7. WAIT TIME: A. Teacher uses wait time after asking questions and after students' responses, particularly during discussions. B. Teacher pauses a minimum of 3 seconds after asking divergent questions to allow student thinking; teacher also pauses after students' initial responses to questions to encourage continued commentary.		

continued

8. STUDENT QUESTIONS: A. Teacher requests students to ask questions. B. Teacher encourages students to devise pertinent questions to stimulate thinking at the divergent level; students ask thoughtful questions.		
9. TEACHER STATEMENTS: A. Teacher balances question asking with statement making, particularly during discussions. B. Teacher uses a variety of statement forms (declarative, reflective, interest, speaker referral) to encourage student interaction.		

REFLECTIVE CONSIDERATIONS

Did the questions asked elicit the quality of thinking intended?

How would you describe the questioning strategy (or pattern) used by the teacher?

If the teacher used both questioning and statements, which do you think was more effective in stimulating interaction and thinking? Why?

Of all the questioning techniques used, which do you think was the most influential in encouraging critical thinking?

How do you know?

ANALYSIS SCALES

TEACHER _____

OBSERVER _____

CLASS _____

DATE _____

OCCURRENCE	EFFECTIVENESS
1. Not evident	1. Not effective
2. Slightly evident	2. Slightly effective
3. Moderately evident	3. Moderately effective
4. Quite evident	4. Quite effective
N Not applicable	N Not applicable

CATEGORIES (Parts A+B Correspond to Occurrence and Effectiveness in the Analysis Scale)	A. OCCURRENCE	B. EFFECTIVENESS
1. ACCEPTANCE OF FEELINGS: A. Teacher recognizes and accepts students' feelings. B. Teacher responds to students' expression of feelings with sensitivity, possibly empathy.		
2. PRAISE: A. Teacher expresses approval of students' efforts. B. Teacher uses a variety of verbal and nonverbal praise; praise is stated simply and genuinely; accomplishment is specified.		
3. ENCOURAGEMENT: A. Teacher requests students to participate. B. Teacher uses expressions of encouragement to stimulate students to initiate or continue with a task or learning activity.		
4. USE OF IDEAS: A. Teacher acknowledges students' ideas. B. Teacher repeats or paraphrases students' comments; elaborates on students' ideas; refers back to previous ideas of students.		
5. COURTESY: A. Teacher thanks students for help or contributions. B. Teacher uses expressions indicating appreciation for students' assistance, ideas, and efforts; teacher contributes to students' feelings of belonging and having worth and dignity.		

REFLECTIVE CONSIDERATIONS

What evidence is available of the effect of the teacher's supportive behavior on students?

How would you describe the social-emotional climate of the classroom?

223

ANALYSIS SCALES

TEACHER _____

OBSERVER _____

CLASS _____

DATE _____

OCCURRENCE	EFFECTIVENESS
1. Not evident	1. Not effective
2. Slightly evident	2. Slightly effective
3. Moderately evident	3. Moderately effective
4. Quite evident	4. Quite effective
N Not applicable	N Not applicable

CATEGORIES (Parts A + B Correspond to Occurrence and Effectiveness in the Analysis Scale)	A. OCCURRENCE	B. EFFECTIVENESS
SPONTANEOUS 1. CLARITY: A. Teacher presents information clearly to the students. B. Teacher defines difficult terms and concepts; examples and illustrations are used to aid comprehension.		
2. FEEDBACK: A. Teacher obtains feedback from students during or after information giving. B. Teacher asks students if they have questions, requests they summarize key points, or directly asks review questions.		
MINILECTURE 3. INTRODUCTION: A. Teacher prefaces minilecture with an introduction. B. Teacher communicates to students what content will be covered, why it is important, and how it relates to the lesson/unit being studied.		
4. ORGANIZATION: A. Teacher presents a cohesive body of information/content to the students. B. Teacher's presentation is logically organized; teacher moves from simple to complex ideas, skills, concepts; teaching aids are employed; new content is related to students' current knowledge.		
5. CLOSURE: A. Teacher makes a discrete closure to the minilecture. B. Teacher reviews, or has students review, what was presented; bridge to the next learning activity is made.		

REFLECTIVE CONSIDERATION

How would you describe the students' behaviors during the presentation?

ANALYSIS FORM   LISTENING SKILLS

ANALYSIS SCALES

TEACHER _____

OBSERVER _____

CLASS _____

DATE _____

OCCURRENCE	EFFECTIVENESS
1. Not evident	1. Not effective
2. Slightly evident	2. Slightly effective
3. Moderately evident	3. Moderately effective
4. Quite evident	4. Quite effective
N Not applicable	N Not applicable

CATEGORIES (Parts A + B Correspond to Occurrence and Effectiveness in the Analysis Scale)	A. OCCURRENCE	B. EFFECTIVENESS
NONVERBAL 1. EYE CONTACT: A. Teacher maintains eye contact with the students. B. Teacher uses continuous eye contact as the students respond to questions, initiate comments, etc.; eye contact is accompanied with positive facial expressions; teacher does not create discomfort by staring.		
2. FACIAL EXPRESSIONS: A. Teacher facial expression in response to students' comments is evident. B. Teacher shows interest in what the students are saying by smiling, nodding, and changing expressions as appropriate.		
3. BODY POSTURE: A. Teacher "body language" in response to students' comments is evident. B. Teacher uses postures indicating attention and interest; gestures using body, hands, fingers are appropriate and not distracting.		
4. PHYSICAL DISTANCE: A. Teacher moves with apparent purpose regarding student-teacher communication. B. Teacher establishes and maintains close proximity in order to hear when working with individual students and small discussion groups.		

continued

VERBAL

5. SILENCE: A. Teacher maintains silence as students speak responsibily. B. Teacher uses congruent nonverbal behaviors including eye contact and body posture while listening; does not interrupt except to use brief verbal acknowledgements, paraphrases, or subsummaries.		
6. VERBAL ACKNOWLEDGMENTS: A. Teacher uses verbal acknowledgments while listening to students' extended communications. B. Teacher interjects brief comments communicating interest, concern, and encouragement.		
7. SUBSUMMARIES: A. Teacher responds with minisummaries during lengthy communications. B. Teacher displays congruent and appropriate nonverbal behaviors while using subsummaries.		

REFLECTIVE CONSIDERATIONS

Describe the general demeanor of the teacher as a listener.

What is the apparent effect of the teacher's listening behavior on students?

REFERENCES

Allen, D., & Ryan, K. (1969). *Microteaching*. Reading, MA: Addison-Wesley.

Atwood, V., & Wilen, W. (1991). Wait time and effective social studies instruction: What can research in science education tell us? *Social Education, 55*(3), 179–181.

Berliner, D. C. (1984). The half-full glass: A review of research on teaching. In P. L. Hosford (Ed.), *Using what we know about teaching*. Alexandria, VA: Association for Supervision and Curriculum Development.

Bloom, B. (Ed.). (1956). *A taxonomy of educational objectives: Handbook I. Cognitive domain*. New York: McKay.

Brophy, J. (1981). Teacher praise: A functional analysis. *Review of Educational Research*, 51, 5–32.

Brophy, J., & Good, T. L. (1986). Teacher behavior and student achievement. In M. Wittrock (Ed.), *Handbook of research on teaching*. New York: Macmillan.

Brophy, J., Rohrkemper, M., Rasid, H., & Goldberger, M. (1983). Relationships between teachers' presentations of classroom tasks and students' engagement in those tasks. *Journal of Educational Psychology, 75*, 544–552.

Chance, P. (1992). The rewards of learning. *Phi Delta Kappan, 74*(3), 200–207.

Christenbury, L., & Kelly, P. (1983). *Questioning: A path to critical thinking*. Urbana, IL: ERIC Clearinghouse on Reading and Communication Skills and the National Council for Teachers of English.

Costa, A., & Lowery, L. (1989). *Techniques for teaching thinking*. Pacific Grove, CA: Midwest Publications.

DeCecco, J. P. (1968). *The psychology of learning and instruction: Educational psychology*. Englewood Cliffs, NJ: Prentice-Hall.

Dillon, J. T. (1988). *Questioning and teaching: A manual of practice*. New York: Columbia University.

Dillon, J. T. (1990). Conducting discussions by alternatives to questioning. In W. Wilen (Ed.), *Teaching and learning through discussion*. Springfield, IL: Charles C. Thomas.

Dillon, J. T. (1994). *Using discussion in classrooms*. Buckingham, England: Open University Press.

Fisher, C. W., Berliner, D. C., Filby, N. N., Marliave, R. S., Cahen, L. S., & Dishaw, M. M. (1980). Teaching behaviors, academic learning time and student achievement: An overview. In C. Denham & A. Lieberman (Eds.), *Time to learn*. Washington, DC: National Institute for Education.

Flanders, N. A. (1970). Analyzing teacher behavior. Reading, MA: Addison-Wesley.

Gage, N. L., & Berliner, D. C. (1992). *Educational psychology* (5th ed.). Boston: Houghton Mifflin.

Gallagher, J. J., & Aschner, M. J. (1963). A preliminary report on analyses of classroom interaction. *Merrill-Palmer Quarterly, 9*, 183–194.

Garrett, S. S., Sadker, M., & Sadker, D. (1990). Interpersonal communication skills. In J. M. Cooper (Ed.), *Classroom teaching skills* (4th ed.). Lexington, MA: Heath.

Good, T., & Brophy, J. (1991). *Looking in classrooms* (5th ed.). New York: HarperCollins.

Good, T., & Brophy, J. (1994). *Looking in classrooms* (6th ed.). New York: HarperCollins.

Good, T., & McCaslin, M. (1992). Teaching effectiveness. In M. Alkin (Ed.), *Encyclopedia of educational research* (6th ed., Vol. 4, pp. 1373–1388). New York: Macmillan.

Guilford, J. P. (1956). The structure of intellect. *Psychological Bulletin, 53*, 267–293.

Hawes, G. R., & Hawes, L. S. (1982). *The concise dictionary of education.* New York: Van Nostrand Reinhold.

Hunkins, F. P. (1989). Teaching thinking through effective questioning. Boston, MA: Christopher-Gordon.

Kelly, T. E. (1993). *Calling on nonvolunteers in the classroom: Democratic imperative or misguided invasion?* Paper presented at the annual meeting of the American Research Association, Atlanta, GA.

Levin, T., with Long, R. (1981). *Effective instruction.* Washington, DC: Association for Supervision and Curriculum Development.

Rowe, M. (1987). Using wait time to stimulate inquiry. In W. W. Wilen (Ed.), *Questions, questioning techniques, and effective teaching.* Washington, DC: National Education Association, 95–106.

Rowe, M. B. (1974). Wait time and reward as instructional variables, their influence on language, logic and fate control: Part 1. Wait time. *Journal of Research on Science Teaching, 11*, 81–94.

Schuck, R. F. (1985). An empirical analysis of the power of set induction and systematic questioning as instructional strategies. *Journal of Teacher Education, 36*, 38–43.

Shostak, R. (1990). Lesson presentation skills. In J. M. Cooper (Ed.), *Classroom teaching skills* (4th ed.). Lexington, MA: Heath.

Strother, D. B. (1987). On listening. *Phi Delta Kappan, 68*(8), 625–628.

Susi, F. D. (1985). Spatial mapping as a method for observing classroom art instruction. *Studies in Art, 26*, 163–168.

Susi, F. D. (1986). Physical space and the teaching of art. *Art Education, 39*(2), 6–9.

Wang, M., Haertel, G., and Walberg, H. (1994). What helps students learn? *Educational Leadership, 51*, 74–79.

Waxman, H. C. (1987–1988). Effective lesson introductions and preinstructional activities: A review of recent research. *Journal of Classroom Interaction, 23*(1), 5–7.

Wilen, W. W. (1987). Effective questions and questioning: A classroom application. In W. W. Wilen (Ed.), *Questions, questioning techniques, and effective teaching.* Washington, DC: National Education Association.

Wilen, W. W. (1991). *Questioning skills, for teachers* (3rd ed.). In *What research says to the teacher* series. Washington, DC: National Education Association.

Wilen, W. W. (1994). What research says to teachers about classroom questioning. *Social Educator* (Australia), *12*, 94–101.

Wilen, W. W., & Clegg, A. A. (1986). Effective questions and questioning: A research review. *Theory and Research in Social Education, 14*, 153–161.

Wilen, W. W., & White, J. J. (1991). Interaction and Discourse in Social Studies Classrooms. In J. Shaver (Ed.), *Handbook of research on social studies teaching and learning* (pp. 483–495). New York: Macmillan.

Zemelman, S., Daniels, H., and Hyde, A. (1993). *Best practice: New standards for teaching and learning in America's schools*. Portsmouth, NH: Heinemann.

CHAPTER **7** Primary Instructional
Methods

OUTLINE

Experienced teachers accumulate a repertoire of methods and make conscientious decisions on a regular basis about how these methods might be effectively employed to achieve lesson objectives and unit goals.

The focus in the previous two chapters has been on planning and teaching skills. In this chapter we synthesize teaching techniques into instructional methods.

In its most general sense, an instructional method is a pattern of teaching actions designed to achieve student-learning outcomes. Central to this definition is the term *pattern*, which suggests a planned and sequential arrangement of actions. Actions refer to the variety of techniques available to teachers as they plan for lessons. Techniques that are common to all methods are described in chapter 6. A method can be applied in its essential form to many subject areas, and can be used by different teachers recurrently. We are also reminded that there are an indeterminant number of variations of procedure and style as teachers make decisions and plan for the implementation of any one method, or for a combination of methods. This within-method variability should be perceived as a strength (Gage & Berliner, 1992).

FOCUS QUESTIONS

1. Instructional methods are designed to achieve general educational goals. For what purposes do discussion, lecture, inquiry, and simulation gaming serve?

2. In what ways does the discussion method contribute toward students' understanding of the content?

3. Although the lecture method is most associated with university-level teaching, it is used extensively in various forms at the secondary level. How might this method be used most effectively by secondary teachers?

4. How does the teacher's use of the inquiry method teach a process that has application to life outside the classroom as well as to content?

5. A major value of the simulation-gaming method is involving students in

authentic task and problematic situations. In what ways is this purpose related to constructivist-oriented principles?

OVERVIEW

The focus of this chapter is on the presentation of four primary instructional methods representing a wide range of subject areas that can be used by teachers at the middle and high school levels. These methods are discussion, lecture, inquiry, and simulation gaming. Several specific forms of each are presented. Each method is designed to achieve a particular kind of learning outcome and is generally flexible enough to be adapted to the range of student abilities and interests. Each form of the four primary methods is described in terms of the instructional techniques essential for successful implementation. Patterns of sequential phases for the four primary methods are presented to assist teachers in using them practically in the classrooms. Experienced teachers accumulate a repertoire of methods and make conscientious decisions regularly about how these methods might be effectively employed to achieve lesson objectives and unit goals. Analysis forms for the discussion, lecture, inquiry, and simulation-gaming methods are included at the end of the chapter to summarize the major features of each method and to aid in your observation and analysis of their use.

SCENARIO

Robert Carl realized that one advantage of getting to school early was that he did not have to wait in line for the copying machine. This morning he was making a transparency of a map (see Figure 7.1). If all went as well as Mr. Carl had planned, the map would serve as a springboard into a new unit. It was intended to stimulate higher-level thinking in his 2nd-period economics class. Although the students were bright, he thought they would probably not immediately guess that the countries on the map were shaped and sized unusually because they were drawn to depict the countries' gross national product (GNP) rather than their physical size. As he started back to his room, he smiled at the thought of successfully challenging their critical-thinking abilities.

"Today we start a new unit, one that will require you to apply what you have learned for the past two months. We have been studying the separate parts of the economy—the role of the consumer, producer, worker, government, corporation, and labor unions—and how each contributes to the big picture. Now we are going to change our focus from microeconomics to macroeconomics and begin a study of the interrelationships among the sectors of the economy and its performance.

"I would like to introduce some new ideas that contain a kind of puzzle for you to try to solve." Mr. Carl noticed two students toward the rear

Figure 7.1 A GNP Perspective of the World. Adapted from *Newsweek*, October 26, 1981, Marta Norman and Richard Tringali. "The World Turned Upside Down." Reprinted by permission.

233

of the room glance up from their desks upon the mention of a puzzle. He placed the transparency of a miniature world map on the overhead projector. "What do you see?"

The first response was, "It's a map of the world with all of the countries. But the countries are shaped differently, with no rounded edges like on a real map."

Another student jumped in, "China's a lot larger than the United States, but not on this map. It doesn't make any sense."

"The map is divided into northern and southern hemispheres," added another.

At this point Mr. Carl thought the stage was set to begin the formal inquiry. "The map does make sense if you know the key to the puzzle. I would like you to try to discover it by asking me questions. But there is a hitch. I will only answer 'yes' or 'no' to your questions, so you will have to think carefully as you phrase them."

"Why is the United States the largest country on this map?"

"You will need to rephrase your question so I can answer 'yes' or 'no.'"

"Okay (pause). Could the map measure something other than size?"

"What do you mean by size?"

"Size. How big the United States is physically."

"Yes. The map is measuring something else."

One student pointed out the size of Japan in relation to the other countries. Another wondered why Denmark was almost as large as Australia. Another asked why Australia was part of the northern hemisphere and India a part of the southern hemisphere on this map. Still another wanted to know if the map was drawn by a computer. After more discussion a hypothesis was offered. "Does the map measure the number of cars in the world?"

"Our first proposed solution to the puzzle. A good idea! Rather than you getting the answer now, what further questions could you ask me to test your guess?"

"What do you mean?" someone asked with a puzzled look.

"Remember that when we use inquiry you have to gather information related to your proposed solutions to a problem. Here we have the same idea, only different in that your questions try to get from me the necessary information to test your hypotheses. Think about the relationships of the countries. How about a 'what if' question?"

(Pause.) "If Mexico doubled its production of cars, would its size on the map double?"

"No. But its size would increase." Several other students offered hypotheses that also centered on products such as steel, computers, and wheat. Eventually one student hypothesized money as the basis for each country's size, and this quickly led to wealth and GNP. After each hypoth-

esis was tested with more student questions, the solution to the puzzle—
the depiction of GNP—was confirmed.

After discussing what clues led a student to discover that GNP was
the answer, Mr. Carl complimented the students on their perseverance
and perceptiveness. He then defined GNP, gave examples of goods and
services included in the computation of GNP, and provided statistics to
support the size of some of the countries in both halves on the map. He
also explained that the north-south line on the map was not meant to be
the equator but rather roughly 30 degrees north latitude.

"We are going to be spending the next several weeks on the concept of GNP because it is one of the most important indicators of economic growth in the United States, or a thermometer of our economic
health, in a sense. It is also directly related to our standard of living. In
other words, how well we live, what we can buy, and the services available to us."

"Let's take a look at our map again. Why do you suppose the countries roughly south of the 30 degrees north latitude line are smaller than
those in the north?"

"They have smaller GNPs."

"Right. But why are so many of the small GNP nations located south
of the United States?"

One student suggested it might have something to do with climate
because it is hotter in the southern hemisphere. He jokingly followed up
with a comment about people taking siestas every day. Another thought
that the northern countries had more technology. After further discussion,
one student commented that some of the most heavily populated countries, such as China and India, were south of the line.

"You have come up with some fine ideas and possible explanations
for this problem, and we will have an opportunity to pursue our inquiry
further when we learn more about GNP. I have some excellent sources
for you to consult and have made arrangements for a guest speaker to
visit us on Monday. He is a graduate student from Brazil majoring in economics at the university. I think he will be an excellent source of information and that we will learn a lot about those factors that influence economic growth, particularly in those countries to the south of us."

Noticing that class time was almost over, Mr. Carl reviewed the lesson by asking the students what they had learned about GNP today. He
gave chapter 9 as the reading assignment in the text. "I also want you to
watch the news tonight on television or read the paper to find out the lat-
est quarter's GNP figures that are to be reported today. We will use them
tomorrow as we begin formalizing some possible explanations and start
our search for data. Depending on the number of hypotheses we can
come up with, perhaps we can form into small groups for the investigation. So long!"

RESEARCH AND THEORETICAL BASE: INSTRUCTIONAL METHODS

Very little research has been conducted on instructional methods, especially that which attempts to determine the effectiveness of various methods in terms of increasing students' learning gains. Most of the research has focused on comparing one method with another. This avenue has not been fruitful because, in general, for most students the use of different teaching methods does not seem to make a difference in learning. Different methods have yielded similar average results when the criterion measured has been achievement. In addition, based on a review of available research, students with varying aptitudes will probably be affected differently by particular methods. This is only one of several factors, including instructional costs, time, and student attitude, that will need to be considered when choosing among different methods and strategies and making other decisions about instruction (Berliner & Gage, 1976).

Another generalized research finding indicates that using a variety of methods increases the probability that student interest will be maintained and that higher achievement gains will be made. Based on their review of research, Good and Brophy (1987) noted that the "systematic use of a variety of techniques produces better results than heavy reliance on any one technique, even a good one" (p. 342).

Although research suggests that different instructional approaches should be used with low- and high-achieving students, Evertson (1982) found that this does not occur in practice. Her study investigated the differences in instructional methods and activities in higher- and lower-achieving English and mathematics classes at urban junior high schools. Each teacher selected for the study had higher- and lower-ability sections of students. After a year of observation she noted that the teachers did not vary their activity patterns for the different sections of students. In other words, these teachers did not instruct their high- and low-achieving students differently. Furthermore, she found definite instructional patterns for English and mathematics teachers.

What are teachers' preferences for various teaching methods and strategies? Thompson (1981) used a rating form to get at urban and suburban elementary and secondary teachers' preferences for Joyce and Weil's (1992) teaching models. Their choices indicated that secondary teachers placed more emphasis on strategies stimulating intellectual skills and growth than elementary teachers, who emphasized the social growth of students.

RESEARCH AND THEORETICAL BASE: DISCUSSION METHOD

Along with lecture and recitation, discussion supposedly has been one of the most used instructional methods at all levels. In their review of descriptive studies on interaction patterns, though, Gall and Gall (1976) suggested that discussion is used infrequently. They characterized discussions by "student-to-student interaction and educational objectives related to complex thinking processes and attitude change" (p. 168). In his review, Dillon (1984) indicated that there was a problem because almost all teacher-student interaction sessions were labeled "discussions," when most should have been labeled recitations because of the use of a highly structured interaction pattern to facilitate students' recall of knowledge.

A primary difference between recitation and discussion is the teacher's willingness to encourage students to assume discussion leadership responsibility. Based on their review of research on interaction in social studies classrooms, Wilen and White (1991) concluded that teachers excessively controlled classroom dialogue through the prevalent "teacher question–student response–teacher reaction interaction" pattern. They found that a discussion is characterized more as a group conversation during which there is greater equity and power sharing between the teacher and students. This atmosphere is more appropriate for achieving social studies goals related to citizenship education, particularly those associated with democratic processes and practices.

True discussion, in many ways, is synonymous with the purposes of democracy because it is congruous with such democratic values as a concern for rationality, commitment to fairness, and respect for other people's opinions and feelings (Wilen, 1994). Parker (1992) suggested that teachers give students an opportunity to experience conversation with people of different genders and of different age, ethnic, and ability groups—which is characteristic of democracy—by discussing, for example, common societal issues and problems. In their research on the discussion of controversial issues, Harwood and Hahn (1990) found that students benefited from discussion because their civic feelings and attitudes were positively influenced.

In their review of research on teaching for understanding, Brophy (1992) devised generalized principles and practices for all subject areas including one on the need for creating discussion environments. He advocates creating classroom learning communities based on interactive discourse designed to encourage the social construction of meaning and to promote conceptual understanding. "Increasingly, research is pointing to thoughtful discussion, and not just teacher or student recitation, as characteristic of the discourse involved in teaching for understanding" (p. 5). Zemelman, Daniels, and Hyde (1993) also included in their standards for "best practice" in social studies the need to increase student participation in interactive and cooperative study by focusing on the open expression of ideas. The standard for discussion can easily apply to other subject areas, such as science, English, and health, that realistically might have analysis of issues and resolution of problems as two of their curricular emphases.

Based on their extensive review of literature on the discussion method, particularly in the area of group dynamics, Gall and Gall (1976) made several recommendations related to the effective use of discussions in the classroom. Class size is critical, with the optimal group size being five students. To accommodate the reality of the school classroom, it was suggested that dividing classes into small groups might be a useful instructional approach. Another recommendation involved using heterogeneous groups for group discussions because of the potential input from a variety of perspectives represented in a diverse group of students. Moderate cohesiveness should be fostered by the teacher so that minority points of view are respected. Another recommendation suggested that teachers consistently model a democratic leadership style rather than an authoritarian one to encourage student thinking and involvement.

Several extensive reviews of research on discussion practices suggest considerable potential for the use of discussion in classroom practice. Gall and Gall (1990) noted that the discussion method is very effective in achieving five types of learning outcomes: (1) subject-matter mastery, (2) problem solving, (3) moral development, (4) attitude change and development, and (5) communication skills. Based on her review of anthropological research on classroom interaction that involved minority students, White (1990) found that teachers could successfully employ a variety of techniques and strategies to encourage culturally different students to participate in discussions.

In his recent book on classroom discussion, Dillon (1994) described several important characteristics of discussion and suggested guidelines to help operationalize this method for classroom use. In a basic sense he mentioned that logical conditions needed to be in place for a discussion to take place: people must talk, listen, and respond to one another, and when they talk, they must be offering more than one point of view on the subject. Also, their intention in discussion must be to enhance their knowledge, understanding, or judgment of the subject under discussion. The driving force of a discussion is a question that invites joint inquiry. Teachers need to take care in formulating a key question "which captures the class' present predicament over the subject matter" (p. 61). Once under way, the discussion is run primarily on nonquestioning alternatives rather than questions because Dillon's research shows that questions foil discussion while a variety of statement forms, wait time, signals, and student questions encourage it. These alternatives are discussed under Phase III (investigation) of the discussion method in the "Application to Practice" section.

Research indicates that the discussion method is as effective as other approaches in learning subject matter. It may be even more effective than other methods, including the lecture, if achieving higher cognitive-level outcomes is the goal (Gall & Gall, 1976). Gage (1969) offered that research emphasis should not be put on comparing methods, such as lecture and discussion, but rather on determining which methods are most effective in achieving specific objectives.

APPLICATION TO PRACTICE: DISCUSSION METHOD

In its most basic form, a discussion is an "educative, reflective, and structured group conversation" with and among students (Wilen, 1990, p. 3).

An examination of the concepts included with the general definition of discussion just provided enhances our understanding of its potential use in the classroom. A key word in the definition is *conversation*, which is a form of social intercourse among familiar people, an informal exchange of thoughts and feelings. By intending that the conversation be *educative*, emphasis is placed on providing purpose and direction through attaining instructional objectives. *Reflective* refers to encouraging students to think critically and creatively at the higher cognitive levels. *Structured* suggests that the conversation is organized and conducted by one or more leaders. A *group* to most teachers means, of course, a class of 20 to 30 students.

One "quasi discussion" and three types of discussion are used by teachers: recitation, guided discussion, reflective discussion, and small-group discussion. They share a common thread requiring the teacher and students to interact verbally for learning to occur. Each differs in terms of purpose, structure, interaction pattern, and levels of student thinking stimulated.

Recitation (Quasi Discussion)

Recitation has been labeled a quasi discussion primarily because it is not intended to be a group conversation. Whereas it is similar to discussion in that it is structured, involves interaction with students, and is designed to achieve objectives, it is not reflective interaction. Discussions have different purposes and interaction patterns, and are used to stimulate higher levels of student thinking (Wilen, 1990). The convention of referring to recitations as quasi discussion was used by Roby (1988) in his research report on discussion models. A teacher uses a recitation primarily to ascertain the extent to which students have memorized pertinent facts. The interaction pattern typically is teacher question, student response, and teacher reaction, a pattern Bellack, Kliebard, Hyman, and Smith (1966) found common in their studies. The pace of the interaction is fairly rapid. Level I low-order convergent questions are the primary ones asked by the teacher to stimulate recall of knowledge. Questions at this level are who, what, when, and where questions. (See chapter 6 for a description of the four types of questions.) The intent of the teacher using recitation is to engage students in what Hudgins (1971, p. 129) termed "reproductive thinking," as opposed to productive thinking, in which students demonstrate understanding or ability to apply learning. An important questioning technique teachers need to use consistently during a recitation is directing questions to both volunteering and nonvolunteering students to get them all involved and to diagnose their knowledge.

Recitation is highly structured with the teacher clearly in control and directing the learning. Roby (1988, p. 166) referred to recitation as a "quiz show" because students try to discover the right answers to topic-oriented teacher questions. If, for example, the students have been diligent in reading the chapter from the literature text, observing the history film or physics demonstration, practicing the pronunciations of French vocabulary, and memorizing the spelling words or mathematics formulas, the teacher will be able to cover the content quickly. Recitation is generally efficient in terms of time demands, which is one reason why it is the most widely used form of discussion. Furthermore, only brief planning or preparation time is required. Teachers can conveniently fit it into practically any part of a lesson. There is a drawback, however, because teachers tend to rely on it too much. Recitation should, ideally, serve as a means to diagnose student progress in learning basic information and their readiness to use that information to develop meaning and deeper understanding.

Guided Discussion

The purpose of guided discussion is to promote understanding of important concepts, generalizations, ideas, values, problems, or issues (Wilen, 1990). The interaction pattern of the guided discussion is similar to recitation in that the teacher generally asks questions, students respond, and the teacher reacts. Differences are apparent, though, because of the emphasis on higher-level thinking. When a teacher asks a question, more than one student may respond, particularly if differences in opinion are expressed. In addition to the possibility of more students responding to each question, some interaction among students may occur. This is certainly not common during recitations, but is more prevalent during reflective discussions (explained in the next section) and is an absolute necessity during small-group discussions. We should also expect some students to begin asking questions for the purpose of explanation and clarification.

The cognitive levels of a teacher's questions appropriate to achieve the goals of a guided discussion generally are Level II high-order convergent and Level III low-order divergent. Convergent questions might, for example, request students to make comparisons between country and bluegrass music, explain South Africa's former policy of apartheid, describe how safety is a critical consideration in an industrial arts laboratory, or interpret a political cartoon. Divergent questions might involve students in drawing conclusions to a difficult chemistry laboratory experiment. During a guided discussion, a teacher may probe some students' responses because clarification is needed, or to extend thinking. Wait time becomes more important because students need time to think of responses to higher-level questions. The teacher will also want to encourage students to begin asking questions.

A guided discussion is moderately structured in that the teacher still assumes the major role of directing learning. As one might surmise, it is not as structured as a recitation, but more structured than a reflective discussion. The discussion is guided because the teacher wants to lead students to predetermined higher-level understandings. However, students have more freedom to present, explore, and test their ideas. Guided discussions still focus primarily on the cognitive dimension of subject matter in contrast to reflective discussions, which also involve affective learnings.

Reflective Discussion

The reflective discussion is potentially the highest level of discussion in terms of stimulated student thinking and student interaction with others related to the content. It is also the least structured, has the potential to generate the most student-student interaction, and generally requires a greater investment of time than the other modes of discussion. It is probably the most difficult form of discussion to conduct, and, in any case, is the discussion format least used by teachers.

The purpose of a reflective discussion is to require students to engage in high-level critical and creative thinking as they synthesize and evaluate information, opinions, and ideas. Students solve problems, clarify values, explore controversial issues, and form and defend positions during reflective discussions (Wilen, 1990). In many ways it is the most exciting of the discussion strategies because of its potential to push students to the highest levels of cognition. For students to respond reflectively to a teacher's questions, they must have a solid understanding of the subject matter that serves as a basis of the discussion. If not, the discussion may turn into what Roby (1988, p. 169) referred to as a "bull session" in which both teachers and students think they have the right answers, freely shared without any supportive data. Reflective thinking requires students to learn the facts, perhaps through class recitations, and to develop understanding, perhaps through teacher-guided discussions. Without knowledge and understanding, opinions cannot be supported and, therefore, are useless in achieving the goals of a reflective discussion.

The interaction pattern is flexible and can range from a traditional approach characteristic of guided discussions to one in which a student, or several students, have assumed leadership and guide the discussion and inquiry themselves. This is the most open form of a reflective discussion. It permits students considerable freedom for direction and expression. This situation will more likely result if the group is smaller than regular class size and the students are particularly responsible and motivated to learn and participate. The effectiveness of a reflective discussion is also influenced by too much teacher questioning, which may forestall and frustrate student participation, primarily because of the control the teacher may exercise over the discussion (Dillon, 1983). There are several interaction patterns that a teacher needs to consider when employing discussion. The decision will probably depend on the size of the group and capability of the students.

Levels III and IV low- and high-order divergent questions are the most appropriate to achieve the objectives of a reflective discussion. At Level III, students draw conclusions, make inferences, form generalizations, and analyze information, among other intellectual behaviors. Level IV questions require students to engage in original and evaluative thinking, such as predicting the future in terms of technological advances given current trends and research findings; speculating on how history might have changed if a particular vice president, given his political beliefs, had become president; defining their stands on abortion; or evaluating the impact a famous conductor/composer had on his or her musical era.

As teachers conduct reflective discussions they must keep in mind a variety of questioning techniques that will increase the probability that their objectives will be attained. Implementing a recitation requires only basic communication skills, with the most important questioning technique being to involve the widest possible number of students in reviewing factual material. Wide participation is not necessarily important in a reflective discussion because some students may feel uncomfortable sharing their opinions, views, or ideas. The content in reflective discussions often involves students' feelings, attitudes, and values. The questions are on a higher level and therefore are more complex, so question clarity is critical. Teachers will need to use ample wait time with higher-level questions consistently during a reflective discussion to provide students enough time to think of responses. Probing is necessary to encourage students to clarify, expand, and support their responses. Finally, the teacher will need to use a variety of statement forms and encourage students to formulate questions as alternative nonquestioning means to stimulate thinking.

The structure of a reflective discussion, that is, the degree of freedom students have to frame an answer, can range from moderate to very low depending on several factors. The most important is the ability and interest level of the students. If students are not stimulated, and are not mature enough or capable of assuming responsibility for their own learning, the most open form would be difficult to implement. Reflective discussions focusing on problem solving have similar outcomes to the inquiry method, to be presented later in this chapter. Both require teachers to assume a more dominant role as facilitator than as an instructor in the traditional sense. A facilitator guides, advises, and keeps students directed toward the goals established, and often serves as a resource person for the group. As the structure normally provided by the teacher in the discussion decreases and students assume more responsibility, a more democratic atmosphere develops. Students are involved in more decision making as they use the power delegated by the teacher. This characteristic is particularly evident in the inquiry method and also in small groups.

Small-Group Discussion

Dividing the large classroom into small groups of students to achieve specific objectives permits students to assume more responsibility for their own learning, develop social and leadership skills, and become involved in an alternative instructional approach. The small-group approach does not have a specific place within the hierarchy of discussion approaches because it is flexible enough to be used to attain the objectives generally associated with guided and reflective discussions, and even recitation.

Although small groups are most appropriate for promoting problem solving, attitudinal change, and critical and creative thinking that coincides with the purposes of reflective discussions, they can also promote the understanding of subject matter and the learning of facts. To illustrate how reflection about a controversial issue might be stimulated, a government teacher could organize students into groups based on their points of view regarding the need for the Equal Rights Amendment to the Constitution. Each group might be charged with determining how they would gather evidence to support their points of view, collecting and organizing the evidence, and presenting it to the class in the form of a panel presentation. A variety of critical-thinking skills would be developed as the students reflectively gathered and organized information and supported their points of view. This process is similar to the inquiry method.

To teach students how to understand subject matter, a teacher could have students in a general science class explore the advantages and disadvantages of several forms of energy: gas, solar, nuclear, wind, and coal. The class could be divided into small groups—each assigned to investigate one energy source—to gather information in the library, draw conclusions about its effectiveness, and report on it in written form. A teacher interested in teaching basic facts using an alternative instructional approach could arrange the class into small groups of five or six students and challenge them, in a gaming fashion, to use their textbooks and accurately complete a worksheet of concept definitions in the shortest time possible. Another approach to "teaching" a test or using it as a learning activity is to permit small groups to review their texts or search other sources to correct answers they missed. In these cases small groups would be formed only for the limited period of time necessary to complete the task.

The structure a teacher establishes for small-group instruction depends primarily on the maturity level of the students. If students are to be involved in problem solving they need freedom to determine direction and make decisions. The teacher monitors group progress and serves as a resource person to assist them in accomplishing their task. More structure may be needed when the objectives center on developing subject-matter understandings and learning facts. Mature students will be able to work without extensive teacher supervision. A problem may occur with less mature students who will need a more structured atmosphere to accomplish a task. These students tend to handle freedom ineptly; thus they probably should not be involved in small-group activities requiring considerable freedom of decision making.

Discussion-Method Phases

Although different kinds of discussions encompass a wide range of purposes, a sequence of phases can be generalized for guided and reflective discussion. They are *entry, clarification, investigation,* and *closure.* The intention in providing a sequence of phases is to describe the discussion strategy in action. This provides for a better understanding of its application in the classroom under differing circumstances, and presents a flexible step-by-step approach to implementation. Our intent is not to prescribe the only way to conduct discussions. The discussion strategy is probably the most flexible of all the strategies presented in this chapter. Therefore, teachers should feel free to modify the sequence of phases but maintain the integrity of the method to suit their own classroom situations, students, subject matter, and course goals.

Phase I. Entry: Identification of Problem, Issue, or Topic

    A. Springboard and/or attention-getter used
    B. Identify problem, issue, or topic
    C. State objectives and rationale

As a teacher begins the lesson and introduces the discussion, the entry is important. There are many ways to enter a discussion depending on the nature of the students and their previous learning, the topic, issue, or problem, and the size of the group. The purpose of the entry is to inform students what is to be accomplished and why it is important. The most straightforward way to do this is to inform students of the objective(s) and rationale. This basic approach would be most appropriate for a recitation, and could also be used for the other forms of discussion. A more stimulating way to enter a discussion is to use a springboard to arouse student interest. In a guided discussion, for example, an industrial arts teacher could use a brief series of national statistics related to accidents in school shops—what kind and how many—to lead into a discussion on safety. A more dramatic approach would be to show slides of actual shop accidents or to describe graphically an accident that may have occurred in the classroom in the past. Springboards and attention getters are also appropriate for reflective discussions. As an illustration, a home economics teacher could role-play a fortune teller and have students ask questions about what the home of the future might be like. The answers the teacher gives could be based on a recent article, made up at the moment, or a combination of both. This would serve as an attention-getting lead-in to a reflective discussion on future technology. The entry to a small-group activity could range from the basic introduction specifying the objective and a rationale to a dramatic entry, depending on the imagination and inclination of the teacher.

Phase II. Clarification

    A. Establish procedures
    B. Define terms and concepts related to the problem, issue, or topic

Informing students of the procedures for a discussion may only be necessary at the beginning of the year or if a particular discussion the teacher has in mind requires specific guidelines. Common rules, of which students may need to be reminded, stipulate that they respect the opinions of others and are not allowed to talk when the teacher or another student is talking. This is particularly appropriate for a reflective discussion. If a controversial issue is to be discussed, the teacher may have other guidelines. A teacher may wish to provide more structure in cases involving less mature students who require more supervision. Small-group discussions may need more structure, especially when first initiated, because students may attempt to take advantage of the social dynamics created by small groups. It is important to keep in mind that too much structure and control will stifle student participation and initiative. This is particularly self-defeating for a reflective discussion in which the emphasis is on encouraging student freedom. Another factor influencing the extent of rules is the size of the group, which determines whether or not more structure may be necessary.

Clarification of the problem, topic, or issue may be necessary if the subject to be discussed is particularly complex and difficult for some students to understand. This becomes critical if the text or other material students have read in preparation for a discussion is ambiguous and confusing. In such a case definition of terms, clarification of concepts, and elaboration of ideas may be all that is necessary to increase the probability that most of the students will participate and understand. For example, clarification may be necessary at the beginning of a reflective discussion on abortion because of the conflict between legal definitions and the many interpretations by special-interest groups. On the other hand, the teacher may consider clarification of these positions to be an objective of the discussion.

Phase III. Investigation

   A. Ask appropriate levels of questions to achieve desired levels of student thinking
   B. Use questioning, and alternative nonquestioning, techniques to maintain discussion and stimulate student involvement and thinking
   C. Encourage student initiative and leadership
   D. Request that students support opinions offered
   E. Ensure sufficient coverage of the problem, issue, or topic being discussed

The investigation is the main body of any discussion because the teacher uses questioning and alternative nonquestioning techniques during this phase to interact with students to achieve the objectives of the discussion. The teacher will ask questions congruent with the levels of student thinking desired: predominantly lower-convergent questions (Level I) during a recitation, predominantly upper-convergent and lower-divergent questions (Levels II and III) during a guided discussion, and lower- and upper-divergent questions (Levels III and IV) during a reflective discussion. The levels of questions specified here are only suggestive because of the need to be flexible. For example, a teacher may want students to compare and contrast the views of citizens representing various economic and social groups regarding the Constitution during the time it was being ratified. If students had not read the assignment they would not know what the various groups were and how they felt. In this case, after having the students read the chapter section, the teacher will conduct a recitation before having them engage in higher-level thinking involving comparisons and conclusions.

The use of appropriate questioning techniques is critical to conducting effective discussions. Misuse can defeat the purpose of most discussions. This particularly applies to reflective discussions. On the other hand, recitations require a minimal application of questioning techniques. During a recitation a teacher is concerned, for example, with determining what students know about the important facts of a reading assignment. Questions are used to diagnose students' knowledge. For this to be accomplished, all students should ideally be called on several times. This is obviously not the case in the schools because generally less than half of the students are called on to recite and most of them are volunteering students who usually get most of the attention. Also consider that recitation rarely occurs in its pure form with all teacher questions categorized at Level I low convergent. More often teachers incorporate Level II high-convergent questions to encourage students to display some understanding of the facts. In this case the recitation has assumed some of the characteristics of the guided discussion.

The guided discussion requires an emphasis on other techniques to achieve its goals. Phrasing, balance, and sequence become more important because the questions are at differing and generally higher cognitive levels. Also, adapting questions to the language and ability levels of the students, particularly in a heterogeneous class, becomes important. Pausing after asking questions and using probing questions to encourage students to complete, clarify, and expand their responses may also be necessary, particularly at the low-divergent level (Level III). Furthermore, student questions can be encouraged.

When the teacher involves students in reflective discussions, all questioning, and alternative nonquestioning, techniques need to be conscientiously and consistently employed. The emphasis is on developing critical and creative thinking, so it is necessary to probe students' responses to expand their thinking and provide support for points of view. Another crucial technique is wait time. The majority of questions generally asked in reflective discussions are at the low- and high-divergent levels (Levels III and IV), so teachers need to pause at least three seconds after asking questions to give all the students time to think. Pausing several seconds after a student gives a response will also increase the probability that the response will be extended with higher-level thinking involved. Students should be encouraged to ask questions during a reflective discussion. For example, in a discussion dealing with issues related to abortion, a teacher may ask students to pause and come up with some questions they would ask a convicted abortion-clinic bomber if that person was in class. Also, what responses might this person give to the questions? High-level divergent thinking can be accomplished by having students devise questions.

A note of caution about the use of questions and questioning, particularly in reflective discussions, needs to be given. As has been previously mentioned, students' participation in discussions can be diminished if teachers misuse questioning techniques. Reflective discussions characterized by too many questions, too rapid a pace, too little attention paid to listening, and too little support for students' contributions will regress to an inappropriate recitation or even a lecture. A sure sign that this is happening is when teachers begin to answer their own questions.

Effective discussions should also involve nonquestion alternatives to stimulate student thinking and participation. In his analysis of several tapes of high school classes, Dillon (1985) found that students spoke more extensively, exhibited more complex thought, and became more personally involved in discussions when the teacher used alternative approaches. Examples of nonquestioning alternatives include a variety of statement forms. For example, a teacher might express a thought that has come to mind in response to what a student has just said ("Well, you know that . . ."), paraphrase or summarize what has been said ("So far, we have been saying that . . ."), express an opinion ("I'm not sure I agree with you . . ."), or refer to what another student has said ("But just a few moments ago, Kim mentioned . . ."). Other alternatives are wait time, student questions and signals that are fillers ("mm-hmm"), verbal encouragers ("go on") and phatics ("interesting") (Dillon, 1994). Our view is that teachers should attempt to integrate these nonquestioning techniques into their overall questioning approach to provide balance so that a more informal and conversational approach is created that encourages student involvement and thinking.

During the investigation phase of a small-group discussion, the students serve as the principal questioners and respondents as they search for information or attempt to propose solutions to a problem. As a facilitator, the teacher may ask questions in working with individual groups to help guide their inquiry and keep them on target. The teacher assumes a secondary role as a questioner in most small-group discussions.

Phase IV. Closure: Summary, Integration, Application

> **A.** Summary in the form of consensus, solutions, insights achieved in relation to topic covered, issue explored, or problem investigated
> **B.** Integrate lesson with goals and previous learning
> **C.** Apply discussion outcomes to other situations

Closure is least important in a recitation and most important in reflective and small-group discussions. In a recitation, closure may center on reviewing those areas in which students displayed the least understanding. Guided discussions involve higher-level thinking, so the teacher needs to use closures to help students summarize important points and integrate understanding with previous learning. Transitions to the lessons following recitations and guided discussions are also appropriate to prepare students for upcoming activities.

Closures are extremely important to reflective discussions because, for many students, this is where ideas, points of view, generalizations, and conclusions are summarized and synthesized and where important learning occurs. Syntheses can bring it all together for students who may have been confused at some point during the discussion. Application and transition are also appropriate within the closure because it is often at this point that decisions students reached in connection with a course of action, for example, might be further examined and evaluated in the real world. Suppose that after reflective discussion students reached the decision to support actively a welfare-reform bill being considered in Congress. Near the end of the lesson the teacher could suggest some of the problems students will face as they become actively involved, focusing on cost in terms of time and money or opposition from fellow students, parents, and so on. This would be an ideal problem for further investigation that could be the focus of the next day's class. More than likely the teacher has the inquiry method in mind as a means to involve students in dealing with this reality.

The closure of a small-group discussion is the point where students generally present what they have found as a result of their investigations. If the students were guided by higher-level thinking questions and activities, each group might report, for example, the benefits and disadvantages of the energy source it investigated, or support for their positions on a balanced-budget amendment. At the end of the lesson we would expect the teacher to follow with a summary and integration of the various points of view, and perhaps a consensus if it was the objective. In the case where the teacher "taught the test" using small groups of students to search out the answers to the objective test items, the closure could simply be a review of the test with the right answers based on students' findings. The closure is important because it provides the teacher with a final opportunity at the end of a lesson to ensure that objectives have been achieved, learning has occurred, and that students will be prepared for the next lesson.

Scenario Analysis

In the introductory scenario, Mr. Carl engaged in considerable interaction with the students, but the students did most of the questioning. He was using guided inquiry (presented later in this chapter). After the students discovered the solution to the "puzzle," Mr. Carl engaged them in another form of the inquiry method that required him to conduct a minidiscussion to get students to hypothesize reasons why countries of the world generally to the south of the United States have lower GNPs. At two other points Mr. Carl had "discussions," but they were, in essence, simply short episodes of reflective interaction facilitating inquiry. The lesson could have been easily conducted as a guided discussion. Instead of having the students question him, Mr. Carl could have used Levels II and III high-convergent and low-divergent questions to stimulate thinking about what the map depicted—for example, "What do you think is the reason why the countries are shaped the way they are?" (key entry-level question); "How do the sizes of the United States and India compare on a real map?"; "Why is the United States the largest country on this map?"; "If GNP increases by 10% this year, what will that do to the size of the United States on this map?"; "How can we summarize what this map is trying to show us?"; and "Why is GNP important?" (key closing question). A recitation would have been appropriate if the objective was for students to recall the countries with the largest GNPs and other characteristics that distinguish them from one another. As a natural follow-up to the inquiry lesson, Mr. Carl could have as his objective for a reflective discussion that the students evaluate U.S. foreign policy toward several developing nations in terms of the approaches we are using to help these countries raise their standard of living.

SUMMARY POINT

Discussion is one of the most useful instructional methods because of its potential to stimulate students' application of knowledge and active involvement in learning at a variety of levels of thinking. Three types of discussion and one quasi discussion have been presented. The recitation has as its purpose the diagnosis of student knowledge of basic facts. The guided discussion aims to promote student understanding through processing information. The goal of the reflective discussion is to stimulate students' critical thinking about issues and problems.

Finally, use of small-group discussions is an alternative to large-group discussion. It encourages students to assume more responsibility for their own learning. The decision about which form of discussion to use when planning will depend on the level of student understanding and thinking desired. And this, of course, will be reflected in the teachers' objectives for the lesson.

A discussion-method analysis form is included at the end of the chapter to aid in your observation and analysis.

REVIEW: IMPORTANT PRACTICES — PHASES OF A GENERALIZED
DISCUSSION METHOD

Entry: Identification of Problem, Issue, or Topic

A. Springboard and/or attention getter used
B. Identify problem, issue, or topic
C. State objectives and rationale

Clarification

A. Establish procedures
B. Define terms and concepts related to the problem, issue, or topic

Investigation

A. Ask levels of questions appropriate to achieve desired levels of student thinking
B. Use questioning, and alternative nonquestioning, techniques to maintain discussion and stimulate student involvement and thinking
C. Encourage student initiative and leadership
D. Request that students support opinions offered
E. Attempt to ensure sufficient coverage of problem, issue, or topic

Closure: Summary, Integration, Application

A. Summary in the form of consensus, solution, insights achieved in relation to topic, issue explored, or problem investigated
B. Integrate lesson with goals and previous learnings
C. Apply discussion outcomes to other situations

RESEARCH AND THEORETICAL BASE: LECTURE METHOD

The instructional method most associated with higher education is the lecture, and it is within this setting that most of the research on it has been conducted (McLeish, 1976). In their review of the research literature on lecturing across all levels, Gage and Berliner (1992) concluded that it is as effective as other methods.

Furthermore, they suggested that the lecture was superior to other methods when "(a) the basic purpose is to disseminate information; (b) the material is not available elsewhere; (c) the material must be organized and presented in a particular way for a specific group; (d) it is necessary to arouse interest in the subject; (e) the material need be remembered for only a short time; and (f) it is necessary to provide an introduction to an area or directions for learning tasks to be pursued through some other teaching method" (p. 457).

Several studies compare the lecture with a variety of diverse methods. In one study three methods were compared in lessons with 9th-grade social studies students. The lecture-recitation approach was found to be superior over inquiry and public-issues discussion in terms of student achievement. However, the relative effectiveness of the three methods was dependent, in part, on student ability (Peterson, 1979).

Three other studies conducted at the university level found that the traditional didactic lecture was ineffective compared to approaches that involved students in the lectures in some way. In one study, biology students perceived lecture as more effective when they completed a handout that accompanied the lecture (Butler, 1992). In another study, students were more successful at solving chemistry problems after participating in an interactive lecture treatment during which students answered and asked questions (Robinson and Niaz, 1991). In a study involving three groups of university remedial-reading and study-skills students, the group that generated and answered questions and the group that wrote original summaries based on the lecture performed better than the group that took and studied notes in the traditional fashion (King, 1992). It appears that lectures can be more effective if students are more actively participating with the subject matter in some way.

The findings of several other research studies have implications for the use of the lecture method in secondary classrooms. Based on their review of the literature, Good and Brophy (1994) advocate the use of advance organizers, first proposed and investigated by Ausubel (1968), to help students organize and structure their thoughts in preparation for receiving information through a lecture. In addition to using advance organizers, lecturers need to capture and hold attention. Research has shown that expressiveness, as demonstrated through verbal and nonverbal behaviors, affects students' ratings of lecturers and may enhance learning (Cooper and Galvin, 1984; Michael and Weaver, 1984).

APPLICATION TO PRACTICE: LECTURE METHOD

The lecture method is essentially a teacher-centered, one-way presentation of information and ideas. This method, like the discussion method, consists of a generalized sequence of phases easily adaptable to several varieties of lecture commonly used by teachers in secondary level classrooms. Information giving, a technique presented in chapter 6, was described as a minilecture, or a shortened and informal form of the lecture. These primarily spontaneous introductions, explanations, and demonstrations can last from less than a minute when the teacher is responding to a student's question to 5 to 10 minutes that a teacher might devote to introducing a guest speaker or simulation game. The lecture method is generally reserved for more formal presentations of subject matter and demonstrations lasting for as long as a full class period. It is appropriate for more extensive and complex one-way communication.

The research has indicated the lecture method is as effective as other methods in achieving its intended goals. Compared to other methods, lecturing is particularly effective when the purpose is presenting information that is not readily available elsewhere. It is also effective when information presentation needs to be tailored to a particular group and there is an intended follow-up using other methods. Furthermore, it is useful when long-term retention of the information presented is not the major consideration (Gage & Berliner, 1992). A lecture has its strengths and limitations that are consistent with the objectives for which it is intended.

Although all teachers need to be able to give information effectively in the classroom, not all teachers can lecture effectively, nor should they be expected to. Critical to the success of presenting a lecture is the effective application of communication skills. Another related factor is the personality of the presenter. The ideal lecturer is dynamic, and presents material in a well-organized and convincing manner. In order to be effective, teachers need to make a thoughtful selection of those skills that help hold students' interest and attention and stimulate their mental involvement. Particular attention needs to be paid to those motivating behaviors and skills presented in the previous chapter: physical movement, nonverbal behaviors, voice, lesson pace, and instructional variation. Each contributes to the creation of an enthusiastic teaching image. The application of these qualities is desirable whenever a teacher is instructing. They seem most pertinent and necessary, however, when a teacher is presenting information over extended periods of time. When communication is two-way, such as during discussions, students' attention is not directly focused on the teacher every minute. The teacher's ability to induce motivation seems to be more critical during one-way communication.

The most important quality of a good lecturer is the ability to present material in an organized manner so that it is well understood by the listeners. A teacher delivering a lecture will obviously need to be well prepared on the topic. The most dramatic and flamboyant lecturers will be ineffective if they do not deal with matters of substance! Some lecturers rely on planned notes to deliver a talk. The well-planned teacher will incorporate visual aids to assist in the presentation of the content. They may range from a single transparency of a lecture outline to an elaborate demonstration involving numerous materials and artifacts. Styles of lecturers will vary as widely as their personalities and mannerisms; the effectiveness of a presentation is better measured in terms of outcomes rather than delivery style.

Three of the most common forms of the lecture method are discussed here: formal lecture, interactive lecture, and demonstration. They have in common the primary emphasis on one-way communication over an extended period of time (more than 10 minutes), and they differ with respect to the degree of student interactive involvement.

Formal Lecture

The formal lecture at the secondary school level is the least used form of the lecture method. It is the most common strategy at the university level. An average student's attention span at the secondary school level is not extensive. After approximately 20 minutes, students' minds wander, even at the high school level. Younger students have even shorter attention spans. The exception is noticed in advanced-placement, honors, and college-preparatory classes where coverage of content is emphasized and many teachers feel obligated to prepare their students for teaching and learning in the typical university classroom.

The formal lecture is sometimes noticed in schools that have flexible scheduling and emphasize other instructional approaches that complement lectures. Scheduled small-group classes are arranged to discuss the material presented in large-group sessions, and independent-study projects fulfill the needs of the more capable and motivated students who want to pursue topics, problems, and issues in depth. In these cases, large-group lectures are sometimes presented by guest speakers who have a particular field of expertise, such as a local historian, president of the chamber of commerce, a labor union official, or a politician. The large-group lecture, in which students are, for the most part, passively involved, would not be effective if it was not supported by a variety of other instructional approaches to encourage and stimulate students' active involvement in learning.

Interactive Lecture

This is the most common form of the lecture method in secondary schools. When teachers describe themselves as lecturers, they usually mean that they teach using interactive lectures. Teachers realize that students' attention spans are not long. Therefore, they attempt to involve students through the use of questioning by encouraging them to ask questions at various points during the presentation. Although some may wait until the presentation is completed before entertaining questions and comments, most lecturers encourage their students to contribute their thoughts and questions during the lecture.

The objectives teachers have for the interactive lecture will primarily determine the level of questions they will ask during or after the presentation. It is common to hear all four levels of questions asked during an interactive lecture. For example, a world history teacher in an interactive lecture on the Protestant secession might pause to review key facts and ask students the names of the six popes who ignored calls for reform during the Renaissance and brought the papacy into disrepute (Level I). At another point the teacher might ask students to compare the reigns of Leo X and Clement VII in terms of acts that inadvertently helped pave the way for the secession (Level II). To stimulate some higher-level thinking near the end of the lecture, the teacher might ask students for some principles that future popes might have learned from the six decades of papal misrule (Level III). At the end of the lecture, time permitting, a final high-divergent question might be asked: Which pope do you think could have had the greatest influence and opportunity to avert the Protestant secession? Questions judiciously interspersed throughout a lecture can successfully stimulate students' active involvement and increase the probability of longer-term learning.

Demonstration

Demonstrations, as typically used by teachers at the middle, junior, and high school levels, are basically formal or interactive lectures depending on the extent that student involvement is encouraged. Although many demonstrations are brief, not extending beyond 10 minutes, others are complex and attempt to provide students with more information. Demonstrations provide teachers with an opportunity to show students a procedure or illustration from which they will be able to learn. For example, a physics teacher performs a demonstration using the Van de Graaff generator to show the effects of static electricity to the students. In an art class, the teacher demonstrates the technique of the Pointillists by creating a painting in their once-popular style. The teacher's intention in this case is not for the students to learn the technique but to appreciate and understand more about this school of painters, especially Georges Seurat and his devotees. The demonstration has the potential to contribute substance and immediacy to a lecture, to breathe life into it!

Teachers more commonly use demonstrations to model particular skills that students are expected to learn. Often, specific levels of performance are demonstrated. Examples include a basketball lay-up shot in a physical education class, computation of compound interest within a consumer mathematics unit, or turning wood on a lathe in a technology class. If students are expected to practice and perform the skill the teacher has demonstrated, the teacher is training students using the demonstration as a model.

Lecture-Method Phases

Phase I. Entry: Preparation for Learning

   A. State objectives and rationale
   B. Provide a context for the new material to be presented
   C. Focus attention on a key concept, generalization, or principle that encompasses the lecture (advance organizer)

The purpose of the entry to a lecture or a demonstration is to inform students what the teacher intends to accomplish, why it is important, and to prepare students to understand what will be presented. The objectives could be verbally stated generally or more formally in specific terms. They might even be listed on a handout or transparency. In this way the students will know what the teacher expects them to learn as a result of the presentation.

A rationale provides students with a purpose for the presentation and how it fits into the unit being studied. This generally satisfies students' urge to know why they are studying something. Teachers often overlook this component of a lesson because they assume it should be obvious to students. Following a rationale could be a brief summary of what has been covered to a certain point to provide a learning context for students. Another approach to providing a learning context is to preview or give an overview of what will be covered in the presentation. The order of lecture-entry components is flexible, and depends on the level of structure of the presentation.

Preparation for students to assimilate information to be presented in a lecture would not be complete without an organizer. The purpose of the organizer is to focus students' attention on and help them understand the "big idea" of the lecture. In many respects the organizer is the common thread weaving through all the information presented. Ausubel (1968) stated that "organizers are introduced in advance of the learning material itself and are also presented at a higher level of abstraction, generality, and inclusiveness" (p. 148). The purpose of the organizer, Ausubel continued, "is to bridge the gap between what the learner already knows and what he needs to know before he can successfully learn the task at hand" (p. 148). In short, it is the glue that holds together in a meaningful pattern the information that is presented; or, stated another way, it is a hook on which to hang ideas.

The key to the effective use of organizers is to identify a central concept, generalization, term, or principle that encompasses the material to be presented and then relate it to what students already know or have experienced. Research confirms that organizers can increase students' comprehension of new learning material. It is logical that the more difficult the learning material, the more useful and necessary an organizer. To prepare students for a formal lecture on the Romantic period of poetry, a teacher might use the organizer "love" to help students understand the works of Keats, Shelley, and Byron. The teacher could start off with formally defining it from the dictionary and including some other diverse definitions from several other sources, including some teenagers' definitions. This would help relate the concept to students' lives. If using an interactive lecture approach, the teacher might ask students what love means to them. Going a step further might involve comparing and contrasting the love students have for parents, pets, friends, and the nation. The interactive approach significantly increases the chance that students will understand the concept and, therefore, the subsequent information on the Romantic period.

Another illustration of an organizer applies in a middle school science class. A science teacher wants to use an interactive lecture to demonstrate the principle of air pressure. An organizer can be used to ensure that students understand the concept of pressure. The teacher might explain the concept and use examples of pressure within the realm of students' experiences, such as tires on a bicycle, a shaken can of soda, or blood pressure. Once the teacher is sure the students understand what pressure is, several planned demonstrations may proceed.

Phase II. Presentation

    A. Sequence content from simpler to complex understandings
    B. Enhance presentation with visual aids
    C. Stimulate attention with verbal and nonverbal behaviors

During the presentation phase the main body of the lecture is presented or the demonstration occurs. Comprehension will be enhanced if the learning material is sequenced from simple to complex understandings and visual aids are used to illustrate key or difficult concepts, processes, or other content. For example, in a formal or interactive lecture on the Constitutional Convention's "Great Compromise," a U.S. history teacher might use as an organizer the principle that a compromise results when one gives up something to get something else. The teacher could easily relate it to students' lives by describing a conflict between a brother and sister over watching television at a particular time. An even more effective and appropriate question for an interactive lecture would be to ask students about their conflicts with brothers and sisters and how they were resolved. After presentation of the organizer, the teacher would need to present logically the differing views on a plan of government of the large and small states. The Virginia and New Jersey plans could be compared by analyzing their strengths and weaknesses from the perceptions of the delegates to the convention and, perhaps, by consideration of current political scientists' views on that episode in history. Finally, the formation, presentation, and acceptance of the Connecticut Plan, or "Great Compromise," would need to be explained, and the process of compromise analyzed.

In this illustration, the teacher progressed from the presentation of basic facts and information related to the Virginia and New Jersey plans to the more complex analysis of the role of compromise in resolving the conflict. The ability of the students to comprehend the lecture is increased because of the logical development and presentation of content. We can also imagine the teacher using several colorful transparencies detailing the provisions of each of the two plans, another of the Connecticut Plan that was finally accepted, and one on the process of compromise.

Phase III. Closure: Review of Learning

    A. Integrate with students' knowledge and experiences
    B. Transition to next lesson or activity

A teacher has the opportunity during the closure of a formal lecture to reinforce what has been presented with a review of key points, concepts, and ideas. Students should also be able to raise questions and make comments, all of which will help teachers determine how effective they were in presenting the lecture. In the case of the interactive lecture illustration, the teacher might use questions to have the students examine the process of compromise they have used with friends and parents to get what they want, and compare it with the one that led to the formation of our legislative branch of government. In this way the teacher can diagnose the students' understanding of the content in the lecture by having them apply it to their own lives. This is a powerful approach to integration. The same approach could be applied to the closure of a demonstration.

The last component of the lecture, whether it is formal, interactive, or a demonstration, is the transition during which the teacher bridges the gap to the next lesson. The lecture is primarily one-way communication; thus, students' higher levels of thinking are generally not being stimulated directly through questions. This, of course, is a major advantage the interactive lecture has over the formal lecture. In the case of a formal lecture or an interactive lecture in which little high-level thinking has been encouraged, the transition is the ideal time to challenge students with a problem or assignment that will serve as the basis for the next lesson. This follow-up should be aimed at engaging students in divergent thinking (Levels III and IV). For example, the U.S. history teacher might have students attempt to locate in the newspaper at least one instance of a compromise that was reached at any level of government over any issue, and evaluate the decision reached based on their perceptions of the criteria for a compromise. Several goals are accomplished through such transition. The bridge to the next lesson is made, students are applying what they have learned in the lecture, and students' higher-level divergent thinking is involved. The closure provides teachers with an opportunity to evaluate directly students' understanding of the information presented and to encourage their application of what has been learned. Student performance during the closure and during the next class session is, indirectly, an evaluation of the teacher's effectiveness in applying the lecture method.

Scenario Analysis

Mr. Carl used the inquiry method that incorporated guided discussion in the hypothetical teaching situation. After the students had discovered the solution to the map "puzzle," he provided some background information on the concept of GNP—definition, examples of goods and services, and statistics comparing the GNP of different countries. His instructional approach could be classified as *information giving* rather than *lecture*, primarily because of the brevity of the explanation.

The lesson could have been a formal or interactive lecture. The entry might have focused on the organizer "standard of living," with Mr. Carl giving illustrations of families with different living standards. He then could have related it to students' lives by asking them to examine their own and family members' needs now and in the future. The lecture would naturally be on several aspects of GNP intended to be covered, supplemented, perhaps, with transparencies illustrating some of the more complex concepts and processes: circular flow of money and products, categories of spending, and leading economic indicators. During the presentation Mr. Carl could use the transparency of the map depicting countries, each with a different size GNP. Another possibility would be to use it in the closure for the purpose of summarizing and reviewing.

SUMMARY POINT

The lecture method is the most straightforward instructional approach. It is the most effective way to convey large amounts of information not readily available to students. It also presents an opportunity for teachers to lay the groundwork for higher-level thinking during follow-up class sessions.

Three closely related forms of the lecture method have been presented: formal lecture, interactive lecture, and demonstration. They all have as their primary purpose the presentation of content using a one-way communications approach. The interactive lecture is the most familiar. This requires that teachers purposely incorporate questions at several levels to stimulate student involvement and thinking during the lecture. The formal lecture is the noninteractive form of the lecture method. Demonstration is essentially an interactive lecture, featuring display or performance, and explanation. Teacher decision making in relation to the lecture during the planning stage involves selecting which form to use to achieve the lesson's objectives. Selection of the form will primarily depend on the amount of content to be covered, the ability level of the students, and the extent of interaction desired.

A lecture-method analysis form is included at the end of the chapter to aid in your observation and analysis.

REVIEW: IMPORTANT PRACTICES: PHASES OF A GENERALIZED
LECTURE STRATEGY

Entry: Preparation for Learning

A. State objectives and rationale
B. Provide a context for the new material to be presented
C. Focus attention on key concept, generalization, or principle that encompasses the lecture

Presentation

A. Sequence content from simpler to complex understandings
B. Enhance presentation with visual aids
C. Stimulate attention with verbal and nonverbal behaviors

Closure: Review of Learning

A. Integrate with students' knowledge and experiences
B. Transition to next lesson or activity

RESEARCH AND THEORETICAL BASE: INQUIRY METHOD

Inquiry is a generic term that applies to methods with which teachers engage students' critical-thinking skills to analyze and solve problems in a systematic fashion. Whereas lecture and recitation are used extensively by teachers, inquiry is used sparingly. Most of the research literature on inquiry centers on comparing it with other methods. One dissertation surveyed studies comparing discovery and expository approaches from 1908 to 1975 and could not conclude one was superior to the other (Weimer, 1974). Ponder and Davis (1982) found a tendency in students taught by methods requiring students' use of critical-thinking skills, such as inquiry, to perform as well as students taught by methods of factual learning. Two other studies conducted since then favored inquiry over expository approaches (Andrews, 1984; Selim and Shrigley, 1983).

As has been previously mentioned, there is a growing movement on viewing teaching and learning from a constructivist vantage point. Theorists believe that students should no longer be relegated to the role of passively receiving information, but rather, teachers should encourage them to mediate it actively by relating it to what they know and developing and applying it in meaningful ways. Inquiry, or problem solving, is being advocated by researchers as one approach to help students achieve the goal of subject-matter understanding. Several of the components of Good and Brophy's (1994) model describing good subject-matter teaching relate directly to the need for learning activities that call for students to engage in critical thinking, problem solving, and decision making. Zemelman, Daniels, and Hyde (1993) likewise strongly advocate the use of the inquiry or problem-solving approach as best-practice instruction in the subject areas of science, mathematics, and social studies.

APPLICATION TO PRACTICE: INQUIRY METHOD

Inquiry is an extremely versatile instructional method because it can be used to teach content, problem solving, critical thinking skills, and decision making. Many consider inquiry to be synonymous with discovery, inductive teaching, reflective teaching, and problem solving. Writers vary somewhat in their interpretation of what it is. In its most general form, inquiry is the analysis of a problem in a systematic fashion. Several key words help us to understand more about inquiry. A *problem* is central to inquiry and can take many forms. It could be academic problem solving, such as mathematics students attempting to discover the process by which an answer was obtained. The problem could occur in social studies, such as, What can the students of a government class do to help get a particular candidate they support elected to the city council? Or the problem could be personal, such as a student's attempt to decide what to do to help a friend in a personal crisis. The word *analysis* suggests that the problem will be dissected into parts and studied; *systematic* means that the problem will be methodically studied through a step-by-step procedure. Inquiry is a process that students can learn and experience as they solve problems through reflective thinking.

Although the steps of inquiry vary depending on the specific objectives the teacher intends to achieve, there is general agreement on a basic form. That form is Dewey's model of reflective thinking (1910). An adaptation is presented here:

1. Identify and clarify the problem.
2. Form hypotheses.
3. Collect data.
4. Analyze and interpret the data to test hypotheses.
5. Draw conclusions.

The problem is created out of a discrepancy in perceptions of data. The more puzzlement involved and the more personal attachment the students have toward the problem, the better the potential for inquiry. Hypotheses are the students' proposed solutions to the problem based on experiences and information they have related to the problem. Data collection requires consulting resources for information related to the hypotheses. Once data have been collected, they need to be analyzed and interpreted to reduce the hypotheses. As a result of this process, a conclusion will be drawn that reflects an acceptance, rejection, or modification of the hypotheses. Depending on the problem, the conclusion could be a solution, generalization, or explanation.

With the inquiry method, both content and process are taught at the same time. Whether content or process is more important and therefore emphasized will depend on the objectives for the lesson and the teacher's judgment. Research confirms that inquiry is as effective as other methods in teaching content and may be better than most in teaching other learnings, especially the process of inquiry.

Teaching the process of inquiry is an opportunity for students to learn and practice skills associated with critical thinking. Helping students develop the ability to think is receiving increased emphasis because of the realization that students will benefit from being independent and reflective thinkers in the real social world (Paul, 1984). For example, in the area of social studies particularly, there is major concern that as much emphasis needs to be placed on the "4th R"—reasoning—as on "reading, 'riting, and 'rithmetic." According to this rationale, responsible citizens are those who are aware of and approach societal issues, concerns, and problems rationally, and are active in working toward their resolution (National Council for the Social Studies, 1979). Mindlessness occurs when citizens act without reflective thinking, and being able to think critically increases the potential for effective citizenship.

Byer (1984) proposed a series of critical-thinking skills and several practical approaches to teaching these skills sequentially within a K–12 curriculum. The skills include: "(1) distinguishing between verifiable facts and value claims; (2) determining the reliability of a claim or source; (3) determining the accuracy of a statement; (4) distinguishing between warranted or unwarranted claims;

(5) distinguishing between relevant and irrelevant information, claims, or reasons; (6) detecting bias; (7) identifying stated and unstated assumptions; (8) identifying ambiguous or equivocal claims or arguments; (9) recognizing logical inconsistencies in a line of reasoning; and (10) determining the strength of an argument" (p. 557). Most of these skills can be taught and practiced as students engage in inquiry in connection with analyzing and solving social issues and problems. In this case the process taught would be inquiry, with the content being information related to a current social issue such as updating immigration laws, corruption in law enforcement, increase in teenage suicides, violence in movies, or the growing influence of political action committees. Specific critical-thinking skills could also be thought of as the content that is to be taught.

When we think about preparing students to deal with personal problems, the skills associated with decision making come to mind. It should be apparent that there is considerable similarity between the processes of inquiry and decision making. To a great extent, both are appropriate in solving social and personal problems. However, personal attitudes and values generally play a greater role in decision making. Personal values need to be considered along with information gathered from sources. Solutions can then be proposed for which the consequences of each need to be considered. Finally a decision is reached, implemented, and eventually evaluated to determine its appropriateness (Armstrong, 1980).

Three forms of the inquiry method are presented: guided inquiry, open inquiry, and the individualized inquiry investigation. All three are primarily subject-matter oriented and have as their structure the process of inquiry. These forms differ in the extent of guidance provided by the teacher, and in the case of the individualized form, the number of students involved.

Guided Inquiry

The extent of the teacher's involvement during the implementation of inquiry is the primary difference between the guided and open forms. As the teacher becomes more involved, more structure is provided, and this results in less freedom for students to take initiative and direction for their own learning experiences. The teacher assumes these responsibilities. During guided inquiry the teacher provides the data and the students are questioned to help them inductively arrive at an answer, conclusion, generalization, or solution. The teacher generally has the "right" answer in mind, or a narrow range of acceptable answers, so the students are led to the conclusion (Shulman & Tamir, 1973). In this case the teacher, being actively involved, is more a director of students' learning and thinking than a facilitator. The guided inquiry form of the method is especially appropriate as a way to introduce the inquiry process to students. The structure serves as security as they venture into a new area involving different kinds of thinking.

The necessity of providing guidance makes the teacher's questioning behavior important in the guided-inquiry process. Although the questions asked by the teacher cover the full range of thinking levels, the most effective questions to stimulate inductive thinking are those classified at Levels II, III, and IV—high-convergent, and low- and high-divergent thinking. As a result of the direct involvement of the teacher in questioning students, the effective use of a full range of questioning skills becomes critical.

One illustration of guided inquiry takes place in an 8th-grade science classroom. The teacher shows the students three test tubes, all half-filled with clear liquid. A few drops from the first test tube are poured into the second and the liquid turns bright purple. Some of the clear liquid from the third tube is poured into the second and the purple liquid becomes completely clear again. As the students stare in amazement, the teacher asks them, "What happened?" to start the inquiry with a review of the facts. Once the problem has been clarified, hypotheses are generated as tentative explanations for the unusual event. The most difficult part is using questions to lead them to test their ideas, such as "What is this liquid?"; "Suppose we poured the liquid from the first tube into the third?"; and "What would happen if . . . ?" The teacher needs to probe students' responses to focus, clarify, extend, and expand their thinking as they are guided to discover that the first tube contained a base (ammonia), the second contained a small amount of phenolphthalein in water, and the third was an acid (white vinegar). Phenolphthalein is an indicator of a base and the acid serves as a neutralizer. As the result of being guided by the teachers' questions, the students are able to discover inductively the explanation for the puzzling event.

Open Inquiry

Students' freedom to initiate and think is expanded in open inquiry. In essence, they assume more responsibility for their own learning and, as a result, lessen their dependence on the teacher. The inquiry process remains the same with the focus on inductive thinking as students propose solutions, gather data, and draw conclusions. A primary difference lies in the data-collection phase. During guided inquiry the teacher provides the data to help students draw conclusions; during open inquiry the students gather the data (Shulman & Tamir, 1973). Student questioning becomes more important during open inquiry because they ask questions and search for the answers. Teacher questions generally guide structured inquiry. The teacher's role is to facilitate by assisting students within the phases of the process. As part of this role the teacher also serves as a resource person, suggesting sources students might consult, such as those in the library, and helping arrange other sources, such as people in the community. Although the teacher usually commences open inquiry with a problem related to what is being studied and assists students in hypothesis formation, the students assume responsibility for data collection and generalizing. This is an essential component in open inquiry.

An illustration for an open-inquiry lesson centers on a class of U.S. government students interested in establishing a recycling center in their community. Assume the class has been studying environmental issues with a particular emphasis on what they perceive as their community's problems. Inquiry was initiated when students decided to focus on ascertaining the extent of community support for a recycling center. Naturally they were hopeful that this would lead to the development of a center. The teacher guided them as they proposed ideas about how they could get support. Some of their brain-stormed approaches were interviewing city officials for their suggestions and their perceptions of problems and issues associated with building a center, conducting a survey of citizens, attending a city council meeting to propose the center, contacting a nearby community that has a center to find out how they got support, and writing to the state and federal governments to see what guidelines might exist. Clarification was achieved as their purpose was more sharply defined and the list of ideas was reduced to four. The data-gathering phase was initiated when it was decided that the class could be divided into small groups, each assuming responsibility for investigating one of the pro-posed approaches. For example, one group planned to present the idea of a re-cycling center to the city council formally to find out if it had been considered in the past, if the council might give tentative support to the idea now, or if council members had suggestions for getting more support or for proceeding to get the idea approved.

The data gathering could take several weeks, most of it being conducted by the groups outside of the regular class sessions. After the information is gathered and analyzed by the groups, a class session will need to be set aside for the pre-sentation of the group findings. The culminating activity of the inquiry process is drawing a conclusion and, in this case, finding out the extent to which the com-munity supports the construction of a recycling center. In the open form of the in-quiry method, the students are more involved in determining the direction of the learning process as they start with a problem of concern to them, propose solu-tions, gather and analyze the data, and draw conclusions.

Individualized Inquiry Investigation

The individualized inquiry investigation method (Wilen & McKenrick, 1989) in-volves identifying able and interested students who will benefit from engaging in independent study. This interpretation of the inquiry method most closely ap-proximates the format of the open-inquiry form because of the freedom given to students. The issue or problem devised should naturally relate to the unit cur-rently under study and, most importantly, have personal meaning for the stu-dent. Examples are an American literature student who, after reading several of Ernest Hemingway's novels and short stories for a class assignment, wants to find out more about how his work has influenced other writers, or a U.S. history student who wants to find out more about how the Japanese treated U.S. prison-ers during World War II because his uncle survived the infamous Bataan "death march." Once a willing student has been identified, and preliminary research has yielded a general issue or problem area, a contract should be drawn up to specify the conditions of the inquiry investigation. The contract could be formal or infor-mal, written or verbal, depending on the needs of the teacher and student. Im-portant questions need to be directly answered: How much time should the stu-dent devote to the investigation? Under what conditions should the student be excused from class sessions to pursue the inquiry? Should that student take the tests with other students? What is to be the method of reporting the investigation? How will the student's effort be evaluated? How will this grade influence the marking-period grade? The contract needs to be designed to clarify mutual expectations.

Once the contract has been agreed on, the investigation should continue with a formal statement of the problem in question form. This will help ensure specific direction. The teacher then needs to assist the student to reflect on tentative explanations or solutions to the problem to guide the inquiry. It is important for the teacher to be supportive and nonjudgmental to encourage intellectual freedom. After assistance from the teacher, and perhaps the librarian or media specialist, in identifying key sources, the student should be left alone to pursue the inquiry. The role of the teacher is to encourage and facilitate, offering assistance when necessary. The method of reporting the project could take many different forms including a paper (the traditional approach), display, oral report, media presentation, videotape, or bulletin board. The individualization of inquiry investigations provides teachers with an opportunity to encourage responsible students to pursue their own interests within an agreed-upon structure.

Inquiry-Method Phases

The phases of the inquiry method basically have their roots in the steps of reflective thinking as conceived by Dewey (1910) and reported in many other current references. Although there is flexibility, the sequence of phases is considered more important than in the other methods presented in this chapter because inquiry is designed to teach an investigative process as well as content.

Phase I. Entry: Presentation and Clarification of a Problem, Issue, or Query

    A. Statement of objectives; provide rationale
    B. Identification of a problem, issue, or query
    C. Relation to students' experiences and lives
    D. Clarification of the problem

The nature of the problem or issue selected as the basis for the inquiry investigation is important for motivational purposes. Although it probably will be at least indirectly related to the unit currently under study, students' attachment to the problem can be greatly enhanced if it in some way relates to their lives. Another motivational approach is to select a problem that causes a discrepancy between what students expect to happen and what actually does happen. A way to accomplish this is to present statistics that can be interpreted differently. The diverse interpretations can serve as a springboard to an inquiry problem. Statistics related to drug usage and abuse might stimulate inquiry in a health class, for example.

The objectives and rationale can be presented before or after the problem is presented, depending on a teacher's preference for an entry format. A problem may evolve naturally out of lesson content and be suggested by a student or a small group. Student initiation is a powerful motivator, particularly if a majority of students express an interest. The teacher generally plans for the investigation. Although a teacher-selected problem can be presented conveniently during the rationale, it should be presented in an interesting way in order to grab students' attention. For example, a vivid description of the final days of the Waco tragedy in 1993 would be an interesting way to lead sociology students into investigating why and how people can be brainwashed into committing themselves so completely, and sometimes tragically, to religious cults.

How the problem, issue, or query is presented in the entry is equally important to all forms of the inquiry method. The opportunity for students to explore problems with which they feel close attachment probably occurs more often with the individualized approach because the student has a choice, and therefore would not be engaging in inquiry without interest. Open inquiry should also be a stimulus to some extent because of the freedom students have in gathering data. In the case of the guided-inquiry approach, teachers tend to control students' involvement more directly because it is more structured.

Phase II. Formation of Hypotheses

A. Encourage the formation of tentative explanations or solutions
B. Clarify hypotheses

A hypothesis is a plausible but tentative explanation for a discrepancy in information or student beliefs, or a proposed solution to the problem. They are considered tentative until they have been tested by data that will be gathered in the next phase. The teacher initially wants to encourage as many solutions as possible. In some cases few solutions may be offered because students are unfamiliar with the inquiry process, so the teacher will have to encourage them. Creativity may even be one of the teacher's objectives during this phase, and the students are therefore expected to brainstorm solutions. In this case quantity is the primary emphasis, with the quality of proposed solutions being the focus later as the hypotheses are clarified.

The teacher can encourage hypotheses to be generated in the large-group situation or in small groups, or in the case of the individualized approach, in a one-to-one meeting. Using small groups to form hypotheses may take somewhat more time than in the large group, but students may not feel as inhibited and may therefore contribute more. Once the students have generated hypotheses in their small groups, they need to be reconvened in the large group to share solutions and devise a list reflecting their collective thinking. While the hypotheses are being discussed for inclusion on the final list, terms are defined and assumptions clarified. The result should be a list of tentative solutions clearly understood by the students.

Phase III. Collection of Data

A. Facilitate the identification of sources for evidence
B. Assist in the evaluation of the evidence

The purpose of the data-collection phase is to provide information leading to the acceptance or rejection of each hypothesis. By this stage the students have shared some information about the problem by virtue of the fact that the problem was clarified and tentative solutions were formed. Sharing common knowledge and experiences is important in the initial phases of inquiry, but at some point information needs to be gathered from a greater diversity of sources and from more authoritative sources outside the classroom. Sources may range from references in the school library to interviewing experts in the field via the Internet. Students may also wish to create the data themselves, as in the case of a survey form to be administered to peers in school, parents, or a sample of community members. In other cases, students may need to generate data through observation and experimentation in a science laboratory. The quality of generalizations students reach at the end of an inquiry investigation can often be directly related to the quantity and quality of sources consulted during this phase.

The teacher's role is to assist students in their identification of sources for evidence and to facilitate the collection and evaluation of the data. This interpretation of the teacher's role applies primarily to the open-inquiry form of the strategy. Thoughts about sources might be shared immediately after the hypotheses are clarified. Of course, the range of sources will be limited by the problem under investigation. The teacher will have to take a more active role in acquainting students with possibilities for sources, particularly if they are neophytes to the inquiry process. The rich possibility of finding evidence to support hypotheses from nonprint sources such as films and videotapes, filmstrips, records and audiotapes, and computer databases is often forgotten. The teacher's responsibility during this phase is to serve as a resource person who continually encourages students to keep an open mind as they consult and explore a variety of sources.

The teacher also needs to help students evaluate the quality of the sources from which they are gathering information. All sources consulted should not be given equal weight when deciding their influence on validating students' hypotheses. Students will need to know the differences between primary and secondary sources, how a writer's frame of reference influences the work, and how to detect a writer's biases and prejudices, for example. Standards for judging sources should apply to all sources, including nonwritten ones.

A major difference between the three forms of the inquiry method is noticed in the data-gathering phase. In guided inquiry the teacher provides the data and structures how students will use it to support or refute their hypotheses. In the case of the open and individualized forms, the students gather the data with the assistance of the teacher, whose role is to facilitate rather than direct. As an illustration, in Suchman's (1962) interpretation of the inquiry method, the teacher provides a science-related discrepant event and the students inductively proceed through the stages by asking questions to which the teacher responds "yes" or "no." During the hypothesis formation and data-gathering phases, the teacher structures the inquiry so that students' questions are focused on the variables and conditions of the event. This knowledge is used to hypothesize and test relationships within the data. The formation of causal relationships leads to an explanation for the event. In essence, the students first hypothesize then collect and analyze the data through their questions, as guided by the high structure provided by the teacher. Suchman's inquiry-training form of the method is essentially guided inquiry. It becomes more open as students gather data themselves as, for example, in the case when they literally test their hypotheses by performing experiments in a laboratory situation.

Phase IV. Testing Hypotheses

  A. Assist in organizing the data
  B. Assist in the analysis and evaluation of the data

The purpose of this phase is to examine the evidence that has been gathered to determine the extent to which it validates or invalidates the hypotheses. In essence, the students are testing the hypotheses. As the information is gathered and recorded, students will need to be concerned with how to handle the quantity of data, some of which might be incomplete and conflicting. Organization and presentation of the data are particularly important for the beginner in the inquiry process. Armstrong (1980) suggested that the data be recorded and categorized in chart form so that students might analyze and evaluate them more easily. For example, each proposed solution or explanation might be placed on a separate large piece of paper or transparency. Three columns might be set up labeled: "evidence supporting," "evidence not supporting," and "evidence neutral." Students can then categorize the evidence they have found based on its worth in supporting or refuting each hypothesis. This structure will make it easier for students to evaluate the data.

This phase is similar for the guided, open, and individualized forms of the inquiry method. The structure the teacher provides for the process will depend on the capacity of the students to pursue inquiry. This is another reason for selecting a particularly capable and responsible student for individualized inquiry investigations. Once students have analyzed and evaluated the evidence, they are ready to draw a conclusion.

Phase V. Closure: Drawing Conclusions

  A. Develop a generalization, explanation, or solution
  B. Integrate into the unit of study

The final stage of inquiry is the acceptance, rejection, or modification of the hypotheses. Drawing a conclusion is the natural follow-up to analyzing and evaluating the data that have been gathered. In fact, these phases often run together, depending on the nature of the problem being investigated and how the teacher structures the hypothesis testing. Although the data may strongly suggest that a particular hypothesis be accepted over others, the teacher should encourage students to support their view by reexamining the evidence. Questions that may need consideration are: Have enough data been gathered to arrive at a conclusion? Does the evidence support only one conclusion or could others be considered? How final is the conclusion? The conclusion reached, whether a generalization drawn from a collection of data, an explanation of a phenomenon or observations, or a solution to a problem, should be considered tentative. Students may tend to accept a conclusion, particularly to a major investigation, that involves the opinions of experts as the final answer or the truth. Reality suggests that any conclusions drawn should be considered tentative because all the evidence related to any issue, topic, or problem can never be available at one time. Students and teacher may have missed several key and influential sources. Furthermore, a conclusion reached may have to be rejected completely if new evidence is reported that refutes it.

The final stage of the inquiry method is basically the same for the three forms discussed in this section. In the case of the individualized approach the teacher may meet with the student doing the investigation to review the conclusions drawn before writing the paper, if this is to be the means for reporting findings from the inquiry. The review made and questions raised during this final phase will increase the chances the student will arrive at a conclusion consistent with the evidence gathered.

Scenario Analysis

Mr. Carl used guided and open inquiry to achieve his objectives. The first part of the lesson centered on applying an adaptation of Suchman's (1962) inquiry-training approach to stimulate students to explain the discrepant event as represented by the puzzling world map. Clarification was achieved as the students responded to "What do you see?" The inquiry was formally begun after Mr. Carl explained the procedure of student questioning as the means to gather data from the teacher. The second phase began after a series of student questions related to specifics about the map were asked and a tentative solution was offered. At that point Mr. Carl asked the student to test his hypothesis by gathering more evidence with more questions. He wanted the student to begin forming causal relationships ("Think about the relationships of the countries. How about a 'what if' question?").

After several other student questions yielded other hypotheses and more data, one student eventually came up with the correct explanation that the map depicted countries' GNPs. Mr. Carl rounded out this part of the lesson with a brief discussion on the clues, or pieces of evidence, that led to the discovery of the explanation. Guided inquiry was used effectively by the teacher to grab students' attention initially through the use of a discrepant event. Student questioning was structured to stimulate inductive thinking that eventually led to the explanation for the event.

After providing some information on GNP, Mr. Carl initiated the final phase of the lesson with a shift to open inquiry. He referred students back to the map and asked why there was a tendency for the smaller GNP countries to be located south of approximately 30 degrees north latitude. Students responded with several tentative explanations and then he suggested that inquiry would be pursued in the next class period. We can envision him beginning the next class period with a review and clarification of the hypotheses offered so far. One indication of a data source was a guest speaker from one of the lower GNP countries to the south. The suggestion was also made that small groups might be formed for the investigation based, perhaps, on the hypotheses formed. If Mr. Carl continues with open inquiry we can expect the students will assume the major responsibility for gathering the data. Although time-consuming, open inquiry provides students with the opportunity to examine significant issues and problems in-depth, using a process practiced by both physical and social scientists.

SUMMARY POINT

Inquiry is a versatile instructional method used to involve students in a process to analyze a problem or issue in a logical and systematic way. The problem is defined generally and can be identified within subject matter content, societal issues, or personal situations. The process of inquiry begins with the problem, issue, or query for which an explanation or solution is desired. Students propose hypotheses, gather data, analyze and evaluate the data, test hypotheses, and draw conclusions. A key consideration teachers need to take into account when deciding if the inquiry method is appropriate is the extent to which inductive thinking and learning the inquiry process itself are among the objectives. The inquiry method teaches content, but its unique strength lies in its ability to teach an investigative process that has applications to life.

Three forms of the inquiry method have been presented with their commonality being the process itself. Their differences lie in the extent to which the teacher structures the students' inquiry by directing or facilitating the collection of data. With the guided and open forms, whole classes of students are generally involved, and in the case of the individualized approach, one or more responsible students are usually encouraged.

An inquiry-method analysis form is included at the end of this chapter to aid in your observation and analysis.

REVIEW: IMPORTANT PRACTICES—PHASES OF THE GENERALIZED INQUIRY METHOD

Phase I—Entry: Presentation and Clarification of a Problem, Issue, or Query

A. State objectives; provide rationale
B. Identify a problem, issue, or query
C. Relate to students' experiences and lives
D. Clarify the problem

Phase II—Formation of Hypotheses

A. Encourage the formation of tentative explanations or solutions
B. Clarify hypotheses

Phase III—Collection of Data

A. Facilitate the identification of sources for evidence
B. Assist in the evaluation of the evidence

Phase IV—Test Hypotheses

A. Assist in organizing the data
B. Assist in the analysis and evaluation of the data

Phase V—Closure: Draw Conclusions

A. Facilitate the reaching of a generalization, explanation, or solution
B. Integration and transition

RESEARCH AND THEORETICAL BASE: SIMULATION-GAMING METHOD

Teachers would probably agree that the instructional method most associated with active student interest and involvement is simulation gaming in either of its two primary forms: simulation and role playing. Although discussion and inquiry as methods can stimulate high levels of participation and excitement, depending on the issue being discussed or the problem being solved, simulation gaming generally exceeds them in inducing motivation because of its emphasis on role playing and decision making to achieve goals. When we think of peak experiences in our schooling, a simulation is often recalled. Some of those powerful roles may have been: a married couple trying to raise a child on a limited budget in a sociology class, an environmentalist trying to avert a community ecological disaster in a science class, a foreman trying to solve a building-construction problem in an industrial arts class, or an investor trying to make the most money in the stock market in an economics class. The dynamics of these peak experiences are remembered long after the regular content taught in traditional ways has been forgotten.

Some definitions are needed before pursuing a review of research. The following terms associated with this method are often used synonymously: *simulation, game, role playing, simulation game, instructional game*, and *gaming simulation*. A *simulation* is a dynamic model illustrating a physical (nonhuman) or social (human) system that is abstracted from reality and simplified for study purposes (Greenblat, 1982; Gilliom, 1977). It may or may not involve competition and winners and losers as the key ingredients of a game. This definition also applies to a wide variety of computer simulations that serve the same purpose. *Role playing* is acting out or dramatizing hypothetical or real-life characters, often in problem situations (Clegg, 1991; Gilliom, 1977). Role playing is an important component of all human simulations, but it is not synonymous with them. The simulation-game instructional method, then, is a hybrid form involving a simulated situation during which roles are played which may or may not involve gamelike activity (Greenblat, 1982). For the purposes of this discussion, the terms *game* and *simulation* will be used interchangeably, as they are generally found in the literature.

Three major comprehensive reviews of research on simulation gaming provides us with a realistic picture of the potential for the application of this method in classrooms (Clegg, 1991; Greenblat, 1982; Randel, Morris, Wetzel, and Whitehill, 1992). The vast majority of the literature on simulations are anecdotal accounts, game descriptions, handbooks of guidelines for playing, and books on the general theme of simulations. Comparatively little research has been conducted and the findings from these, for the most part, have been mixed (Clegg, 1991).

Evaluation of simulations has been difficult because of their diversity. Research generally shows that cognitive learning takes place during simulations, but it is not greater when simulations are compared to traditional techniques (Greenblat, 1982). In their review of research, Randel et al. (1992) found that students reported more interest in simulations compared with traditional methods. They concluded that "subject matter areas where very specific content can be targeted are more likely to show beneficial effects for gaming" (p. 261). Greenblat (1982) concluded that limited evidence seems to support the claims that gaming helps to develop general and interpersonal relations skills and problem-solving abilities.

Computer simulations are on the rise with the increasing incorporation of this technology in the schools. But, as a result of its newness, little research has been conducted. Clegg (1991) reported some tentative directions related to research in social studies education: "Students using computer simulations demonstrated increases in affective outcomes such as interest, motivation, enjoyment, sense of personal control, and willingness to persevere in completing learning tasks" (p. 527). He concluded that there is good learning potential for computer simulations that involve students in problem solving and decision making.

APPLICATION TO PRACTICE: SIMULATION-GAMING METHOD

As a method, simulation gaming has potential in helping to facilitate the goals associated with constructivist theory. Constructivism, as has been previously reported, emphasizes encouraging students to make connections between new information and their existing networks of prior knowledge and experiences. This is accomplished, in part, by providing opportunities for students to process and apply new learning in authentic task and problematic situations. The more the application situations are social, involving interaction with other students about the content being taught, the better, because students learn from each other (Brooks and Brooks, 1993; Good and Brophy, 1994). A primary purpose of simulation gaming is for students to become actively and thoughtfully involved in problematic situations that represent in-depth extensions and applications of the content being taught. In addition, most simulations involve students in highly interactive team situations as they make decisions and work to solve problems. Simulation gaming seems to be an ideal method to operationalize the constructivist-oriented principles and practices of good subject-matter teaching that Brophy (1992) offered based on his review of research. An instructional strategy that also meets this constructivist criteria is cooperative learning, which is presented in chapter 8.

Simulation
Simulations are designed to help students study and analyze a real-world social situation or process while being active participants within it. As students are involved in simulations, they role play by acting out characters and interacting with each other. They also make decisions and experience the consequences of their decisions. Many simulations have been commercially prepared as simulation games and therefore include the element of competition. But competition, producing winners and losers, is not a means or an end in a simulation unless the simulation focuses on analyzing the processes and forces of the competition in order to understand better the real social situation being portrayed. The teacher's role is to structure and facilitate the simulation and to conduct the debriefing discussion.

Simulations help prepare students to make the transition from the classroom to the real world. Traditionally, the emphasis of most subject areas has been on the transmission of information to passive students with little regard for the understanding and application of what has been "learned." Students saw little relevance in what was taught because it did not relate to their present or future lives. In the area of social studies, for example, for which many of the simulations have been developed, the goal is to develop students' critical-thinking skills as they engage in inquiry, decision making, and social action. The ideal end product is citizens equipped with the necessary skills and dispositions to reflect critically on societal issues and problems and participate actively in their resolution. Ideally, simulations encourage students to see relevance in what they are being taught and to encourage them to become actively involved in their own preparation to make political, economic, social, and personal decisions as young adults.

The range of simulations available to teachers at all grade levels in all subject areas is impressive. Simulations have been used in classrooms from kindergarten through adult levels. A list of 88 simulations for elementary social studies classrooms was compiled for *Social Education* by Muir (1980). Catalogs of simulations by the company Simile II are for universities and colleges, and can be used for businesses and the military as well. Some familiar names are Plea Bargaining, Starpower, Access, and Crisis. Simulations can be free, as many published teacher-made simulations are, or quite expensive, especially if they involve multimedia packages. The journal *Simulation and Gaming* publishes at least one simulation each month for a wide audience of readers (for the cost of a subscription or free at many libraries). Two relatively recent cross-cultural games are Visit to an Alien Planet (Powers, 1993) and Upside Down (Neves & Sanyal, 1992). At the other end of the price continuum are technologically oriented simulations published by Tom Snyder Productions (1994), for example, that involve Macintosh, MS-DOS, Apple II, and Windows software, and videodisc, video, and CD-ROM applications. One of the most expensive is the complete series of the Decisions, Decisions computer simulations costing more than $1,000. While most simulations are designed to be completed in one or two class periods, some are quite long. Dig 2 for grades 9 through 12 (Interact, 1993) takes 15 to 21 hours, while Congress in the Classroom (Schlemmer & Hill, 1977) was designed for high school government courses to be completed in as few as six weeks but could easily be run for a full semester.

A brief description of one popular simulation will help you get a sense of the potential this method has for classrooms studying units related to values, ethics, or futuristics. In Humanus (Simile II), students role-play survivors of a worldwide catastrophe. They are linked to the outside world through their survival computer, Humanus. Humanus monitors and controls them through a "voice print-out" recorded on audiotape and requires the survivors to make a variety of decisions: what 10 items do they want the computer to provide beyond basic life-support needs? How can the members of the cell create an environment in which each person's viewpoint is valued? Should a potentially contaminated survivor be allowed to enter the cell?

The debriefing phase involves the different groups of students in guided and reflective discussions sharing the decisions they have made and the reasons for their decisions. Students analyze the emotional aspects of their decisions and the cultural, philosophical, and experiential backgrounds contributing to their views. This simulation can be played over two class periods with a regular-sized class of students and requires minimal preparation time and no consumable forms. Only a tape recorder is necessary.

Role Playing

Role playing is a critical component in all of the simulations mentioned because most simulations are socially oriented and interaction between participants is necessary. While there are some simple role-playing situations, particularly at the elementary level, in which a student might dress up in the character of a famous political, social, or military leader and read an important speech, most role playing used in secondary classrooms involves problematic situations. While all social simulations involve role playing, not all role playing involves socially simulated situations. Shaftel and Shaftel (1967) commented on the parallels between simulation, gaming, and role playing. They have a mutual concern in: "1. conflict of interests, personal or interpersonal or intergroup, in which players 2. face alternatives from which to choose, and 3. must make individual decisions" (p. 12).

Role playing is designed to help students understand the perspectives and feelings of other people regarding a wide range of personal and social issues. This is accomplished by having several students act out, or dramatize, situations in which people are in conflict or faced with a dilemma of some sort. Role playing provides an opportunity for students to step into the shoes and get into the minds of others confronted with problematic situations. Shaftel and Shaftel (1967, p. 8) referred to this process as helping students become "inner-directed" so that they might learn to live in groups and develop intelligent concern for others. The majority of the class not directly involved in the role playing will be indirectly involved by observing and analyzing the words and actions of the role players. Their roles are equally as important because of their source of feedback. Just as in a simulation, the teacher's role is to structure and facilitate the role playing and conduct the critical follow-up debriefing discussion.

A brief description of a role-playing episode will help clarify the procedure and suggest the potential this method has for many classrooms. The subject is U.S. history and the topic for the role play is women and the Constitution. The objective is for students to role-play a conversation between Abigail Adams, Mercy Otis Warren, and John Adams, reflecting accurately the values of the players and the period. In preparation for assuming their roles, the students have read a variety of primary and secondary sources. Role cards for the three roles are distributed and the scene created: Abigail has just read John's negative response to her letters pleading that women not be omitted from the Constitution. She and her friend, Mercy, a strong feminist of the time, are discussing the letters and the issues over tea. Part way through the discussion, John enters and joins them.

The ensuing conversation is intended to depict the ideas and feelings of the participants. The observers are to focus on the values being held by the participants as reflected in what they say and how they behave. The enactment might last for three to six minutes, followed by the debriefing. The discussion is comprised of reviewing the events, values, positions, realism, and accuracy of the role play. A reenactment may be necessary if the teacher and students feel that other values need to be portrayed or emphasized. The final discussion centers on comparing colonial and contemporary women and, most importantly, generalizing the role women play, and do not play, in society today and the inherent problems in inequality. An essay in which students individually and privately reveal their points of view might follow (Shelly and Wilen, 1988).

The previous example is an illustration of one of several reasons that a teacher might want to use role play—depicting historical or contemporary problems. Other types of role playing center on dealing with immediate human-relations problems. Joyce and Weil with Showers (1992) elaborated on several types in this category. Interpersonal conflicts involve conflicts between people, and role playing can be used to discover approaches to overcome them. Intergroup relations might become problematic when ethnic and racial stereotyping develops, for example. Another reason is authoritarian beliefs. Role playing can help uncover negative attitudes and prejudices. Individual dilemmas occur when a person is caught between two contrasting values or when one person's values contrast with another person's. Role playing might help clarify and suggest solutions for these potentially difficult and sensitive situations.

Simulation-Gaming Phases

The phases of simulation gaming have been generalized for simulation and role playing and have been adapted from the work of Joyce et al. (1992). Our intention is not to prescribe a format for conducting all simulations and role playing but to provide a general structure that teachers can modify to suit their own classroom situations. Providing suggested phases will help operationalize simulation gaming by providing a mind's-eye view of how this method might unfold in the classroom.

Phase I. Orientation

    A. Explain simulation/role playing
    B. Overview of simulated/problem situation
    C. Objectives to be achieved

Students need to be oriented to simulation and role playing, particularly if they have not previously encountered these methods. The general purpose of using simulation or role playing over other methods and the general goals that you hope this method will achieve should be mentioned and discussed to help students understand why you are taking this different approach.

The most important component of this introductory phase is presenting the problem situation in role playing or the overview of the simulation. Students need to understand the problem fully to step into the shoes of a character in the case of role playing. Another consideration is that emotions may be quite high if the problem to be dealt with is based on an interpersonal classroom conflict. In this case a particularly positive and supportive classroom environment needs to be created for the role playing to be effective. In both role playing and simulations, the teacher should inform students of the objectives he or she wants to achieve through the play or game to provide a sense of direction and tie in to the content being taught.

Phase II. Participant Preparation

    A. Set up and interpret scenario/problem
    B. Establish procedures
    C. Organize teams/select participants

The specific roles participants assume in the simulation or role playing may call for more specific interpretation and this should be encouraged to increase the probability that goals will be met. For both simulations and role playing, setting the stage and establishing lines of action are necessary so roles can be understood. In role playing, those students who are not directly participating need to be prepared as observers. Perhaps a list of questions that different groups observing the action are to answer as they view the enactment and reflect on it may help structure their involvement. This will depend on the characteristics of the students involved.

Procedures need to be established and understood; this includes classroom-management standards. One of the major advantages of simulations and role playing is that students assume considerable freedom in determining the direction of their learning. Those students who are immature and irresponsible may decide to abuse this freedom so different behavioral standards may need to be established.

Phase III. Simulation/Enactment Operations

    A. Commence simulation/role play
    B. Facilitate operations
    C. Close simulation/role play

This phase is the main body of the method—the actual simulation or enactment. It is during this phase that all the efforts made previously come together to provide the learning experience. Students are to assume their roles and the teacher's primary responsibility is to facilitate the enactment or simulation. One role of the teacher is to serve as a resource person to provide the materials and sources necessary or to suggest where they may be found to keep the operation moving. Facilitating is an important role because, on one hand, you want to allow students enough freedom to analyze situations, solve problems, and make decisions without intervening too much. Students may sense they are doing things (displaying the "right" attitudes and values in a role play, for example, or the "right" decisions or solutions in a simulation) for the teacher rather than themselves if intervention is too heavy-handed. On the other hand, the teacher needs to provide structure and direction when necessary, particularly to keep students on-task. The teacher will also need to determine when to terminate the role play or simulation and begin the debriefing, or prepare for reenactment in the case of a complex role-playing situation.

Phase IV. Debriefing Discussion

    A. Review action, perceptions, and problems
    B. Relate simulation/enactment to real world
    C. Connect to previous learnings and future goals

The role play and simulation are learning experiences, but learning really can't be determined until the debriefing discussion. This phase cannot be emphasized too heavily. Often, students get so wrapped up in the role play or simulation that they need to step back and reflect on their actions and intentions and make connections to the real world outside the classroom. In her research on debriefing,

Lederman (1992) stated, "The debriefing sessions, like the experiential activity, is learner-based: it is discovery learning in which participants are provided with incentives to examine and analyze their inner thoughts and reflections" (p. 154). The experiences the students have undergone essentially become the raw data for learning, and the process of debriefing makes connections possible.

Stadsklev (1980) proposed the following structure for debriefing: (1) experience, (2) identify, (3) analyze, and (4) generalize (EIAG). The *experience* part is the actual simulation. *Identify* means to describe the experience in terms of decisions made or data gathered, for example, and the reasons for engaging in specific behaviors. In a role play, feelings need to be described and consequences identified. During the *analyze* phase, higher-level reflection is required to look back on the role play or simulation for deeper meanings and understandings. Cause-and-effect relationships should be explored, alternative approaches and decisions should be considered, and the impact of problem solutions should be reasoned. The final phase is to *generalize*. At this point students should be ready to express what they have learned in terms of the simulation or role play. Further, because the simulation was an abstraction of reality, they should be able to make connections to the real world. Students also need to see the connection of the simulation or role playing to content taught before and content to be taught. Teachers also need to ensure that the original objectives guiding the method be reviewed.

The teacher's role during the debriefing is more active and directive than during the role play or simulation because of the discussion responsibilities involved. A major responsibility is guiding students to discover what has been learned, whether positive or negative, rather than being didactic. It would be entirely appropriate to implement either the guided or reflective discussion depending on the nature of the simulation or role play and the interest and ability level of the students.

One other possibility is to incorporate journal writing as a final phase. Petranek, Corey, and Black (1992) contended that learning from simulations occurs on three levels: participating in the game, debriefing in discussions, and writing in a journal. "Journal writing is . . . a means to validate knowledge, to organize material, to understand ideas, and to substantiate the experience" (p. 183). Students can write about their personal experiences, problems, and growth resulting from the simulation. Further, they can write more specifically about the integration of their experiences with real life.

Scenario Analysis

Mr. Carl did not use role playing or simulation in the introductory economics-class scenario. One simulation he might consider implementing during the GNP unit is Development, which is available from Science Research Associates, Inc., and presented in Gordon (1972). Development explores the relations between the major world powers and the developing nations of the world. The two major powers are labeled *East* and *West,* and they compete for the loyalty of the developing countries. The competition partly centers on the distribution of foreign aid.

The goal for the developing countries is to improve their standard of living by accepting foreign aid without giving up political independence and freedom of action on the world stage.

SUMMARY POINT

The method of simulation gaming is experiential and, therefore, a different alternative to the other methods presented. Here lies its strength and appeal to students because they get an opportunity to assume a more active role as they "do" science, health, history, or sociology. The appeal to teachers who are oriented toward constructivism is that, through an authentic learning experience such as a simulation or role playing, students learn by making connections between their own knowledge and experiences and the real world. This method encourages students to go deeper into an issue or problem as they engage in social interactions with their peers. The result is a higher probability that meaning will be constructed and understanding of more complex ideas will result.

A simulation-gaming analysis form is located at the end of the chapter.

REVIEW: IMPORTANT PRACTICES — PHASES OF A GENERALIZED SIMULATION-GAMING METHOD

Orientation

A. Explain simulation/role playing
B. Overview of simulated/problem situation
C. Objectives to be achieved

Participant Preparation

A. Set up and interpret scenario/problem
B. Establish procedures
C. Organize teams/select participants

Simulation/Enactment Operations

A. Commence simulation/role play
B. Facilitate operations
C. Close simulation/role play

Debriefing Discussion

A. Review action, perceptions, and problems
B. Relate simulation/enactment to real world
C. Connect to previous learnings and future goals

SUMMARY POINT

1. Many factors need to be considered in choosing a particular strategy or method.
2. No one method can be totally relied on.
3. If a method is to be used effectively, the teacher needs to become proficient in its use.
4. The most effective teachers potentially are those who effectively use several modes.
5. The teacher's choice of methods has been less often a rational decision than defaulting to a comfortable pattern.
6. Making instructional choices based on instructional purposes is a potential approach to improving instructional effectiveness.
7. Specific methods are effective for particular sorts of learning outcomes; compatibility is the key factor.

Instruction is the means for "turning knowledge into learning" (Jones, Bagford, & Wallen, 1979, p. 1). Without a knowledge of and practical experience with a variety of instructional techniques and methods, Mr. Carl would not have been able to accomplish what he had intended in his lesson. The implementation of a planned sequence of instructional approaches brought the concept of GNP to life. The probability is high that the knowledge the students gained from reading was turned into learning by the teacher as a result of decisions he made while planning the lesson. Effective decision making is basic to effective teaching.

QUESTIONS FOR REFLECTION

1. Mr. Carl, in the scenario introducing the chapter, used a discrepant event to stimulate guided inquiry. The discrepancy created a clever puzzle that students were to solve through their questioning. What is one discrepant event you can devise in your subject area that might have the same impact on students' curiosity?
2. Research shows that teachers generally do not teach their high- and low-ability students differently. What are some of the disadvantages of not individualizing instruction more for these groups of students?
3. Why is there a persistence of teachers' use of recitation even though the literature is much more supportive of discussion as the primary method to teach for understanding?
4. What would you recommend to your cooperating teacher as to how he or she might promote more equity and power sharing with students during a large-group discussion?
5. What can you learn as a teacher from watching a talk-show host effectively conduct a discussion with guests and live and call-in audiences?
6. Considering that reflective discussion is the most difficult form of dis-

cussion, what might you do in your classroom to make it easier to conduct a reflective discussion?

7. What are some entries you might devise to commence a guided or reflective discussion in your subject area?

8. Do you think it is appropriate to offer your personal opinion or position on an issue during a discussion? Provide evidence to support your view.

9. What are approaches that you might use to encourage students to generate questions during a discussion to encourage their participation and thinking?

10. What do you think are some of the assumptions teachers have about how students learn when they use lectures in one form or another as the primary instructional method?

11. Some theorists suggest that the lecture is the most difficult instructional method to use in the classroom, whereas others suggest it is the easiest. What support could you provide to support both points of view?

12. Think of a complex topic in your subject area that you might be teaching. What advance organizer might you use to help students understand your topic better?

13. What have you read that would help to distinguish the terms generally used synonymously with inquiry: discovery, reflective teaching, inductive teaching, and problem solving? Based on your readings, what definitions would you apply?

14. Think of a topic or theme that you are or will be teaching. What are some problematic situations you could devise for which the inquiry method might be appropriate?

15. Who is one of the students you are, or will be, teaching that you would classify as above average in terms of ability and motivation? Would you encourage this student to engage in an individualized inquiry investigation? If so, how might you go about it?

16. Observe a videotape of a teacher using one of the forms of discussion, lecture, or inquiry. What would you suggest to the teacher as to how the performance might be improved based on the information presented in the chapter? Use the appropriate analysis form as a structure to observe the lesson.

17. Supposedly, simulations and role-playing situations are peak experiences that people readily recall as being exciting and memorable learning activities long after being out of school. Can you recall such a simulation or role-playing situation from your schooling? Why do you think it had such an impact?

18. If you had the time and opportunity to design a simulation for a topic, event, issue, or problem that you teach or will be teaching, what would it look like?

19. Think of a human relations problem that a small group of students in one of your classes is having, or possibly could have. How might role playing be a useful method to help clarify or solve the problem?

ANALYSIS FORM   DISCUSSION METHOD

TEACHER _____

OBSERVER _____

CLASS _____

DATE _____

	OCCURRENCE	EFFECTIVENESS
	1. Not evident	1. Not effective
	2. Slightly evident	2. Slightly effective
	3. Moderately evident	3. Moderately effective
	4. Quite evident	4. Quite effective
	N Not applicable	5. Not applicable

CATEGORIES (Parts A+B Correspond to Occurrence and Effectiveness in the Analysis Scale)	A. OCCURRENCE	B. EFFECTIVENESS
PHASE I: ENTRY: IDENTIFICATION OF PROBLEM, ISSUE, OR TOPIC A. Springboard and/or attention getter used		
B. Identify problem, issue, or topic		
C. State objective and rationale		
PHASE II: CLARIFICATION A. Establish procedures		
B. Define terms and concepts related to the problem, issue, or topic		
PHASE III: INVESTIGATION A. Ask the appropriate levels of questions to achieve the desired levels of student thinking		
B. Use questioning techniques such as probing, wait time, and redirection to maintain discussion, and stimulate student involvement and thinking		

C. Use nonquestioning alternative techniques such as various statement forms to maintain discussion and encourage student involvement		
D. Encourage student initiative and leadership		
E. Request that students support opinions offered		
F. Ensure sufficient coverage of problem, issue, or topic		
PHASE IV: CLOSURE: SUMMARY, INTEGRATION, APPLICATION A. Summary in the form of consensus, solutions, insights achieved in relation to topic covered, issue explored, or problem investigated		
B. Integrate lesson with goals and previous learning		
C. Apply discussion outcomes to other situations		

REFLECTIVE CONSIDERATIONS

How would you describe the interaction pattern of the discussion?

To what extent was student discussion leadership evident?

Based on the nature of your students and content to be taught, why did you decide on the discussion method to achieve objectives? (self-analysis)

To what extent did you achieve your purpose? (self-analysis)

How do you know? (self-analysis)

ANALYSIS SCALES

TEACHER _____

OBSERVER _____

CLASS _____

DATE _____

OCCURRENCE	EFFECTIVENESS
1. Not evident	1. Not effective
2. Slightly evident	2. Slightly effective
3. Moderately evident	3. Moderately effective
4. Quite evident	4. Quite effective
N Not applicable	5. Not applicable

CATEGORIES (Parts A + B Correspond to Occurrence and Effectiveness in the Analysis Scale)	A. OCCURRENCE	B. EFFECTIVENESS
PHASE I: ENTRY: PREPARATION FOR LEARNING A. State objectives and rationale		
B. Provide a context for the new material to be presented		
C. Focus attention on a key concept, generalization (advance organizer), or principle that encompasses the lecture		
PHASE II: PRESENTATION A. Sequence content from simpler to complex understandings		
B. Enhance presentation with visual aids		
C. Stimulate attention with verbal and nonverbal behaviors		
PHASE III: CLOSURE: REVIEW OF LEARNING A. Integrate with students' knowledge and experiences		
B. Transition to next lesson or activity		

REFLECTIVE CONSIDERATIONS

Why did you decide using the lecture method was the best approach to teach the content?

What verbal and nonverbal behaviors did students display to indicate they understood the content of your lecture?

To what extent did you achieve your objectives?

ANALYSIS FORM — INQUIRY METHOD

ANALYSIS FORM   INQUIRY METHOD

TEACHER _____

OBSERVER _____

CLASS _____

DATE _____

ANALYSIS SCALES

OCCURRENCE	EFFECTIVENESS
1. Not evident	1. Not effective
2. Slightly evident	2. Slightly effective
3. Moderately evident	3. Moderately effective
4. Quite evident	4. Quite effective
N Not applicable	5. Not applicable

CATEGORIES (Parts A +B Correspond to Occurrence and Effectiveness in the Analysis Scale)	A. OCCURRENCE	B. EFFECTIVENESS
PHASE I: ENTRY: PRESENTATION AND CLARIFICATION OF A PROBLEM, ISSUE, OR QUERY A. State objective; provide rationale		
B. Identification of a problem, issue, or query		
C. Relate to students' experiences and lives		
D. Clarification of the problem		
PHASE II: FORMATION OF HYPOTHESES A. Encourage tentative explanations or solutions		
B. Clarify hypotheses		
PHASE III: COLLECTION OF DATA A. Facilitate the identification of sources for evidence		
B. Assist in the evaluation of the evidence		
PHASE IV: TEST HYPOTHESES A. Assist in organizing the data		
B. Assist in analysis and evaluation of data		
PHASE V: CLOSURE: DRAWING CONCLUSIONS A. Facilitate the reaching of a generalization, explanation, or solution		
B. Integration and transition		

REFLECTIVE CONSIDERATIONS

What variation in the inquiry process did you use to achieve your goals?

How did students respond and react to your guidance as they were led through the inquiry process?

To what extent did students assume a leadership role as they engaged in inquiry?

What evidence do you have that the students were engaged in critical and creative thinking?

283

ANALYSIS FORM

ANALYSIS SCALES

TEACHER _____

OBSERVER _____

CLASS _____

DATE _____

OCCURRENCE	EFFECTIVENESS
1. Not evident	1. Not effective
2. Slightly evident	2. Slightly effective
3. Moderately evident	3. Moderately effective
4. Quite evident	4. Quite effective
N Not applicable	5. Not applicable

CATEGORIES (Parts A +B Correspond to Occurrence and Effectiveness in the Analysis Scale)	A. OCCURRENCE	B. EFFECTIVENESS
PHASE I: ORIENTATION A. Explain simulation/role playing		
B. Overview of simulated/problem situation		
C. Objectives to be achieved		
PHASE II: PARTICIPANT PREPARATION A. Set up and interpret scenario/problem		
B. Establish procedures		
C. Organize teams/select participants		
PHASE III: SIMULATION/ENACTMENT OPERATIONS A. Commence simulation/role play		
B. Facilitate operations		
C. Close simulation/role play		
PHASE IV: DEBRIEFING DISCUSSION A. Review action, perceptions, and problems		
B. Relate simulation/enactment to real world		
C. Connect to previous learnings and future goals		

REFLECTIVE CONSIDERATIONS

What was there about the simulated (simulation) or problem (role playing) situation that was motivating to the students?

What criteria were used to select students for the teams (simulation) or enactments (role playing)?

Was your amount of involvement during the simulation or enactment correct? Why or why not?

What were some of the direct and indirect clues that you picked up from the students during the debriefing that indicated they learned about the real world?

REFERENCES

Andrews, J. (1984). Discovery and expository learning compared: Their effects on independent and dependent students. *Journal of Educational Research, 28,* 80–89.

Armstrong, D. (1980). *Social studies in secondary education.* New York: Macmillan.

Ausubel, D. (1968). *Educational psychology: A cognitive view.* New York: Holt, Rinehart & Winston.

Bellack, A., Kliebard, H., Hyman, R., & Smith, F. (1966). *The language of the classroom.* New York: Columbia University Press.

Berliner, D., & Gage, N. (1976). The psychology of teaching methods. In N. Gage (Ed.), *The psychology of teaching methods: 75th Yearbook of NSSE.* Chicago: University of Chicago Press.

Brooks, J., & Brooks, M. (1993). *The case for constructivist classrooms.* Alexandria, VA: Association for Supervision and Curriculum Development.

Brophy, J. (1992). Probing the subtleties of subject-matter teaching. *Educational Leadership, 49*(7), 4–8.

Butler, J. (1992). Use of teaching methods within the lecture format. *Medical Teacher, 14*(1), 11–25.

Byer, B. (1984, April). Improving thinking skills. *Phi Delta Kappan, 65*(8), 556–560.

Clegg, A. (1991). Games and simulations in social studies education. In J. Shavers (Ed.), *Handbook of research on social studies teaching and learning.* New York: Macmillan.

Cooper, P., & Galvin, K. (1984). *What do we know about research in teacher training in instructional strategies?* Paper presented at the Annual Meeting of the Central State Speech Association, ERIC, Chicago.

Dewey, J. (1910). *How we think.* Lexington, MA: Heath.

Dillon, J. (1983). *Teaching and the art of questioning.* Bloomington, IN: Phi Delta Kappa.

Dillon, J. (1984). Research on questioning and discussion. *Educational Leadership, 42*(3), 50–60.

Dillon, J. (1985). Using questions to foil discussion. *Teaching and Teacher Education, 1,* 109–121.

Dillon, J. (1994). *Using discussion in classrooms.* Buckingham, England: Open University Press.

Evertson, C. (1982). Differences in instructional activities in higher and lower achieving junior high English and math classes. *Elementary School Journal, 82,* 329–350.

Gage, N. (1969). Teaching methods. In R. L. Ebel (Ed.), *Encyclopedia of educational research.* London: Macmillan.

Gage, N., & Berliner, D. (1992). *Educational psychology* (5th ed.). Boston: Houghton Mifflin.

Gall, J., & Gall, M. (1990). Outcomes of the discussion method. In W. Wilen (Ed.), *Teaching and learning through discussion* (pp. 25–44). Springfield, IL: Charles C. Thomas.

Gall, M., & Gall, J. (1976). The discussion method. In N. L. Gage (Ed.), *The psychology of teaching methods: 75th yearbook of the NSSE*. Chicago: University of Chicago Press.

Gilliom, M. (1977). Simulations. In E. Gilliom (Ed.), *Practical methods for the social studies*. Belmont, CA: Wadsworth.

Good, T., & Brophy, J. (1987). *Looking in classrooms* (4th ed.). New York: Harper & Row.

Good, T., & Brophy, J. (1994). *Looking in Classrooms* (6th ed.). New York: HarperCollins.

Gordon, A. (1972). *Games for growth*. Chicago: Science Research Associates.

Greenblat, C. (1982). Games and simulations. In H. Mitzel (Ed.), *Encyclopedia of educational research* (Vol. 2). New York: Macmillan.

Harwood, A., & Hahn, C. (1990). *Controversial issues in the classroom: ERIC Digest*. Bloomington, IN: Clearinghouse for Social Studies/Social Science Education.

Hudgins, B. (1971). *The instructional process*. Chicago: Rand McNally.

Interact (1993). *Catalog*. Lakeside, CA: Author.

Jones, A., Bagford, L., & Wallen, E. (1979). *Strategies for teaching*. Metuchen, NJ: Scarecrow Press.

Joyce, B., & Weil, M., with Showers, B. (1992). *Models of teaching* (4th ed.). Boston: Allyn & Bacon.

King, A. (1992). Comparison of self-questioning, summarizing, and notetaking-review as strategies for learning from lectures. *American Educational Research Journal, 29*(2), 303–323.

Lederman, L. (1992). Debriefing: Toward a systematic assessment of theory and practice. *Simulation and Gaming, 23*(2), 145–160.

McLeish, J. (1976). The lecture method. In N. Gage (Ed.), *The psychology of teaching methods: 75th yearbook of the NSSE*. Chicago: University of Chicago Press.

Michael, T., & Weaver, R. (1984). Lecturing: Means for improvement. *Clearinghouse, 57*, 389–371.

Muir, S. (1980). Simulation games for elementary social studies. *Social Education, 35*–39.

National Council for the Social Studies (1994). Curriculum standards for social studies. Washington, D.C. NCSS.

Neves, J., & Sanyal, R. (1992). Upside down: A cross-cultural simulation. *Simulation and Gaming, 23*(3), 370–375.

Parker, W. (1992, November). *The possibilities of discussion*. Paper presented at the annual meeting of the College and University Faculty Assembly of the National Council for the Social Studies, Detroit, MI.

Paul, R. (1984). Critical thinking: Fundamental to education for a free society. *Educational Leadership*, 4–14.

Peterson, P. (1979). *Aptitude-treatment interaction effects of three teaching approaches: Lecture-recitation, inquiry, and public issues discussion* (ERIC Document Reproduction Service No. ED 186427). Madison, WI: Research and Development Center for Individualized Schooling.

Petranek, C., Corey, S., & Black, R. (1992). Three levels of learning in simulations: Participating, Debriefing, and Writing. *Simulation and Gaming, 23*(2), 174–185.

Ponder, G., & Davis, O. (1982). Social studies education. In H. Mitzel (Ed.), *Encyclopedia of educational research*. New York: Free Press.

Powers, R. (1993). Visit to an alien planet. *Simulation and Gaming, 24*(4), 509–518.

Randel, J., Morris, B., Wetzel, C., & Whitehill, B. (1992). The effectiveness of games for educational purposes: A review of recent research. *Simulation and Gaming, 23*(3), 261–276.

Robinson, W., & Niaz, M. (1991). Performance based on instruction by lecture or by interaction and its relationship to cognitive variables. *International Journal of Science Education, 13*(2), 203–215.

Roby, T. (1988). Commonplaces, questions and modes of discussion. In J. Dillon (Ed.), *Classroom questions and discussion*. Norwood, NJ: Ablex.

Schlemmer, D., & Hill, R. (1977). *Congress in the classroom*. Washington, DC: Congressional Quarterly.

Selim, M., & Shrigley, R. (1983). Group dynamics approach: A sociopsychological approach for testing the effect of discovery and expository teaching on the science achievement and attitude of young Egyptian students. *Journal of Research in Science Teaching, 20*, 213–224.

Shaftel, F., & Shaftel, G. (1967). *Role playing for social values: Decision-making in the social studies*. Englewood Cliffs, NJ: Prentice-Hall.

Shelly, A., & Wilen, W. (1988). Sex equity and critical thinking. *Social Education, 52*(3), 168–172.

Simile II. *Catalog*. Del Mar, CA: Author.

Shulman, L., & Tamir, P. (1973). Research on teaching in the natural sciences. In R. Travers, (Ed.), *Second handbook of research on teaching*. Chicago: Rand McNally.

Suchman, J. (1962). *The elementary school training program in scientific inquiry: NDEA Project 216*. Urbana, IL: University of Illinois.

Thompson, B. (1981). Teachers' preferences for various teaching methods. *NASSP Bulletin, 65*, 96–100.

Tom Snyder Productions (1994). *Catalog*. Watertown, MA: Author.

Weimer, R. (1974). A critical analysis of the discovery versus expository research studies investigating retention or transfer within the areas of science, mathematics, vocational education, language, and geography from 1908 to the present. (Doctoral dissertation, University of Illinois, 1975). *Dissertation Abstracts International, 35*.

Stadsklev, R. (1980). *Handbook of simulation gaming in social education*. University, AL: Institute of Higher Education Research & Services.

White, J. (1990). Involving different social and cultural groups in discussion. In W. Wilen (Ed.), *Teaching and learning through discussion*. Springfield, IL: Charles C. Thomas.

Wilen, W. (1990). Forms and phases of discussion. In W. Wilen (Ed.), *Teaching and learning through discussion*. Springfield, IL: Charles C. Thomas.

Wilen, W. (1994, June). *Democracy and reflective discussion in social studies classrooms.* Paper presented at the International Social Studies Conference, Nairobi, Kenya.

Wilen, W., & McKenrick, P. (1989). Individualized inquiry: Encouraging able students to investigate. *Social Studies, 80,* 36–39.

Wilen, W., & White, J. (1991). Interaction and discourse in social studies classrooms. In J. Shaver (Ed.), *Handbook of research on social studies teaching and learning.* New York: Macmillan.

Zemelman, S., Daniels, H., and Hyde, A. (1993). *Best practice: New standards for teaching and learning in America's schools.* Portsmouth, NH: Heinemann.

8 Teaching Strategies
for Promoting Achievement

OUTLINE

> *There is not one single teaching strategy that is the best approach; but certain strategies, used in certain contexts, have been documented by researchers as improving achievement.*

FOCUS QUESTIONS

1. What instructional practices characterize a teacher who uses direct-teaching methods?
2. For what learning purposes is the direct-teaching approach most suited?
3. What is the essential belief that is the basis for mastery learning?
4. What is the role of the teacher in mastery learning?
5. What are the five basic elements of cooperative learning?
6. How does cooperative learning differ from mastery learning?

The preceding chapters have discussed teaching techniques verified by effective-teaching research, supported by learning theory, tested by teachers, and essential to every teacher's practice. This chapter examines strategies that have been identified as promoting achievement and student learning. A strategy for the purpose of this chapter is a general approach to instruction. It subsumes a variety of methods such as were described in the previous chapter. A strategy serves as an organizer for the delivery of instruction by guiding decision making about the teacher's role, the students' role, the selection of methods, and instructional materials. A strategy helps the teacher make optimal use of methods and resources in achieving particular goals. This chapter examines strategies that have been identified in the research as promoting achievement on standardized tests.

The strategies presented in this chapter emerged from the effective-teaching research (Roberts & Kenney, 1985; Teddlie, Kirby, & Stringfield, 1989; Cruickshank, 1990) but are very much a part of the nineties' educational restructuring efforts. Direct teaching is widely promoted for secondary classrooms because it increases time-on-task and focuses on achieving learning objectives. Mastery learning is a key instructional practice in Outcome-Based Education—a movement for school reform with more than 2,000 schools in its network (Ellis & Fouts, 1993). Cooperative learning is the strategy widely identified as a viable approach for the heterogeneous classroom with its inclusion of multicultural, multiethnic, multilingual, at-risk, disabled, and multitalented students where "diversity is celebrated within a cooperative content" (Putnam, 1993, p. 6). Cooperative learning also fits comfortably into the constructivist classroom.

As Joyce and Weil pointed out in their influential work, *Models of Teaching* (1992), in which they described more than 20 models to teaching, there is no single teaching strategy that is the best approach. Teachers need a variety of approaches to address their many instructional purposes and students' varied learning styles and needs. Teachers will have a better command over their instructional decisions if they employ a variety of strategies and methods. Strategies provide teachers with an organizational pattern or plan with which to structure the curriculum, determine curriculum materials, and guide teacher behaviors with students. Strategies are the pedagogical arsenal to accommodate a wide range of instructional maneuvers. However, keep in mind that classroom research has not "identified specific instructional behaviors that are ideal for all types of students and situations" (Good & Brophy, 1994, p. 377).

OVERVIEW

This chapter describes three general strategies of teaching in sufficient detail to enable teachers to recognize their potential and consider their use. The direct-teaching strategy emphasizes structure, high teacher visibility, focused objectives, and effectiveness in promoting on-task student behavior. Mastery learning establishes minimum levels of performance that every student or group is expected to achieve. Whereas traditional approaches consider time to be a constant and achievement a variable, mastery learning does just the opposite. The cooperative-learning strategy takes advantage of students' natural inclination to sociability.

After learning the skills of communication, group process, and leadership, students become an effective source of instruction for each other as they work together in small groups.

At the end of the chapter, analysis instruments are included to help the reader examine the strategies described in this chapter.

SCENARIO

Millie Blaine, a second-year high school English teacher, was reviewing her plans for her next unit on "The Hero/Heroine of the 90s" with the fifth-hour class. She thought about the difficulties she had encountered in her first try at cooperative learning that year and what she was going to change in the second try as a result.

Millie felt that a cooperative-learning approach for this new unit on literature, writing, and self-reflection was the strategy to use because of the diverse makeup of her classes that continued to present difficulties for her in terms of management and achieving learning outcomes. Having come from a small midwestern town, she has been continually challenged by the mix of students in her classes that include diverse cultural, racial, and socioeconomic groups, as well as special-needs students.

With such diverse needs and strengths in that section, Millie felt that another cooperative group project would be appropriate. She would make changes in her practices based on what she had learned and what the students had learned from the first attempt. She would start the unit tomorrow with a discussion on the final self-evaluation reports the class had submitted at the conclusion of the initial cooperative-learning unit. She would solicit suggestions from them as to how to make this attempt successful for everyone. She would encourage much discussion about how they built (or were not able to build) group interdependence.

Building interdependence had been a problem. She recalled the written self-evaluation from Junko:

> I really do not prefer working in groups because I fear that others in my group may not work as hard as I do to do my best, and I would end up having to do the group's project. However, I was satisfied to find that all but one in my group did their part and contributed to the group project. I am not sure if I could have done as well by myself because I do not have the artistic ability two people in my group had. But, I still like to depend only on myself.

Millie was not sure how much she should try to change attitudes about cooperative learning similar to Junko's. However, this time she thought that she would structure the groups even more carefully to ensure a heterogeneous balance of cultures, races, and special needs, as well as distribution of students with leadership abilities now that she knew her students better. She would start her class the next day with a think-pair-share activity in which partners within the groups would think about their past cooperative experiences and how to improve them, and then form ideas together to share with the group and with the whole class.

Fortunately, Millie had her own team partner down the hall—Miguel Fernandez—who had been her mentor her first year. Now they both were using the cooperative-learning approach and sharing ideas on meeting the challenges of teaching diverse student populations.

In Millie Blaine's building, other teachers were trying varied approaches to instruction to raise achievement and learning. Max Rosenberg had been using a mastery-learning approach in his 9th-grade algebra class since the beginning of the semester. He had spent much of the summer organizing his curriculum with support materials in several units complete with pretests and posttests and specific instructional objectives that indicated the level of mastery the students must reach. He had arranged a file cabinet with numerous practice sheets and tests and had also obtained some software packages on beginning algebra to use on the computer in the back of the room.

He had initially expected to have each student work individually, but having talked to Millie Blaine and Miguel Fernandez, he had decided to group the students according to their present mathematical knowledge level. No group was larger than five students, and students were continually regrouped as they achieved learning objectives and delved further into new materials.

Max was troubled at first by the achievement-level grouping he had created because he was against any identification of lower-ability groups. However, as he saw students moving easily among groups and turning to group members as tutors, he decided to keep the group approach.

Max had reported to Millie that the students were handling the approach to instruction well. Several groups were four to five units behind but were working and progressing, even though their pace was slower than others in the class. Overall, he was pleased with the improved achievement and attitude of the students in the class.

Also, upstairs in the science lab Rose Fortunato, using the direct-teaching approach, was ready to move from the presentation phase of the lesson, in which she had conducted a model demonstration on chemical bonding, into the group-practice stage. During the group practice she would review the concept using overheads and models and ask the students a number of questions to check on their understanding of the principle before they did their small-group practice in the laboratory.

Rose Fortunato felt comfortable with the use of the six instructional functions of direct teaching to structure her chemistry lessons because they facilitated her lesson planning and helped her maintain much student involvement through comprehension checks and group practice. She was pleased with the achievement level of the class.

All three of these teachers were encouraged by their principal to examine and extend their instructional practices to accommodate strategies that were reported in educational research as increasing students' achievement. They had received information and an orientation to these strategies in a series of in-service meetings held in the district. Small summer stipends had been made available for curricular planning to implement the strategies. The school district was committed to focusing on the improvement of instruction to increase achievement and student learning.

RESEARCH AND THEORETICAL BASE

The first achievement-raising strategy to be examined is direct teaching. Direct teaching refers to the instructional approach emerging from the works of Berliner, Bloom, Harnischfiger, and Wiley (in Peterson & Walberg, 1979) on the impact of time and content covered on student success. It is also based on the system of direct instruction developed by Good, Grouws, and Ebmeier (1983) for the teaching of mathematics following a structured approach that became identified as lesson functions. Although most of the research on direct teaching comes from studies of elementary school classrooms, the strategy is presented here for secondary teachers so that it can be used at appropriate times and with the appropriate students, as explained later in this chapter. Direct teaching refers to academically focused, teacher-directed classrooms using sequenced and structured materials. It also refers to teaching activities in which goals are clear to students, sufficient time is allowed for instruction, coverage of content is extensive, performance of students is monitored, and feedback is academically oriented (Rosenshine, 1979). Rosenshine included the teaching functions from Good et al. (1983) to provide a six-stage sequenced structure to instruction.

In a report on direct teaching, Rosenshine and Stevens (1986) indicated that across a number of studies the more effective teachers (in terms of promoting student achievement) were those who maintained a strong academic focus and spent less time in nonacademic activities. Studies by Soar (1973), Stallings and Kaskowitz (1974), and Solomon and Kendall (1979) showed that teachers who most successfully stimulated gains in achievement played the role of a strong leader. Researchers found that classrooms organized so that children had a great deal of choice about the activities they would pursue had lower academically engaged time and achievement (Rosenshine, 1979). Rosenshine described the direct teacher as the more successful instructor in teaching content measured by achievement tests. This type of teacher structures and selects activities within a controlled classroom.

In the past, the picture of the direct teacher was that of a grim, didactic authority figure who instructed the class as a whole and dominated the class time with much teacher talk. This teacher made the instructional decisions and taught through lecture and drill for a high percentage of correct rote-memory responses. This picture caused many educators to question the negative side effects that this approach could produce. However, researchers confirmed to the contrary that direct teachers in more structured, formal classrooms with higher achievement results are warm, concerned, and flexible, and allow more freedom of movement (Rosenshine, 1979). These studies reported that direct teaching is effective in teaching skill subjects such as reading and mathematics and does not produce a negative classroom climate. Other strategies may be more appropriate for achieving creative and expressive goals. As was stated in chapter 2, there is no single strategy for effective instruction, just as there is no single list of teaching behaviors that will guarantee achievement. These strategies and teaching behaviors need to be part of a teacher's information so that they can be tied to the accomplishment of certain goals, such as teaching basic skills to students who may react most positively to much teacher direction.

The teaching functions considered part of the direct-teaching strategy reflect the information from researchers, working independently, who arrived at similar findings on the systematic approach to instruction being used by teachers whose students had higher rankings on achievement tests (Rosenshine & Stevens, 1986). These studies were conducted mainly in elementary settings in which teachers implemented direct-teaching behaviors and their students obtained higher achievement or higher academic engaged time than did students in classrooms where direct instruction was infrequently practiced.

Two noteworthy studies for secondary teachers using direct instruction that reported positive gains in student achievement need to be mentioned: the Texas Junior High School Study (Emmer, Evertson, Sanford, Clements, & Worsham, 1982) and Organizing and Instructing High School Classes (Fitzpatrick, 1982).

The second strategy for instructional variety and achievement improvement is the mastery-learning model developed by Bloom (1980) and Block & Burns (1976) and derived from the work of Carroll (1963). This strategy is based on the idea that learning depends largely on time—the time allowed for learning and the time needed for learning (Carroll, 1963).

Bloom developed the mastery approach, maintaining that all students in an ordinary classroom can master a subject given sufficient time. This instructional approach is an individualized, diagnostic method in which students receive immediate remediation if they cannot pass the formative test at the prescribed level. They continue to study and test until they have reached that prescribed mastery level.

The research literature on mastery learning is largely positive. A 1990 analysis of findings from 108 research studies showed "that mastery learning programs have positive effects on the examination performances of students in colleges, high schools, and the upper grades in elementary schools. The effects appear to be stronger on the weaker students in a class. . . . Mastery programs have positive effects on student attitudes toward course content and instruction but may increase student time on instructional tasks" (Kulik, Kulik, & Bangert-Drowns, 1990). Benjamin Bloom and his associates' research in 1984 showed even higher impressive achievement gains for students moving from a group-based mastery learning to an individual-focused mastery approach (Bloom, 1984).

The mastery approach gives students more control over the amount of time for learning the content, so their success rate is expected to be higher. This expectation that success can be achieved through effort has been shown by achievement theorists to affect motivation positively (Dweck & Goetz, 1978) (see chapter 2). Many advocates of mastery learning recognize this expectation for success from the teacher and the student as the strongest feature of this model.

Mastery learning has its critics because of its possible effects of limiting teacher time with brighter students, its narrow view of the curriculum in terms of defined sets of skills, and its very structured and mechanistic approach to instruction (Stallings & Stipek, 1986). However, the research literature in mastery learning is largely positive. Ellis & Fouts (1993), in their survey of the research, reported study after study indicating the superiority of mastery learning over traditional learning in raising test scores.

The third instructional strategy for promoting achievement is the cooperative-learning approach, which uses peer tutoring and team cooperation to encourage student learning. It emphasizes motivation, as does mastery learning, and like the other two models can be implemented by teachers in both elementary and secondary school classrooms using the instructional materials of that system. The key components of the strategy are peer interaction, cooperation, and communication (Roberts & Kenney, 1985).

In their review of the research on cooperative learning, Stallings and Stipek (1986) found that this learning strategy has been used to accomplish at least four purposes: (1) to raise the value of academic achievement among students and encourage students to help each other learn; (2) to use cooperation and peer instruction to benefit both high- and low-ability students; (3) to provide an alternative cooperative model to the competitive model most used in schools; and (4) to improve human relations among races and ethnic groups in a school.

Of the many cooperative-learning methods that have been researched and evaluated, five seem particularly appropriate and effective for teaching and learning at the middle school through high school levels. The Student Teams–Achievement Division (STAD) and Teams-Game-Tournament (TGT) forms of cooperative learning were developed at Johns Hopkins University by Slavin and his associates (1990) and are among the oldest and most heavily researched. Jigsaw was developed by Aronson, Blaney, Stephan, Sikes, and Snapp (1978), with a variation devised by Slavin (1990). Johnson and Johnson and their associates (1987) developed the Learning Together model, which is also widely used, and Sharon and Sharon (1976) developed the Group Investigation Approach. All of these approaches emphasize cooperation rather than competition, with students helping and encouraging each other in groups to learn.

Cooperative learning is one of the most heavily researched instructional methods, with close to 200 studies conducted (Slavin, 1990). In a review of research, Slavin (1991) concluded that cooperative-learning approaches enhance student achievement when they incorporate group goals and individual accountability. Achievement effects of cooperative learning were found to be consistently positive in 37 of 44 experimental/control comparisons of at least four weeks' duration. Further achievement effects were found to be equally positive for students at all grade levels (2–12), in all major subject areas, in all types of schools (urban, rural, and suburban), and for high, average, and low achievers. Finally, cooperative learning has also consistently and positively influenced a variety of other outcomes including students' self-esteem, intergroup relations, acceptance of academically handicapped students, and attitudes toward school (Slavin, 1991). The amount of empirical research data on cooperative learning as an effective teaching strategy is tremendous (Ellis & Fouts, 1993).

The effectiveness of cooperative-learning strategies with students with disabilities is important to note for today's inclusive classrooms (Tateyamo-Sniezek, 1990). In studies involving the mildly handicapped (those with learning disabilities, mental retardation, or sensory and physical impairments), the reviews by Johnson and Johnson (1981, 1989) and Slavin (1990) showed increased achievement and social acceptance for the disabled students.

Cooperative-learning investigations with moderate and severe disabilities have been conducted in both elementary and secondary schools with varied activities such as science projects, art, cooking, music, academic and preacademic tasks, and group recreation activities. Putnam (1993) reports that cooperative learning in these studies is found to produce certain positive social and verbal interactions, greater interpersonal attraction, and academic gains comparable to those in competitive and individualistic situations (Putnam, 1993). Kagan (1992) cited a significant finding from the research that showed the lowest-achieving students and minority students benefiting the most academically from this approach.

Because an essential dimension of cooperative learning is training in social skills that encourages students to interact with each other and to learn how people can work together, it has been cited as an effective approach to accommodate needs of students from many different backgrounds (Kagan, Zahn, Widaman, Schwarzwald, & Tyrrell, 1985). In the multicultural classroom, in second-language education, and with students with limited English proficiency, research findings cite cooperative-learning strategies as encouraging confidence, self-esteem, and social skills in learners (Parrenas and Parrenas, 1993). At-risk students can benefit from cooperative learning experiences as well (Slavin, 1989). Sudzina and Douvre (1993), in their review of the research on use of cooperative learning with at-risk students, concluded that "cooperative learning can enable teachers to concentrate on the risk factors that can be influenced"—learned helplessness, limited student strategies for handling learning tasks, and student avoidance of literacy tasks.

There is a general consensus that cooperative-learning methods enhance student achievement and learning, but the vast majority of studies, which were strongly supportive, were conducted in grades 2 through 9. Only a few studies support effectiveness in grades 10 through 12. Another concern is the appropriateness of cooperative-learning approaches for developing higher-order conceptual learning. Most of the studies have focused on the basic skill areas of mathematics, language arts, and reading, but relatively few studies have been conducted in other areas. Several, however, have found strong effects of higher-order understanding in creative writing, reading, and social studies (Slavin, 1990). Although the research evidence is quite strong in favor of cooperative learning as an instructional strategy, teachers' use of a variety of instructional strategies is still recommended when considering all the dynamics of classroom teaching and learning. Also, one must keep in mind that this strategy requires training, motivation, and determination to keep trying it if students are to reap the benefits.

APPLICATION TO PRACTICE

Each of these three achievement-improvement strategies—direct teaching, mastery learning, and cooperative learning—is examined in this chapter regarding how they fulfill the following aspects of their instructional design:

>Purpose
>
>Focus
>
>Role of teacher
>
>Method
>
>Role of learner
>
>Structure
>
>Evaluation
>
>Appropriate subjects and types of learners

Direct Teaching

Direct-teaching strategy does not fit the constructivist approach to teaching when it separates the curriculum into smaller pieces of knowledge with emphasis on skill and content acquisition. Constructivist classrooms approach curriculum by working with larger concepts and encouraging students to identify the skills and additional content they will need to build the larger cognitive structure. However, if direct teaching moves away from emphasis on the "correct answer" to building on the understanding of the students concerning concepts, then it can be both teacher directed and student centered.

In direct instruction, teachers are actively involved by introducing content, demonstrating skills, directing large-group experiences with the content, checking students' understanding and monitoring individual or small-group work, as well as providing review. The focus is on teacher interaction with students rather than students interacting mainly with materials after a brief explanation by the teacher.

Direct instruction is examined here as a key strategy because it emphasizes meeting specific objectives keyed to learning outcomes and is particularly effective for acquisition of basic skills. This approach continues to be widely used today because it helps increase on-task learning time (Gettinger, 1986) that contributes to student achievement.

This strategy also may be called *systematic teaching* or *active teaching*. The information about this strategy was obtained mainly from the following authors: Rosenshine (1979), Barnes (1981), Good (1982), Rosenshine and Stevens (1986), and Stallings and Stipek (1986). For more detail on this instructional approach, readers are urged to examine these key sources, as well as the work of Hunter (1994) and Russell (1981).

Purpose. The purpose of direct teaching is to increase achievement by the teacher's attention to specific, analytical, academic objectives, by coverage of objectives to be tested, and by active engagement of the student in academic tasks. Attention is to be given to promoting student success through a variety of means, such as those described in chapter 2. The teacher takes charge of the classroom to provide a climate for learning that is student involved and task oriented.

Focus. The focus of the strategy is academic and teacher centered, with a structured curriculum useful for teaching skills and acquiring new information. Within this focus the teacher conveys that the business of the classroom is learning.

Role of Teacher. This is a teacher-directed strategy, which means that the teacher chooses the activities and controls the time spent on the phases of the lesson. The strategy requires the teacher to be a good motivator to keep students on task. There is much interaction of the teacher with the students in all phases of the lesson. The teacher's immediate, corrective feedback is important for student learning. When teachers are not involved in the presentation or in leading group practice, they are monitoring students' progress by moving around the room, keeping students on task, giving feedback, and working with individuals.

The teaching practices described in chapters 5 and 6 are those appropriate for direct instruction.

Method. A teacher planning to use direct teaching would want to divide the curriculum into small segments or steps through such curriculum techniques as skill analysis and conceptual mapping. First, skills, processes, and concepts are identified and arranged in a meaningful order. Then they can be presented in small steps, after which students are provided with classroom time for practice and feedback. Therefore, the basic elements of direct or systematic instruction include: (1) preparing students for the lesson, (2) presenting the lesson, (3) students' practicing the lesson, (4) evaluating and providing feedback on student learning (Barnes, 1981).

The structuring of the lesson is important in this model. Rosenshine (1983) and Rosenshine and Stevens (1986, p. 379) produced from a number of research sources a list of six instructional functions that are essential to the structure of direct teaching. These functions include daily review, structuring and presentation, guided practice, feedback and correctives, independent student practice, and weekly and monthly reviews. These functions do not have to be in every lesson. Teachers must decide which functions are necessarily dependent on the complexity of the material and students' needs. Details of the functions as described by Rosenshine and Stevens (1986) are as follows:

1. *Daily Review*
   Checking homework (routines for students to check each other's papers).
   Reteaching when necessary.
   Reviewing relevant past learning (may include questioning).
   Review prerequisite skills (if applicable).
2. *Structuring and Presentation*
   Provide short statement of objectives.
   Provide overview and structuring.
   Proceed in small steps but at a rapid pace.
   Intersperse questions within the demonstration to check for understanding.
   Highlight main points.
   Provide sufficient illustrations and concrete examples.
   Provide demonstrations and models.
   When necessary, give detailed and redundant instructions and examples.
3. *Guided Practice*
   Initial student practice takes place with teacher guidance.
   High frequency of questions and overt student practice (from teacher or materials). Questions are directly relevant to the new content or skill.
   Teacher checks for understanding (CFU) by evaluating student responses. During CFU, teacher gives additional explanation, processes feedback, or re peats explanation where necessary.
   All students have a chance to respond and receive feedback; teacher ensures that all students participate.
   Prompts are provided during guided practice (where appropriate).
   Initial student practice is sufficient so that students can work independently.
   Guided practice continues until students are firm.
   Guided practice is continued (usually) until a success rate of 80% is achieved.

4. *Feedback and Correctives*

Quick, correct responses can be followed by another question or a short acknowledgment of correctness (i.e., "That's right").

Hesitant correct answers might be followed by process feedback (i.e., "Yes, Linda, that's right because . . . ").

Student errors indicate a need for more practice.

Monitor students for systematic errors.

Try to obtain a substantive response to each question.

Corrections can include sustaining feedback (i.e., simplifying the question, giving clues), explaining or reviewing steps, giving process feedback, or reteaching the last steps.

Try to elicit an improved response when the first one is incorrect.

Guided practice and corrections continue until the teacher feels that the group can meet the objectives of the lesson.

Praise should be used in moderation; specific praise is more effective than general praise.

5. *Independent Practice (Seat Work)*

Sufficient practice.

Practice is directly relevant to skills/content taught.

Practice to overlearning.

Practice until responses are firm, quick, and automatic.

Ninety-five percent correct rate during independent practice.

Students alerted that seat work will be checked.

Students held accountable for seat work.

Actively supervise students, when possible.

6. *Weekly and Monthly Reviews*

Systematic review of previously learned material.

Include review in homework.

Frequent tests.

Reteaching of material missed in tests.

The instructional functions need not be present in every lesson, nor do they limit instructional methods to the lecture mode. Within the function phases a variety of methodologies may be used. Direct teaching does not mean lecturing.

For example, in the presentation stage the teacher may use modeling with a demonstration, followed by small groups trying another approach to the demonstration. Even guided inquiry can be part of a presentation phase. Many different learning activities should be planned for students during the guided practice, as well. Guided practice could involve a guided large- or small-group discussion on a focused topic related to the concept presented, such as 10th graders developing an expanded understanding of the concept *revolution*—by discussing meanings of Revolutionary War, Industrial Revolution, cultural revolutions, and sexual revolution. As a result of the guided discussion, students would then write papers on the topic of revolution. Role playing, in which students follow the steps of a process or enact parts of a concept, also could be used as a method. Both independent and guided practice could be conducted in three ways: students working alone using written materials or computer materials, students working with others, and the teacher leading the practice. Certainly all the techniques including entry, closure, and motivation must be used, as well as the skills of informing, supporting, questioning, managing, and listening.

To summarize, the methodology of direct teaching needs to be varied and should include many methods with a systematic approach to instruction.

Role of Learner. Within this academically focused classroom, the role of the learner is to follow, stay on-task, and perform. If this structure appears to be stifling the creativity of the learner, the teacher can provide opportunities for the learner to use divergent and creative thinking in some of the learning experiences planned for the independent and review functions. For example, the student could demonstrate knowledge of the problem-solving process by describing a situation and the different steps groups of people might use to solve a problem (i.e., solving the problem of dealing with a class bully in an 8th-grade gym class).

Evaluation. The direct-teaching strategy includes both formative (during instruction) and summative (conclusion of instruction) evaluation. The teacher giving corrective feedback during guided practice and independent practice is a key to students' achievement. Frequent tests are given during the weekly and monthly reviews so that reteaching of key material can take place as needed.

Appropriate Subjects and Types of Learners. This direct-instruction strategy is reported to work best with teaching skill subjects such as reading, writing, mathematics, grammar, computer literacy (Gelder & Maggs, 1983), and factual parts of science and history (Rosenshine & Stevens, 1986). Those bodies of knowledge that are hierarchical in structure with step-by-step progression can best be taught with the direct-instruction model.

As to which types of learners benefit most from this systematic approach, research tells us that it is helpful for young children, slower learners, and students of all ages and abilities during the first stages of learning informative material or material that is difficult to learn (Berliner, 1982). This strategy has been widely adapted by those teaching basics and special education (Condon & Maggs, 1986). Opportunities are provided for students to have considerable feedback and practice. Teachers can make adaptations in the model by shortening the time spent on guided practice and independent practice for more mature learners and increasing the presentation time for new material.

Another Model Using Direct Teaching. Madeline Hunter's Instructional Theory Into Practice (ITIP) contains many of the features of the direct teaching strategy and has been implemented via in-service workshops in many parts of the country. The program includes identifying clear instructional objectives, teaching at the correct level of difficulty, structuring instruction with lesson functions almost identical to those named by Rosenshine and Stevens (1986, p. 377), and emphasizing the importance of comprehension checks and use of the principles of learning, such as motivation theories and reinforcement theories. It is a teacher decision-making model based on learning theory applied to practice.

During the 1980s many school administrators adopted the ITIP model as the effective way to teach. Teachers were evaluated as to their ability to follow the ITIP principles. At its peak the Hunter program was being used in districts in all 50 states (Ellis & Fouts, 1993).

The ITIP model was the subject of a thorough longitudinal study done from 1981 to 1985 in two schools in Napa Valley, California (Stallings, 1987). The findings were that achievement did improve in the target schools over four years, but took a considerable drop in the fourth year. The study raised many questions about the model's effectiveness in improving student achievement. The ITIP model was based on psychological research in the area of learning, but the model had no research base concerning its effectiveness in raising student achievement (Ellis & Fouts, 1993).

From the Hunter movement, educators have learned that effective teaching that raises achievement develops students' thinking skills and problem-solving abilities and uses a variety of teaching methods and strategies rather than a single method, such as direct instruction that is geared more appropriately for basic-skill teaching.

Mastery Learning

This strategy focuses on the student's ability to learn through providing enough time and the right conditions using a diagnostic-prescriptive approach to determine instructional decisions. Mastery learning is not a constructivist approach. It does provide an individualized instruction or small-group approach using a structured curriculum divided into small groups of knowledge and skills to be learned. The strategy is taught with the belief that all students, given enough time, can reach reasonable instructional objectives. The strategy is part of outcomes-based education—a school restructuring process that organizes the whole school around the outcomes the school wants to achieve. Mastery learning is a key instructional component in the OBE model that is being adopted in many states. It also is widely used in many other countries (Hymel & Dyck, 1992).

Many of the components of direct instruction are included in this strategy with these important differences: It emphasizes flexible, structured time with the content, diagnostic/prescriptive teaching, and successful completion of all objectives by all students.

Purpose. The purpose of mastery learning is the accomplishment of a specific learning task at a designated performance level by all the students. It assumes that through this approach learning can be improved, and the variability in what students learn can be decreased. Accordingly, it also assumes that all children without learning handicaps can master learning tasks, given the necessary amount of time and instruction needed to learn the task.

Focus. The focus of mastery learning is an academic one concentrating on the individual acquiring specified skills and knowledge within a flexible time frame. The complete model developed by Carroll (1963) included the following equation for learning (Gage & Berliner, 1984):

$$\text{Degree of learning} = \frac{\text{time allowed for learning} \times \text{motivation}}{\text{time needed to learn} \times \text{quality of instructor} \times \text{ability to understand instructor}}$$

Role of Teacher. This strategy is teacher intensive, with considerable responsibility on the teacher to promote student success. The teacher starts by breaking the curriculum into units with prerequisite skills and identified knowledge. Objectives are arranged according to the scope and sequence of the units. During instruction, the teacher presents the material in a variety of forms, monitors students' work, and tests students' progress in mastering the objectives. Using diagnostic/prescriptive techniques, the teacher identifies the areas that need remediation. Whole-class instruction, lecturing, and inquiry strategies can be used if the amount of time for individual students to achieve mastery remains flexible. In addition, the teacher must be able to provide alternative learning strategies for students when they encounter difficulties. Recording student progress and success in meeting defined performance objectives is an important part of the teacher's role. Students need to know how they are progressing in accomplishing goals.

The role of the teacher differs in two approaches to mastery learning— Bloom's Learning for Mastery (LFM) and Keller's Personalized System of Instruction (PSI) (Stallings & Stipek, 1986). In Bloom's LFM, the teacher uses interactive verbal instruction with the whole group as well as with individuals, whereas in PSI, the teacher monitors the curriculum as instruction proceeds through the self-paced instructional materials. LFM is similar to the direct-teaching strategy in that it relies on teacher interaction with students, whereas PSI has students interacting more with materials.

Method. The diagnostic/prescriptive approach is used in this strategy. The teacher identifies prerequisites, assesses students' present knowledge, and formulates testing to determine students' progress in reaching objectives. The emphasis of instruction is usually on the individualized approach with the teacher-to-student relationship being the key. Peer instruction and small-group work also can be used. Indeed, the entire variety of instructional methods may be used with the total class or with a small group when the teacher covers the same part of the curriculum with everyone together. Supplemented alternative approaches must be used to accommodate different learning styles if students have not learned the content. However, methodology relies heavily on tutorial approaches with small-group sessions, one-to-one tutoring, programmed instruction, alternative workbooks, games, and computer-based instruction.

In Keller's PSI the method is tutorial, with students moving through the structured curriculum via sequenced learning materials. "Thus a visitor to a PSI classroom would see students working independently at their desks with a teacher and possibly several aides moving from student to student to offer assistance" (Stallings & Stipek, 1986, p. 743).

Role of Learner.   The learner in mastery learning has more control than in direct instruction by determining the amount of practice time needed. This means that students are given considerable freedom in deciding how fast they move through the objectives. In Bloom's (1980) LFM approach, the students take responsibility for mastering the task by working on their own, even though the class may be moving on to the next unit. In PSI classrooms, the students control their rate of progress by working through structured materials and experiences at their own speed throughout the course. The progress of the students rests heavily on individual effort and perseverance.

Structure.

Phase I.   The structuring of a course or a unit for mastery learning can be considered in five phases (Bloom, 1971). The first phase involves breaking down the content into small units of learning so students can learn and be evaluated on each incremental step. These units are arranged hierarchically with clear instructional objectives, and component skills and concepts are identified. Bloom recommended breaking the unit into a number of elements ranging from specific terms or facts to more complex and abstract ideas such as a hierarchy of learning tasks and concepts and principles.

Phase II.   Phase II involves decisions concerning the use of appropriate instruction to enable students to accomplish the objectives. The methods of instruction are not prescribed in this model and are open to any number of strategies that accommodate the teacher's teaching style and the students' learning styles.

Phase III.   The teacher designs and administers formative diagnostic tests that can be scored by the students to give themselves feedback on their progress. A formative test is given after each learning unit is completed.

Phase IV.   Students who have not achieved mastery are provided in Phase IV with additional materials or individualized instruction, such as teacher or peer tutoring, or small-group instruction to help them learn the information. Students who have achieved mastery are provided with enrichment materials until the class is ready to move to the next unit. In Bloom's LFM model, students are to relearn the material on their own time if mastery has not been reached when the class moves on to the next unit. In Keller's PSI model, students work individually through these phases at their own pace throughout the course.

Phase V. The final phase involves summative testing to determine mastery. Students receive an incomplete until they have reached the mastery level.

A caution needs to be raised here concerning the structuring of this strategy. Teachers must be careful in planning this strategy to allow for much teacher and peer interaction and to de-emphasize the use of worksheets and workbook materials. Students working through set after set of programmed materials on their own will accomplish fewer objectives and ultimately may become unmotivated and resistant.

Student progress is rewarded in terms of individual mastery of specific objectives. Mastery is defined by the school system and is usually at the 80% level for the objectives in a unit (Roberts & Kenney, 1985).

Evaluation. As has been mentioned throughout the discussion of the strategy, formative diagnostic testing is critical to the program. Students may score the tests themselves to identify areas of difficulty immediately. These errors are targeted in subsequent instruction. Finally, summative tests are administered at the end of a unit or several units to determine grades. Most students are expected to reach mastery level; therefore, it is essential that realistic mastery levels are carefully set by each school or district.

This grading system is criterion referenced (based on reaching objectives at a specified level), so it is essential that the principal be informed of the teacher's use of mastery learning. This approach is accommodated best in an ungraded school where students move through the entire curriculum at their own rate.

Appropriate Subjects and Types of Learners. Bloom (1984) pointed out that mastery learning works best for subjects that can be sequenced with hierarchical objectives, such as mathematics or reading in the lower grades. In secondary schools, subjects that have no prerequisites, such as algebra and science, work best. Obtaining mastery with students who have a history of difficulties with a subject such as 8th-grade arithmetic may necessitate too much time to make this approach feasible for them.

Keller's PSI is used more often in secondary and college classrooms (Stallings & Stipek, 1986). This approach, which enables students to work through materials at their own pace, works better with more mature students who have more intrinsic motivation.

Low-ability students or students with learning difficulties would be expected to benefit from the mastery strategy (Stallings & Stipek, 1986) because time is available for practice, remediation, and teacher and peer interaction. Certainly students who have poor self-concepts in terms of their learning ability could benefit from this approach with its emphasis on success within the student's own time frame. Students' errors are considered an expected happening in the learning process; therefore, students' fear of failure can be eliminated. It is this positive motivational thrust that may be the strongest feature of mastery learning in promoting achievement.

Outcome-Based Education. Since mastery learning has been widely associated with Outcome-Based Education (OBE), a brief description is appropriate here. Its originator, William Spady, described it as follows:

> Outcome-Based Education means organizing for results: basing what we do instructionally on the outcomes we want to achieve; whether in specific parts of the curriculum or in the schooling process as a whole. (Spady, 1988, p. 5)

The three major principles of OBE (Ellis & Fouts, 1993) are the following:

1. All students can learn and succeed. Students are capable of learning the essentials of the school curriculum but not at the same rate or in the same way.
2. Success breeds success. Success of all students is essential to build strong self-concepts for learning and behavior.
3. Schools control the conditions of success. Schools can provide positive learning conditions for all students by such practices as (1) specifying learning outcomes, (2) expecting all students to perform at high levels of learning, (3) ensuring opportunities for student success, (4) varying the time for learning according to students' needs, (5) determining students' assignments through continuous formative assessment of student learning.

Cooperative Learning

For the third achievement strategy, the reader may recall Mrs. Blaine's classroom in the scenario in which she was planning to implement a cooperative-learning approach for her next unit. She had carefully considered the heterogeneous makeup of the class and decided that this cooperative strategy could benefit her students. She anticipated increases in both achievement and positive attitudes for her students caused by their working together. Mrs. Blaine knows that this third instructional-improvement strategy—cooperative learning—uses a noncompetitive, student-centered approach to learning, as did the mastery-learning strategy. However, this model emphasizes students working together in cooperative-learning projects, engaging in peer tutoring, and possibly receiving a grade based on the group's performance as well as individual performance.

SCENARIO

We return to Millie Blaine to examine more of her thinking about cooperative learning.

As Mrs. Blaine was considering her next attempt at teaching a unit—"The Hero/Heroine of the 90s"—she thought fondly of Mrs. Duea,

her methods teacher at the state university, who had stressed cooperative-learning strategies as one approach to help meet the diverse needs
of students. Now that this class had completed one experience with cooperative learning with mixed success—three groups functioned well,
two groups floundered but did produce a group project, and one group
fell apart—she was eager to try again with the fifth-hour class, knowing
that a teacher needs much experience and knowledge about cooperative
learning to use it successfully.

She chose the fifth-hour class because it had the most diverse
needs, with the following mix of students:

(1) seven academically weak students who had reading skills at the
    fourth-grade level and lacked motivation to turn in assignments;
(2) several students with excellent writing skills;
(3) four students who were social isolates, ignored by the rest of the
    class (two of these were low-achieving students, and one was from
    Mexico and had minimal English skills in reading and speaking En-
    glish);
(4) class of mixed races and cultures—African-American, Latinos, Euro-
    pean-Americans, and Asian-Americans;
(5) two students with learning disabilities, one who also had motor-skills
    impairment.

Millie thought about the positive self-report she had received from
Jeffrey, who had resource-room support for his learning disability and
had failed English once before. He was an isolate in her class last year,
preferring to be uninvolved. In the first group experience this year he became a helper to Carmen, the student with minimal English skills. In a
think-pair-share task, he helped her understand and they began to work
together often. He also was taking seriously his role of keeping the group
on-task. Millie learned from that experience the importance of selecting
at least one student who might be a potential friend for an at-risk student
and to limit one or two at-risk students to a group.

Millie's concerns resurfaced as she recalled group four, which never
did accomplish a group project. The group broke into two pairs, each pair
of good friends working separately, while the fifth member chose to work
on his own. The projects were satisfactory but the objectives of developing intergroup cooperations, communications, and interpersonal skills
were not met.

She knew that she would have to work with the groups this time on
building cooperative group skills and seeing themselves as interdependent. She would identify a role for each individual while building the analogy of the football team. The quarterback is dependent on the line to
block the defensive team while he throws the ball to the receiver, who is

also looking for blocking protection. No touchdown results unless everyone does his job. She hoped the girls would provide a sports analogy of their own.

The objective Millie would emphasize as a result of the class's first cooperative attempt would be building cooperative skills, such as practicing active listening, paraphrasing what others say, providing positive feedback to each other, and examining different points of view without criticizing each other. To emphasize the learner approach, the first piece they would read would be an Updike short story about a former football player. Thereafter, the groups would choose the stories and novels to read and films to watch in pursuit of the 90s heroes and heroines. She would provide them with a list to guide their choices, but they might add others. The group project would be a report on the 90s hero/heroine as developed from their review of the literature, and an individual paper on themselves as a hero or heroine. All writing would be edited by the group.

Purpose. The purpose of this strategy is (1) to increase achievement through group collaboration that enables students to learn from each other; (2) to provide an alternative to the competitive structure of most classrooms today that discourages the poorer student; and (3) to improve human relations in the classroom by promoting interdependent activities that teach collaborative skills.

A number of cooperative-learning programs are in operation around the country, and the impact of several of these programs has been evaluated (Stallings & Stipek, 1986). Cited were Teams—Games-Tournaments, Student Teams–Achievement Divisions, and Jigsaw; other programs include Learning Together, Group Investigation, and Team-Assisted Instruction.

Focus. The focus of cooperative learning is both academic and affective, with emphasis on achievement of shared goals through cooperative efforts. To accomplish this focus, five basic elements must be included (Johnson, Johnson, Holubec, & Roy, 1990):

1. establishment of positive interdependence;
2. promotion of face-to-face interpersonal interaction and small-group skills;
3. maintenance of individual accountability for mastering learning tasks;
4. promotion of social skills; and
5. ensurance that groups process their achievement and maintenance of effective working relationships.

Role of Teacher. The teacher role differs considerably in this strategy from traditional approaches to instruction. Teachers act as facilitators in cooperative learning by establishing groups whose members work together on shared goals. However, the teacher may teach basic concepts and skills. As facilitator, the teacher must monitor the functioning of the groups, intervene whenever necessary to teach small-group skills, provide assistance when needed, and evaluate students and groups as to how well members work together (Johnson, Johnson, & Smith, 1991). Essential to the teacher's role is his/her interpretation along with student input of what is happening in the classroom in terms of students' thinking and understanding and the changes that need to be made as a result of that information. In the planning stage the teacher's responsibilities include (1) structuring the curriculum into units with objectives that can be achieved cooperatively and (2) establishing groups to work together on reaching shared objectives. These objectives must be clearly specified with both cognitive objectives and collaborative skill objectives.

In the preparation stage, the teacher must work with the students in helping them learn how to perform each of the roles in the group (see "Structure" section, Phase II, number 6). Also, students need to be introduced to the learning skills, such as pacing, giving specific feedback, and research skills they will be using. Students, in addition, need to become aware of the social skills they will be expected to employ, such as using active listening, communicating feelings, praising, giving constructive criticism, and providing support (Goor & Schween, 1993).

In the instructional stage, the teacher's role involves the following (Johnson, Johnson, Holubec, & Roy, 1984): (1) clearly explaining the task, goal structure, lesson objective, and learning activity to the students; (2) monitoring the effectiveness of the cooperative-learning groups, providing assistance as needed, and giving feedback on students' work with content and group skills; and (3) evaluating students' achievement and encouraging their self-evaluation.

Method. The major methodology used is the small-group approach. Within that approach, discussion, inquiry, and modeling methods may be used by the teacher. Certainly the strategy of cooperative learning would not be used exclusively for all class work. Students need to experience independent work and some competitive experiences as well. At times the teacher will teach the whole class, using a range of instructional methods. However, the methodology utilized most frequently will include methods that accommodate group-process skills and cooperative-learning skills.

Five common formats used for cooperative-learning activities are the following (Goor & Schween, 1993):

1. Student Teams–Achievement Divisions—Students complete common work assignments in groups of four or five, then are tested individually. A team score is calculated by noting result of individual students' improvement over past performance (Lewis & Doorlag, 1991).
2. Think-Pair-Share—Students first try to answer a question or learn material by themselves, then discuss their thoughts and understandings with partners, and finally share with their whole group or the class (Kagan, 1992).

3. Jigsaw—Each group member is given one piece of information and is responsible for teaching it to the group. In Jigsaw II, students obtain their own information and share it with the group. Students then are tested individually (Kagan, 1992).

4. Team Accelerated Instruction—This approach involves individualized instruction because students are assigned materials at their own achievement level and are assisted by their group members in learning the material. Group points are obtained through improvement on individual tests (Olson & Platt, 1992).

5. Group Investigation—A constructivist approach to challenge groups at a higher level in which students take responsibility for their own learning. The group decides what to investigate, what contribution each will make, and how each will communicate what he/she has learned (Lewis & Doorlag, 1991).

The teacher may set up a base group—a long-term, heterogeneous cooperative-learning group with stable membership whose main responsibilities are to provide support, encouragement, and assistance in completing assignments and striving to learn (Johnson, Johnson, & Smith, 1991). These base groups act as support groups to monitor and look out for each other, and to care about each other's growth and welfare throughout the year.

Formal cooperative-learning groups are set up to accomplish a task or handle a unit of content from a few days to a few weeks with such approaches as those previously described.

Role of Learner. This strategy gives students much control within the group structure. They become both teachers and learners as they practice communication and group-process skills, as well as leadership skills. Each student is expected to utilize these skills to promote group success. Students are to give and receive assistance, feedback, reinforcement, and support to each other. Students are to be in a positive interdependent role in which one cannot succeed without all succeeding. Positive interdependence encourages students to see how their work benefits others and their group members' work benefits them. They are responsible for each member's learning. The reward structure promotes group importance and interdependence. In most cooperative-learning models, the students work in small groups of four or five and receive an individual grade for their work with the group.

The students are held responsible for determining whether cooperative skills are practiced within the group. They are encouraged to analyze the progress of the group in light of each member's role. Peer feedback and self-evaluation are solicited. Therefore, the student's role involves responsibility to the group as well as to oneself for academic progress.

Structure. As one can observe in the scenario describing Mrs. Blaine's planning for a unit, cooperative learning is structured around a curriculum designed to be learned through cooperative groups of students who have individual responsibilities for accomplishing their group's goals. Specific lesson objectives are established within a group task. Much time must be spent in planning how to implement the curriculum and to prepare students for this cooperative approach to instruction.

The following steps for implementing cooperative learning are from Johnson et al. (1984, 1990), *Circles of Learning*, as well as Johnson, Johnson, & Smith (1991), and provide an outline of the procedure to use in structuring this model. Note the number of steps in the planning and preparation phases.

PHASE I: PLANNING

1. Specification of instructional objectives—both academic objectives and collaborative-skills objectives
2. Decisions on the size of the group—range from two to four or five
3. Assignment of students to groups—heterogeneity recommended
4. Arrangement of room to accommodate working groups
5. Arrangement of instructional materials to promote interdependence—all given same materials or each given different resources

PHASE II: PREPARING STUDENTS

6. Assignment of roles to ensure interdependence—each member given a responsibility, such as reader, taskmaster, recorder, calculator, checker, reporter, materials handler, reflector, encourager of participation, praiser, checker for understanding (Johnson, Johnson, & Smith, 1991)
7. Explanation of the academic task
8. Communication of group's interdependency—reward structure explained, mutual goals established, materials shared, roles assigned
9. Communication of individual's accountability—each individual, as well as the group, will be assessed by such measures as quizzes and student work assessed by group
10. Promotion of intergroup cooperation—encouragement of groups working together through giving rewards or praise
11. Explanation of criteria for success
12. Specification of desired behaviors, such as contributing, helping, listening to others, encouraging others to participate, asking for help or clarification, using self-monitoring skills, using quiet voices (Johnson et al., 1991)
13. Teaching collaborative skills—active listening, paraphrasing what others say, giving compliments, resolving controversy without criticism, summarizing, checking for understanding

PHASE III: MONITORING AND INTERVENING

14. Encouraging face-to-face interaction with oral summarizing, giving and receiving explanations, and elaborating
15. Monitoring students' behavior—giving feedback, reinforcement, and praise
16. Assistance provided, where needed
17. Intervention to teach collaborative skills

PHASE IV: EVALUATION AND PROCESSING

18. Evaluation of quality and quantity of students' learning
19. Assessment of how well group functioned—groups can list things they did well in working together and things they need to improve
20. Providing closure to the groups and individual learners—both teacher and students can summarize, share groups' work, review.

Evaluation. Formative evaluations of individual and group progress, as well as self-monitoring, are important throughout. Formative evaluations of groups can take place each week, with the group analyzing strengths and weaknesses in accomplishing group goals. Summative evaluation includes group and individual assessment measures. A criterion-referenced approach may be used to assess that the specified objectives within the assigned concepts and skills were accomplished. Students may receive both a group grade and an individual grade. Their grade may be contingent on a group project or the average of each student's progress toward meeting group objectives. Having to share the same grade encourages students to provide support for those members who are having trouble reaching goals, be they academic goals or the performance of cooperative learning skills. However, individual accountability should be maintained to meet specified objectives. Students may also receive a grade as to their individual ability in functioning within the group. Teachers may require a work log to be kept by each group that includes what each student was to have contributed, what they did contribute, and how the group evaluated the effort.

Johnson et al. (1991) describe the individual test followed by a group-test approach in which an examination is given to each individual for a grade. The teacher scores the answers, then gives the test again to the cooperative groups. In the group examination the students confer on the answers to each question. The task is to answer each question correctly. The cooperative goal is for all group members to understand the material. The group is to agree on one answer and identify how it arrived at that answer. Each group is responsible for ensuring that all students understand the material they missed on the individual test. Bonus points can be given if all members of the group score 90% or better on the group test. These bonus points are added to students' individual scores to determine their individual grades for the test.

The preceding is an example of an approach to grading in a cooperative group. The decision as to how grades will be arrived at depends on the type of interdependence the teacher wants to establish among the students. Johnson et al. (1991) provide the following suggestions:

1. Individual score plus bonus points based on all members reaching the criterion (see example preceding).
2. Individual score plus bonus points based on lowest score.
3. Link individual score to group average.
4. Individual score plus bonus based on improvement scores over past tests.
5. Total members' individual scores; all members receive the total.
6. Average members' individual scores.
7. Group score based on a single product produced by group.
8. Randomly select one member's paper to score and to decide group grade. All papers in the group have been certified as correct and acceptable.
9. Randomly select one member's exam to score and all group members receive that score.
10. All members receive lowest member score. Group members have prepared each other for the exam.
11. Average academic scores plus collaborated skills performance score.
12. Give dual academic and nonacademic award, such as a pass on homework. Members receive an individual grade and a group reward if group meets the group goal.

Appropriate Subjects and Types of Learners. The cooperative-learning approach can be used with most learning tasks, especially concept attainment, verbal problem solving, categorizing tasks, skill attainment, and judging tasks. Any lesson can be structured into a group-learning situation that promotes collaborative skills. Cooperative learning has been used in such diverse subject areas as business classes and computer training (Johnson et al., 1984). The approach has been used with kindergarten students up through adults in college. In Johnson et al. (1984), a list of schools and teachers around the country that use cooperative learning was printed. This listing included teachers in all grade levels, as well as in higher- and continuing-education classes.

It appears that low-achieving students can benefit considerably by cooperative learning because they are coached and helped to achieve objectives through group support. The effect on their self-image and motivation can be very positive. High achievers can benefit also because they are working toward group success rather than their individual achievement, and hence feel less isolated. They also can find challenges in the opportunity to learn decision making, leadership roles, and conflict management skills. Putnam (1993) maintains that cooperative learning is a major strategy for the inclusion classroom because it enables teachers to meet the needs of diverse learners by the tasks assigned to students and the group's responsibility to team learning. She says children with varying cognitive abilities, developmental and learning disabilities, sensory impairments, and different cultural, linguistic, and socioeconomic backgrounds will benefit both academically and socially in cooperative-learning classrooms. Although student achievement is improved because students help each other, it is in the area of human relations that the strength of this strategy appears to lie. Students develop interpersonal and group skills that encourage them to work well with others and accept each other's differences. Students from a variety of racial and ethnic backgrounds may be perceived more positively in cooperative-learning situations.

Cooperative-Learning Methods in Action: Student Teams–Achievement Divisions. One of the most versatile forms of cooperative learning is Student Teams–Achievement Divisions (STAD). As Slavin (1990, 1991) explained, STAD has been used in many subject areas including mathematics, social studies, science, and language arts, where the focus is on teaching specific objectives emphasizing the learning of factual knowledge with single, right answers. Students representing a range of ability levels, gender, and ethnicity are assigned to four-member teams. The teacher presents a lesson, and then the students work within their teams to learn the content or master the skill. They work cooperatively to ensure that all team members know the material. The students then individually take quizzes in the traditional way, without helping one another.

The following is an actual illustration of STAD that has been applied in a 7th-grade mathematics class based on a chapter on percentage (Wilen, 1991). Prior to involving students in a cooperative-learning unit the teacher prepared her students by informing them of the purposes, procedures, and expected outcomes. She also identified important small-group social and communication skills and had her students describe appropriate verbal and nonverbal behaviors characteristic of these skills. Students were told that evaluation was based on their quiz and team improvement scores. Quizzes were administered once each week. Individual improvement scores were computed after every quiz and were based on how well students were doing compared to their base score. An important goal for students was to work toward maintaining or increasing their base scores. Team improvement scores were based on the averages of the team members' individual improvement scores and they became 20% of the final grade for each student.

Four-member teams were formed representing a cross section of each of the classes in terms of academic performance and gender. The classes contained only one minority student. Academic performance was based on students' base scores, which were computed from previous test averages. Each team contained one high- and one low-achieving student, and two average-achieving students. The students were informed of the formula for team composition and accepted the arrangement with minimal concerns.

The daily procedure provided the structure for this application of STAD. At the beginning of each period, while the class was studying percentage, students met with their teams to check and discuss their assignment related to percentage problems that they had completed individually prior to class. A good deal of the time was spent answering questions different team members had about the assignment. This phase lasted about 10 minutes. The teacher then presented a short lesson of about 10 to 15 minutes about percent of increase and percent of decrease, for example, and gave a homework assignment based on it. The students then returned to their teams to help each other start the homework. Once a week a quiz was given that each student took individually. Team improvement scores were computed once per week and students were informed of their status. During the orientation period the students were told that there were three major sources for help, the most important of which was the students themselves. The other sources to be consulted by the students were the textbook and the teacher, in that order. The emphasis was on decreasing student dependency on the teacher and increasing it on team effort. The teacher spent class time circulating among the teams listening to students' interactions. Interventions were often necessary and served as opportunities for the teacher to model appropriate cooperative-learning behaviors, such as asking questions and giving responses. Classroom management was accomplished by keeping students on task, maintaining close proximity, and encouraging students' efforts.

Cooperative Learning Methods in Action: Jigsaw. The original Jigsaw was developed by Aronson and his colleagues (1978) and a version was produced by Slavin (1990), which he called Jigsaw II. Jigsaw is appropriate for every subject area that has academic material that can be broken down into sections. English, science, and social studies are particularly appropriate subjects because they deal with written material that is generally in narrative form. In Jigsaw, according to Slavin (1990, 1991), students are assigned to four- to six-member heterogeneous teams with the task of working on content material that has been divided into different sections. Students are responsible for their own section that contains specific and unique information. After reading the material, one student from each team having the same material meet as "expert" groups to discuss the material, help each other to learn it, and then design ways to teach it to others unfamiliar with it. Students return to their teams to teach their pieces of the puzzle to team members who, in turn, also teach their puzzle pieces. An evaluation exercise can follow, such as a test or report, that requires all the students to know all parts of the material.

The following is an 11th-grade U.S. history lesson that uses the original Jigsaw method as the primary instructional approach (Vocke & Capps, 1990). According to the objective, the students will "write a description of the changes in Mary Chestnut's personal views and attitudes toward the South's chances for success during the Civil War" (p. 8). The focus of this lesson is on learning from a primary source, which in this case is the diaries of Mary Chestnut (1823–1886), who was married to Brigadier General James Chestnut, an aide to Jefferson

Davis, and had lived in several southern states during the war. Four "expert" groups of students were formed, each having different diary entries: July 24, 1861; June 29, 1862; August 19, 1864; and March 30, 1865. Their task for each entry was to identify the main event about the war Mary was describing, her reaction to the event, and other ideas and attitudes from the diary entry. After the students return to their teams to teach their parts of the puzzle, a culminating activity such as a quiz could be used to get at key facts, or an essay could be used to synthesize information from the parts of the diary.

Another approach appropriate for U.S. history classes using Jigsaw is to have students read quotations and excerpts from various people and sources related to the use of the atom bomb at the end of World War II. Four "expert" groups could be formed to investigate the arguments for using the atom bomb, arguments for not using the bomb, impact of the bomb on Hiroshima and its people, and reactions to the bombing of Japan. After the four sections of material are taught to team members, a culminating activity could center on having students assume the role of President Truman, with the benefit of hindsight, and make a reasoned decision as to whether or not the bomb should have been used to end World War II (Vocke & Capps, 1990).

Jigsaw II. This adaptation of Jigsaw by Slavin (1990) is similar to the original except that students read a common narrative instead of different sections. In Jigsaw II no students possess unique knowledge; instead, students teach each other common knowledge such as that found in a short story in an English literature class, or a chapter from a science text, or a journal article in a government class. Students work in heterogeneous teams as in STAD with "expert" teams formed to learn and teach sections or topics of the narrative. Students in their "expert" groups answer and discuss questions from worksheets designed by the teacher for the purpose of having students recall important information and to relate the content to broader themes. For example, if the students had been reading a chapter of *The Adventures of Huckleberry Finn*, several questions might relate to specific facts associated with Huck deciding not to turn Jim in to the authorities. Other questions might deal with the broader themes of friendship or slavery that cut across several chapters. Students then return to their original teams to teach what they have learned about their topics. Next they take a quiz that covers all of the topics and team scores are computed as in STAD. Students' individual improvement scores are the basis of the team scores and the high-scoring teams get the rewards, also as in STAD. As Slavin (1990) summarized, "The key to Jigsaw is interdependence: every student depends on his or her teammates to provide the information he or she needs to do well on the quizzes" (p. 104).

Peer Tutoring. In cooperative learning, students are arranged to help each other reach certain outcomes identified by the teacher or the group. Peer tutoring does occur as part of the cooperative-learning experience or may be arranged in the classroom following constructivist principles that emphasize student-to-student interaction.

Selected studies on peer tutoring and teaching show that both the tutor and the tutee benefit from the experience. Waggoner (1971, p. 98) summarized a series of studies that identified the following advantages of peer teaching:

1. Peer teaching can reduce anxiety caused by differences in age, status, and background between students and teachers. A peer tutor may communicate more easily with other students, as well.
2. More individualized instruction is possible.
3. The tutor may increase his or her own understanding as well as self-esteem and self-confidence.
4. Peer tutors may be more patient with a slower learner.
5. Peer teaching reinforces learning, may reorganize knowledge more effectively, and increase understanding.

As Pierce (1982) reported, evidence suggests that the tutoring experience can sharpen the understanding and abilities of the tutor, as well as increase a student's self-esteem and positive attitude toward school.

The important point here is that students should realize that we learn from one another and that we all are teachers and learners at different times. Good and Brophy (1994) recommend that teachers model this understanding by pointing out to their students what they—the teachers—have learned from the class. We need to remind students that the goal is their learning, not the comparison of their progress to others in the class.

Good and Brophy (1994, pp. 307–308) provided some guidelines for arranging peer tutoring as follows:

1. The teacher provides guidance to the tutor with suggestions on how to approach the content for that student being tutored and the materials to use.
2. The teacher switches tutoring assignments every couple of weeks.
3. The teacher arranges for all students to be tutors at times so that they feel that everyone can help each other learn.
4. A tutor or tutors may work with a small group. A mixture of students with various talents who use their skills to accomplish a learning objective help students appreciate different approaches and each other's talents. One student may be able to develop metaphors or creative examples while another one can depict information with a diagram.
5. The teacher needs to monitor the tutoring to see when he/she needs to provide some assistance, such as modeling appropriate instructional behaviors for a pair or for the class.
6. Careful planning of pairings is necessary. Best friends may not be able to stay on task or may become too critical of each other.
7. Tutors are not to test their fellow students to establish a grade for their learning. This responsibility needs to remain with the teacher.

8. Communication to the parents and to the principal is important. Let them know that you are using peer tutoring, what your purpose is, and what you hope the outcomes will be.

SUMMARY POINT

This chapter has focused on three strategies—direct teaching, mastery learning, and cooperative learning—whose positive effects on achievement have been studied and documented. These approaches developed from compensatory education programs in the late sixties and early seventies for urban elementary school children but have since been used throughout the country in all school settings and with students of all ages.

Both direct teaching and mastery learning are structured approaches and require sequenced curriculum materials. Students are continually tested to see if they have learned the material, then recycled and/or retaught until objectives are reached. Mastery learning allows students time flexibility in attaining the mastery level. In comparison, direct instruction moves the class along as a group, but allows for individual differences in learning through individual practice activities and group work. Cooperative learning emphasizes improved achievement through collaborative learning with positive group identity.

In the three preceding strategies, the cooperative-learning approach is the one most compatible to the climate of the constructivist classroom. By challenging groups to construct their own understandings of concepts and principles through shared group experiences, learning takes on personal meaning. Direct instruction, if it creates a dependent role, de-emphasizes student independent thinking by the teacher giving too much explanation and guidance. Mastery learning provides the students time to explore and develop their own understandings, but the curriculum for mastery learning is usually divided into small segments presenting a part-to-whole approach rather than emphasizing whole-to-part with concentration on big concepts (Brooks & Brooks, 1993).

None of these three should be used as the sole approach to instruction. There is no one model for effective instruction. Each has much to offer in presenting strategies for accomplishing particular learning objectives. Teachers' decision making enters in when determining which parts of the curriculum can be accomplished most effectively by using a particular strategy. Beginning teachers need opportunities to instruct various units of the curriculum using these strategies and others to develop a varied teaching repertoire. The more techniques, methods, and strategies the teacher is able to use, the better decisions the teacher can make in choosing appropriate instruction to help each learner understand the curriculum content. Remember, however, that learning only takes place within the learner. The teacher cannot ensure student learning with the best of lesson plans and instructional strategies. The key to student learning is to have students actively involved in meaningful experiences that help them form connections with the knowledge and skills they need to make decisions and build their understanding of the world.

As you choose the instructional strategies for your lessons, you must consider your students, their developmental level, cultural background, academic abilities, special talents, and socioeconomic background. Also, the curriculum content must be considered—the major concepts and skills and their interrelation to other knowledge students are learning. With all these considerations, teachers are continually challenged by the complex decisions they must make concerning instruction.

REVIEW: IMPORTANT PRACTICES FOR ACHIEVEMENT STRATEGIES

Direct Teaching

1. is large-group instruction on specific objectives;
2. is academically focused and teacher directed;
3. uses designated teaching functions to provide a sequenced structure for instruction;
4. emphasizes effective use of class time and coverage of content; and
5. is recommended for teaching skill subjects.

Mastery Learning

1. is an individualized, diagnostic/prescriptive approach that can include whole-group instruction;
2. involves the student controlling the time needed for obtaining mastery;
3. uses pretesting and posttesting, and recycling with remediation;
4. is recommended when mastery of information is essential; and
5. uses sequenced and structured materials.

Cooperative Learning

1. is the instructional use of small groups to enable students to work together to enhance their other group's learning;
2. uses peer interaction, positive interdependence, individual accountability, and cooperation to accomplish group-learning projects and to receive group award;
3. involves teacher structuring the curriculum into units with objectives that can be achieved cooperatively;
4. is most effective in teaching collaborative skills and promoting group identity; and
5. is an effective strategy to use when teaching diverse groups of students.

QUESTIONS FOR REFLECTION

1. Why do you think the strategies presented in this chapter have a link to student achievement?
2. Do you foresee any time in your teaching future when you might decide to try mastery learning? If so, with what types of students and content would you think this strategy is most effective?
3. Considering some of the different approaches to assessing students in cooperative learning, which do you feel is the one you would use in your preferred grade level or subject area?
4. In the cooperative-learning strategy the teacher has the least control over the class. Would this bother you as a teacher? How would you deal with giving so much control to your students?
5. What advice would you give Millie Blaine about the way she is structuring her next cooperative-learning venture? Is she overlooking any important step in the preparation process?
6. The direct-teaching approach is widely used in today's classrooms. How is it, or is it, incompatible with constructivist thinking about instruction?
7. What must the teacher keep in mind as factors to consider when planning instruction? Explain how they may influence the teacher's decision about methods or strategies to use.
8. Which of the instructional strategies in this chapter would you be most comfortable using in your classroom? Explain why. What does this decision tell you about your comfort zone in teaching? What are the advantages and disadvantages?

ANALYSIS FORM	ACTIVITIES FOR OBSERVATION DIRECT TEACHING

ANALYSIS SCALES

	OCCURRENCE	EFFECTIVENESS
TEACHER _____	1. Not evident	1. Not effective
OBSERVER _____	2. Slightly evident	2. Slightly effective
CLASS _____	3. Moderately evident	3. Moderately effective
DATE _____	4. Quite evident	4. Quite effective
	N Not applicable	N Not applicable

CATEGORIES (Parts A +B Correspond to Occurrence and Effectiveness in the Analysis Scale)	A. OCCURRENCE	B. EFFECTIVENESS
1. Is this a teacher-directed classroom in which the teacher makes decisions about activities and materials and teacher controls students' time in the classroom?		
2. Does the instruction have a stated academic purpose?		
3. Is there considerable interaction between teachers and students?		
4. Is the amount of off-task time for students kept to a minimum?		
5. Does the teacher have the curriculum divided into small units with skills, process, and concepts identified?		
6. Has the teacher prepared the students for the lesson with review and overview?		
7. Do the students know the objective of the lesson and how it fits in with the unit being studied?		
8. Does the teacher use a variety of approaches to presenting lessons including a. presenting material in small steps? b. presenting outlines when material is complex?		

continued

9. Does the teacher provide time for guided practice with teacher and students working together as a group?		
10. Is there a high frequency of questions and overt student practice?		
11. Does the teacher conduct comprehension checks while involved in the presentation and group practice phase?		
12. Does the teacher give immediate corrective feedback?		
13. Does the teacher reteach when necessary?		
14. Does the teacher provide time for individual practice with evaluation and feedback?		
15. Does the teacher monitor the class during the group practice and independent practice phases?		
16. Does the teacher plan weekly and monthly reviews?		

ANALYSIS FORM

MASTERY LEARNING

ANALYSIS SCALES

TEACHER _____

OBSERVER _____

CLASS _____

DATE _____

OCCURRENCE	EFFECTIVENESS
1. Not evident	1. Not effective
2. Slightly evident	2. Slightly effective
3. Moderately evident	3. Moderately effective
4. Quite evident	4. Quite effective
N Not applicable	N Not applicable

CATEGORIES (Parts A + B Correspond to Occurrence and Effectiveness in the Analysis Scale)	A. OCCURRENCE	B. EFFECTIVENESS
1. Is the curriculum structured into small hierarchical units with prerequisite skills and knowledge identified?		
2. Are specific objectives with a designated mastery level identified?		
3. Are a variety of instructional techniques used to instruct students?		
4. Are students working independently as the teacher provides input where needed?		
5. Does the teacher administer formative tests to give students feedback on their progress?		
6. Are students given additional instruction and study materials if they have not reached the mastery level?		
7. Is ample time provided for students to accomplish the unit objectives at mastery level?		
8. Is student progress recorded in terms of individual mastery of specific objectives?		
9. Are realistic mastery levels set for the abilities of students in the class?		
10. Are students given corrective feedback as well as scores on tests?		
11. Is the student permitted to move to the next unit without mastering the previous unit?		
12. Do the class grades reflect success with mastery objectives?		

ANALYSIS FORM   COOPERATIVE LEARNING

TEACHER _____

OBSERVER _____

CLASS _____

DATE _____

OCCURRENCE
1. Not evident
2. Slightly evident
3. Moderately evident
4. Quite evident
N Not applicable

EFFECTIVENESS
1. Not effective
2. Slightly effective
3. Moderately effective
4. Quite effective
N Not applicable

CATEGORIES (Parts A+B Correspond to Occurrence and Effectiveness in the Analysis Scale)	A. OCCURRENCE	B. EFFECTIVENESS
1. Has the teacher structured the curriculum into units with objectives that can be achieved cooperatively?		
2. Is group collaboration evident in the classroom?		
3. Are students encouraged to learn from one another?		
4. Is there an emphasis in the room on the use of communication and group-process skills?		
5. Is it evident from observing the groups that the following elements have been addressed: a. positive interdependence? b. cooperative learning skills? c. individual accountability for completing tasks? d. promotion of face-to-face interaction?		
6. Does the teacher give feedback on students' progress with group skills as well as progress with academic objectives?		
7. Are students encouraged to self-evaluate their academic and group success?		

REFERENCES

Aronson, E., Blaney, C., Stephan, C., Sikes, J., & Snapp, M. (1978). *The jigsaw classroom.* Beverly Hills, CA: Sage.

Barnes, S. (1981). *Synthesis of selected research on teaching findings.* Austin, TX: Research and Development Center for Teacher Education, University of Texas.

Berliner, D. (1982). Should teachers be expected to learn and use direct instruction? *ASCD Update, 24,* 5.

Block, J., & Burns, R. (1976). Mastery learning. In L. S. Shulman (Ed.), *Review of research in education* (Vol. 4). Itasca, IL: F. E. Peacock.

Bloom, B. (1971). Mastery learning and its implications for curriculum development. In E. W. Eisner (Ed.), *Confronting curriculum reform.* Boston: Little, Brown.

Bloom, B. (1980). Learning for mastery. In K. Ryan & J. Cooper (Eds.), *Kaleidoscope, readings in education.* Boston: Houghton Mifflin.

Bloom, B. (1984). The search for methods of group instruction as effective as one-to-one tutoring. *Educational Leadership, 41*(8), 4–17.

Brooks, J., & Brooks, M. (1993). *The case for constructivist classrooms.* Alexandria, VA: Association for Supervision and Curriculum Development.

Carroll, J. (1963). A model of school learning. *Teachers College Record, 64,* 723–733.

Condon, D., & Maggs, A. (1986). Direct instruction research: An international focus. *International Journal of Special Education, 1,* 35–47.

Cruickshank, D. (1990). *Research that informs teachers and teacher educators.* Bloomington, IN: Phi Delta Kappa Educational Foundation.

Dweck, C., & Goetz, T. (1978). Attributes and learned helplessness. In J. Harvey, W. Ickes, & R. Kidd (Eds.), *New directions in attribution research.* Hillsdale, NJ: Erlbaum.

Ellis, A., & Fouts, J. (1993). *Research and educational innovations.* Princeton Junction, NJ: Eye on Education.

Emmer, E., Evertson, C., Sanford, J., Clements, B., & Worsham, M. (1982). *Organizing and managing the junior high classroom.* Austin, TX: Research and Development Center for Teacher Education, University of Texas.

Fitzpatrick, K. (1982). *The effect of a secondary classroom management training program on teacher and student behavior.* Paper presented at the annual meeting of the American Educational Research Association, New York.

Gage, N., & Berliner, D. (1984). *Educational psychology* (3rd ed.). Boston: Houghton Mifflin.

Gelder, A., & Maggs, A. (1983). Direct instruction microcomputing in primary schools: Manipulation of critical instructional variables. *Research in Science and Technology Education, 1,* 221–238.

Gettinger, M. (1986). Issues and trends in academic engaged time of students. *Special Services in the School, 2,* 1–17.

Good, T. (1982). *Classroom research: What we know and what we need to know.* Austin, TX: Research and Development Center for Teacher Education, University of Texas.

Good, T., & Brophy, J. (1994). *Looking in classrooms* (6th ed.). New York: HarperCollins.

Good, T., Grouws, D., & Ebmeier, H. (1983). *Active mathematics teaching*. White Plains, NY: Longman.

Goor, M., & Schwenn, J. (1993). Accommodating diversity and disability with cooperative learning. *Intervention in School and Clinic, 29*(1), 6–16.

Hunter, M. (1994). *Enhancing teaching*. New York: Macmillan.

Hunter, M., & Russell, D. (1981). Planning for effective instruction: Lesson design. In *Increasing your teaching effectiveness*. Palo Alto, CA: Learning Institute.

Hymel, G., & Dyck, W. (1992). *An international perspective on mastery learning*. Paper presented at the 25th International Congress of Psychology, Brussels, Belgium. (ERIC Document Reproduction Service No. ED 359 260)

Johnson, D., Johnson, R., Holubec, E., & Roy, P. (1984/1990). *Circles of learning: Cooperation in the classroom*. Alexandria, VA: Association for Supervision and Curriculum Development.

Johnson, D., Johnson, R., Holubec, E., (1990). *Circles of learning: Cooperation in the classroom*. Edina, MN: Interaction.

Johnson, D., Johnson, R., & Smith, K. (1991). *Active learning: Cooperation in the college classroom*. Edina, MN: Interaction.

Johnson, D., & Johnson, R. (1987). *Learning together and alone* (2nd ed.). Englewood Cliffs, NJ: Prentice-Hall.

Johnson, R., & Johnson, D. (1981). Building friendships between handicapped and non-handicapped students: Effects of cooperative and individualistic instruction. *American Educational Research Journal, 18*(4), 415-423.

Johnson, R., & Johnson, D. (1989). *Cooperation and competition: Theory and research*. Edina, MN: Interaction.

Joyce, B., Weil, M., with Showers, B. (1992). *Models of Teaching* (4th ed.). Boston: Allyn & Bacon.

Kagan, S. (1992). *Cooperative learning*. San Juan Capistrano, CA: Resources for Teachers.

Kagan, S., Zahn, G., Widaman, K., Schwarzwald, J., & Tyrrell, G. (1985). Classroom structural bias: Impact of cooperative and competitive individuals and groups. In R. Slavin, S. Sharan, S. Kagan, R. Hertz-Lazarowitz, C. Webb, & R. Schmuch (Eds.), *Learning to cooperate*. New York: Plenum.

Kulik, C., Kulik, J., & Bangert-Drowns, R. (1990). Effectiveness of mastery learning programs: A meta-analysis. *Review of Educational Research, 60*(2), 265-299.

Lewis, R., & Doorlag, D. (1991). *Teaching special students in the mainstream*. New York: Merrill/Macmillan.

Olson, J., & Platt, J. (1992). *Teaching children and adolescents with special needs*. Columbus, OH: Merrill/Macmillan.

Parrenas, C., & Parrenas, F. (1993). Cooperative learning, multicultural functioning, and student achievement. In L. Malave (Ed.), *Annual conference journal of the national association for bilingual education conferences*. National Association for Bilingual Education. (ERIC Document Reproduction Service No. ED 360 877)

Peterson, P., & Walberg, H. (Eds.). (1979). *Research on teaching: Concepts, findings and implications*. Berkeley, CA: McCutchan.

Pierce, M. (1982, April 13). *Partner learning: Concept and rationale*. Paper presented at 60th CEC Conference, Houston, TX.

Putnam, J. (Ed.). (1993). *Cooperative learning and strategies for inclusion*. Baltimore: Paul H. Brookes.

Roberts, J., & Kenney, J. (1985). *Implementing four models of instructional improvement: Research for Better Schools, Philadelphia, Pa*. Paper presented at Annual Meeting of American Educational Research Association, Chicago. (ERIC Document Reproduction Service No. ED 256 742)

Rosenshine, B. (1979). Content, time, and direct instruction. In P. Peterson & H. Walberg (Eds.), *Research on teaching: Concepts, findings and implications*. Berkeley, CA: McCutchan.

Rosenshine, B. (1983). Teaching functions in instructional programs. *Elementary School Journal, 83*(4), 335-351.

Rosenshine, B., & Stevens, R. (1986). Teaching functions. In M. Wittrock (Ed.), *Handbook of research on teaching*. New York: Macmillan.

Sharon, S., & Sharon, Y. (1976). *Small-group teaching*. Englewood Cliffs, NJ: Educational Technology Publications.

Slavin, R. (1989). Students at risk of school failure: The problem and its dimensions. In R. Slavin, N. Karweit, & N. Madden (Eds.), *Effective programs for students at risk*. Needham Heights, MA: Allyn & Bacon.

Slavin, R. E. (1990). *Cooperative learning: Theory, research, and practice*. Englewood Cliffs, NJ: Prentice-Hall.

Slavin, R. E. (1991). Synthesis of research on cooperative learning. *Educational Leadership, 48*, 71–82.

Soar, R. (1973). *Follow through classroom process measurement and pupil growth*. Gainesville, FL: University of Florida, Institute for Development of Human Resources.

Solomon, D., & Kendall, A. (1979). *Children in classrooms: An investigation of person-environment interaction*. New York: Praeger.

Spady, W. (1988). Organizing for results: The basis of authentic restructuring and reform. *Educational Leadership, 46*(2), 4–8.

Stallings, J. (1987). For whom and how long is the Hunter-based model appropriate? Response to Robbins and Wolfe. *Educational Leadership, 44*, 62–63.

Stallings, J., & Kaskowitz, D. (1974). Follow through classroom observation evaluation, 1972–1973 (SRI Project URU\M7370, Stanford, CA: Stanford Research Institution). In M. Wittrock (Ed.), (1986), *Handbook of research on teaching*. New York: Macmillan.

Stallings, J., & Stipek, D. (1986). Research on early childhood and elementary school teaching programs. In M. Wittrock (Ed.), *Handbook of research on teaching* (3rd ed.). New York: Macmillan.

Sudzina, M., & Douvre, S. (1993). *Using cooperative learning to teach "at risk" students*. Paper presented at the annual meeting of the Association of Teacher Educators, Los Angeles, CA. (ERIC Document Reproduction Service No. ED 355 221)

Tateyamo-Sniezek, K. (1990). Cooperative learning: Does it improve the academic achievement of students with handicaps? *Exceptional Children, 56*, 426–437.

Teddlie, C., Kirby, P., & Stringfield, S. (1989). Effective versus ineffective schools: Observable differences in the classroom. *American Journal of Education, 97*, 221–236.

Vocke, D. E., & Capps, K. (1990, November). *Cooperative learning: Why and where in the American history curriculum*. Paper presented at the Annual Conference of the National Council for the Social Studies, Anaheim, CA.

Waggoner, K. (1971). Higher math in lower school. *Yale Alumni Magazine, 34*(9), 24–25.

Wilen, W. (1991, February). Interview with Kathryn L. Wilen, mathematics teacher, Davey Junior High School, Kent, Ohio.

CHAPTER **9** Evaluation of Classroom Performance

> *Evaluation can no more be a totally rational process than instruction. Teachers' sensitivity and values are inevitable factors in the effectiveness of their evaluations.*

Evaluation is one of the three major components of teaching, along with planning and instruction. Yet in the informal view of teachers, evaluation is often perceived as the stepchild of teaching. Writing tests, grading them—especially essay tests—and reporting students' grades are grudgingly executed as onerous chores of teaching. Very few teachers are attracted to teaching by this aspect of the job. It is not surprising, then, that evaluation is probably the major aspect of teaching that receives the least professional attention from teachers, and so is an area in which many teachers can substantially improve. This chapter is designed to initiate thinking toward the development of a sound concept and effective practices of evaluation.

Although evaluation has been described here as one component of teaching, it is not mutually exclusive from the other parts. Evaluation occurs in planning in the selection of particular topics and strategies. As objectives are being written, it is intended that they will become the basis for subsequent evaluation. Teachers need to plan daily for collecting data on student progress. And during instruction, evaluation occurs as teachers observe student behaviors, consider student responses, provide feedback and correction to students, and judge the extent to which instruction has been effective. At the completion of a unit of work, written tests and other demonstrations of achievement typically occur. When teachers think of evaluation, this latter aspect is generally what comes to mind. However, the many aspects of evaluation deserve thoughtful consideration by teachers if evaluation principles and practices are to contribute optimally to the effectiveness of teaching.

In a fundamental sense, evaluation means placing a value on some entity, thus expressing an indication of its worth. Implied within the process is a standard, usually in the form of a criterion or a comparison, and a decision. Evaluation as decision making should conform to the principles of decision making described in chapter 1. Evaluation should be made on the basis of the best information or evidence available and should be, as much as possible, a rational process.

FOCUS QUESTIONS

1. Evaluation is conceived by some persons primarily as tests at the end of units and grades on a report card. In contrast, what other factors are included in an informed teacher's concept of evaluation?
2. How have research findings contributed to teachers' evaluation practices? How might they contribute even more?
3. How can evaluation be integrated with instruction rather than being treated essentially as an add-on?
4. What evaluation policies and practices might a teacher use to cause students' focus to shift somewhat away from grades as the incentive for learning, and toward worthy outcomes?

OVERVIEW

This chapter describes the role and process of teacher classroom evaluation. This broad perspective will serve as a framework for the teacher's continuing development of an informed comprehensive approach to this component of the teacher role. Brief commentary on two major components of teacher classroom evaluation is also presented: grading and test writing.

This limited treatment of the topic is intended to help the reader understand evaluation as a pervasive and integral part of teaching. It does not make a pretense at being comprehensive. Many fine texts devoted entirely to assessment and evaluation are readily available to provide in-depth information and methodology.

SCENARIO

The end of the second six-week grading period at Jefferson County Local High School was approaching. John Sykes, the school's art teacher, remembered clearly the end of the first grading period. As a teacher with several years' experience, he had proceeded to assign the first six weeks' grades in his Art I class much the same as in the past years. Art was not considered to be one of the difficult courses in the school, but this particular class had less apparent ability than any John remembered. He had assigned quite a few C grades as well as two Ds and an F.

John's approach to assigning grades had always been rather casual. He examined the artwork each student turned in and made an overall judgment of its quality. He prided himself on his connoisseurship approach, including the critique he wrote on every project, but he also tempered his evaluation with compassion when he thought students deserved it. In the academic aspect of the course dealing with art principles and art history, he examined the numerical scores, looked for natural breaks throughout the range of scores, and assigned letter grades by inspection.

After grades had gone out, John got calls or visits from four of his students' parents from that class, in his experience a surprisingly large number. The parents did not understand why their children had gotten grades as much as two letters below expectation. He explained the basis for the grade as best he could and tried to enlist parents' cooperation in urging students to take their artwork seriously and conscientiously. Mrs. DeTano, a parent and herself a teacher in another district, was one of the parents to visit. Her daughter, Lynn, had gotten a D, and Mrs. DeTano was not satisfied with John's explanation of how he determined the grade. She pointedly referred to the explanation as "unconvincing," and asked John to produce his explicit standards. She used the term "rubric" in referring to the standards, a term John had not heard before in this context. Her Lynn, she said, had been unable to produce a copy of any such standards or inform her of any that had ever been communicated to the class.

John spent an uncomfortable half hour with Mrs. DeTano. She was obviously knowledgeable but rather self-righteous, he thought. He was shaken and had therefore responded defensively in the conference, but in later reflection he was willing to grant that she might have a point. He felt she was being condescending when she insisted on sending him a copy of the rubric she used to assign grades, but nevertheless he examined it when it arrived. He also talked with several fellow teachers whose judgment he respected. Then he set about rethinking his approach to evaluation.

Art, he reasoned, is not only for artists. But as he examined the grade distribution for the first six weeks, he realized that the students who had a knack for art had been rewarded with the high grades. He intended to encourage these students, but he wondered if it had been at the expense of some of the others. What, in fact, is important in a beginning art course? Is it the same for everyone? Can individual differences be accommodated without abandoning reasonable standards? His implicit answers to these questions were reflected in the new grading criteria he established after a week of thoughtful consideration. Three categories for evaluation were included:

> Artistic rendition
>> Technical skill
>> Creativity
>
> Attitude and effort
>> Attendance and punctuality
>> Work habits
>> Preparation and initiative
>
> Academic achievement
>> Quality of participation
>> Test scores

John Sykes was especially pleased with the final touch to his system. The categories were weighted 2-1-1, but students would individually select which category was to be given the highest weight. This would be considerably more fair to students with only moderate talent. When he initiated the new system, including his first attempt at developing a rubric, he spent a whole period describing it to the class and inviting their comments. He was encouraged by their enthusiasm.

The following day, after making minor modifications based on the students' feedback, he provided a copy of the system to each student. He asked them to share it with their parents and to decide which weighting alternative they each preferred. He also set up a system whereby he would keep anecdotal notes on each student that would be useful for evaluating attitude and effort. It would be more work, he realized, but if 50% of some of the students' grades was to be determined by this sort of information, he would need credible documentation; enough, he thought, to satisfy Mrs. DeTano.

As John talked with his colleagues prior to setting up his own new system, one of them impressed him with the idea that evaluation should be an integral part of instruction, and that students needed thoughtful feedback and correction to contribute to the learning process. "I certainly do this as they are doing their projects," John thought, "but not while we are focusing on principles and history." He decided, therefore, to occasionally use quizzes in class that would include several objective items and a short essay item. In most cases, John did not collect the quizzes.

The correct answers to the objective items were given immediately, then the papers were passed on to another student to critique the essay. Following this phase, they were passed on once more and both the essay and the first critiquer's comments were critiqued. When the papers were returned to the writer, John solicited questions about the essay and the critiques. On the several occasions he had done this over the past five weeks, animated discussions that featured thoughtful insights occurred. Using these "teaching quizzes," both he and his students had the opportunity to engage in feedback and correction. At first he thought the students might object to their peers reading their papers, but they actually enjoyed this approach. When John Sykes did plan to collect quizzes and grade them himself, he announced it a day ahead.

Now, as grades were about to be assigned for the second six weeks, John felt reasonably comfortable with this new, more accountable approach. But one student, Ricky, still concerned him. Ricky had missed school sporadically throughout the term due to complications following a summer bout with mononucleosis. Ricky was an average student, but a wholly undistinguished artist. Now he had fallen behind considerably in all aspects of his work. His grade for this period, based on the established criteria, was clearly an F.

Mr. Sykes called Ricky in and informed him of the situation. Almost in tears, Ricky nodded his understanding. "But, Ricky," said Mr. Sykes, "suppose I assign you a C grade because I'm sure you could have made it if your health had been up to par. However, it would be conditional. I will ask you to sign a contract specifying what you'll need to make up from these past several weeks in addition to the regular work for the next grading period. And we will need to see improvement over your work so far. By the way, how is your health now? Are you up to it?"

Ricky's eyes had lit up. "Oh, yeah. You bet, Mr. Sykes. I sure appreciate the chance. I just can't afford to get any Fs in high school. I won't disappoint you—or myself."

As a delighted Ricky retreated down the hall, John thought, "So what's a grade for after all? I feel better about grades this grading period than I ever have before." Then he smiled as he uttered half aloud to himself, "Thank you, Mrs. DeTano."

RESEARCH AND THEORETICAL BASE

Although research has accumulated at a rapid rate in education as a total enterprise throughout this century, the attention has been uneven from area to area. One of the areas about which the available research is limited is teachers' classroom-evaluation practices (Lazar-Morris, Polin, May, & Burry, 1980; Stiggins, Conklin, & Bridgeford, 1986). The relative effects of various evaluation approaches and the effect of particular student testing and grading practices are not well documented in the literature. On the other hand, the treatment of the principles of evaluation and measurement is extensive.

Teachers tend to feel comfortable in the testing aspect of evaluation (Gullickson, 1984). They generally feel confident with and rely heavily on their own judgment (Lazar-Morris et al., 1984). On the other hand, grading is a painful responsibility (Gage & Berliner, 1991). This apparent paradox is at least partly explained by the findings that teachers are often not well prepared to conduct classroom evaluation and their formal training is minimal and narrow in scope (Rudman et al., 1980; Stiggins et al., 1986). Furthermore, teachers learn their evaluation techniques primarily from their colleagues, as well as from personal experience (Stiggins, 1985). As the findings indicate, teachers tend to employ intuitive and expedient practices in evaluation. They express little concern about the mechanical aspects of test writing and grading. Yet they do not, as a rule, have a well-developed, pedagogically defensible system of evaluation that they trust. Dealing with the affective implications of evaluation is thus often emotionally stressful.

Much of the literature on evaluation in recent years has been on authentic assessment, also termed alternative, naturalistic, or performance assessment (Perrone, 1991; Herman, Aschbacher, & Winters, 1992; Marzano, Pickering, & McTighe, 1993; Madaus and Kellaghan, 1993; Zemelman, Daniels, & Hyde, 1993; and Wiggins, 1993). These authors recognize the shortcomings of assessment as it has traditionally been conducted using paper-and-pencil tests primarily to ascertain students' acquisition of factual knowledge. Recently recommended practice targets students' ability to acquire personal meaning and to use knowledge in realistic tasks. Wiggins (1993) maintains that "we are not preparing students for real, 'messy' uses of knowledge in context—the 'doing' of the subject" (p. 202). Also, broader sampling of students' achievements over time is encouraged, with the use of portfolios to collect and preserve appropriate evidence (Graves & Sunstein, 1992; Grady, 1992). In a review of the research on the use of portfolios, Herman and Winters (1994) reported that relatively few studies were available on the effectiveness of portfolios. They did comment that most educators were positively disposed in principle to the use of portfolios, but that portfolios posed a demanding evaluation task to the teacher, a characteristic that limits their potential.

The area of standardized testing has been given a disproportionate amount of attention in the evaluation literature as compared with other areas (Stiggins & Bridgeford, 1985). A substantial body of literature describes large-scale standardized testing for accountability; however, teachers consider standardized tests to be of little importance (Salmon-Cox, 1981; Stiggins et al., 1986). Standardized testing has had limited impact in the classroom. It does not lead to higher achievement, nor do test results influence subsequent teacher practice (Kellaghan, Madaus, & Airasian, 1982). In fact, standardized test results and teachers' ratings produce very similar information on student performance for teachers (Pedulla, Airasian, & Madaus, 1980). Standardized tests clearly have their greatest influence outside the classroom and are primarily useful for administrative and public relations purposes. They constitute an essentially neutral factor in classrooms (Stiggins, 1985).

Evaluation is a complex—perhaps deceptively complex—aspect of teaching. In addressing this concern, Stiggins et al. (1986) stated, "We begin to comprehend the complexity of classroom assessment as we explore the range and frequency of teachers' decisions and the plethora of student characteristics they must consider in making those decisions" (p. 10). They go on to report that a review of several studies produced 66 student characteristics used by the sample teachers in evaluation-related decision making. One may conclude from this report that evaluation can no more be a totally rational process than instruction can. Teachers' sensitivity and values are inevitable factors in the effectiveness of their evaluation.

Teacher-made tests are a staple in most teachers' approaches to assessment of student progress. Rudman et al. (1980) found that teachers prefer norm-referenced tests (i.e., graded on an in-class comparative basis) over criterion-referenced tests (i.e., graded on the basis of a predetermined absolute standard). However, Lazar-Morris et al. (1980) reported that norm-referenced tests are considered by most experts to be characterized by narrowness of focus, bias, and unreliability. The preferred alternative is the criterion-referenced test because of its diagnostic, placement, and remediation uses, and its ease of interpretation. Except in those instances in which ranking of students' performance is necessary, criterion-based measures are recommended.

Tests work to teachers' and, in a sense, to students' advantage because by their very nature they are an incentive to students. Halpin and Halpin (1982) reported that students increase their study efforts when they know a test is imminent. Every experienced teacher knows this, for teachers commonly exhort students with the reminder that certain material will be on a test. In some cases it is virtually posed as a threat. Nungester and Duchastel (1982) found that students' retention of learned material was enhanced if they were tested on it. Tests, therefore, are useful in serving both instructional and evaluative purposes.

A clear similarity is apparent between teachers' verbal questioning and the items they write for classroom tests: both tend to emphasize factual recall. Fleming and Chambers (1983) indicated that teachers preferred matching questions and used few essay questions. Carter (1984) reported both from her own study and a review of the literature that teachers had a limited repertoire of test-writing skills and found it difficult to write items for testing higher-order thinking skills, in particular inference and prediction. One may conclude that, to a large extent, teacher-made tests are superficial. If teachers are, in fact, concerned about students' higher-order thinking skills, it is not always apparent from their tests.

The grading system affects the curriculum in the view of teachers (Agnew, 1983). They feel that it trivializes learning because it establishes a predisposition for readily assessed low cognitive-level learning; the curriculum is "covered" rather than "uncovered." Furthermore, from the students' viewpoint, grades as the measure of achievement replace achievement itself as the prized outcome of classroom learning activities. Grades become the hidden—but not very well hidden—curriculum.

From the research on classroom evaluation, we discern that the problems affecting evaluation practices in the classroom tend to involve human complexity and diversity more than mechanical or technical issues. The philosophical and emotional aspects of assessment are more difficult to deal with than matters of form or measurement. We realize that we search in vain for final solutions to the most vexing problems of evaluation. In the final analysis, ongoing judicious decision making based on a sound understanding of the principles of evaluation holds the greatest promise. In this aspect of teaching, as in planning, instruction, and discipline, there is simply no substitute for informed teacher decision making.

APPLICATION TO PRACTICE

Role of Evaluation in the Classroom

Why evaluate? A good question. The simplest answer a teacher might give is, "Because I am required to assign grades to students." That answer expresses an unassailable fact of teaching. But there is much more to it. Would teachers evaluate if it were not for the necessity of assigning a grade? Certainly teachers committed to excellent instruction would use evaluation in several ways: to diagnose students' readiness, to individualize learning, to ascertain the interim progress of students, to decide when tutoring or reteaching is advisable, and to assess the effectiveness and the outcomes of instruction.

Evaluation is sometimes considered to be an add-on to the instructional process, or something that occurs only after a unit of study to assign a grade to a student. This is a decidedly myopic view. As is implied in the opening section of this chapter and the subsequent comments, evaluation is an integral part of the teaching process. Evaluation is an important aspect of planning as content is selected, objectives are written, and remediation and enrichment are considered. During a unit of study, evaluation provides continuing feedback to the teacher and students and is an important information source for making adjustments.

At the completion of a unit of study, evaluation focuses on assessing the level of learning students have attained, assigning grades, and obtaining evidence of instructional effectiveness. In one sense, some of these aspects of evaluation tacitly occur regardless of teacher intentions. It is important to note that purposeful attention to evaluation enhances the several kinds of contributions that evaluation potentially makes to classroom outcomes.

The Process of Classroom Evaluation

Goals and Objectives. Written goals and objectives serve nominally as the beginning of the evaluation process. However, because evaluation is cyclical (i.e., the evaluation from one unit of study may affect planning for the next), there may be no absolute starting point. Care must be taken during the writing of objectives, especially at the unit and specific-outcomes levels, that they lend themselves to evaluation. Improperly or vaguely written objectives seriously impede evaluation of learning. John Sykes, in his art course, may have had as a program goal:

> Students will understand the contribution of color to the intent of an artwork.

Obviously, there is no way that Mr. Sykes could see inside the students' minds to assess the level of understanding of this concept. Therefore, he would need to have at least one—and probably more—specific objectives, which, when fulfilled, he would accept as evidence of probable understanding. Such specific objectives might be:

> Students will match a list of color tones to a set of possible intents.
>
> Students will explain Klee's use of color to emphasize the graphic dimension of his art.
>
> Students will produce a colored-pencil sketch in which they use color tone to express a feeling level.

If teachers are to evaluate learning at the various levels of thinking (six levels were presented in the planning chapter), then objectives must be written at the respective levels. The various levels of objectives, if used as guides to direct instruction, result in developing learning activities conceived at those levels. However, evaluation would have to occur in terms of the objectives at those levels to determine the actual learning outcomes.

Goals and objectives are also used as the basis for building tests with a table of specifications. In its simplest form, each goal that the test covers is listed and assigned a percent weighting. Within each goal, each objective is assigned a percent. In writing or selecting items to be included on the test, the appropriate number of items may then be included for each objective and goal to ensure a sampling of subject matter. Table 9.1 is a general example.

Authentic Assessment. Until the mid-1980s, the literature on classroom assessment dealt almost exclusively with the traditional sorts of topics that are described in the other sections of this chapter. Previous editions of this book have included the statement that the last major change in assessment practices was adoption of the letter grade (ABCDF) scale based on research conducted by Starch (1913, 1918). That assertion is no longer accurate. A new perspective based on practices that are termed authentic (or alternative, performance, or naturalistic) assessment has been given an increasingly prominent place in the literature, and we can predict with a fair degree of confidence (we in education know better than to go too far out on a limb!) that the several practices of authentic assess-

Table 9.1 Generalized Table of Specifications

GOAL 1 60%	
Objective 1.1	30%
Objective 1.2	15%
Objective 1.3	15%
GOAL 2 40%	
Objective 2.1	25%
Objective 2.2	15%
	100%

ment will continue to gain in prominence. One major reason is that teachers are becoming increasingly convinced that traditional practices, while they will continue to be used for the purposes they serve well, are insufficient to fulfill all the functions evaluation should serve in modern classrooms. A second major reason is that teachers are increasingly approaching their teaching and their students' learning in constructivist terms, as has been described throughout this book. This places the emphasis on students doing more than simply knowing. Zemelman et al. (1993) said it this way:

> Today, teachers are no longer satisfied to assess students' growth solely on the basis of classroom quizzes and standardized achievement tests, which tend to treat the curriculum as a pyramid of atomized subskills, and which often miss what kids can really do with coordinated, higher-order activities like writing, researching, experimenting, or problem solving. Instead, innovative teachers are increasingly using kidwatching, observational notes, interview questionnaires, checklists, student artifacts and work samples, performance assessment, student self-evaluation, evaluation conferences, portfolios, and other tools to get a better understanding of kids' learning and more clearly explain their progress. (p. 185)

Zessoules and Gardner (1991) investigated classroom environments that supported what they termed an assessment culture as opposed to a testing culture. Four critical conditions for an assessment culture were identified: "nurturing complex understandings, developing reflective habits of mind, documenting students' evolving understandings, and making use of assessment as a moment of understanding" (p. 51). These conditions exist minimally, if at all, in classrooms in which virtually all evaluation occurs as tests administered following instruction, and in which students view learning as the means to "earn" a grade. Authentic assessment requires that learning be recognized as an evolving event, that its occurrence (or nonoccurrence) is evident in a variety of ways to the alert and concerned teacher, and that it should, where feasible, be evaluated as students' demonstrated ability to use knowledge or skill to accomplish meaningful tasks.

In some learning settings, authentic learning is a virtual aspect of the activity. In art, music, technology education, and physical education classes, for example, the respective outcomes are usually performances or artifacts that reflect the level of learning that has been achieved. No contrived and noncontextual "test" is necessary. Teachers in other content areas that do not lend themselves by their essential nature to authentic assessment have been generally complacent in their efforts to employ authentic assessment practices, although in fairness we must acknowledge that many informed and conscientious teachers have used creative and realistic methods of evaluation. The following several examples provide a sense of what teachers may do.

- In mathematics classes, teachers use realistic word problems that require students to use problem-solving skills. Also, teachers challenge students to write their own realistic problems that they own as a class.
- In economics class, the teacher conducts a stock-market competition between student groups in the class. Each group is allowed a $5,000 credit at the beginning to invest and each group vies to make the greatest profit on their investment. Working in groups and having to discuss and agree on investment decisions is a further benefit of this activity.
- In biology class, the students accept the task of identifying the plant life along the metropolitan park nature trails and producing plaques with pertinent information for the benefit of nature enthusiasts.

The authentic activities described above, and the many more that you undoubtedly can think of once you are on a roll, appear to be learning activities more so than assessment practices. And that is just the point! Authentic assessment is, as much as possible, integral to the learning itself. The question then arises, What about a grade? It is a fair question, even though a glib first response might be, So who needs a grade? But until schools have evolved considerably from their current posture, teachers will be required to grade students on the ABCDF scale.

One means of translating authentic assessment into letter grades is through use of a rubric. A rubric is a set of descriptions of behaviors, outcomes, or criteria identified with each grading symbol. "The current interest in rubrics comes as educators throughout the United States try to define learning outcomes, set standards for student achievement, and expand the use of performance assessments to evaluate what students know and can do" (O'Neil, 1994). Developing rubrics is acknowledged to be difficult, but they do make explicit the standards that may otherwise be vague to both the teacher and students. Marzano et al. (1993) provide many sample rubrics for a variety of settings. The following four-level rubric is from their book (p. 99):

Demonstrates effective interpersonal skills

4   Consistently and actively helps promote effective group interaction and expresses ideas and opinions in ways that are sensitive to the feelings or knowledge base of others.

3   Consistently participates in group interaction without prompting and expresses ideas and opinions in ways that are sensitive to the feelings and knowledge base of others.

2   Sporadically participates in group interaction without prompting and expresses ideas and opinions in ways that are sensitive to the feelings and knowledge base of others.

1   Rarely, if ever, participates in group interaction without prompting or expresses ideas and opinions in ways that are sensitive to the feelings and knowledge base of others.

Portfolios. Portfolios have achieved prominence among teachers as an alternative assessment approach. Originally, the term was associated with artists' collections of their works. The portfolio expedited the examination, evaluation, and possible sale of their products. This idea of a collection of artifacts has been extended into the classroom, and it takes myriad forms as teachers and students in a range of classrooms assemble and organize materials representing students' progress and achievement.

A *portfolio*, originally a folder or large envelope containing artwork, has been appropriated by educators to incorporate any collection of classroom-produced artifacts. It may take the form of a folder, notebook, box, or drawer—whatever is a convenient organizing device. The concept of an organized collection is the key to portfolio development.

Portfolios have two characteristics that make them valuable as an assessment approach. First, they provide an ongoing means of monitoring students' progress. They include the actual products—an evolving contextual record—rather than only isolated grades in the teacher's gradebook. Second, they may be controlled to a significant degree by the students—that is, the students decide what to include in the portfolio that best represents their ability, interests, and achievement. Grady (1992) described it this way:

> Students have a vested interest in the creation of their portfolios, certainly more than they have for a file of test scores in the main office. The portfolio represents a range of efforts and tangible achievement; it presents a learning history. In a well-designed portfolio system, the students select the pieces of work to be included in the portfolio. The student has the chance to revise it, perfect it, evaluate it, and explain it. It is different from work completed just to fulfill an assignment or written for the teacher's eyes; a piece created for the portfolio bears a piece of the student's identity. Whether the work is a self-generated word problem in math or a persuasive essay, the student claims ownership. It represents

the student in a concrete and authentic way that a stanine score cannot do. . . . With portfolios, assessment is an important part of the learning cycle, rather than being merely a result. (pp. 12–13)

As mentioned in the case of authentic assessment, the grading of portfolios needs special consideration. It is especially appropriate that the teacher and students cooperatively decide on the expectations that pertain, and develop a rubric for students' self-evaluation as well as the teacher's evaluation. Decisions have to be made about the extent to which various factors will be weighted, such as the amount and quality of content; the effort expended; the students' explanation, insight, and evaluation; and neatness and organization. With standards clearly in place and owned by students, focus is provided for their learning, and motivation is enhanced as well.

Content Selection. The selection of content and the development of learning objectives occurs more or less simultaneously, each complementing the other. From the curricular point of view, courses are essentially a body of content; from an instructional point of view, courses are a sequence of learning activities.

John Sykes probably views his art course both in terms of knowledge to be learned and activities to engage in, and each becomes very much a part of the other. For this group of students, basic information about art will have to be presented, including principles of form, balance, perspective, and medium. He will also want students to be aware of the role of art in our cultural setting, and the contribution of art in the practical and aesthetic dimensions. Finally, of course, he will want students to create works of art at whatever level they are capable.

A variety of levels of learning and several types of learning outcomes are implied by the content this teacher intends to teach. He must make two kinds of decisions: What content in what sequence is most pertinent for this group of students, and what learning activities are most appropriate to achieve the objectives related to that content? By knowing his content well, making reference to the course syllabus, and becoming increasingly familiar with his students, Mr. Sykes will correlate content and activities. However, continuing evaluation of achievement and instructional effectiveness will be used to redirect and fine-tune teaching as necessary.

Data Collection. Evaluation has two components: information on achievement or performance and a standard that provides a base for measuring. Information on achievement is obtained in a variety of ways. Informally, teachers make evaluations continuously as they observe students. Students' willingness to attend class, ability to respond, and demonstration of interest and initiative provide the teacher with a sense of how things are going and what adjustments are expedient. Teachers also notice patterns of behavior in individual students and begin to determine where extra help may need to be given, where enrichment is possible, and where additional monitoring is required. John Sykes noticed that Ricky had a unique problem, and he devised a unique approach in the form of a conditional grade and a contract to accommodate him.

More formally, teachers use instruments to collect data useful for evaluation. They may be in the form of checklists and various kinds of tests. Also, data collection may involve such assignments as homework papers, journals and notebooks, reports, and creative projects. During the course of a unit, evaluation based on these sources, often through the use of student-developed portfolios, should be used to assess students' progress, diagnose students' problems, and provide continuous feedback to students. Teachers should make sure that students are well informed about their progress through the systematic use of feedback and correction procedures, and that no student's learning and achievement problems go unattended for long.

We observe John Sykes using "teaching quizzes" as a means of providing useful interim evaluation to students and the opportunity for immediate correction. In this regard, the most important consideration was student learning, not assigning grades.

Establishing a standard against which data are compared is the second aspect of evaluation. Teachers' astute judgment is required for this task. In some cases, teachers allow their standards to remain implicit, as John Sykes initially did. This may lead to difficulty, as is illustrated in the scenario. Standards must be clearly stated to be as useful as possible, and they must be communicated to the students, often in the form of a rubric. Students are thus provided with a benchmark that clarifies levels of achievement and performance.

Applying Standards. Teachers sometimes think of their grading scales as standards, such as 65% or a D mark as passing. These are only a part of the standards. It still leaves open the questions, 65% of what? Or, a D based on what? A teacher's well-written course and program goals provide the basis for establishing the "what" part of the standard. However, the teacher must still determine how the level of compliance with the standard is to be measured and the appropriate scale to express the level of compliance.

In the case of John Sykes, a program objective is: "Students will understand the contribution of color to the intent of an artwork." He may establish, according to the specific objectives related to this goal, that (1) students must match with at least 70% accuracy color tone with possible intent; (2) students must show in a brief paragraph that they are aware of the concept "graphic dimension" and how color may contribute to it; and (3) students will render a sketch that in his practiced view expresses (marginally at least) feeling through the use of color tone. This is about as explicit as standards for performance can be for this type of learning. Students who do not achieve the minimums stated will have to be retaught until they do. If Mr. Sykes is using the ABCDF scale, then the correct number of matching items, the extent of students' understanding of Klee's use of color tone, and the quality of the sketch will all have to be translated into grade symbols. He will have to depend on his judgment to do this. Experience will be helpful in making these judgments. Consequently, new teachers will find this to be one of the more difficult aspects of teaching.

Reporting and Using the Results of Evaluation. The foregoing commentary implies that evaluation is useful only if it is communicated to concerned parties. Teachers, of course, immediately use the results of evaluation for making decisions about appropriate strategies, pacing, individualizing, and assessing instructional effectiveness. Students need to know the results of evaluation to guide them in their ongoing work and possibly to provide incentive for their continued efforts. Others who are indirectly involved with classroom learning—counselors, administrators, and parents—also have the need to be informed at least periodically about students' classroom achievement.

The results of evaluation procedures are reported to students both informally and formally. Casual comments by the teacher in class in response to students' answers or during a supervised study period constitute a useful kind of feedback. Marks and comments on homework papers provide a somewhat more structured means for assessment reporting. Conferences with students to attend to exceptional situations are useful, as was John Sykes's conference with Ricky. Quizzes administered in class, the results of which may or may not be recorded as a grade in the gradebook, constitute an even more structured form of evaluation. Formal evaluations usually occur in the form of weekly or unit tests, or assessments of some type of performance such as timed athletic events or the quality of a creative effort. In chapter 2, a section is devoted to describing effective feedback and corrective practices that the teacher uses as a component of instruction.

All the separate evaluations that occur during a grading period, usually six to nine weeks in duration, are accumulated, processed according to the teacher's predetermined plan, and entered on a report form as the official grade assigned to the student. These grading-period grades are averaged again at the end of the semester and at the end of the year so that ultimately all the student's academic achievement in a course is reported as a single mark.

When grades are viewed in this perspective, their possible shortcomings are apparent. Are they reliable? Are they valid? Do they really convey meaning? Generally speaking, they are, in fact, as reliable as any other predictor of future academic achievement. They are also useful in that they have become the basis of a convention of communication that is widely understood among the many parties who ultimately make use of them. Finally, no alternative assessment or evaluation method has become widely enough accepted that one can predict that in the foreseeable future standard letter grades will be de-emphasized, let alone replaced.

Test Writing

In the course of comprehensive classroom evaluation, both formal and informal data will be obtained in several ways. Observation of students provides a continuing series of impressions. Anecdotal records, checklists, and rating scales are used to collect and record more substantive information. But, on the whole, paper-and-pencil tests are the source of most of the formal evaluation-related information that teachers obtain.

Paper-and-pencil tests are made up of essay and objective items. The essay items may be short-answer questions that require a sentence or two, or they may be extended to involve several paragraphs. The most common types of objective items are true-false, completion, matching, and multiple choice.

Essay Items. Essays are especially useful for measuring higher-order thinking, including analysis, synthesis, and evaluation. However, they take a relatively long time to answer compared with objective items, so only a limited sample of learning can be measured with essay items. Factual information and basic comprehension are much more efficiently measured with objective test items.

Essay tests take much less time to write than multiple choice tests primarily because far fewer items are included. However, a thoughtfully written essay item may require a considerable expenditure of time to get it just right. Care must be taken to write the items clearly and specify precisely what the response should address. An essay item can cover only a relatively limited range of information; thus, items should be judiciously selected, based on a priority of objectives. In other words, sampling is a prime concern.

In John Sykes's class, we can imagine as a test item: "What is the contribution of art to our culture?" Obviously, entire books have been written on the topic and whole courses are devoted to investigating certain aspects of it. Although he may want students to begin to appreciate the contribution of art in his course, we can imagine students' frustration in attempting to respond to such a broad question. We also wonder how a teacher would grade their responses.

A more limited question in this class might be: "What was Paul Klee's contribution to the art of the first half of this century?" Here again, however, we recognize some problems. Did Paul Klee make only one contribution? Should the students simply name the contribution in a brief phrase or sentence, or should they provide a context, some description, and the impact? How much should the student write? The item does not meet the criteria of clearness and preciseness.

Consider one more example: "In a one-page essay (approximately 150 words) describe the single most identifiable characteristic of Paul Klee's painting in the 1920s and 1930s, and give an example of how his work influenced other artists of his time." In this item, three things are made clear to the students: the length of the essay, the expectation that they will describe the single most identifiable characteristic of Klee's painting, and that they must produce evidence supporting the assertion that Klee had professional influence. Although writing essay items may be done more quickly than writing most objective items, much care must still be taken to write selectively and precisely. The time spent writing such items will pay off when teachers grade them. It is so much easier when teachers know exactly what to look for!

Grading essays that students write both in response to test questions and as general term-paper assignments is laborious, mentally fatiguing work. Reading dozens of papers all addressing the same topic challenges the teacher's mind to remain alert and discriminating. But it is unlikely that there will ever be a mechanical or electronic device to do it for you, so be prepared. Many teachers avoid this unsavory task by simply not using essay items or assignments. This self-serving practice is unacceptable in any class in which constructivist teaching and students' higher-order learning (meaning making) is involved.

The following suggestions are helpful in grading essays fairly, quickly, effectively, and with a minimum of mental fatigue.

1. Write the essay question or the statement of the essay assignment incisively, as described previously.
2. Inform the students clearly about the expectations you have for their essays; a rubric for this purpose is recommended.
3. Determine what components will be assessed and the weighting to be used: for example, comprehensiveness—60%, expressive quality—20%, insight and creativity—20%. Points may be used rather than percent if one chooses.
4. Make a list of the points that the essay should address to ensure focus and consistency in your marking.
5. Read several selected papers before marking to get a feel for the manner in which students have responded.
6. Respond to students' papers with praise where deserved and with constructive corrective feedback that will be helpful. Keep in mind that essays (and all tests) are most useful as instruments for students' learning.

The art course that has been used as a setting for the previous examples is not a language arts course, which presents another concern. To what extent do students' word-comprehension skills related to reading and interpreting an item and their expressive skills related to responding to an item become factors in the evaluation of a student response? In other words, teachers may find themselves grading students' language skills as much as their acquisition of understanding in the art course. This is a dilemma without an immediate solution. At the very least, students should be made aware of the extent to which expression will count as a factor in grading—if it counts at all. Also, every effort should be made to use clear, basic language in writing test items. Finally, students who are known to have limited comprehension and expressive skills should be given whatever consideration is helpful and fair. Within the context of these considerations, the goal should be informed teacher decision making that focuses on the students' best interest.

Objective Items. Most tests are made up primarily or entirely of objective items. They have the advantage of covering a lot of material efficiently, of being easy to score, and of being easy to translate into students' grades. On the other hand, they are most commonly used to test at the lower thinking levels, primarily recall and comprehension, although it is possible to have objective items at all levels of thinking. Teachers tend to use objective items because of these advantages, but there is a danger of trivializing the evaluation of learning outcomes. Objective means of measuring learning are necessary but not sufficient as a comprehensive approach to evaluation.

Matching, completion, and true-false items are the usual means of assessing students' recall. To the extent that some information is very important to students' understanding and becomes the "raw material" for subsequent information processing, these types of assessment are useful. However, it is clear from the research that these items are used with disproportionate frequency, or at the very least they are not supplemented by a sufficient number of items that test at the higher levels of thinking.

Although these three kinds of objective test items are straightforward in form, they nevertheless must be carefully written. True-false items, for example, deal in absolutes. However, absolutes that are also not self-evident are rather difficult to find. Students become testwise and realize that an absolute or specific determiner such as "always" or "never" usually signifies a false answer. Ambiguity is a problem as well. For example, a true-false statement might be: Michelangelo was a 16th-century artist. A knowledgeable student would realize that Michelangelo produced one of his greatest sculptures, the Pieta, in the last years of the 15th century, and in the absolute sense the statement is false. Yet the teacher would probably intend this as a true statement. In writing any objective test item, a teacher must constantly keep in mind the concern for avoiding ambiguity.

The multiple-choice form is the most difficult to write but the most useful objective test item. It involves producing a stem that describes the substance of the item and from three to five possible answers from which to select. This type of item can potentially assess all the levels of thinking, but it is most useful for measuring recall and comprehension. In some cases it may also measure application and analysis.

The best approach to writing a multiple-choice item is to write a stem and correct response that deals with a pertinent and important aspect of the unit of study and is directly related to a unit goal. Then write at least two, but preferably three or four, so-called distractors, or possible responses that would be attractive to a person who was insufficiently informed. This latter task is the most difficult, and the effectiveness of the item is especially dependent on the finesse with which the distractors are written. But plausible distractors are difficult to write, so most multiple-choice items include four instead of five possible responses from which the student picks one. In some cases, only three possible responses are included, but the chances of guessing right considerably reduces the discriminating power.

Some examples of multiple choice questions provide a basis for examining their qualities.

1. Michelangelo is associated most closely with which Italian city?
   a. Bologna
   b. Rome
   c. Milan
   d. Florence

This is a straightforward example of a recall-level item. Of course, one might have used a true-false item to test for the same knowledge. One might also have embedded this bit of information in a format that requires matching artists with locales.

2. Michelangelo's greatest artwork is
   a. *David*
   b. Mona Lisa
   c. *Pietà*
   d. Sistine chapel ceiling

This item has at least two flaws. First, one will probably encounter more argument than agreement about which was the greatest work of art. There is clearly no best response, and ambiguity results. Second, Mona Lisa is a ringer in this list, because another artist painted it. Students might very likely form unintended impressions if Mona Lisa is included as a distractor. In a more general sense, Mona Lisa lies outside the range from which appropriate distractors should be selected; it is of a different genre.

3. The "power" in Michelangelo's art lies primarily in his ability to
   a. give embodiment to a transcendent level of human experience.
   b. create a perfect mirror image of reality in both sculpture and painting.
   c. use line and perspective to produce unusual spatial relationships.
   d. represent common and familiar objects in unique, emotionally charged images.

This analysis level item may be appropriate for a college-level course in art history or art appreciation. However, if this were a question asked in Mr. Sykes's 9th-grade class or in any level of high school class, students could not handle the language level. It would be as much a test of reading comprehension as of art knowledge.

4. Michelangelo can appropriately be formally considered a "Renaissance man" primarily because
   a. he lived in the 15th and 16th centuries.
   b. he was a master of several forms of art.
   c. he was a friend of powerful people in his time.
   d. his art was not limited to the traditions of his time.

This example of an analysis level item meets the criteria presented later for writing effective multiple-choice items.

Writing multiple-choice test items, according to Gage and Berliner (1991), is "a kind of art form" (p. 645). This should not discourage teachers from writing them. Rather, it advises teachers not to take the skill for granted and to work at developing it. The previous examples begin to give a sense of the intellectual task involved in producing these items. A set of suggestions will help to guide the writing of such items. Practice in developing a feel for them will contribute to improving the skill.

1. Keep the language at the students' level; use good grammatical form.
2. Write the stem and correct response first, then add three or four plausible distractors.
3. Express as much of the substance of the item as possible in the stem.
4. Avoid ambiguity; be certain that one response is clearly the best response.
5. Keep the responses in an item consistent in type and length.
6. Avoid specific determiner words and absolutes such as *every, none, always,* and *never.*
7. Avoid the use of negative words (*no, not*) in the stem if possible; always avoid a double negative, or a word used both in the stem and in the response.
8. Do not use "all of the above" as a distractor.

Purposes of Evaluation

Diagnostic Evaluation. Students in a typical secondary classroom present teachers with a staggering range of individual differences. In an ungrouped 9th-grade class, reading-comprehension levels alone may span up to eight years. Especially in classes in which cumulative learning is a factor (mathematics and language), diagnostic tests provide the teacher with useful information about students' levels of previous achievement. Involving students in studies for which they have insufficient background is self-defeating; teaching students material that they have already mastered is uselessly redundant.

Diagnostic tests may be of two sorts. Standardized tests may be used to determine how a particular student or entire class compares with typical students at that level (a norm group). Also, standardized tests are available that measure students' learning skills (reasoning and computational). The *Tenth Mental Measurements Yearbook* (Conoley & Kramer, 1989) is a standard reference for teachers in this area.

The second sort of diagnostic test is sometimes referred to as a *pretest*. This teacher-made test is written to reflect the goals/objectives of an imminent unit of study. It may be quite similar to the test intended to be administered at the completion of a unit of study. Students' scores and success rate on these diagnostic tests will provide valuable information for planning learning activities within the unit and individualizing learning to the extent it is feasible. If, for example, grading contracts are used, diagnostic test information provides the basis for specifying the terms of the contract. It should be noted here that a separate and unique contract for each student (which could involve more than 100 contracts per teacher!) is unrealistic, although separate contracts may be developed for occasional exceptional situations. However, contracts written at three levels of student learning within a course of study is manageable for most teachers and will help the teacher avoid teaching only the mythical average student.

Formative Evaluation. This aspect of evaluation asks the question, "How am I doing?" It is not particularly different in form from the other tests, although it may be somewhat informal. These are tests or other approaches to evaluation that are administered at opportune times to provide feedback to the teacher and students regarding achievement. They serve a diagnostic function within a course of study. They serve as a basis for the teacher in ascertaining instructional effectiveness, making midunit curricular decisions, determining the impact of instructional innovations, and deciding whether reteaching should occur. They serve as a means for the student to gauge progress at any point and identify gaps or weaknesses in the mastery of the unit goals. Grades from formative evaluation tests may be recorded and counted as part of the student's achievement for the grading period, but this is not their major purpose.

For example, during a unit of painting in John Sykes's art course, a particular student may have been found to be quite adept in sketching the outlines of an intended painting. This student would be introduced to the next phase involving mixing colors, while other students continued to improve their sketches. In the scenario, another sort of formative evaluation occurred as John Sykes used "teaching quizzes." These not only gave the students information on the extent to which they were meeting the teacher's expectations, but were also an incentive to study efforts.

Summative Evaluation. When most people—especially nonteachers—think of evaluation, summative evaluation is what they have in mind. Summative evaluation occurs at the completion of a unit of study, and its primary purpose is to determine the extent to which each student has achieved the unit goals/objectives. Summative evaluation can occur in a variety of forms (including timed performances, written reports, or presentations to the group), but usually occurs as a written test. The scores derived from summative evaluation exercises are usually the primary source for determining students' grades.

If evaluation is considered to be a cyclical process, summative evaluation may also serve a diagnostic function. The end-of-unit test indicates to the teacher the extent to which students have benefited from a unit of instruction. Some students in an algebra class, for example, simply may not be ready to proceed to second-order equations if they have not mastered simple linear equations. Remediation may be prescribed based on diagnosis from the summative evaluation outcome.

Classroom Tests

Teacher-made tests are a traditional and indispensable part of evaluation. They serve several functions, including, of course, measuring achievement. The items on a test provide the teacher with the opportunity to select for the student those aspects of the unit of study that are most important, and thus reinforce learning of the material one last time during the study of the unit. Furthermore, students' attention is entirely devoted to the test for the duration of the time, resulting in some of the most intense learning that occurs in a classroom. This is a strong rationale for writing powerful tests.

A test score has no meaning until it is compared to a referent. Three types of referents are presented in this chapter. The teacher's purposeful choice of the appropriate referent is an important evaluation-related decision.

Norm-Referenced Tests. The referent for norm-referenced tests is the average of the students' scores on that particular test. It is an attractive approach to teachers because it lets them off the hook regarding making prior decisions about levels of achievement. Either by eyeballing a set of scores after the fact and assigning letter grades using break points in the range, or even by using a more sophisticated approach involving normal curve statistics, teachers establish norm-referenced student grades. It has the effect of neutralizing the teacher's possible shortcomings as an instructor because the highest score made is the highest score possible.

Many standardized tests are norm referenced, using what Gage and Berliner (1991) referred to as the "distant peer group." Teachers or administrators often wish to know how their students compare with their cohort group districtwide, statewide, or nationwide. Teachers may make curriculum decisions or revise expectation levels based on the results of such tests.

Also, students may wish to know their standing within a certain population. The Student Achievement Test (SAT) and American College Test (ACT) are examples of norm-referenced standardized tests that provide college-bound students with important information about their current levels of achievement, which in turn are predictors of future academic achievement.

The use of norm referencing is widely criticized in the literature. In their evaluation-related decisions, teachers tend to default to norm referencing even when it is not the pedagogically recommended approach. However, norm referencing is a useful—in fact, indispensable—means of addressing the evaluation purposes for which it is intended.

In cases in which it is useful to rank students in the class, to cite achievement in terms of percentiles, or to employ a competitive approach usefully, norm-referenced grading is appropriate. However, it does allow the teacher to get by with unclear objectives and expectations and with marginally effective instruction. In general, teachers should think carefully before using norm-referenced tests in the classroom.

Criterion-Referenced Tests. As the term implies, students are required to meet a predetermined level of performance to be assigned a particular grade. Establishing the appropriate level, or criterion, may be a difficult task for the teacher, especially an inexperienced teacher. A criterion set too low results in unreasonably high grades and little grade dispersal. At the other extreme, a criterion set too high dooms a disproportionate number of students to low grades. This results in disappointed students and a grim teacher who is shaken by the specter of personal failure. Setting appropriate criteria is an important but risky part of evaluation.

Although the major disadvantage of criterion-referenced testing is the difficulty of establishing appropriate standards, the advantages far outweigh this disadvantage. The criterion-referenced approach allows teachers to establish, in their judgment, reasonable targets for student performance. If a target is not met, the teacher may need to analyze the possible causes and perhaps revise expectations, but it is not a reason to abandon the use of the approach. Criterion-referenced testing also allows the teacher to set a level of mastery that determines when reteaching should occur. Each student's level of competence is clearly represented because this approach is based on an absolute referent.

The objectives within a unit of study may, in fact, be written in terms of criteria. In an art class, the teacher may set as an expectation: "Students will mix three shades of each of the secondary colors within the ranges displayed on the classroom chart." This statement clearly establishes what students are to accomplish and further specifies the criterion against which it is to be compared. Other objectives in chapter 5 on planning are examples of the relationship of objectives to criterion-referenced approaches to evaluation.

Self-Referenced Tests. For some learning under particular conditions, the only appropriate evaluation approach is an assessment based on past performance. In a typing class, a criterion of 60 words per minute (wpm) may be established to get an A grade. However, a student with poor motor skills could never hope to attain anything close to that level. A more reasonable approach is to determine through several trials the student's current speed level, then establish a reasonable target, such as a weekly increase of two wpm for the next six weeks. A subsequent dilemma arises: Should a student who achieves only 32 wpm get a higher grade than one who may type 45 wpm? It can be resolved only in terms of the teacher's philosophy as it relates to evaluation: What, in fact, is the purpose of grades?

Students' Grades

Grades (the term marks is also used) have been called the coin of the students' realm. They usually are the object of the students' ardent desire. Getting high marks is a satisfying experience for students; getting low marks may be devastating. School marks are an important factor in students' determination of their self-images.

In the most basic sense, school marks are symbols with which the teacher communicates to students and other interested parties an estimate of each student's academic performance. From an academic point of view, grades convey pertinent and useful information. But grades are so emotionally charged that the academic uses of grades are frequently overshadowed.

The academic functions of grades are straightforward. Wrinkle (1947) and Adams and Torgerson (1964) identified four functions: (1) administrative, for determining such things as promotion, transfer, class standing, and eligibility for honors; (2) guidance, for identifying characteristics of strength and weakness, advising on enrollment in particular programs, and planning for careers; (3) informing, for communicating the results of evaluation to interested parties, primarily students and parents; and (4) motivation, for providing an incentive for students when innate interest in learning is minimal. On the other hand, grades have certain suspect qualities. After reviewing the literature, Kindsvatter (1969) concluded that school marks may have the following shortcomings:

1. Marks are variable, subjective, contaminated, even capricious.
2. Marks create a condition of unfair competition.
3. Marks reflect an aristocratic rather than democratic attitude.
4. Marks preoccupy students and their parents.
5. Marking practices deny the psychological principle of individual differences.
6. Marking practices tend to influence teaching in the direction of memorization and regurgitation at the expense of concept formation and creativity.
7. Marking practices encourage student dependency. (p. 331)

Although there is general agreement that grades are necessary (some might say a necessary evil), an informed and sensitive approach to evaluation can attenuate some of the negative outcomes of grading. A teacher who takes an arbitrary, self-righteous approach to grading will almost certainly hurt some students unnecessarily. On the other hand, a teacher who uses a positive, developmental approach to determining grades, as Mr. Sykes did in the case of Ricky, can take advantage of the contribution that grades can make to promoting classroom achievement while minimizing contingent negative effects.

As you develop your personal approach to assessing students' work and assigning marks, establish clearly for yourself those principles and beliefs that reflect your philosophy of teaching. In the authors' view, democratic values, including respect for the worth and dignity of every student and acceptance of individual differences, are fundamental propositions for teachers in American classrooms. What values emerge, then, in your approach to classroom evaluation? Following are some suggestions for your consideration.

1. Assessment practices should be consistent with modern methodology as presented in the professional knowledge base of teaching.
2. The primary purpose of classroom evaluation is to contribute to the learning process.
3. Assessment practices should demonstrably be in the best interest of the students.
4. Any classroom marking practice or individual mark that induces discouragement, disillusionment, resignation, or defeat is suspect. Further, a failing mark given to a student is in some measure a failure of the teacher as well.
5. A system of classroom evaluation should include opportunities for self-evaluation, and, where feasible, cooperative evaluation.

The Teacher's Personal Grading System. The system the teacher uses to compute a student's grade is, by and large, a personal invention. Although the teacher must operate within the school's grading policy, which at the very least specifies what is marked (e.g., achievement, effort, citizenship, attitude), what scale and symbols are used, and the length of grading periods, the teacher generally has a wide range of freedom in selecting or devising personal marking practices. No one system is recognized as the best.

One factor in determining a grading system is the nature of a particular course. In a case in which grades are accumulated from a series of periodically administered, objectively scored tests, straightforward averaging is sufficient. If a variety of sources of evaluation is involved, matters of accumulating and weighting add complexity to grading. Three general criteria apply for any system: it should be functional, fair, and clear.

Informing the students early and clearly regarding the teacher's approach to grading is more important than what approach is used. The students deserve to know what factors are taken into consideration, what relative weight is assigned to each factor, and the minimum expectations for achieving each grade. Describing this information in writing and delivering it to students with explicit directions on the sheet that it is to be shared with parents is the best approach; no student or parent can claim not to have been informed insofar as the teacher is culpable.

SUMMARY POINT

Classroom evaluation is an inevitable component of teaching. However, it is underused as a contributor to teaching effectiveness. Potential will be realized through a comprehensive understanding of the several dimensions of classroom evaluation and the discerning and imaginative application of its pertinent principles. This potential includes greater scope in planning, more informed decision making during instruction, and an increased base of information for assessing achievement.

REVIEW: IMPORTANT PRACTICES FOR EVALUATION

1. Write incisive, unambiguous unit goals and objectives that are both guides for instruction/learning and the bases for standards of achievement.
2. Gather evaluative data from as wide a range of sources as is feasible, both formal and informal.
3. Write tests that reflect the objectives at all the levels of thinking and that become powerful teaching tools as well as well-designed data-gathering instruments.
4. Use authentic assessment practices to enrich and personalize the evaluation process.
5. Develop a comprehensive approach to evaluation incorporating its diagnostic, formative, and summative functions.
6. Use a criterion-referenced approach for interpreting test results unless there is a specific reason to use another approach.
7. Develop a personal grading system that is functional, fair, and clear.

QUESTIONS FOR REFLECTION

1. At the close of the scenario, John Sykes asked the rhetorical question, "So what's a grade for after all?" Your own philosophical approach to grading can be brought to the level of explicit awareness by writing a paragraph in response to John Sykes's question.
2. Given a typical unit of study in your subject area, what evaluative data will you obtain, and how will you obtain it, to accomplish the diagnostic, formative, and summative functions of evaluation?
3. In developing a grading system for your classroom that is functional, fair, and clear, what will be the major features you will incorporate?
4. How do the principles of constructivist teaching contribute to a fuller understanding of the concept of authentic assessment?
5. How would you deal with the evaluation implications of the following situations?
   a. A student has been placed in your class who is clearly unable to achieve at what you consider to be a minimally acceptable (mastery) level of accomplishment. (The principle of inclusion is especially pertinent here.)
   b. Both knowledge and performance (or creative) outcomes are included in the course, yet you are limited to assigning only one final mark.

c. A student is found to have cheated on an important unit test.

d. A student has a poor attendance record, has completed only about half the homework assignments, was often late turning in work, but scored well on the unit test.

REFERENCES

Adams, G., & Torgerson, T. (1964). *Measurement and evaluation in education, psychology, and guidance.* New York: Holt, Rinehart & Winston.

Agnew, E. (1983). *A study of the letter grade system and its effect on the curriculum.* Paper presented at the annual meeting of the AERA, Montreal. (ERIC Document Reproduction Service No. ED 238 143)

Carter, K. (1984). Do teachers understand the principles for writing tests? *Journal of Teacher Education, 35*(6), 57–60.

Conoley, J., & Kramer, J. (Eds.). (1989). *Tenth mental measurements yearbook.* Lincoln, NE: Buros Institute of Mental Measurement.

Fleming, M., & Chambers, B. (1983). Teacher-made tests: Windows on the classroom. In W. E. Hathaway (Ed.), *Testing in the schools: New directions for testing and measurement.* San Francisco: Jossey-Bass.

Gage, N., & Berliner, D. (1991). *Educational psychology* (5th ed.). Boston: Houghton Mifflin.

Grady, E. (1992). *The portfolio approach to assessment (Fastback series).* Bloomington, IN: Phi Delta Kappa Educational Foundation.

Graves, D., & Sunstein, B. (1992). *Portfolio portraits.* Portsmouth, NH: Heinemann.

Gullickson, A. B. (1984). Teacher perspectives of their instructional use of tests. *Journal of Educational Research, 77*(4), 244–248.

Halpin, G., & Halpin, G. (1982). Experimental investigations of the effects of study and testing on student learning. *Journal of Educational Psychology, 72,* 32–38.

Herman, J., Aschbacher, P., & Winters, L. (1992). *A practical guide to alternative assessment.* Alexandria, VA: Association for Supervision and Curriculum Development.

Herman, J., & Winters, L. (1994). Portfolio research: A slim collection. *Educational Leadership, 52*(7), 48–55.

Kellaghan, T., Madaus, G., & Airasian, P. (1982). *The effects of standardized testing.* Boston: Kluwer-Nijhoff.

Kindsvatter, R. (1969). Guidelines for better grading. *Clearinghouse, 43*(6), 331–334.

Lazar-Morris, C., Polin, L., May, R., & Burry, J. (1980). *A review of the literature in test use* (Rep. No. 144). Center for the Study of Evaluation, University of California.

Madaus, G., & Kellaghan, T. (1993). The British experience with authentic testing. *Phi Delta Kappan, 74*(5), 458–469.

Marzano, R., Pickering, D., & McTighe, J. (1993). *Assessing student outcomes.* Alexandria, VA: Association for Supervision and Curriculum Development.

Nungester, R. J., & Duchastel, P. C. (1982). Testing versus review: Effects on retention. *Journal of Educational Psychology, 74,* 18–22.

O'Neil, J. (1994). Making assessment meaningful. *Association for Supervision and Curriculum Development Update, 36*(6), 1, 4–5.

Pedulla, J. J., Airasian, P. W., & Madaus, G. F. (1980). Do teacher ratings and standardized test results of students yield the same information? *American Educational Research Journal, 17*(3), 303–307.

Perrone, V. (1991). *Expanding student assessment.* Alexandria, VA: Association for Supervision and Curriculum Development.

Rudman, H., Kelly, J., Wanous, D., Mehrens, W., Clark, C., & Porter, A. (1980). *Integrating assessment with instruction* (Research Series No. 75). Lansing, MI: The Institute for Research on Teaching, Michigan State University.

Salmon-Cox, L. (1981). Teachers and standardized achievement tests: What's really happening? *Phi Delta Kappan, 62*(8), 631–634.

Starch, D. (1913, October). Reliability and distribution of grades. *Science, 38,* 630–636.

Starch, D. (1918). *Educational measurements.* New York: Macmillan.

Stiggins, R. J. (1985). Improving assessment where it means the most: In the classroom. *Educational Leadership, 43*(2), 69–74.

Stiggins, R. J., & Bridgeford, N. J. (1985). The ecology of classroom assessment. *Journal of Educational Measurement, 22*(4), 271–286.

Stiggins, R. J., Conklin, N. F., & Bridgeford, N. J. (1986). Classroom assessment: A key to effective education. *Educational Measurement: Issues and Practice, 5*(2), 5–17.

Wiggins, G. (1993). *Assessing student performance.* San Francisco: Jossey-Bass.

Wrinkle, W. (1947). *Improving marking and reporting practices in secondary schools.* New York: Rinehart.

Zemelman, S., Daniels, H., & Hyde, A. (1993). *Best practice: New standards for teaching and learning in America's schools.* Portsmouth, NH: Heinemann.

Zessoules, R., & Gardner, H. (1991). Authentic assessment: Beyond the buzzword and into the classroom. In V. Perrone (Ed.), *Expanding student assessment.* Alexandria, VA: Association for Supervision and Curriculum Development.

CHAPTER **10** Toward Effective Teaching

OUTLINE

The hope [for improving the profession] lies in the expanding knowledge base of the profession and teachers subscribing to it as the defining trait of their practice.

This book has presented dozens of ideas about teaching, and especially about instruction. No reader could or should remember them all separately. What the reader should have acquired as a synthesis of the book's content is a sense of what a mature and professional teacher is; the respect this teacher has for the science of teaching; the approach this teacher takes to decision making; the model this teacher provides for students as a scholar and a leader; the skill with which this teacher employs a range of teaching methods; and the tolerance this teacher has for conditions that cannot be directly controlled.

The challenge to the novice teacher, as is perhaps now clear, is not to emulate precisely some expert model but rather to be an effective decision maker. Training is most useful in highly predictable and repetitious situations. Teaching is not like that. At any moment the situation in the classroom is shaped by the interplay of numerous dynamic variables. Conditions change quickly within a classroom and vary markedly from class to class. The task of the teacher is to control as many variables as possible and be able to react with assurance to those that are not directly controllable. Teachers, therefore, depend much more on knowledge and judgment than on training to be effective decision makers. The fact that the answers are not "out there" to be found is at first difficult to accept. The fact is that the answers—or at least the decisions—come from within. This sometimes makes teaching a lonely job, and not a job for the fainthearted or the insecure.

The effective teacher is not a single, readily described entity. Effective teachers share some common general traits, but in practice those traits are exhibited in unique and personal ways. In a real sense, aspiring teachers must reinvent the effective teacher based on their knowledge, beliefs, perceptions, personality, and interaction with students in various contexts. Assistance with this task is available from this book, from teacher educators, and from practicing teachers. However, the ultimate responsibility for acquiring identity in the teacher role and integrity as a professional educator lies with each prospective teacher.

We presume that by now the reader has considered the many ideas in this book and the image of the effective teacher has begun to take shape. The next likely step is to develop one's teaching skills through extensive teaching. This phase usually occurs as student teaching or the internship. This book was designed for teacher-education students, student teachers, and first-year teachers to provide direction in applying instructional skills. Activities were devised to aid beginning teachers and supervisors in obtaining data to help measure the effectiveness of these skills on students and in turn influence instructional decisions. The data-collection instruments included in many chapters are intended for this purpose. We suggest, therefore, that this book's contribution, more than one of informing per se, has the potential to contribute to one's actual entry into teaching.

FOCUS QUESTIONS

1. In chapter 1 the proposition was presented that decision making was the basic teaching skill. Now, nine chapters and a healthy measure of development later, what support can you give to affirm that proposition?
2. How will you use the concept of praxis—the application of scholarship to practice—as a key to your professional development?
3. What means are available to teachers to improve their practices in systematic and purposeful ways?
4. To what extent are teachers justified in considering themselves to be professional practitioners?

STUDENT TEACHING AND INTERNSHIP

Student teaching or an internship is the usual culmination of the teacher-education program. In the view of student teachers or interns, it is the most important phase because they finally encounter the real demands of the teacher role. It is typically approached with some anxiety and perceived to be a trial-by-fire or a sink-or-swim proposition. Realistically the possibility of this exists, but students who have been reasonably successful in preparation experiences prior to student teaching have little rational basis for fear. It is essentially a very special time for learning in ways that have been previously unavailable because preparation prior to this phase has taken place primarily in college classrooms and has focused on the knowledge base. Now as the preparation responsibility for the development of preservice teachers is carried over into the first years of in-service teaching, more personalized and practical assistance is available to the beginner through and beyond student teaching. The profession is acknowledging that an optimally effective teacher develops only after a substantial period of study and practice. The support increasingly provided to novice teachers is the sign of a maturing profession.

As student teachers or interns adjust to their first intensive periods of teaching, their focus shifts from the cognitive, or intellectual, preparation to experiential engagement. This shift presents a new set of demands to the student teachers or interns about which they will feel some measure of stress. This stress can cause a beginning teacher to abandon newly acquired, pedagogically endorsed ideas and revert to more comfortable intuitive ones. This is a time for tough-minded decision making on the part of the student teacher or intern. Student teaching and the internship will be a more valuable experience if deliberate efforts are made to employ approaches and practices as they are described in this book. Resisting the temptation to practice without consideration of effective teaching techniques will diminish the extent of necessary relearning later to function as an optimally effective teacher. Those who play golf by first using a flawed swing and then learning a proper swing will appreciate the logic of this suggestion.

Student teaching and the internship enlist the services of a successful practicing teacher, variously referred to as the cooperating or mentor teacher, to supervise the beginner. The function of the cooperating teacher is far more than simply making a classroom available to the student teacher. An important contribution made by this person is in observing the student teacher's or beginning teacher's performance to provide descriptive and evaluative feedback. Receiving impressions and advice from a perceptive observer is valuable. To the extent that the data provided are focused, systematically obtained, carefully analyzed, and thoughtfully interpreted, it is especially valuable. The entire process that is referred to as "clinical supervision" in the literature is facilitated by the instruments provided in this book. Further, the process of action research contributes meaningfully to teachers' efforts to improve their teaching.

SCENARIO

Denton Coleman had been student teaching in a Spanish III class for six weeks. He had gotten by the initial jitters and uncertainty and was beginning to establish his own teaching style. He realized he tended not to be as structured in his approach as his cooperating teacher, Kay Obrock; however, she did not insist on more structure. She was willing to let Denton experiment and find his own most comfortable and effective way. Denton had felt a sense of relief after the first three weeks when he realized he was able to manage acceptably well as a teacher. With the relief came a surge of confidence and exhilaration about teaching. Now, however, at the six-week point, he experienced some self-doubt and a decided letdown. The students in his Spanish III class seemed complacent. They had not been well prepared for class nor had they been as enthusiastic in their participation as he remembered they were for Ms. Obrock.

When he shared his concern with his cooperating teacher, she responded, "I've noticed it, Denton. Part of it, I guess, is that the honeymoon is over. When you are a new face and a different personality the kids are naturally curious and interested. Every teacher experiences that, and it usually works to your advantage at first. When you don't have that going for you any more you have to look more carefully at what is happening." They talked for a few more minutes, but he still felt uneasy and didn't have any clear notion of what to do about it. Then something Kay Obrock had said came to mind: "Look more carefully at what is happening." He remembered the text he had used in his principles and methods course that included a series of instruments for analyzing instruction.

Denton took the book from the bookshelf when he got home and began to look through it. As he revisited the familiar pages he thought it just might be what he needed. The next day, in their first-period conference, Denton showed the book to Kay—especially the analysis instruments. "We didn't have anything like this when I was in college," she said, "but it looks interesting." She spent some time during the day looking through the book. When they met again after school for their daily wrap-up, each had some ideas. Denton said, "The problem seems to be motivation. They aren't working very hard, and they are fooling around in class more and more. Isn't there something in the book about motivation?"

"Yes," Kay replied. "But motivation is a big topic. A lot of things contribute to motivation. As I see it, that is one of the advantages of the book, that it helps make you aware of the parts and gives you a way to examine them." After some discussion, Kay went on to say, "Look, there is an instrument in chapter 6 called 'Motivating Behaviors.' It includes six different aspects of motivation. Why don't I use this in class tomorrow, and it will help us focus more specifically on something we can handle. The book suggests making a videotape so that you can do some analysis, too. Maybe I can get the video camera away from the football coach for a day or two. You know, maybe the coaches are on to a good thing with the video camera. I never thought about that."

Denton Coleman taught while Kay Obrock observed with the instrument before her. Then they both viewed the videotape later. Their analysis, done independently and then compared, revealed a similar pattern. Denton used his voice well enough, changed the instructional mode frequently, and controlled the pace appropriately. He did less well in displaying enthusiasm. However, moving about the classroom and using purposeful nonverbal behaviors were identified as the motivation areas of most need in both of their analyses.

They discussed the results of their analyses at some length. Then Kay said, "Denton, you can't change everything at once. Let's take one thing at a time. Suppose we concentrate on your movement about the class. We agree that you tend to plant yourself next to the desk too much of the time. We can get to nonverbal behavior later. Okay?" Denton agreed. They examined what was involved in moving about the class, including the monitoring that was facilitated by that movement. "Why don't I make a diagram of the room and chart your movements for a whole period. I'll also identify situations that should be monitored and see if you respond by moving there."

"Sounds good to me," Denton agreed enthusiastically. "Now maybe I should give some thought to just how I can move effectively. You know, maybe I'll start class from the back of the room tomorrow. I wonder what they'll think about doing the warm-up drill that way?"

APPLICATION TO PRACTICE

Clinical Supervision

Clinical supervision is the highly structured and intensive means with which the cooperating teacher contributes to the process of systematic analysis. Goldhammer (1969) and Cogan (1972) originally described clinical supervision, and numerous authors have written more recently on the topic (Bryan & Copeland, 1978; Goldhammer, Anderson, & Krajewski, 1980; McFaul & Cooper, 1984; Snyder, 1981; Sullivan, 1980).

In a regular in-service setting, clinical supervision tends to be somewhat unwieldy because of the extensive amount of time required of the supervisor unless it is part of an assistance program for beginning and marginal teachers. With a designated mentor or support teacher to give the beginning teacher feedback on teacher behaviors and their effect on student behaviors, the clinical supervision model can be a valuable tool to promote informed decision making for the beginning teacher. Clinical supervision is ideally suited for the internship and the student-teaching phases because the student teacher and cooperating teacher or support teacher necessarily work in a close relationship over a considerable period of time. The time the cooperating teacher or support teacher spends observing the beginning teacher will be used to maximum advantage if clinical supervision is implemented.

Clinical supervision varies in its number of steps from author to author, but in essence the process is the same. The following four steps describe the process in its simplest form using the student teacher–cooperating teacher titles, but the process is the same for intern–support teacher, and beginning teacher–supervisor.

Step 1—Preobservation Conference. The student teacher and cooperating teacher decide together what aspect of the student teacher's performance will be targeted. This idea is then behaviorally defined in terms of its discrete components. An instrument comprised of a series of components such as those in this book provides such a definition. Next, a criterion or goal stated in measurable terms is established. Finally, if an instrument is not already available for collecting pertinent data, one will have to be devised.

Step 2—Observation and Data Collection. The cooperating teacher may actually use the instrument to collect data during the student-teaching episode. However, the cooperating teacher might more usefully operate a video camera to ensure that the episode is expertly taped. The tape can then be used later for obtaining data. Ideally, both the student teacher and cooperating teacher will tabulate and analyze data independently for later comparison, discussion, and evaluation.

Step 3—Analysis of Data. Whatever the situation is regarding data-collection, it is essential that the cooperating teacher use the data-collection instrument. Examination of the data, either independently or cooperatively, should reveal patterns that in turn suggest underlying meanings. The cooperating teacher needs to be certain that thorough analysis does occur and the implications are translated into appropriate teaching strategies.

Step 4—Postobservation Conference. The cooperating teacher and student teacher compare their respective analyses and implications. Considerable attention should be given to probing underlying meanings together and discussing promising strategies. A new target or goal should be agreed on and the student teacher should be made responsible for developing a plan to reach it. This initiates a new cycle of clinical supervision, and the cycle continues as long as it is productive in any area of teaching improvement. In the scenario we find Denton Coleman and Kay Obrock beginning the process of clinical supervision that has the potential to help Denton make measurable improvement in his teaching.

SUMMARY POINT

Effective teacher decision making about instructional improvement or any other aspect of teaching requires an informed belief system. Although a popular aphorism postulates experience as the best teacher, teaching experience alone provides no guarantee of instructional improvement over time. However, decisions made in the interest of improving instruction that are based on systematically obtained data are virtually certain to produce targeted gains.

REFLECTIVE TEACHING

The term reflective teaching is used rather loosely in the literature to refer to teachers' scrutiny of and decision making about their teaching practices. Boud, Keogh, and Walker (1985) considered reflection to be "an active process of exploration and discovery" (p. 7). Ginsburg and Clift (1990) defined reflection as "the systematic and concerted synthesis of theory and practice—praxis" (p. 454). Kennedy (1990), in synthesizing references from the literature, concluded that "reflection is an ongoing process that enables teachers to continually learn from their own experiences by considering alternative interpretations of situations, generating and evaluating goals, and examining experiences in light of alternative goals and hypotheses" (p. 817).

We hope that teachers have always reflected in the ways described, and certainly it has occurred in varying degrees. However, relatively little study was made of teachers' reflectivity. Dewey's treatise on the topic, *How We Think* (1933), was widely applauded, but had little impact on teaching generally. In the mideighties, educators rediscovered the book and have made wide reference to it in the literature. In it Dewey asserted that problem solving is a matter of systematic inquiry to determine a preferable course of action, but that any course of action is subject to continuing review and revision.

The Process of Reflective Teaching

Feiman-Nemser (1990) considered reflective teaching to be a generic professional disposition. This is true in the sense in which it has already been described. On the other hand, it has also been referred to as a process. It is not a single specific process that is once and for all written in stone, but it is a general process that incorporates the spirit of inquiry. Van Manen (in Zeichner & Liston, 1987) postulated three levels of reflectivity: technical rationality, practical action, and critical reflection, as depicted in Figure 10.1.

Technical rationality refers to "delivering" the curriculum in much the way it is presented in the official documents of the school. Practical action involves

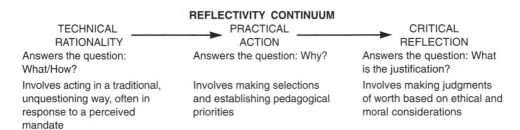

REFLECTIVITY CONTINUUM

TECHNICAL RATIONALITY	PRACTICAL ACTION	CRITICAL REFLECTION
Answers the question: What/How?	Answers the question: Why?	Answers the question: What is the justification?
Involves acting in a traditional, unquestioning way, often in response to a perceived mandate	Involves making selections and establishing pedagogical priorities	Involves making judgments of worth based on ethical and moral considerations

Figure 10.1 Levels of Reflectivity

teacher selection from among alternatives that are available in light of the pro-jected practical outcomes of each. "At this level every action is seen as linked to particular value commitments, and the actor considers the worth of competing educational ends" (Zeichner & Liston, 1987, p. 24). Critical reflection transcends practical action by asking questions in the ethical and moral dimension, involv-ing "concerns for justice, equity, and concrete fulfillment, and whether current arrangements serve important human needs and satisfy important human pur-poses" (p. 25).

Teachers are encouraged to engage in reflectivity at the highest level that is pertinent in a given situation. Ongoing decisions are necessary at the level of technical rationality, of course, as teachers conduct the routines of teaching. A teacher's personal teaching style is largely defined by the nature and pattern of decisions at this level, for example, the methods the teacher prefers, the rules es-tablished for behavior, and the frequency and type of homework assignments.

Meanwhile, many opportunities will occur for making practical action deci-sions. The teacher needs to be alert to these occasions and consider pedagogical priorities and the particular characteristics and needs of the students. At this point the teacher may decide not to have the class read *Romeo and Juliet* as the course of study stipulates but instead see a videotape of *West Side Story* with the intention of reading brief excerpts from the play that illustrate the relationship between them.

Relatively few instances of critical reflection will occur, but these are ones that will profoundly affect educational experiences within a classroom. Should birth control information be made explicitly available to students? Should a stu-dent be failed who has passed the tests but attended irregularly? Should different standards be applied to the students who are bused in? Should ethnic versions of English usage be accepted in the classroom? Should students who are found smoking be reported if the automatic three-day suspension will seriously affect their chance of passing?

Scenario Reprise

The scenario at the beginning of this chapter depicted Denton Coleman, a stu-dent teacher, and Kay Obrock, his cooperating teacher, involved in reflection on teaching. Denton, after reflecting on his teaching, speculated that the problem was students' motivation. Kay extended the reflection process, and suggested a systematic analysis based on an instrument designed for the purpose. When this was done, further analysis revealed more specific problem areas within the scope of motivation, and a plan was made to address one of them. This type of inquiry is a simple, straightforward application of the principle of reflective teaching.

Consider on the other hand what might have occurred. Denton could have assumed that the Spanish III students were lazy or they were staging a conspir-acy. He may immediately have resorted to using a verbal reprimand or threat or other punitive measure at the expense of any good will that had accrued in the six weeks he had been their teacher. His approach, instead, represents the application of sound pedagogical principles, and he has a good chance of achieving his intended outcome of providing additionally for the students' motivation. Meanwhile, this learning about teaching experience is valuable for Denton.

THE TEACHER AS RESEARCHER

The professional development of a teacher is a career-long concern. Obtaining a teaching certificate, even an advanced certificate or degree, or tenure in one's position does not exempt one from the expectation of engaging in continuing development. Only the most arrogant of teachers would claim to have reached a level of optimum effectiveness beyond which further improvement is impossible. And teaching is a dynamic, evolving profession in which changes are ongoing. To remain static in one's skills and methods assures that one's practice will become outmoded. Consequently, there is the expectation that teachers will keep up with literature pertinent to their practice, attend courses and workshops as part of their inservice education, engage in professional dialogue with their colleagues, and be open to promising new ways of providing effective education for youth.

In recent years a new emphasis has been placed on the role of the teacher as researcher, an aspect of reflective practice, as a means of improving teaching (Johnson, 1993). However, acceptance of this new role has been met with considerable reluctance by teachers. They have tended to view research with suspicion when they have viewed it at all (Bennett, 1993). They consider research to be closely associated with theory, and that theory is something that educational theorists are involved with that has little relevance to hands-on teaching. Research conjures up mountains of data in support of jargony-stated hypotheses. When teachers are asked how they use research in their classrooms, they typically reply, in effect, that they make no overt use of research in their teacher decision making. Teacher educators and researchers must accept some measure of blame for having failed to convince prospective teachers—who then become practicing teachers—of the potential of research to be a mainstay of their beliefs and practices.

All teachers conduct a kind of "soft research" in their classrooms, if research is broadly conceived as making thoughtful decisions about instruction based on information derived from their observation and experience. In this current context, however, research is defined as systematic problem solving based on data obtained for that purpose. Basically, we are construing research in a somewhat more formal way than that with which teachers routinely address concerns in their classrooms. We refer to it as *action research*, a term coined in 1949 by Stephen Corey (1953) based on a concept introduced by John Dewey in the 1920s and further developed by Kurt Lewin in the 1940s. Kemmis and McTaggart (1982) stated that action research "provides a way of thinking systematically about what happens in the school or classroom, implementing action where improvements are thought to be possible, and monitoring and evaluating the effects of the action with a view to continuing the improvement" (p. 5). They go on to say that "action research can be seen as a method for practitioners to live with the complexity of real experience while, at the same time, striving for concrete improvement" (p. 6).

In the words of McCutcheon and Jung (1990), "Action research is characterized as systemic inquiry that is collective, collaborative, self-reflective, critical, and undertaken by the participants of the inquiry. The goals of such research are the understanding of practice and the articulation of a rationale or philosophy of practice in order to improve practice" (p. 148). Finally, action research is strongly endorsed on the basis of 12 purposes it serves (International Reading Association, 1989):

> Helps solve classroom problems.
> Encourages effective change.
> Revitalizes teachers.
> Empowers teachers to make decisions in their classrooms.
> Identifies effective teaching and learning methods.
> Promotes reflective teaching.
> Verifies what methods work.
> Promotes ownership of effective practices.
> Widens the range of teachers' professional skills.
> Provides a connection between instructional methods and results.
> Helps teachers apply research findings to their own classrooms.
> Enables teachers to become change agents.

Avery (1990), reporting on her use of action research, made these comments:

> Teaching was more exciting than it had ever been. I was no longer implementing someone else's instructional program. Instead, I was developing a responsive mode of teaching based on the needs of learners. As I listened to and observed children actively engaged in learning, I found myself becoming enthused and energized by the richness and multiplicity of ways in which they learned. I became involved in demonstrating strategies for writing and reading and in exposing my students to more literature as their appetite for literacy increased. Teaching had taken on new dimensions, and I was changing as a professional. (pp. 34–35)
>
> I do not conduct investigations with findings that can be duplicated. I pursue questions that I find relevant within the context of my own teaching to better understand and respond to individual learning processes. (p. 35)
>
> The connections between theory and practice became a reality for me because of my own classroom research. (p. 41)

Further testimony is provided by Bennett (1993) based on a study of 90 teachers who used action research in their classrooms:

> Experienced teacher-researchers stated that their research brought them many personal and professional benefits, including increased collegiality, a sense of empowerment, and increased self-esteem. Teachers-researchers viewed themselves as being more open to change, more reflective, and better informed than they had been when they began their research. They now saw themselves as experts in their field who were better problem solvers and more effective teachers with fresher attitudes toward education. They also saw strong connections between theory and practice. (p. 69)

This sort of testimony on behalf of action research recommends it for use by any teacher or student teacher. What is more pertinent for student teachers especially than a process that helps them achieve their primary mission—to become increasingly effective teachers over the duration of student teaching?

The Process of Action Research

Action research may take place in at least three modes: individual-teacher research, collaborative-action research, and schoolwide-action research (Calhoun, 1993). For our purposes in this chapter, only the first is addressed, but we do acknowledge the others for their potential as approaches to team problem solving, faculty-development activities, and school reform.

The action-research process is predicated on the general question, "What might I do to improve my teaching?" Embedded within this question is a tacit concern for apparent or suspected problems or deficiencies, as well as purely developmental interests. With the general intent of improvement in mind, more specific questions may be posed as a response to some particular problem or need that concerns the teacher. These can be framed as "if" questions; for example, will my teaching be more effective if I:

> change my movement pattern?
>
> ask more higher-level questions?
>
> use cooperative-learning activities?
>
> use classroom meetings to address group concerns?

This list could be extended to include many dozens of questions. A teacher planning to engage in action research might list several possible areas for attention, then prioritize on the basis of what is most pressing and what is readily doable.

Step 1 in the action-research process is determining which question has the greatest potential to immediately affect one's teaching effectiveness. In student teaching, the student teacher and cooperating teacher as a team would do this. The question should be sufficiently limited in scope so that it is manageable.

Step 2 is devising a new approach/behavior that is an intended improvement over the current practice. This essentially becomes a hypothesis—that is, the teacher is taking the position that the new practice has the possibility of being more effective than the current practice, and eliminates or mitigates a perceived problem in current practice.

Step 3 involves determining the nature of the data that will be required to test the hypothesis, and making provision to obtain them. Depending on the question asked, data may be collected by means of students' test performance, anecdotal records or journals, observation instruments or simple frequency counts, questionnaires, interviews, video recording, or any available source. The observation instruments included at the end of many of the chapters in this book would serve to provide data regarding the practices they reflect. Step 3, it should be noted, would probably occur more or less concurrently with Step 2.

Two approaches are especially useful for collecting comparable data. The "pre-post" method involves obtaining baseline data prior to the new treatment, then obtaining data on the same sample (usually a group of students) following the treatment. The control-group method involves treating one group but withholding treatment from a second reasonably similar group. In either case, a difference in the data collected will be a measure of the change that has occurred.

Step 4 is implementing the new approach. The idea for the approach may be suggested in the educational literature or it may be the teacher's creative response to a classroom situation.

Step 5 is tabulating and analyzing the data, and reflecting on the outcome of the new practice, especially as it compares to the former practice.

An example of action research conducted by a student teacher was reported by Brooks (1994) based on her role as supervisor of that teacher. We note that the fact that the teacher involved is a student teacher is incidental; any teacher might have done this research.

> Jackie was a nontraditional student teacher assigned to me for supervision. When I first conferenced with her, I was struck by her maturity, depth of preparation, and reflective skills. Her first formal observation gave credence to this initial impression. By the fourth week of the ten-week student teaching experience, Jackie approached me with an idea for her required action research project. Although her instructional work was outstanding, Jackie was not pleased with her students' scores on the first test she had administered. She began her analysis of the problem, low student grades, by looking at her reviewing techniques. As a result of much reading and brainstorming with her cooperating teacher, Jackie devised a series of daily reviews over previously learned

material and supplemented this with a full day's review prior to the next test. The class period review utilized a spelling bee format with teams using books and notes rather than individual players working from memory. When the tests were scored, the grades were just as disappointing as previously. In fact, several students scored lower on the second test than on the first. In discussions with students after the return of papers, it became clear to Jackie and me that because of the extensive in-class reviews, the students did not think they needed to study beyond that amount for the test! Obviously, emphasis on review was not the key to the correction of poor student performance on the tests.

At this point, I suggested that we begin to look at the evaluative instrument, the test itself. To determine if students missed more of one type of question than another, the cooperating teacher ran an item analysis of the test questions. No pattern emerged; students missed each and every question with similar frequency. Jackie then began to examine each test item, searching for ambiguities of language, trickiness of wording, complexity of concept. She found a few items of dubious nature, but not in sufficient quantity to explain the problem. That evening on the phone, I suggested another tactic: examine the questions for content, relate them to the lesson in which that material was covered, analyze the lesson plan, reflect on its enactment, and determine whether the information was covered appropriately for its subsequent importance. The following evening, an excited Jackie called. Through reflection, she discovered that the problem was far more subtle than even I had thought. Her lesson plan objectives for each day were not explicit enough to give her the guidance she needed. Therefore, even though the elements of a "good" workable plan were present, they were not adequate to help her to focus on the important material and to assist her students in making sense of all the information.

That weekend as Jackie reworked her plans for the coming week, she continually examined her objectives. Were they clearly worded? Was the focus sharp? Had she been explicit in stating what her students were to learn from each lesson? How could she help each student achieve understanding? How would she measure that understanding? The scores on the next tests were somewhat improved. Jackie continued to work on objectives, focusing, rewording, analyzing. By the completion of her student teaching, every student's scores had risen, several more than doubling from the first test. Further, Jackie believed that even though her earlier test construction was not that much at fault, her later tests which built on the clearly stated objectives were better measures of her students' understanding of major social studies concepts than her earlier tests.

EMPOWERING TEACHERS

This chapter has addressed the concern for empowering teachers. The conditions that attend teaching are well-known, although unevenly reported, and a litany of them here is not necessary. The overwhelming task that has been given the school and its teachers in current society is unrealistic. In many instances teachers feel beleaguered in the face of it. Maeroff (1988) made the point that "the situation that currently exists for many teachers, especially in problem-plagued urban school districts, produces not empowerment, but impotence" (p. 474).

These conditions are not going to go away. If teachers, and the education profession generally, are waiting for that to happen, they are naive. Of course teachers need to be well organized politically to use whatever influence they can mount to affect legislation and funding, but this essentially only allows education to "stay even." If teachers are to make a breakthrough toward higher status and greater empowerment, it will occur more in pedagogical than political terms. Doing what they do better—teaching—and doing it so convincingly that it cannot be ignored by the community they serve, which ultimately is the nation, is the key to empowerment.

Shulman (1986) commented insightfully on the nature of a profession:

> What distinguishes mere craft from profession is the indeterminacy of rules when applied to particular cases. The professional holds knowledge, not only of how—the capacity for skilled performance—but of what and why. The teacher is not only a master of procedure but also of content and rationale, and capable of explaining why something is done. The teacher is capable of reflection leading to self-knowledge, the metacognitive awareness that distinguishes draftsman from architect, bookkeeper from auditor. A professional is capable not only of practicing and understanding his or her craft, but of communicating decisions and actions to others. (p. 13)

Teachers need to frame their understanding of their role in these terms, and to set about ordering their practice to conform to them. A suggested beginning is to attend to Francis Bacon's admonition long ago that knowledge itself is power. The profession will not be moved ahead very far by those gifted individual practitioners who practice their craft with insight and panache, but whose intuitive gifts retire with them. The hope lies in the expanding knowledge base of the profession and teachers subscribing to it as the defining trait of their practice. Teachers will think of themselves as more than technicians who implement pedagogy; they will be agents in the continual redefining of that pedagogy. Oberg and Mc-Cutcheon (1990) referred to this as they described the expansion of the role of the teacher into research:

The teacher-as-researcher is based on teachers liberating themselves from ideas solely imposed by others outside the classroom. In a sense it constitutes an acknowledgement that teaching belongs to teachers and as the experts about their own practice, teachers are the ones most able to understand and refine their work. (p. 142)

Understanding one's discipline in terms of its organizing schemes and its structure, being able to use the concept of pedagogical content knowledge, having a repertoire of effective teaching strategies that are available to promote optimal learning, being committed to reflecting on one's teaching, using systematic approaches to analyze one's practice, and utilizing information from and methods of research in one's classroom are the bases for achieving empowerment. And through these, teaching will reach its potential to be a fulfilling profession.

QUESTIONS FOR REFLECTION

1. What are the most common variables that affect the continuously emerging classroom scene, and what is the influence of each one you identify?
2. What aspects of clinical supervision qualify it to be considered an application of action research? And how does action research, in turn, qualify as an aspect of reflective teaching?
3. How can you use the levels of reflectivity—technical rationality, practical action, and critical reflection—to help you translate the concept of reflective teaching into substantive teacher practice?
4. The notion of the teacher as researcher has emerged prominently in recent years. Why, in your view, has this happened, and what is the likely broad impact of it on teacher attitudes and teaching practice?
5. The nation broadly, and many states individually, have established higher standards and optimistic expectations for schools as the next century approaches. Given the commentary on teacher empowerment and teaching as a profession in this chapter, what can teachers do as individuals and as a profession to make gains toward those goals, as well as help define (redefine?) pertinent and realistic goals?

REFERENCES

Avery, C. (1990). Learning to research, researching to learn. In M. Olson (Ed.), *Opening the door to classroom research*. Newark, DE: International Reading Association.

Bennett, C. (1993). Teacher researchers: All dressed up and no place to go? *Educational Leadership, 51*(2), 69–70.

Boud, D., Keogh, R., & Walker, D. (1985). What is reflection in learning? In D. Boud, R. Keogh, & D. Walker (Eds.), *Reflection: Turning experience into learning*. New York: Nichols.

Brooks, E. (1994). *Action research and teacher supervision.* Unpublished manuscript, Kent State University.

Bryan, N., & Copeland, W. (1978). *Instructional supervision training program*. New York: Merrill.

Calhoun, E. (1993). Action research: Three approaches. *Educational Leadership, 51*(2), 62–65.

Cogan, M. (1972). *Clinical supervision*. Boston: Houghton Mifflin.

Corey, S. (1953). *Action research to improve school practice*. New York: Teachers College, Columbia University.

Dewey, J. (1933). *How we think*. Boston: Heath.

Feiman-Nemser, S. (1990). Teacher preparation: Structural and conceptual alternatives. In R. Huston (Ed.), *Handbook of research on teacher education*. New York: Macmillan.

Ginsburg, M., & Clift, R. (1990). The hidden curriculum of preservice teacher education. In R. Huston (Ed.), *Handbook of research on teacher education*. New York: Macmillan.

Goldhammer, R. (1969). *Clinical supervision: Special methods for the supervision of teachers*. New York: Holt, Rinehart & Winston.

Goldhammer, R., Anderson, R., & Krajewski, R. (1980). *Clinical supervision*. New York: Holt, Rinehart & Winston.

International Reading Association (1989). *Journal of Reading, 33*(3), 216–218.

Johnson, B. (1993). *Teacher as researcher*. Washington, D.C.: Office of Educational Research and Improvement (ERIC Digest No. ED 355 205).

Kemmis, S., & McTaggart, R. (1982). *The action research planner*. Victoria, Australia: Deakin University.

Kennedy, M. (1990). Choosing a goal for professional education. In R. Huston, (Ed.), *Handbook of research on teacher education*. New York: Macmillan.

Maeroff, G. (1988). A blueprint for empowering teachers. *Phi Delta Kappan, 69*(7), 472–477.

McCutcheon, G., & Jung, B. (1990). Alternative perspectives on action research. *Theory into Practice, 29*(3), 144–151.

McFaul, S., & Cooper, J. (1984). Peer clinical supervision: Theory vs. reality. *Educational Leadership, 41*, 4–9.

Oberg, A., & McCutcheon, G. (1990). Teacher as researcher. *Theory into Practice, 29*(3), 142–143.

Shulman, L. (1986). Those who understand: Knowledge growth in teaching. *Educational Researcher, 15*(2), 4–14.

Snyder, K. (1981). Clinical supervision in the 1980s. *Educational Leadership, 38*, 521–524.

Sullivan, C. (1980). *Clinical supervision: A state of the art review*. Alexandria, VA: Association for Supervision and Curriculum Development.

Zeichner, K., & Liston, D. (1987). Teaching student teachers to reflect. *Harvard Educational Review, 57*(1), 23–48.

Index